BODHICARYĀVATĀRA WITH COMMENTARY

ŚĀNTIDEVA

SONAM TSEMO

Translated by
ADRIAN O'SULLIVAN

Dechen Foundation

Published and distributed by Dechen Foundation. Dechen Foundation is an association of Sakya and Karma Kagyu Buddhist centers founded by Lama Jampa Thaye under the authority of Karma Thinley Rinpoche.

www.dechen.us

First edition 2019
Printed in the United States of America

© Copyright 2020 by Adrian O'Sullivan
All rights reserved. No part of this publication may be reproduced in any form or by any means, without permission in writing from the publisher.

Library of Congress Control Number: 2018968586
ISBN:
978-1-7335560-0-2 (hardback)
978-1-7335560-2-6 (paperback)

For my Parents

CONTENTS

Foreword   vii
Introduction   ix

BODHICARYĀVATĀRA WITH COMMENTARY

PART I
THE PURPOSES OF THE COMPOSITION
1. In Praise of Bodhicitta   5

PART II
THE PRIMARY BASIS
In Praise of Bodhicitta (2)   21

PART III
THE PRODUCTIVE CAUSE
In Praise of Bodhicitta (3)   27
2. Confession of Faults   45
3. Fully Holding Bodhicitta   69

PART IV
THE COOPERATING CONDITION
4. Concern   91
5. Clear Comprehension   117
6. Patience   161
7. Effort   217
8. Meditation   247
9. Wisdom   317

PART V
THE SUBSEQUENT RESULTS
10. Dedication   459
    Colophon   477

Translator's Afterword: Logic	479
Glossary	485
Bibliography	489
Notes	497

FOREWORD

I am delighted to welcome the appearance of this major work of Buddhist scholarship in English translation. It is the fruit of several years of labour by the translator, Adrian O'Sullivan, who has already established himself as one of the new generation of Buddhist practitioner/translators.

The present volume contains both the root text of the celebrated 'Entering the Bodhisattva Conduct' by the 7th-8th century Indian master Śāntideva and the superb commentary composed by Sonam Tsemo (1142-1182), one of the most celebrated masters of the Sakya school in Tibet. The two works together provide an extensive and brilliant guide to the entire practice of the Mahāyāna path to enlightenment as maintained in the Madhyamaka school of tenets. Sonam Tsemo's commentary, reflecting his many years of study with philosophical luminaries like Chapa Chokyi Sengge, stands today as one of the pinnacles of Sakya scholarship.

It is my prayer that this English translation contributes greatly to the flourishing of our great Sakya tradition in the West for the benefit of all beings.

Lama Jampa Thaye
August 28th, 2018, France

INTRODUCTION

The present work contains translations of two texts—Śāntideva's *Bodhicaryāvatāra*, or 'Entering the Bodhisattva Conduct', and a commentary upon that text composed by the second hierarch of the Sakya school of Tibetan Buddhism, Sonam Tsemo (*bsod nams rtse mo*, 1142-1182). Śāntideva was an Indian Ācārya (master scholar) and meditator who lived in the 7th-8th centuries. His *Bodhicaryāvatāra* remains to this day one of the most popular and referenced works of the Mahāyāna Buddhist tradition. It is well known in the West and has several English translations, including some based on the Tibetan translation of Ngok Loden Sherab (*rngog blo ldan shes rab*, 1059-1109) et. al., as is the present edition. Though such English translations are widely available, a new translation of the *Bodhicaryāvatāra* is nevertheless presented here together with Sonam Tsemo's commentary, allowing the root text and its commentary to be read together with consistency across the two translations. Entitled simply 'Commentary on the *Bodhicaryāvatāra*',[1] Sonam Tsemo's text is a work of consummate scholarship and clarity, bathing in brilliant light every detail of Śāntideva's classic text. In particular, it has a detailed exegesis of the *Bodhicaryāvatāra's* ninth chapter, 'Wisdom', comprising about forty percent of the Tibetan edition of the commentary, which does not include the entire root text but only fragments of and references to it. Hence, we have two translations interposed—a new English translation of the *Bodhicaryāvatāra* in ten chapters and the first full

English translation of the detailed twelfth century commentary written by Sonam Tsemo.

Śāntideva

According to Tāranātha's (1575-1674) history of Buddhism in India,[2] Śāntideva was a prince who, from an early age, had visions of the bodhisattva Mañjuśrī. When Śāntideva came of age and was due to succeed his father to the throne, Mañjuśrī appeared to him in a dream, seated upon that very throne, and told Śāntideva it would be improper for the student to sit upon the teacher's seat. He also dreamt of Ārya Tārā blessing him and advising him that to possess a kingdom would lead him to hell. Inspired by this, he left the royal palace to seek a new life. He encountered Tārā in the form of an ordinary woman who led him to meet Mañjuśrī himself, appearing to him as a hermit in the forest, and Śāntideva was able to attain meditative samādhi and insight.

After this, Śāntideva became a minister in another Indian kingdom to help spread the Buddhist teachings. He kept a wooden sword about his person as a token of Mañjuśrī. When commanded by the king and the other ministers to show this wooden sword, Śāntideva warned them that doing so would harm them. The king insisted however, so, asking the king to cover at least one of his eyes, Śāntideva drew the sword and its light blinded the king's unprotected eye. The king was filled with amazement and promised to protect the Buddhist teachings. From then on, Śāntideva was known as an accomplished master ('siddha').

Śāntideva then took ordination at the great monastic institute of Nalanda. Inwardly, he meditated upon Mañjuśrī's presence and received further teachings from the deity but, outwardly, he ate a lot of rice and appeared to be sleeping most of the day and night. It was during this time that Śāntideva composed his *Śikṣā-samuccaya*, a text largely comprising quotations from the sutras concerning training, and the shorter *Sutra-samuccaya*, which is unfortunately lost.

The monks felt Śāntideva was not doing his fair share around the place, so they contrived a plan to get rid of him. Bidding him sit upon a high seat to recite teachings, Śāntideva complied and asked if they would like to hear something old or something new. Eagerly anticipating his impending humiliation and expulsion, the monks requested something new. Śāntideva began to recite the *Bodhicaryāvatāra*. In due course, he recited the now famous verse (9.34):

> When neither existence nor non-existence
> Remain before the mind,
> Since there is no other category at that time,
> There is a complete non-conceptual pacification.

At this point he seemed to rise up into the sky and become invisible, whilst his recitation continued without interruption. Having completed the *Bodhicaryāvatāra*, Śāntideva departed the monastery, despite the requests of the amazed monks for him to stay.

After this, in the south, Śāntideva defeated the magical powers of some non-Buddhists by dispelling a mandala they had constructed in the sky, allowing the Buddhist teachings to spread. He used his powers to provide food for five hundred Buddhist converts and over a thousand beggars, and brought an end to a war when he entered the battlefield.

Tāranātha summarizes the life of Śāntideva as these seven extraordinary deeds: the visions of Mañjuśrī, the king, benefitting Nalanda, winning over the monks, benefitting the Buddhist converts, benefitting the beggars and defeating the non-Buddhists. Such is the life of Śāntideva according to our Mahāyāna tradition.

Sonam Tsemo

The present commentary on the *Bodhicaryāvatāra*, one of the earliest of many Tibetan commentaries on Śāntideva's great work, was composed by the Tibetan Ācārya (Tib. *slob dpon*), Sonam Tsemo. As the son of Sachen Kunga Nyingpo (1092-1158), he became the second of the 'five founding fathers' of the Sakya lineage and thus an important figure in the history of Tibetan Buddhism. According to Dhongthog Rinpoche's *The Sakya School of Tibetan Buddhism: A History* (2017), when Sonam Tsemo was born in 1142, the child announced that he was finished with childish activities, and always sat thereafter with crossed legs. Like Śāntideva before him, the young child had visions of Mañjuśrī and Tārā, as well as other tantric deities, and was able to recite tantras and śāstras by heart.

After Sachen Kunga Nyingpo's death in 1158, Sonam Tsemo travelled to the monastery Sangphu Ne'uthog (*gsang phu ne'u thog*) in central Tibet, where he studied for eleven years with the great scholar Chapa Chokyi Sengge (*phywa pa chos kyi sengge*), receiving and mastering the entirety of the Buddhist scriptural collections, including detailed teachings on the *Bodhicaryāvatāra*. He became a great Ācārya and tantric master, and appeared to his students in forms of Mañjuśrī, Virūpa and Avalokiteśvara.

In addition to the present commentary, Sonam Tsemo composed influential explanations of Vajrayāna, such as his *General Presentation of the Four Sets of Tantras*, and other dharma works. He held the dynastic seat of Sakya, mostly in absentia, from 1159-1171. Then, having passed authority to his younger brother, Drakpa Gyaltsen, Sonam Tsemo left for a lakeside retreat at Chumig in the far west of the Sakya realm to focus on yogic practice. He passed away in 1182 and is said to have attained the 'rainbow body', one of the highest possible signs of accomplishment for a Buddhist practitioner.[3] Sonam Tsemo's works attest to someone who achieved a consummate understanding of Mahāyāna and Vajrayāna. From his works, we modern students, though separated from him by many tumultuous centuries, can directly receive the pure, uncorrupted dharma.

The Translation

Both the root text and commentary assume familiarity with Mahāyāna tenets and terminology, so for those who lack this, studying an introductory text on the principles of Mahāyāna will be an indispensable prerequisite. I recommend *Rain of Clarity: Stages of the Path in the Sakya Tradition*, composed by my own teacher, Lama Jampa Thaye, as it is an English-language work presenting the Mahāyāna in accord with the Sakya tradition. Also, since Sonam Tsemo's commentary makes use of the Buddhist logic system (Tib. *tshad ma*, Skt. pramāṇa) and since this topic has not been studied by most English-speaking students of Buddhism, I have provided in the appendix a short guide to the logical terminology employed in the present work. For convenience and clarity, where logical terminology is used by Sonam Tsemo as a kind of shorthand, I have made most of these references explicit in the notes.

A very useful aid in the translation of Sonam Tsemo's commentary has been a later Sakya commentary on the *Bodhicaryāvatāra*, that of Lhopa Kunkhyen Rinchen Pal (*lho pa kun mkhyen rin chen dpal*, 13th century[4]), called *The Oral Instructions of Mañjuśrī*, in which the bodhisattva Mañjuśrī of the title is identified with the author's teacher, Sakya Pandita (*sa skya pan di ta kun dga' rgyal mtshan*, 1182-1251), the fourth hierarch of Sakya and the nephew of Sonam Tsemo. This later commentary presents certain explanatory points made by Sakya Pandita but also draws very extensively on Sonam Tsemo's text, often following the same structure and reiterating or paraphrasing many of its passages and key explanatory points. It is normal in Tibetan authorial practice to make uncredited use of antecedent sources in this way. This is because the tradition values the sutras of the Buddha and the śāstras based upon them as sources of truth, as well as personal experience, particularly meditative experience, over originality or personality. The similarity of Lhopa Rinchen Pal's commentary to that of Sonam Tsemo has made it an invaluable aid in translating some of the most difficult passages and identifying textual corruptions in the extant editions of Sonam Tsemo's text.

Both commentaries shed light on the early Tibetan conception of the Svātantrika-Prāsangika distinction. Though this distinction came to have variant interpretations, here, in its near-original form, it is addressed to the related philosophical questions of how sentient beings can comprehend ultimate truth whilst subject to delusion and how Buddhas can comprehend relative truth and act in saṃsāra without being subject to delusion. To add clarity and context to Sonam Tsemo's remarks on this topic, I have included in the notes several of Lhopa Rinchen Pal's passages addressing the Svātantrika-Prāsangika distinction. In general, Sonam Tsemo's commentary reflects the influence of Chapa Chokyi Sengge from whom Sonam Tsemo received teachings on the *Bodhicaryāvatāra* at Sangphu. These teachings were subsequently received and propagated by one of the most influential scholars in the history of Tibetan literature, Sakya Pandita, as is evident from the overlap in content with the commentary of Lhopa Rinchen Pal, Sapan's student, as well as certain comments in Sakya Pandita's own *Clarifying the Sage's Intent*, some of which I have drawn attention to in notes. Thus, Sonam Tsemo's commentary is an important seminal text in the intellectual tradition of Tibetan Buddhism.

The hierarchical structuring of the Tibetan commentarial tradition remains a challenge for English translations. Some enumerate each section by concatenating every hierarchical section number into unfathomable chains of digits (e.g. 3.5.2.3.4.1.1), while others produce indented tables showing the complete hierarchical structure, sometimes running to hundreds of entries and dozens of levels of indentation. Here, I have added hierarchical tables throughout the text which provide ad hoc overviews of certain complex substructures within the master hierarchy, without attempting overall completeness. This breaks up the master hierarchy into somewhat manageable chunks in a manner somewhat compatible with the limitations of ordinary human comprehension. Nevertheless, as with the Tibetan system which gives little or no guidance at all, the onus remains on the reader to do most of the work by regularly flipping pages back and forth to reorient him or herself within the master hierarchy until it can be memorized.

The practice of numbering the root verses is an addition now standard for Western translations of ancient texts, an improvement over the older commentarial systems of both the East and West that quote only one or two syllables from the referenced lines. The letters a, b, c and d indicate the four lines within each verse of the root text, e.g. 'v1cd' indicates the third and fourth lines of the first verse. Square brackets indicate an insertion by the translator.

The reader may notice regular variations in the point of view, especially in the root text, between first, second and third person. These variations are typically present in the original text; I have tried to remain faithful to its point of view when indicated. Yet, whether Śāntideva says 'I' or 'you', he is typically addressing himself, for as he says near the outset:

> I do not expect this to benefit others.
> I composed it only to develop my own understanding.

Therefore, when not explicitly indicated, I have preferred 'I' for the root text and 'one' for the commentary.

As is normal with Buddhist translations these days, common Sanskrit terms such as Buddha, dharma, saṅgha, bodhicitta, and many more, are used without English translation on the assumption of the reader's familiarity with them from other Mahāyāna works, an essential prerequisite for reading this book. A glossary provides the Tibetan translation for a small number of key terms. For any others, the Tibetan text is available online at the Buddhist Digital Resource Center (W2DB4568), for which page numbers are provided throughout the present translation.

Two other terms of translation are worthy of mention. For the Tibetan term *rtag pa*, normally translated as 'eternal' or 'permanent', I have preferred 'sempiternal', invoking an old distinction from Western philosophy between what is outside of time or timeless (the eternal) and what is immutable and everlasting within time (the sempiternal). It is this latter sense in which the Buddhist critiques of the ultimate existence of God, the self and matter are generally founded. For the Tibetan term *nyon mongs*, which has been translated variously as 'defilement', 'affliction' or 'disturbing emotion', 'negative emotion' and so forth, I have preferred 'defilement'. Though 'affliction' is equally suitable, there are reasons to think the meaning of *nyon mongs* differs from what is meant by 'emotion' in important respects.[5]

For this project, I must thank my teacher, Lama Jampa Thaye, from whom I received the transmission of these texts at Sakya Changlochen Ling, France from 1999-2003, and who originally proposed this translation project in Santa Monica, California in December 2013. I also wish to thank Sam van Schaik for his helpful advice and encouragement.

Adrian O'Sullivan
March 2019, North Carolina, USA

BODHICARYĀVATĀRA WITH COMMENTARY

I bow down to the Lion of the Śākyas.

> Lord Mañjughoṣa, famed in the ten directions,
> Resplendent and delightful, peaceful master of speech,
> Completely free from elaborations, with conceptual thought pacified,
> Lord of protectors, I pay homage to your mighty form.

The three main parts of the *Bodhicaryāvatāra* are the introduction, the main body of the śāstra and the conclusion. If distinguished in more detail, there are five parts:

1. The purposes of the composition [chapter 1, v1-3]
2. The primary basis: the individual person [v4-5]
3. The productive cause: the generation of bodhicitta [v6-chapter 3]
4. The cooperating condition: subsequently practising the training [chapters 4-9]
5. The subsequent results of the practice [chapter 10]

PART I
THE PURPOSES OF THE COMPOSITION

Chapter 1

IN PRAISE OF BODHICITTA

There are three explicit subsections and one implicit section on the four branches of purpose and relation.[1] The explicit sections are:

1. Homage and praise
2. The commitment to compose
3. Discarding pride

These concern lines 1ab, 1cd and the next eight lines, respectively:

1.1
To the Sugatas, the dharmakāya they have mastered, and their sons,
And to all those worthy of prostration, I respectfully prostrate.
To enter the vow of the Sugatas' sons,
In accord with the tradition, I will now briefly explain.

1.2
Nothing said here has not been said before,
And I have neither eloquence nor erudition,
So, I do not expect this to benefit others.
I composed it only to develop my own understanding.

1.3
Because of developing virtue like this,
The power of my faith will increase for a little while.
But if others, similar in fortune to me,
Should see it, that is also of benefit.

I will explain each section with respect to the following three points: [248]

1. The purpose of the section
2. A condensed explanation of the section
3. The literal meaning of each section[2]

Section overview: The purposes and relation [v1-3]

1. The purpose of each section
    1. The purpose of homage and praise
    2. The purpose of commitment to compose
    3. The purpose of discarding pride
2. The condensed meaning of each section
    1. The condensed meaning of homage and praise
    2. The condensed meaning of commitment to compose
    3. The condensed meaning of discarding pride
3. The literal meaning of each section
    1. The literal meaning of homage and praise
    2. The literal meaning of commitment to compose
        1. Setting out the subject matter to be elaborated
        2. Abandoning personal invention
        3. Abandoning [the fault] repetition
    3. The literal meaning of discarding pride
        1. The understanding of others is not the primary goal
        2. The author's own understanding is the primary goal
        3. Yet, in dependence upon that, there is benefit for others
4. The implicit fourth section on the four branches of purpose and relation
    1. The purpose of presenting the four branches
    2. The condensed meaning
    3. The literal meaning

1. The purpose of each section

The purpose of homage and praise: while an author may or may not have their own individual purposes, of most importance are the following enumerated results. There are three benefits for the author himself:

1. Those which are worldly: [praise and fame in the world, which though acquired nevertheless are not intended by the author]
2. Those which are intended: [by gaining merit and preserving it from decline, one overcomes outer and inner obstacles to the completion of the composition]
3. The foremost one: [by sowing the seeds of higher rebirth and definitive goodness in the author's mind, the defilements are dispelled and suffering is cast aside]

There are five benefits for others [who receive or hear the teaching]:

1. They completely hold the causes of all goodness [where 'all goodness' is identical to the 'foremost' benefit of self, above]
2. Awareness of the greatness of the teacher
3. Understanding that the śāstra possesses excellent meaning
4. Entering into the conditions by which the author himself attained accomplishments
5. Not losing the means of entering [i.e. in accord with the second ('intended') benefit of self, through the merit generated and preserved, one will be able to complete the hearing of the śāstra]

These eight may be learned in more detail from other sources.[3]

The purpose of the commitment to compose: having made the promise, the composition of the śāstra is sure to be completed because holy beings do not abandon whatever promises they have made.

The purpose of discarding pride: out of the pride of thinking of oneself as learned, one might abandon the composition of the text.

2. The condensed meaning of each section

1. The condensed meaning of homage and praise comprises lines 1ab:

   1. Making homage and praise to the sources of refuge—the Three Jewels is line 1a
   2. Making homage and praise to others who are worthy of respect is line 1b

2. The condensed meaning of the commitment to compose:

   1. Setting out the subject matter to be elaborated – line 1c
   2. Abandoning personal invention - 'In accord with tradition' in 1d
   3. Abandoning the fault of repetition - 'I will briefly explain' also in 1d

3. The condensed meaning of discarding pride: [249]

   1. The understanding of others is not the primary goal - 2a-2c
   2. The author's own understanding is the primary goal - 2d-3b
   3. In dependence upon that, there is benefit for others - 3cd

3. The literal meaning of each section

1. The literal meaning of homage and praise:

> **1.1**
> **To the Sugatas, the dharmakāya they have mastered, and their sons,**
> **And to all those worthy of prostration, I respectfully prostrate.**

The 'Sugatas' means the Buddhas, who have perfected abandonment and realization. 'Su' signifies excellence. 'Gata' means going or having gone to abandonment and realization in this way, in entirety and irreversibly:[4]

- Abandonment is 'excellent' because it is the abandonment of

the obscurations of the defilements, which are fully appropriate to abandon.
- Abandonment is 'in entirety' because it is the abandonment of the obscurations of cognizables, i.e. the clinging to existence, which is the cause of the defilements and, since the defilements are the result, it is abandonment of the cultivation of lower rebirths.
- Abandonment is 'irreversible' because, since the abandonment is final, there is knowledge of non-arising and knowledge of exhaustion.

- Realization is 'excellent' because it is realization of reality as it is—the direct apprehension of emptiness.
- Realization is 'in entirety' because it is the knowledge [of reality] as it seems.
- Realization is 'irreversible' because it never diminishes.

This is the jewel of the Buddha.

'The dharmakāya they have mastered': the jewel of the dharma is the ultimate cessation in the space free from the adventitious defilements and it is the ultimate path of realization with the wisdom without dualistic appearances [i.e. the third and fourth Noble Truths]. Possessing the dharma of realization due to mastery over their stream of existence is a 'kāya' [body] in the sense that it is the basis of all the good qualities of that realization. It is also the body of meaning of the dharma scriptures.

'And their sons' [250] refers to the bodhisattva saṅgha. They are born from the lineage of the Sugatas and are their heirs. Śrāvakas, though they are also born from that lineage, are not their heirs, i.e. not their sons. If the sons of the wheel-turning universal emperors do not possess the marks [of an emperor], they are not heirs to the lineage, i.e. are not sons, as explained in the *Sutra Requested by Kāśyapa*.

To 'prostrate' to them means making homage and praise to the sources of refuge of the Mahāyāna family—the Three Jewels.

'And to all who are worthy of prostration': the Mahāyānist not only takes refuge in these sources of refuge but also makes prostrations to others who are worthy of prostration. This includes śrāvakas, pratyekabuddhas, khenpos, ācāryas and so forth who, while they are not sources of refuge, are worthy of prostration because of their eminent qualities.

2. The literal meaning of the commitment to compose:

1. Setting out the subject matter to be elaborated
2. Abandoning personal invention
3. Abandoning the fault of repetition

1. Setting out the subject matter to be elaborated

To enter the vow of the Sugatas' sons,

This has four aspects:

1. The individuals who undertake the vow: the Sugatas' sons are bodhisattvas in whose minds the vow exists.
2. The essence of the vow: the continuity of the intention to train. This is not a physical characteristic.[5]
3. Its aspects: The nature of the vow itself—the moral conduct of the vow [i.e. abandoning nonvirtues]; the nature of diligence in the vow—the moral conduct of gathering virtuous dharmas; the moral conduct of benefitting sentient beings
4. The meaning of the term 'vow': like a dam across a river stops the water from flowing the wrong way, a vow functions similarly [251] in regard to the methods of practice.

2. Abandoning personal invention

In accord with the tradition, …

Is this an original explanation of the bodhisattva vow by the author's own invention? No, it is in accord with the tradition since it does not contradict the scriptural tradition.

3. Abandoning the fault of repetition

Objection: 'The explanation of the meaning here has already been taught elsewhere. Therefore, since this is repetition, it is pointless.'

... I will now briefly explain.

It would not be possible to give here a detailed explanation of the entire scriptural tradition. This presentation is just a condensed summary of the meaning of the scriptural tradition, so there is no fault of repetition.

3. The literal meaning of discarding pride:

1. The understanding of others is not the primary goal
2. The author's own understanding is the primary goal
3. Yet, in dependence upon that, there is benefit for others

1. The understanding of others is not the primary goal

1.2
Nothing said here has not been said before,
And I have neither eloquence nor erudition.
So I do not expect this to benefit others.

Objection: 'The composition of this śāstra is not of benefit for the understanding of others because, since it has not fully purified you, it cannot ripen others. It is not of benefit for your own understanding either, because your understanding is already complete, so you have no need of it.'

Response: it is not expected to benefit others. In which case, is the benefit of others neglected? No, because there is no possibility of it benefitting others. Why not? Because, regarding the meaning, nothing said here has not been said before, i.e. it will not create any understanding that was previously lacking and because, regarding the words, they are neither eloquent nor erudite, i.e. they will not create any understanding in the manner of beautiful poetics, such as the *Condensed Succession of Lives* by Virācārya [Aśvaghoṣa].

Therefore, there is no possibility of it benefitting others, so there is nothing to be done. [252] In that case, what is the purpose of composing it?

2. The author's own understanding is the primary goal

I composed it only to develop my own understanding.

1.3
Because of developing virtue like this,
The power of my faith will increase for a little while.

Why compose this? Because it will increase the power of faith. What circumstances bring that about? A virtuous act such as composing this śāstra will bring it about, as well as other similar virtues, such as hearing it. How long will that last? A little while. What causes it? The development of virtue, i.e. the habituation of one's mind to virtue. In that case, is the benefit of others disregarded? Will the bodhisattva conduct be impaired? When their benefit is not possible, there is no work to be done for the benefit of others, but when it is possible to do something, the benefit of others should not be disregarded.

3. Yet, in dependence upon that, there is benefit for others

But if others, similar in fortune to me,
Should see it, that is also of benefit.

There is benefit for others similar in fortune to the author and, implicitly, for those who are less fortunate. Although, according to the author, the explanation is poor, it is based upon the words of holy beings. 'Also' means in addition to the benefit for the author.

4. The implicit section: the four branches of purpose and relation

1. The purpose of presenting the four branches
2. The condensed meaning
3. The literal meaning

1. The purpose of the composition

The presentation of the four branches of purpose and relation has three functions: it counteracts doubts that there will be benefit to others, it counteracts the misunderstandings of others and it adorns the main text.

2. The condensed meaning

The four branches of purpose and relation[6] are:

1. The explanandum is 'the entrance to the vow of the Sugatas' sons' [v1c].
2. The immediate purpose is that by 'explaining' [v1d] this, the reader's understanding develops.
3. The metapurpose is indicated in the subject of the homage and praise, i.e. the objects of praise are the state to be attained. [253].
4. The relation: the explanans and the immediate purpose are connected as the depended upon and the dependent dharma.

To elaborate on these:

1. By showing the explanandum, the immediate purpose becomes possible.
2. By showing the immediate purpose, one understands the possibility of accomplishing it.
3. By showing the metapurpose, the immediate purpose is established as a desideratum.
4. By showing the relation, the relation between achieving the immediate purpose by means of the explanans is established.

3. The literal meaning: this has already been explained in the previous section.

If one wishes for an explanation of the meaning of each chapter according to the tradition of the śāstra, it is as follows.

> Textual overview: Summary of textual structure in relation to chapters 1 - 10
>
> 1. The purposes and relation [chapter 1, v1–3]
> 2. The primary basis: the individual person [v4-5]
>   1. The bodily basis
>   2. The mental basis
> 3. The productive cause: the generation of bodhicitta
>   1. The benefits [v6-36]
>   2. The actual practice [chapters 2-3]
>   1. Preliminaries
>   2. Main part
>   3. Conclusion
> 4. The cooperating condition: subsequently accomplishing the training [chapters 4-9]
>   1. Concern
>   2. Mindfulness and clear comprehension
>   3. Patience
>   4. Meditation
>   5. Wisdom
> 5. The subsequent results of the practice: dedication of merit [chapter 10]

Concerning parts 2 - 5:

- Part 2 is the primary basis—the individual person.
- Part 3 is the generation of bodhicitta—the productive cause.
- Part 4 is the practice of the conduct—the cooperating condition, which follows this.
- Part 5 is the subsequent attainment of the result—the direct accomplishment of unsurpassed enlightenment. It is only the path of the Mahāyāna family which is said to possess this result.

Part 2, the primary basis—the individual person: the bodily basis is the attainment of all abundances of freedoms and endowment and the mental basis is the attainment of the merit and intelligence for the expanded potential of the Mahāyāna. This is explained in chapter 1, verses 4-5. On the attainment of the freedoms and endowments of the basis and the expanded potential of the Mahāyāna, one generates bodhicitta, the productive cause. Then, with the awareness of the benefits, enthusiasm is generated in one's mind and, subsequently, one proceeds to the main practice. The first step is taught in chapter 1, which creates enthusiasm through an awareness of the benefits, and the second step follows this.

Part 3, the productive cause—generation of bodhicitta: this comprises the preliminaries, main part and conclusion: [254]

3.1. Preliminaries: To become a suitable vessel for bodhicitta through the diminishment of karmic obscurations, the seven branches of accumulating merit are taught:

1. To become a suitable vessel in one's stream of being through eliminating the karmic obscuration of greed, one makes offerings to the Three Jewels.
2. To become a suitable vessel in one's stream of being through eliminating the karmic obscurations of relying on faulty sources of refuge, one takes refuge in the Three Jewels.
3. To become a suitable vessel in one's stream of being through eliminating the karmic obscurations of nonvirtuous actions of body, speech and mind, one confesses faults. Of these three, since confession is the principal one, the overall chapter is called 'Confession of faults' [chapter 2].
4. To become a suitable vessel in one's stream of being through eliminating the karmic obscurations of envy of others' virtues and creating obstacles for them, one rejoices with the highest happiness in the others' creation of merit.
5. To become a suitable vessel in one's stream of being through abandoning the obscurations of the teachings not remaining and the teacher not being present, which come from the karmic obscurations of abandoning the dharma, one requests the turning of the wheel of dharma and also
6. One supplicates [the Buddhas] not to pass into nirvāṇa.
7. To become a suitable vessel in one's stream of being through eliminating the karmic obscurations of lacking the possibility of a vast and inexhaustible result due to inferior dedications, one dedicates the roots of virtue.

3.2. The main part: Having established the perfectly purified basis, one generates the bodhicitta of aspiration, wishing to actually realize the suchness of all dharmas and to benefit beings through attaining the kāya of complete omniscience. After the preliminary of the threefold-aspiration mind,[7] one then grasps the hook of the vow. [255]

3.3. The conclusion: This comprises generating joy in oneself and others. These three sections comprise chapters 2 and 3.

Part 4, the cooperating condition—subsequently accomplishing the training: the general cause of accomplishing the training is 'Concern' [chapter 4]. The specific trainings are the six perfections. Among these, giving does not have a separate chapter solely on its practice but is taught throughout the text. Moral conduct is taught in the chapter on 'Mindfulness and Clear Comprehension', [chapter 5] because that is the cause of moral conduct not declining. 'Patience' and the rest of the six perfections are directly taught in the next four eponymous chapters.

According to others, the subsequent training is explained according to [Śāntideva's] *Śikṣā-samuccaya*. In that text, the general cause comprises both concern and clear comprehension:

> Learning, moral discipline, giving, patience and so forth—
> As many virtuous qualities as can be named—
> Concern is the root of them all.
> Thus the Sugata has taught it as the attainment of a treasure.[8]

And:

> The practitioner of perfect abandonment
> Will never be separate from concern,
> Nor from mindfulness and clear comprehension,
> Nor moral discipline, all through the mind.[9]

According to this opinion, there are three kinds of specific trainings:

1. Establishing the antidotes and abandoning remaining obstacles
2. Reliance on the accompanying training

3. Seeing the nature of the antidotes: the path of unified calm abiding and insight meditation

The first of these is the 'Patience' chapter which establishes the antidote to impatience with suffering, difficulties and profound dharma. [256] It puts an end to them, i.e. it eliminates them. The second is 'Effort' and the third comprises both 'Meditation' and 'Wisdom'.

These [general and specific trainings] collectively comprise the cooperating condition, which directly establishes the final point.

Part 5, The subsequent results of the practice: this comprises the chapter on 'Dedication', which begins [v10.1]:

> By whatever virtue there is
> In my undertaking
> To enter the bodhisattva conduct...

Therefore, the conduct brings about the results.

PART II
THE PRIMARY BASIS
THE INDIVIDUAL PERSON

IN PRAISE OF BODHICITTA (2)

There are two subsections:

1. The bodily basis: the difficulty of acquiring the freedoms and endowments
2. The mental basis: meritorious intelligence

1. The bodily basis: the difficulty of acquiring the freedoms and endowments

> 1.4
> It is extremely difficult to acquire the freedoms and
>   endowments
> Which make this human birth meaningful.
> If I fail to benefit from it now,
> How will I get a chance like this again?

There are three sections:

1. Their nature
2. Difficult to acquire
3. The extent of the benefits it brings

1. Their nature

Freedom is abandoning the eight non-freedoms: hell-being, hungry ghost, animal, barbarian, long-lived god, wrong views, being devoid of Buddhas, having impaired senses—four human and four non-human states.

Endowment comprises the five endowments of oneself—attaining a human body, unimpaired senses, not having committed any of the inexpiable deeds, being born in a central country and having faith in the remaining [teachings]—and the five endowments from others—the Buddha has appeared, he has taught the dharma, the teachings remain, there are still those who practise and they have compassion for others.

Regarding the freedoms, according to some, the eight non-freedoms are not the opposites of the eight freedoms but their absences. If that were the case, such things as sky-lotuses would also have the freedoms. The freedoms are not absences but the presence of their opposites. It is generally not the case [that the freedoms are mere absences], for then such things as vases would possess the opposite of the non-freedoms, [257] but only sentient beings can have this.

Some say:

- 'The opposite of the four non-human states [freedom] is not distinct from the attaining of a human body [first endowment]
- The opposite of impaired senses [freedom] is having unimpaired senses [second endowment]
- The opposite of holding wrong views [freedom] is engaging in uncorrupted actions [third endowment]
- The opposite of being born in the borderlands [freedom] is being born in a central land [fourth endowment]
- The opposite of being devoid of Buddhas [freedom] is having faith in the remaining teachings [fifth endowment]

Therefore, the freedoms are not distinct from the endowments of oneself.'

According to this opinion, freedom is the negative aspect while endowment is the same thing from the positive aspect. Therefore, they are only distinct in the sense that abandoning the obscurations of the cognizables and realization of reality are also opposite aspects [of a single thing]. However, in *The Biography of Brahmin Jayosmayatana*,[1] the 'difficulty of acquiring the opposite of the eight non-freedoms' and the 'difficulty of acquiring the abundant freedoms' are taught separately, so this opinion does not accord with that text.

2. Difficult to acquire

It is said to be 'extremely difficult' because it is even more difficult for a turtle to put his neck through the centre of a wooden yoke afloat on an ocean.

3. The extent of the benefits it brings

Whilst it may be difficult to acquire, since it is only of slight benefit, why acquire it? A 'human birth' is 'meaningful' because it is the basis for attaining higher rebirths and definitive goodness.

The last two lines of verse 4 indicate that if, having attained it, one did not take hold of the roots of its benefit, then its goodness would subsequently reoccur only very rarely.

2. The mental basis: meritorious intelligence

> **1.5**
> **Just as lightning flashes for an instant**
> **Through the dark, black clouds of the night,**
> **Likewise, only rarely, merit and intelligence arise**
> **Fleetingly in the world through the power of the Buddhas.**

There are five common thoughts:

1. The cause of entering the white dharma in general—the faith of conviction
2. The cause of entering this teaching[2]—the faith of clarity
3. The cause of entering the arising of certainty [258]—the faith of longing
4. The causes of swiftly entering—reflection on the difficulty of acquiring the freedoms and endowments

5. Reflection that the freedom which has been obtained will not last long

There are two uncommon thoughts:

1. The kindness of wishing to benefit sentient beings
2. Faith which becomes certain about the means

The common and uncommon attitudes are the proper basis for the generation of bodhicitta and the subsequent practice of the conduct by someone who is of the awakened Mahāyāna family.

If one wonders how the difficulty of acquiring human birth is being exemplified here, the example is: 'night' means being without the appearance of the sun, 'dark and black' means being without the appearance of the moon, 'clouds' means having little chance of any appearances and 'just as lightning flashes for an instant' means appearing nevertheless, despite those factors. Also, 'through the power of the Buddhas' is the condition of the attitudes, 'merit and intelligence' is the nature, 'only rarely' means arising only very occasionally and 'arise fleetingly' means not remaining for very long.

PART III
THE PRODUCTIVE CAUSE
THE GENERATION OF BODHICITTA

IN PRAISE OF BODHICITTA (3)

The generation of bodhicitta has two main subsections:

1. Praising the benefits of bodhicitta [chapter 1, v6-36]
2. The ritual of taking hold[1] of bodhicitta [chapters 2-3]

1. Praising the benefits of bodhicitta

1. Ordinary benefits
2. Extraordinary benefits
3. The reasons for the benefits
4. Summarizing the benefits of self
5. Summarizing the benefits of others

1. Ordinary benefits

1. Invisible benefits
2. Visible benefits
3. Praising the benefits by analogy

> Section overview: Ordinary benefits [v6-14]
>
> 1. Invisible benefits
>   1. It overcomes all nonvirtue
>   1. The nature of nonvirtue
>   2. How it overcomes them
>   2. It benefits oneself
>   3. It has the power to benefit others
>   4. It fulfils individual worldly wishes
> 2. Visible benefits
> 3. Praising the benefits by analogy
>   1. It transforms the inferior into the supreme, like the elixir of an alchemist
>   2. It is difficult to find but extremely powerful, like a wish fulfilling jewel
>   3. Its fruits know no exhaustion, like the inconceivable tree
>   4. It overcomes the inexpiable evil deeds, like a warrior
>   5. It consumes the inevitable results of nonvirtuous actions, like the fire at the end of time
>   6. Other specific examples

1. Invisible benefits

    1. It overcomes all nonvirtue
    2. It benefits oneself
    3. It has the power to benefit others
    4. It fulfils individual worldly wishes [259]

1. It overcomes all nonvirtue

    1. The nature of nonvirtue
    2. How bodhicitta overcomes nonvirtue

1. The nature of nonvirtue

> **1.6**
> **In this way, virtue is constantly weak and feeble,**
> **And the extremely great power of nonvirtue is unbearable.**

The first line indicates the weakness of the power of the antidote. 'The extremely great power of nonvirtue' indicates the great power of that which is to be abandoned. 'Unbearable' indicates the result of this—suffering. One's nonvirtues are not dominated by virtues; rather, one's virtues are dominated by nonvirtues.

2. How bodhicitta overcomes nonvirtue

> **What virtue, if not perfect bodhicitta,**
> **Could possibly overcome it?**

There is no virtue other than bodhicitta that possesses the power conducive to liberation which overcomes such nonvirtue.

2. It benefits oneself

1.7
The mighty sages, who have known it for many aeons,
Have seen that only bodhicitta has this power.

Since they have meditated on it throughout innumerable aeons, the Buddhas, who perceive what is beneficial and what is not beneficial, acknowledge that bodhicitta is of the supreme benefit.

3. It has the power to benefit others

> **With bodhicitta, limitless multitudes**
> **Will easily attain the supreme bliss.**

When this intention arises in their mind, limitless sentient beings will easily attain the supreme bliss of great enlightenment. Why is this accomplishment so easy, when one must practise with difficulty for three inconceivable aeons? Because bodhisattvas give rise to a mind which takes joy in undertaking difficulties for the benefit of others, because their suffering is accompanied by the result, and because, compared to the limitless sufferings of saṃsāra, the difficulties are very slight.

4. It fulfils individual worldly wishes

1.8

> Those wishing to end the many sufferings of conditioned existence,
> Those wishing the dispel the unhappiness of beings,
> And those wishing for many happinesses,
> Should never abandon this bodhicitta.

The first line refers to the happiness of the śrāvakas, the second to bodhisattvas and the third to the happinesses of the higher realms. [260]

Since the happiness of the śrāvakas and happiness within conditioned existence may arise without the generation of bodhicitta, if they do arise with it, is it not illogical to say they are results of bodhicitta? They are not contrary to it and although they are not part of its nature, results will occur even while generating bodhicitta as mere by-products. Since these are temporarily connected with it, they are presented as the results of bodhicitta. So even those who wish to train in the śrāvaka bhūmis should practise the training of the perfection of wisdom.

2. Visible benefits

> 1.9
> The very instant bodhicitta arises
> In someone tormented in the prison of saṃsāra,
> They will be called an 'heir of the Sugatas',
> And be praised by gods and men.

When bodhicitta arises, a new name is received: one is called an 'heir of the Sugatas', meaning that one is worthy of the praises of worldly gods and men. Who receives this? All beings who are tormented in the prison of saṃsāra. When do they receive it? The very instant that they generate bodhicitta.

3. Praising the benefits by analogy

1. It transforms the inferior into the supreme, like the elixir of an alchemist
2. It is difficult to find but extremely powerful, like a wish fulfilling jewel

3. Its fruits know no exhaustion, like the inconceivable tree
4. It overcomes the inexpiable evil deeds, like a warrior
5. It consumes the inevitable results of nonvirtuous actions, like the fire at the end of time
6. Other specific examples

1. It transforms the inferior into the supreme, like the elixir of an alchemist

> **1.10**
> Like a supreme alchemical elixir,
> Having imbibed it, the impure body is transformed
> Into the priceless jewel of the kāya of a conqueror.
> So, firmly take hold of what is called 'bodhicitta'.

The impure body is transformed. Into what? Into the priceless jewel of the kāya of a conqueror. What transforms it? The 'taking hold', i.e. taking hold of the generation of bodhicitta. How is that exemplified? [261] It is like the transformation of base metals into gold by an alchemical elixir. Alternatively, 'take hold' may refer to [the transformation of] the body itself.

2. It is difficult to find but extremely powerful, like a wish fulfilling jewel

> **1.11**
> If the only guides of beings have, with unfettered minds,
> Seen its value in consummate examination,
> Those of us who want to be free from wandering
> Should firmly grasp the precious bodhicitta.

Who grasps firmly this precious bodhicitta? Those who wish to be free from the saṃsāric state of wandering. Why do they grasp it? Because its value has been seen in consummate examination. Whose examination? The 'guides of beings', i.e. the Sugatas, who have examined it with their enlightened minds.

3. Its fruits know no exhaustion, like the inconceivable tree

> **1.12**

> All other virtues are, like a plantain tree,
> Exhausted after they produce their fruit,
> But the perennial tree of bodhicitta
> Grows with an inexhaustible supply.

Virtues which are not based upon the generation of bodhicitta, once ripened, are exhausted but those which are based upon the generation of bodhicitta, once ripened, will grow in conformity with their cause and their exhaustion will be unknown.

4. It overcomes the inexpiable evil deeds,[2] like a warrior

> **1.13**
> Like facing great terrors accompanied by a warrior,
> Even those who have committed the extremely evil acts
> Will instantly be freed by relying on it.
> Why then would conscientious people not rely on this?

One will be freed from the intense suffering that results from the extremely evil inexpiable acts after just a moment of experiencing it. Although the acts are not purified, temporarily the resultant ripening of the sufferings does not occur, until finally they are discarded. For whom? For whomever relies upon bodhicitta. In what way? Like passing great terrors guarded by a warrior, until the final destination is reached, temporarily one will not be harmed.

5. It consumes the inevitable results of nonvirtuous actions, like the fire at the end of time

> **1.14**
> Like the fire at the end of time, great evils
> Are totally consumed by it.

Bodhicitta consumes the great inexpiable evil deeds and they are gone forever. How long does it take? An instant. What is it like? It is like the fire at the end of time, i.e. the world-destroying fire at the end of the aeon.

6. Other specific examples

Its benefits are limitless,
As Lord Maitreya explained to Sudhana.

Where are the limitless benefits of bodhicitta explained? In the *Āryabuddhavataṃsaka Sutra*. By whom are they explained? By Lord Maitreya. [262] To whom are they explained? They are explained to Sudhana, as follows. The merchant's son Sudhana, having generated bodhicitta before the Bhagavān Mañjughoṣa and having received instructions from many spiritual teachers, finally sought out the Jina Maitreya in the 'Palace of Vairocana Adorned with Ornaments' on the shores of a great lake. Maitreya received him, saying,

> 'Look! You are a being of pure intent.
> Sudhana, a son born into wealth,
> You have approached me. Wise one,
> Have you travelled well? You who have compassion and
>   love...'[3]

And so on. Following this praise, Sudhana, the merchant's son, requested, 'I have generated bodhicitta but I pray you teach me how to train with diligence.'

Maitreya responded, 'Son of noble family, bodhicitta is like the seed of all the Buddha's teachings. Since it makes virtuous dharmas grow in all beings, it is like a field. Since it is the support of the entire world, it is like the earth. Since one is protected by all the bodhisattvas, it is like a father. Since it delivers from all poverty, it is like Vaiśravaṇa. Since it perfectly establishes all benefits, it is like a wish fulfilling gem. Since it defeats the enemy defilements, it is like a lance. Since it envelops the undisciplined mind, it is like clothing. Since it severs the head of the defilements, it is like a sword. [263] Since it protects from all hostility, it is like a weapon. Since it captures those in the river of saṃsāra, it is like a fishing hook. Since it scatters the layer of dust of the defilements, it is like the mandala of wind. Since it collects all the conduct and aspirations of the bodhisattvas, it is like synopsis. Since it is worshipped by the worlds of humans, demigods and gods, it is like a stupa. Son of noble family, bodhicitta possesses these qualities, as well as a myriad of other qualities.'

2. The extraordinary benefits of bodhicitta

1. Divisions
2. Characteristics
3. Benefits of aspiration
4. Benefits of application

1. Divisions

> **1.15**
> **When summarized, bodhicitta**
> **Should be known as having two types:**
> **Bodhicitta of aspiration**
> **And bodhicitta of application.**

The first two lines enumerate the divisions as two and the latter two name each one.

2. Characteristics

> **1.16**
> **Like understanding the difference**
> **Between wishing to go and going,**
> **So the wise should understand the difference**
> **Between these two, respectively.**

Some say that aspiration, as the wish to go, is generating the mind which arises from symbols [or words] because one merely takes motivation as one's object in order to have realization of the path. Application, as the actual going, is generating the mind of the attainment of the ultimate dharmata because one takes actual enlightenment as one's object by directly entering the uncorrupted path of seeing the truth. However, this is not the opinion of the Ācārya [Śāntideva] because he explains in the *Śikṣā-samuccaya* that ordinary individuals also train in application [bodhicitta] and hence the dharmata is attained only by receiving teachings on the practices of application bodhicitta.[4] [264]

According to Ācārya Jetāri, aspiration is the pursuit of enlightenment for the benefit of beings and application is the protection of that intention from decline.[5] However, this is not the opinion of the Ācārya because protection from decline does not fit the example of going somewhere.

According to some others, aspiration is as before [i.e. pursuit of enlightenment] but application is the training itself. However, this was not the intention of the Ācārya because in the liturgy, generating application bodhicitta is separate to undertaking the training.[6] It would also contradict the scriptures, which refer to three bases:

- The fortunate basis—the [bodhisattva or Mahāyāna] family
- The basis for practising the conduct—generating bodhicitta
- The basis for the swift attainment of perfect buddhahood—the bodhisattva training [7]

That is, the teaching on the second basis—generating bodhicitta—is distinct from the teaching on the third basis—the training. The source for the explanation of aspiration and application given by the Ācārya is the *Avataṃsaka Sutra*, where it says,

> It is rare for a person to have the aspiration for enlightenment.
> It is even rarer to pursue the conduct.[8]

Thus, pursuit of the result is the generation of aspiration bodhicitta, while pursuit of the means to achieve that result is application bodhicitta. Therefore, it is also called 'generating the mind endowed with conduct' because the conduct is motivated by the promise to practise it.

3. Benefits of aspiration

1.17
For those wandering in saṃsāra,
Great results arise from aspiration bodhicitta,
But a ceaseless stream of merits does not arise
As it does for application bodhicitta.

With aspiration, since it is not the same as having diligence in actual practice, although one may have abundant happiness even while remaining within saṃsāra, if one's circumstances lack the actual cause which will fulfil that intention, one will not enter a continuous stream of merit because one does not have the intention and seriousness of being committed to the conduct. [265] But if one has the cause which fulfils the gathering of virtue, then merit is present even when one's intention and seriousness are interrupted, such as when asleep or when distracted.

4. Benefits of application

> **1.18**
> **For whoever embraces**
> **This incontrovertible intent to liberate**
> **Limitless realms of beings,**
> **By the perfect adoption of that intent,**
>
> **1.19**
> **From the moment of embracing it, even when asleep**
> **Or distracted, a force of merit**
> **As vast as space**
> **Arises in an uninterrupted stream.**

The one who adopts this intent, from the moment it is embraced, creates a force of merit equal to the sky. What does it mean to 'adopt' the intent? It means that the intent is 'irreversible', i.e. one does not allow the commitment to practise the path to diminish. What is the purpose of not allowing the commitment to practise the path to diminish? It is to completely liberate the limitless realms of sentient beings. Therefore, through adopting the generation of the mind which thinks, 'I will not allow the conduct which will liberate sentient beings to diminish', merit increases. Does it increase only intermittently? No, it is constant, without interruption. When does the cause to fulfil the intent occur? Although the cause is not present when one is sleeping or distracted, it nevertheless arises by the power of adopting the commitment. For example, this is like the continuity of merit that arises for someone who adopts renunciation, even when sleeping or distracted. Regarding this distraction, however, if someone is generating bodhicitta but, out of distraction from training, decides to stop practising, it is not logical that merit still increases.

> Section overview: The reasons for the benefits [v20-35b]
>
> 1. Scripture
> 2. Reasoning
>   1. Aspiration bodhicitta
>   1. The vastness of its intent
>   2. Its rarity
>   1. There is nobody else who has such a benevolent intent
>   2. Nor ourselves
>   3. Establishing the greatness of the benefit of generating this mind
>   3. The greatness of its goodness
>   2. Application bodhicitta
>   1. The actual practice is undertaken
>   2. The many individuals affected
>   1. Those possessing the cause, ignorance
>   2. Those experiencing result, the destitution of happiness
>   3. Those tormented by suffering
>   3. It does not depend on getting anything back
>   4. Establishing vastness
>   5. Explaining how it is particularly powerful

3. The reasons for the benefits

    1. Scripture
    2. Reasoning

1. Scripture

1.20
The Tathāgata himself taught
These benefits along with their reasons
In the *Sutra Requested by Subahu*
For the sake of those inclined to lesser paths.

These benefits were taught by the Tathāgata himself. [266] In what sutra? In the *Sutra Requested by Subahu*. For what purpose? For the sake of benefitting sentient beings inclined towards lesser paths, i.e. they were taught for the benefit of the uncertain Mahāyāna family. Are they merely described? No, their reasons are also explained, i.e. the benefits are demonstrated with the reasons for them, as explained in the next section.

2. Reasoning

1. The reasons for the benefits of aspiration
2. The reasons for the benefits of application

1. The reasons for the benefits of aspiration

1. The vastness of its intent
2. Its rarity
3. The greatness of its goodness

1. The vastness of its intent

1.21
Even if one wishes to dispel merely
The head pains of beings,
The possession of that beneficial intention
Is endowed with boundless merit.

1.22
What can one say then of the wish to dispel
The endless unhappiness of each sentient being,
Wishing to establish every single one of them
In limitless qualities?

The sea-captain Maitra named his son 'Daughter' [to protect him from following his father into a dangerous occupation]. The father died shortly after and when Daughter came of age, he asked his mother about his father's profession. She replied that he was an incense merchant. So Daughter purchased incense to the value of two hundred silver coins and then returned to attend to his mother. He said, 'I am going to become a merchant in the town by selling incense.' He traded incense in the town and then similarly in the city, until he was selling to the whole region. In this way, in the town he accumulated four hundred silver coins, then in the city six hundred, until across the whole region he had made eight hundred silver coins.

He returned each time to attend to his mother. She finally told him that his father was a sea-merchant. Having heard this, he immediately prepared to go to sea. When his mother objected to this, he kicked her in the head and departed. He travelled to the cities called 'Lands above the ocean shores' and spent a year each in four cities called 'Intoxicating', 'Ever-intoxicating', 'Delighting' and 'Guru of Brahmā', in which he consorted blissfully with two hundred, four hundred, six hundred and then eight hundred goddesses respectively. He returned to attend to his mother, [267] and lived out his days.

He departed to the cities of the ephemeral hells and passed through the hell-cities called Intoxicating, Ever-intoxicating, Delighting and Guru of Brahmā, whereupon a voice in the sky spoke, saying, 'Your arrival here is by the power of your actions [karma].' He saw a group of hell-beings with their heads being drilled by wheels and he immediately made the wish, 'May the pains of their heads be dispelled and may they ripen in me!' Whereupon, his was the only head being drilled but, through his kindness, he was then freed from that suffering. Thus, he said, 'This occurred through the full ripening of the harm I did to my mother.'

If even the intention to dispel pains in the head has such benefit, what can one say of the wish to dispel the endless suffering of all the limitless sentient beings and to establish every one of them in limitless happiness?

2. Its rarity

1. There is nobody else who has such a benevolent intent
2. Not even for themselves
3. Establishing the greatness of the benefit of generating this mind

1. There is nobody else who has such a benevolent intent

>**1.23**
>**Do even our father or mothers**
>**Ever have such a benevolent wish?**

Do even the gods, the rishis,
Or even Brahmā harbour such benevolence?

One's parents, who naturally have a strong bond of love with their children, one's personal guardian deities,[9] rishis who always speak the truth and even Brahmā who has trained his mind in the [four] immeasurables certainly wish for our happiness in this life but they do not have the intention to achieve enlightenment for our benefit.

2. Not even for themselves

> 1.24
> Those beings never before,
> Even in their dreams,
> Had an intention like this, even for their own sake.
> How could it arise then for the sake of others?

3. Establishing the greatness of the benefit of generating this mind

> 1.25
> The intention to benefit others did not arise
> For sentient beings even for their own sake.
> The arising of this highest treasure of the mind
> Is an unprecedented wonder.

'Unprecedented' here means it is extraordinary or uncommon.

3. The greatness of its goodness

> 1.26
> It is the cause of joy in all wandering beings.
> It is the elixir remedying the suffering of sentient beings.
> How can the merit of this treasure of mind
> Even begin to be measured or quantified?

It generates both joy in the mind and happiness in the body.

2. The reasons for the benefits of application [268]

   1. The actual practice is undertaken

2. The many individuals affected
3. It does not depend on getting anything back
4. Establishing vastness
5. Explaining how it is particularly powerful

1. The actual practice is undertaken

> **1.27**
> **If the mere intention to help others**
> **Is better than making offerings to the Buddhas,**
> **What can one say about the endeavour**
> **To bring happiness and benefit to all beings without exception?**

This verse describes the intention to help others as superior even to the worship of the Buddhas. As it says in the *Sutra Requested by Candrapradipa*,

> If one filled a myriad of worlds
> With limitless kinds of offerings
> And offered this every day for all time,
> It would not even approach the mind of loving kindness.[10]

It also says in the *Sutra Requested by Vīradatta*,

> To the Buddhas, the one who has
> The intention of bodhicitta
> Is superior to the one who makes offerings
> Of overflowing treasures to the Sugatas.[11]

2. The many individuals affected

> **1.28**
> **Though they long to be free from suffering,**
> **They hurriedly chase after suffering itself.**
> **Though they long for happiness, in their ignorance,**
> **They destroy it as though their own happiness were their enemy.**

1.29
Whoever is destitute of happiness
And burdened with many sufferings
Will be filled with every happiness
And cut off from all their suffering,

1.30
And their ignorance, too, will be dispelled.
What virtue could equal that?
What friend can compare to it?
What merit is remotely comparable to it?

There are three kinds of beings referenced here:

1. Those possessing the cause—ignorance
2. Those experiencing result—destitution of happiness
3. Those tormented by suffering

1. Although they long to be free from suffering, in their ignorance they hurriedly chase after suffering itself and, although they long for happiness, in their ignorance they destroy their own happiness as if it were their enemy. Thus, they possess the cause: ignorance. The benefit for such beings is that 'their ignorance too will be dispelled.' The additional benefit of that is they now accumulate merit. No other kind of merit is known which is remotely like this.

2. The particular benefit for whomever is destitute of happiness is that they are 'filled with every happiness.' The praise is, 'What [virtue] could equal to that?' [269]

3. The benefit for those burdened with many sufferings is they are 'cut off from all suffering.' The praise is, 'What friend is even alike to it?'

3. It does not depend on getting anything back

1.31
If one who repays a helpful deed
Is worthy of some praise,
What can one say of the bodhisattva
Whose excellent deeds are unsolicited?

4. Establishing vastness

> **1.32**
> Worldly people respect someone who briefly
> Gives a little food, contemptuously,
> To a few beings, satisfying them only for half a day,
> Saying, 'That was a virtuous deed.'

> **1.33**
> What can one say then of someone who
> Always gives the unsurpassed happiness
> Of the Sugatas to countless sentient beings throughout time,
> The ultimate perfection of their wishes?

Even the giving of food is praised with the words, 'That was a virtuous deed.' If one wonders why the bodhisattva is superior, it is because the former has an inferior number of beings: a few; inferior time: one moment; inferior substance: mere food; inferior conduct: with contempt; and inferior benefit: satisfying for half a day, while the bodhisattva is superior in always practising vast giving for great fields of countless sentient beings; for a superior time: throughout time; with a superior substance: the unsurpassed bliss of the Sugatas; and a superior benefit: the ultimate perfection of their wishes.

5. Explaining how it is particularly powerful

> **1.34**
> If one should develop a malevolent intention
> Towards such beneficent sons of the conquerors,
> The Sage has taught they will remain in the hells
> For as many aeons as malevolent thoughts developed.

For even a momentary malevolent intent, one can remain in the hells for an entire aeon. In the sutra of the *Display of Completely Definitive Pacification*, it says,

> For however long they develop a mind of hatred and a mind of contempt for bodhisattvas, for as many aeons beings will remain in the hell realms.[12]

Having explained bodhicitta as a particularly powerful field of nonvirtue, next it is explained as a particularly powerful field of merit:

> **1.35**
> **Nevertheless, if one's attitude is good,**
> **The results will be even greater.**

4. Summarizing the benefits of self

> **The sons of the conquerors, with great seriousness,**
> **Never perform nonvirtue and their virtues continuously increase.**

With great dedication, they never perform nonvirtue [270] even at the cost of their lives. Rather, their virtues continuously increase.

5. Summarizing the benefits of others

> **1.36**
> **I bow down before**
> **Those in whom this sacred jewel of mind is born**
> **And I take refuge in those sources of happiness**
> **Who bring happiness even to those who harm them.**

Bringing happiness even to those who harm them means, out of compassion, they bestow happiness on those who do them harm. It does not mean the happiness arises as a result of the harms committed, for that would contradict the earlier assertion in verse 34.

Chapter 2

CONFESSION OF FAULTS

> Textual overview (recap):
>
> 1. The purposes of the composition [chapter 1, v1-3]
> 2. The primary basis: the individual person [v4-5]
> 3. The productive cause: the generation of bodhicitta [v6-chapter 3]
>   1. Praising the benefits of bodhicitta [chapter 1, v6-36]
>   2. Generating bodhicitta in one's stream of being [chapters 2-3]
>   1. Preliminaries
>   2. Main Part
>   3. Conclusion
> 4. The cooperating condition: subsequently practising the training [chapters 4-9]
> 5. The subsequent results of the practice [chapter 10]

Generating bodhicitta in one's stream of being [i.e. part 3.2] has three subsections:

1. Preliminaries
2. Main part
3. Conclusion

1. Preliminaries

This comprises the seven aspects of the seven-branch prayer, beginning with the making of offerings:

1. Offerings
2. Taking refuge
3. Confession
4. Rejoicing
5. Requesting
6. Supplication
7. Dedication of merit

1. Offerings

1. Offering worldly substances owned by oneself
2. Offering unowned worldly substances, i.e. those which exist unappropriated by anyone
3. Offering the physical body
4. Offerings emanated by the mind
5. Unsurpassable offerings
6. Offering homage

The first five are offerings of material goods, while the sixth is the offering of service. Among the material goods, the first four are surpassable, while the last is unsurpassable. Among the surpassable material goods, the first two are outer offerings, while the third is inner.

1. Offering worldly substances owned by oneself

> **2.1**
> **In order to take hold of this treasure of mind,**
> **I make offerings properly to the oceans of good qualities—**
> **The stainless jewels of the Tathāgata, the holy dharma,**
> **And the sons of the Buddhas.**

The basis is the 'Tathāgata' and so forth, i.e. the Three Jewels. 'Stainless jewels' and 'oceans of good qualities' refer to all three of them. Physically and mentally, one 'makes offerings properly'—i.e. the offerings are magnificent and one's intentions are pure.

2. Offering unowned worldly substances [271]

2.2
I offer every flower and fruit there is,
Every kind of restorative,
All the wealth in the world,
And all the clear, refreshing waters.

2.3
Likewise, I offer bejewelled mountains,
Secluded and delightful forest groves,
Trees of paradise rich with blossoming flowers,
Many trees with branches laden with excellent fruit,

2.4
The beautiful fragrances of gods and men,
All incense, wish granting trees and bejewelled trees,
All kinds of crops, cultivated without effort,
And everything else worthy of offering, all ornamented with

2.5
Lakes and pools adorned with lotus flowers,
Mellifluous with the song of wild geese,
In the endlessness of space and in innumerable worlds,
All completely unowned.

2.6
Thinking of these, I offer them properly
To the sages, supreme among men, and their sons.
Holy recipients, out of your compassion,
Please accept my offerings and think of me with kindness.

2.7
I am without merit and completely destitute;
I have no other wealth to give.

> Therefore, protectors, you who think only of the benefit of others,
> Please accept these for my benefit.

The first two verses concern the particular things offered, mostly the objects of mankind, while what follows that is the possessions of other kinds of beings. 'In the endlessness of space and in innumerable worlds' indicates the particular locus. Being 'completely unowned' indicates the particular criterion. 'The sages, supreme among men, and their sons' indicates the recipients. Verse 6 indicates the actual application. Verse 7 indicates the particular cause and purpose.

3. Offering the physical body

> 2.8
> To the conquerors and their sons, I offer
> All my bodies. Sublime beings,
> Please always accept them,
> And I will be your devoted servant.

> 2.9
> When I am under your protection,
> I will fearlessly bring benefit to sentient beings in conditioned existence.
> I will completely overcome my former nonvirtues
> And henceforth cease all other nonvirtues.

The recipients are the conquerors and their sons. The offering substance is all one's bodies. The practice is indicated by 'sublime beings, please always accept them'. The type of offering is indicated in line 8d. The purpose of the offering is indicated in lines 9ab. The practice subsequent to the offering is indicated in lines 9cd.

4. Offerings emanated by the mind

1. Bathing
2. Robes and ornaments
3. Scented oil
4. Flowers
5. Incense

6. Food
7. Lamps
8. Palaces
9. Articles worthy of great beings
10. Offerings not for the purposes of enjoyment—the uninterrupted stream of veneration

1. Bathing

> **2.10**
> **In freshly scented bathing houses,**
> **With crystal floors, clear and bright,**
> **And columns shimmering with jewels,**
> **Decorated with canopies alight with pearls,**
>
> **2.11**
> **To the Tathāgatas and their sons**
> **With many precious vases, filled with**
> **Scented water that delights the senses, and with many songs**
> **And music, I request to bathe the Buddhas' forms.**
>
> **2.12**
> **I then wipe dry their bodies with the finest cloths,**
> **Fresh and fragranced with scents.**

The first verse is emanating the bathing houses; 11a indicates the objects of veneration; 11b-d is requesting to bathe their bodies; and the final two lines indicate drying their bodies.

2. Robes and ornaments

> **To the holy ones I offer**
> **Fragrant robes of appropriate colours.**
>
> **2.13**
> **With all kinds of excellent garments, soft and fine,**
> **And an array of supreme ornaments, I adorn**
> **Ārya Samantabhadra, Mañjughoṣa,**
> **Avalokiteśvara and the others.**

'Appropriate colours' means offering robes of the correct colours for those who dress as monastics, while ornaments and variously coloured garments are offered to those who dress as laypeople. [272]

3. Scented oils

> **2.14**
> With supreme scents that permeate
> The three thousand-fold world system, I anoint
> The bodies of the lords of sages, blazing with light,
> Like polishing pure, burnished gold.

4. Flowers

> **2.15**
> To the supreme objects of worship, the lords of sages, I offer
> Delightful flowers such as mandaras, lotuses
> And utpalas, all sweet-smelling and
> Wonderfully laid out in garlands,

5. Incense

> **2.16**
> And I offer clouds of permeating incense, enchanting to the mind,
> From the finest incense sticks,

6. Food

> And I offer many kinds of
> Ambrosial foods and drinks.

7. Lamps

> **2.17**
> I offer jewelled lamps, arranged upon
> Rows of golden lotus flowers.

8. Palaces

Their grounds fragrant with the perfume
Of flower petals scattered upon it,

2.18
I offer vast palaces, resonant with pleasing songs of praise,
Bright and resplendent with hanging ornaments of pearls and jewels,
Ornamenting the vastnesses of space,
To those who have the nature of compassion.

According to Ācārya Ratnākaraśānti,[1] verse 2.17 is actually arranged,

On grounds fragrant with the perfume
Of flower petals scattered upon it,
I offer jewelled lamps, arranged upon
Rows of golden lotus flowers.

The offerings of lamps and palaces are thus set out as verses 2.17 and 2.18, respectively.

9. Articles worthy of great beings

These articles comprise the precious parasol, lion throne, foot rest, cooling fan with a jewelled handle and so forth. Of these, the parasol with golden handle is described in the first of the next two verses:

2.19
I offer to the lords of sages
Beautiful jewelled parasols with golden handles,
Decorated with handsome designs and
Held aloft in an arrangement joyful to behold,

2.20
And a multitude of other offerings,
With music delightful to hear.
I present billowing clouds of offerings
To soothe the sufferings of sentient beings.

10. Offerings not for the purposes of enjoyment—the uninterrupted stream of veneration

Having offered objects for the purpose of pleasure, now one offers objects which are not for pleasure: an uninterrupted stream of veneration.

> **2.21**
> **May an uninterrupted rain**
> **Of flowers and precious gems descend**
> **Upon all the jewels of holy dharma,**
> **The stupas and statues.**

5. Unsurpassable offerings

The masters of the tenth bhūmi, who have gained mastery over the six higher perceptions, make offerings to the Buddhas by manifesting light rays which arise from their actions:

> **2.22**
> **Just as Mañjughoṣa and others**
> **Made offerings to the conquerors**
> **Likewise I make offerings**
> **To the Tathāgatas and their sons.**

6. Offering homage

   1. Praise
   2. Prostration

1. Praise

> **2.23**
> **I praise these oceans of good qualities**
> **With oceans of melodious praise.**
> **May these pleasing clouds of melodious praise**
> **Always ascend to their ears.**

2. Prostration to the sources of refuge

> **2.24**
> **To the Buddhas of the three times,**

To the dharma, and to the supreme among communities,
With bodies as numerous as atoms
I respectfully prostrate.

The recipient, agent and action of prostration correspond to the first two lines, third and fourth lines, respectively. One also prostrates as follows: [273]

2.25
I prostrate to the bases of bodhicitta,
And to the stupas,
And I prostrate to preceptors, ācāryas,
And the supreme practitioners.

The 'bases of bodhicitta' means forms of the Buddha-body which are extraordinary supports of generating bodhicitta. Some commentaries say it means the bodhisattva pitakas.

2. Taking refuge

The first line indicates the particular time and the following three indicate the particular field and type of refuge:

2.26
Until the essence of enlightenment,
I take refuge in the Buddha,
And likewise in the dharma,
And in the assembly of bodhisattvas.

Taking refuge can be summarized in seven points:

1. Classifications
2. Explaining their distinguishing characteristics
3. Nature
4. Distinction of resultant refuge and generation of aspiration bodhicitta
5. Purpose
6. The meaning of the term 'refuge'
7. The distinct trainings

1. Classifications: ordinary refuge and extraordinary refuge
2. Explaining their distinguishing characteristics

> *Sources*: Śrāvakas emphasize as their source of refuge the result of the śrāvaka [vehicle]—the stage of an arhat. Having abandoned suffering, arhats listen to the dharma in the presence of the Buddha and teach it to others and thus they are the precious jewel of the saṅgha. Pratyekabuddhas, through their realization of the profound dependent origination, emphasize as their source of refuge the precious jewel of the dharma which dispels sufferings. Mahāyānists emphasize as their source of refuge the teacher, the Buddha, who frees them from fear. Taking hold of all three—taking the Buddha as the teacher, the dharma as the path and the saṅgha as companions—is the 'causal' refuge [as opposed to the 'resultant' refuge].[2]
>
> *Durations*: Hīnayānists take refuge for as long as they live; Mahāyānists take refuge until they have attained ultimate enlightenment.
>
> *Causes*: Śrāvakas and pratyekabuddhas, wishing to be liberated from suffering, take refuge out of faith, whilst Mahāyānists [274] take refuge out of a compassion that wishes to free others from their sufferings.
>
> *Motivations*: Śrāvakas take refuge for their own benefit, whilst Mahāyānists take refuge to free others from their sufferings.

These four distinguishing characteristics determine the specific superiorities of the extraordinary refuge.

3. Nature

The one who seeks the result—buddhahood, the source of fearlessness—takes the Buddha as the teacher, the dharma as the path and the saṅgha as companions. While striving for that result, even though one takes the Buddha as teacher and so forth [i.e. dharma as path, saṅgha as companions], if one takes other teachers such as Brahmā, it is not the proper refuge, since one still seeks inferior results.

4. Distinction of resultant refuge and generating aspiration bodhicitta

How then is the resultant refuge different from aspiration bodhicitta? To think, 'Seeking enlightenment for the benefit of sentient beings, I will definitely attain the result' is merely an intention in the context of refuge, whereas in the generation of aspiration bodhicitta, one actually grasps the hook of a vow.

5. Purpose

By taking refuge, one can go on to take the prātimokṣa vows. Furthermore, one takes refuge in order to possess great protection, to restrain the karmic obscuration of erroneous objects of faith, to be counted as a holy person and to be protected by gods who have faith in the dharma.

6. The meaning of the term 'refuge'

When in the grip of a mass of obscurations, fears and sufferings, one seeks a refuge from them.

7. The training which follows refuge

From the ordinary perspective, it is said there are four primary trainings:

> Attending holy beings, listening to the dharma, disciplining one's mind [275] and practising the dharma in conformity with the dharma.

And four associated trainings:

> Being without sensory disturbances, perfectly undertaking the training, having love and compassion for sentient beings and endeavouring in making offerings at the appropriate times.

These quotations are from Ārya Asaṅga.[3] From the extraordinary perspective, it is taught in the *Parinirvāṇa Sutra*:

> After going for refuge to the Buddha,
> One is a perfect follower of virtue,[4]
> And should not take refuge
> In any other deities.

56 | BODHICARYĀVATĀRA WITH COMMENTARY

If one seeks refuge in the dharma
One should abandon the intention to kill any life.
If one seeks refuge in the saṅgha,
One should not prostrate to the tīrthikas.[5]

3. Confession

1. The power of regret
2. The power of reliance
3. The power of antidote
4. The power of desisting

Section overview: The power of regret [v27-46]

1. Consideration of each type of act individually
   1. Supplication to the objects of reliance
   2. Consideration of the natures individually
   3. Consideration of the objects individually
2. Longing to be freed swiftly
   1. The aspects of longing
   2. Ceasing to rely on the unreliable
3. Consideration of individual meaningless acts
   1. Various kinds of nonvirtuous actions have been committed
   2. Consideration of their meaninglessness
   3. Logically establishing that point
   4. Empirically establishing that point
   5. Summary
4. Fear of the results
   1. The inevitable result: transmigration to another rebirth
   2. Fear of experiencing this
   3. The reason why the fear will not abate
   4. The aspects of suffering

---

1. The power of regret

   1. Consideration of each type of act individually
   2. Longing to be freed swiftly
   3. Consideration of individual meaningless acts

4. Fear of the results

1. Consideration of each type of act individually

   1. Supplication to the objects of reliance
   2. Consideration of the natures individually
   3. Consideration of the objects individually

1. Supplication to the objects of reliance

> **2.27**
> **To the perfect Buddhas and bodhisattvas**
> **Who dwell in all directions,**
> **And who possess great compassion,**
> **I supplicate you with joined palms.**

The first three lines indicate the objects of reliance, 'joined palms' indicates the act of outward respect and 'supplication' indicates the act of speech.

2. Consideration of the natures individually

> **2.28**
> **Having wandered without beginning**
> **In this life and in others,**
> **I stupidly performed nonvirtues,**
> **Or commanded them to be done.**

> **2.29**
> **Compelled by ignorance and delusion,**
> **I took pleasure in this.**
> **Now seeing this was a terrible mistake,**
> **I sincerely confess it to the protectors.**

One's own 'stupidity' is the general motivation for nonvirtue. The specific reason is the compulsion by ignorance and delusion. 'Nonvirtues' are one's own inherent misdeeds, attendant misdeeds and the inciting of others to the same. The last two lines indicate the content of the confession.

3. Consideration of the objects individually [276]

2.30
Whatever harm I have done towards
The Three Jewels, my parents, my teachers and others,
Based on the defilements,
And whatever nonvirtues I, burdened with nonvirtue

2.31
And afflicted with many faults, have done
With my body, speech or mind,
These deeds, now utterly unbearable to me,
I confess before the guides of the world.

The first two lines indicate the substantive objects. The next line indicates the motivation. The next three lines indicate the basis. The last two lines are a consideration of results of this.

2. Longing to be freed swiftly

1. The aspects of longing
2. Ceasing to rely on the unreliable

1. The aspects of longing

2.32
I will die before
My nonvirtues have been purified.
So that I may be saved from them,
I pray for your protection to come swiftly.

The first two lines indicate the negative actions which have not been confessed. The next line is the intention and the last line is the supplication to the objects of reliance.

2. Ceasing to rely on the unreliable

2.33
The untrustworthy Lord of Death
Will not wait for me to be ready.

> Regardless of whether I am sick or healthy,
> This fleeting life is unstable.

Although one may have a general intention to confess, if one wonders whether it should be done now or later, consider how unsuitable it is to rely on something unreliable.

3. Consideration of individual meaningless acts

   1. Various kinds of nonvirtuous actions have been committed
   2. Consideration of their meaninglessness
   3. Logically establishing that point
   4. Empirically establishing that point
   5. Summary

1. Various kinds of nonvirtuous actions have been committed

> **2.34**
> Everything must be left behind and I must go, too.
> Yet, without understanding this,
> Because of friends and foes,
> I have carried out all kinds of nonvirtue.

The first two lines indicate the intention; the third line indicates the objects of the intention and the last line indicates the deed itself.

2. Consideration of their meaninglessness

> **2.35**
> My foes will become nothing.
> My friends will become nothing.
> I, too, will become nothing.
> In this way, all of us will become nothing.

Contemplate the fruitlessness of negative acts for their sakes.

3. Logically establishing that point

> **2.36**
> Like experiences in dreams,

> We get involved with this and that,
> But these will become only memories,
> For whatever has passed will never be seen again.

The logical subject is the objects of experience, i.e. that which 'we get involved with'. The conclusion is that they will pass from objects of experience into objects of memory. The reason is that whatever passes away will never be seen again. The example which proves that pervasion[6] is their likeness to 'the experiences in a dream.'

4. Empirically establishing that point

> 2.37
> In the short time of this life,
> Many friends and foes have already passed,
> But whatever unbearable nonvirtues
> I carried out because of them still await me.

The first two lines indicate that the objects of intention are unreliable. Nevertheless, since nonvirtues are impermanent, perhaps they are harmless? Although the nonvirtue itself may have ceased, it is taught that the continuity of imprints remains, as indicated in the second two lines.

5. Summary

> 2.38
> Not even understanding
> That I, too, am just as temporary as they were,
> Out of ignorance, desire and hatred,
> I have done many nonvirtues.

The first two lines indicate that one has not taken the antidote—the understanding of impermanence. [277] The last two lines indicate the various kinds of action.

4. Fear of the results

   1. The inevitable result: the transmigration to another rebirth
   2. Fear of experiencing this

3. The reason why the fear will not abate
4. The aspects of suffering

1. The inevitable result: the transmigration to another rebirth

> **2.39**
> **If, without respite, day and night,**
> **This life is running out,**
> **And there is no granting of an extension,**
> **Why would death not come for someone like me?**

The logical subject is 'me'. The probandum is that death will come, i.e. 'Why would death not come?' The reason is indicated in the first two lines, i.e. the exhaustion of life and the third line, i.e. no extension of life. Therefore, since migrating to the next life is certain, it is inevitable that it will be experienced.

2. Fear of experiencing this

> **2.40**
> **Lying on my death bed,**
> **Though surrounded by all my friends and family,**
> **The sensations of life ending**
> **Will be experienced by me alone.**
>
> **2.41**
> **When seized by the messengers of the Lord of Death,**
> **What good is family, what good are friends?**
> **Merit alone will protect me then,**
> **But I have never really relied on it.**
>
> **2.42**
> **Oh protectors—I was unconcerned and,**
> **Not realizing this would be so terrifying,**
> **I carried out many nonvirtues**
> **For the sake of this impermanent life.**

The first verse indicates the ceasing of life, the second indicates the approach of the suffering of the next life and the third indicates the aspects of regret.

3. The reason why the fear will not abate

> **2.43**
> Even now, when someone is told
> They are to be taken to a torture chamber, they are terrified.
> Their appearance quickly changes:
> Their mouth becomes dry, their eyes bulge and so on.
>
> **2.44**
> What need to mention the utter despair
> Of being in the grasp of the terrifying
> Messengers of the Lord of Death,
> And being sick with terror.

The first two lines give an example of fear for the harms of this life. The next two lines complete the example. The second verse relates the example to the harms of future lives.

4. The aspects of suffering

> **2.45**
> 'Can anyone protect me
> From such a great horror?'
> With gaping eyes and a terrified aspect,
> I will search in the four directions for a refuge,
>
> **2.46**
> But not seeing any refuge in the four directions,
> I will be enveloped in despair.
> Then, when I have no refuge,
> What am I going to do?

2. The power of reliance

   1. Taking hold of the general supports
   2. Taking hold of the particular supports of specific bodhisattvas

3. Having taken hold of the supports, the subsequent practice—
to follow their instructions

1. Taking hold of the general supports

> **2.47**
> Therefore, to the conquerors, the protectors,
> Who strive in their purpose of protecting beings,
> And whose great power dispels all fears,
> I go for refuge from this day forth.
>
> **2.48**
> In the dharma taken to heart,
> Which dispels fear of saṃsāra,
> And in the assembly of bodhisattvas,
> I likewise completely take refuge.

The Buddhas are 'conquerors' of the benefit of self in respect of abandoning the defilements and possessing good qualities. They are 'protectors' of beings in that they fulfil the benefit of others:

> Everything that is harmful,
> Non-methods [of mistaken paths], the lower realms,
> The transitory collections and lesser vehicles—
> Because of protecting from these, he is supreme among
>   refuges.[7]

Thus the protectors of beings [278] strive in these ways, using manifold powers and dispelling fears of saṃsāra. The 'dharma' means the dharma of realization which, when it is taken to heart, is cessation —freedom of the dhātu from adventitious impurities—and the dharma of the path, which dispels fears of saṃsāra. The 'saṅgha' means the community of bodhisattvas.

2. Taking hold of the particular supports of specific bodhisattvas

> **2.49**
> Overwhelmed by fear,
> I offer myself to Samantabhadra.

To Mañjughoṣa
I make an offering of my own body.

2.50
To the protector Avalokiteśvara
Who unerringly acts out of compassion,
I call out with a desperate cry,
Begging him to protect me, someone so burdened with nonvirtue.

2.51
To Ārya Ākāśagarbha
And to Kṣitigarbha, too,
And to all the lords of great compassion,
Seeking refuge, I cry out for their help.

2.52
To Vajrapāṇi, the sight of whom
Makes malevolent beings, like the messengers
Of the Lord of Death, scatter to the four directions,
I go for refuge.

3. Having taken hold of the supports, the subsequent practice—to follow their instructions

2.53
In the past, I defied your advice but,
Now, seeing such great horrors,
I pray that my truly going for refuge to you
Will dispel them.

3. The power of antidote

  1. The reasons to persevere in the antidote
  2. Advice to engage in it quickly

1. The reasons to persevere in the antidote

  1. The example of an illness

2. The example of a precipice

1. The example of an illness

> **2.54**
> **If I need to follow the doctor's advice**
> **Out of fear of just a common illness,**
> **What can be said of being constantly sick**
> **With the hundred faults of desire and so forth.**

'Common illness' means illnesses such as phlegmatic disorders etc. If frightened even of that, what can be said of the necessity to rely upon the antidotes to the illnesses of the defilements?

How is that worse than common illnesses?

> **2.55**
> **If any one of these**
> **Can destroy everyone in the world,**
> **And if no other cure for them**
> **Is anywhere to be found,**

> **2.56**
> **Then the attitude of disregarding**
> **The instructions of the omniscient physician,**
> **Which remediate all these maladies,**
> **Is extremely stupid and contemptible.**

The first two lines indicate the great faults of such illness. The next two lines indicate the rarity of the remedy. The second verse indicates the practice which becomes the supreme remedy.

2. The example of a precipice

> **2.57**
> **If I need to be careful**
> **Near an ordinary, shallow ridge,**
> **What can be said of this abyss**
> **Which plummets for a thousand miles?**

To 'plummet for a thousand miles' indicates wandering in the depths of saṃsāra without beginning or end.

2. Advice to engage in it quickly

> **2.58**
> **'Surely I won't die today!'**
> **It is hardly appropriate to be so casual,**
> **When the time of my end**
> **Will inevitably come.**
>
> **2.59**
> **What can take away this horror?**
> **What can I do to be free from it?**
> **If the end is inevitable,**
> **How can I be relaxed and content?**

The first four lines indicate making certain of impermanence. The next line indicates there being no cause of permanence. The last three lines are an exhortation to be diligent.

4. The power of desisting

1. Restraint for the next life
2. Purifying former lives
3. Conclusion of the chapter

1. Restraint for the next life

1. Fearing the consequences [279]
2. Speciality of the intention to abandon

1. Fearing the consequences

> **2.60**
> **The past was experienced and now it is gone.**
> **What is left of that for me now?**
> **Through my attachment to it,**
> **I defied the instructions of the teacher.**

2.61
If I must leave behind this life
And all its friends and acquaintances,
Going on alone to who knows where,
How can these friends and enemies matter?

The first line is reflecting on the nature of impermanence, the next is on the cessation of any lasting remainder, the next is on attachment to the impermanent remnants not being sensible and the fourth is on wrong practices not being appropriate. The next four lines indicate definitively giving up worldly interests.

2. Speciality of the intention to abandon

2.62
'Suffering comes from nonvirtue.
How can I be definitively freed from that?'
Day and night, I should constantly consider
Nothing but this very thought.

The first line indicates the resultant suffering and the rest is bringing the cause of that to mind.

2. Purifying former lives

2.63
Insensibly and ignorantly,
Whatever nonvirtues, whether inherent
Or attendant,
I have done,

2.64
In the presence of the protectors,
With palms joined and desperately aware of the suffering,
Again and again I prostrate
And confess all of these acts.

'I' (myself) am the one who is to make the confession. An 'inherent misdeed' is an act of nonvirtue unconnected to any vows of training. A misdeed that is 'attendant' refers to nonvirtue which is attendant upon the taking of a vow.⁸

Perhaps then one should not take vows at all, for then it would be impossible to commit the nonvirtues attendant upon them. This is not correct. If a vow is maintained, merit increases, which is why vows are so important. Why does merit increase with the maintenance of a vow? Attendant misdeeds are extremely serious acts, so to prevent their occurrence, it is necessary to maintain a protective cordon around the vow, like maintaining a bamboo fence in order to preserve a fruit grove.

3. Conclusion of the chapter

> **2.65**
> **Guides of the world, please look upon**
> **My mistakes and nonvirtues.**
> **They lack any goodness at all.**
> **From now on, I will not do them anymore.**

In the first two lines, one acknowledges one's faults as faults. In the latter two, having seen those faults, one promises to refrain from them.

Chapter 3

FULLY HOLDING BODHICITTA

Section overview: Preliminaries 4-7 [v1-10]

4. Rejoicing
    1. Rejoicing in worldly virtue
        1. Rejoicing in the outcome of merit, which leads to the higher realms
        2. Rejoicing in the outcome of liberation, which leads to enlightenment
    2. Rejoicing in the virtue of śrāvakas
    3. Rejoicing in the virtue of Buddhas
        1. Rejoicing in the result
        2. Rejoicing in the cause
5. Requesting
6. Supplication
7. Dedication of merit

---

4. Rejoicing

1. Rejoicing in worldly virtue
2. Rejoicing in the virtue of śrāvakas
3. Rejoicing in the virtue of Buddhas

1. Rejoicing in worldly virtue

   1. Rejoicing in the outcome of merit, which leads to the higher realms
   2. Rejoicing in the outcome of liberation, which leads to enlightenment

1. Rejoicing in the outcome of merit, which leads to the higher realms

> **3.1**
> **In the virtue which alleviates the sufferings**
> **Of all beings in the lower realms,**
> **And places those who are suffering in happiness,**
> **I gladly rejoice.**

The first two lines are rejoicing in the cause: virtue which alleviates the sufferings of the lower realms. It is this virtue which creates the higher realms. The next line is rejoicing in the result of that: those who are suffering are placed in happiness—the happiness of saṃsāra, which is like the happiness of scratching an itch.

2. Rejoicing in the outcome of liberation, which leads to enlightenment

> **3.2**
> **In the gathering of virtue**
> **Which causes enlightenment, I rejoice.**

2. Rejoicing in the virtue of śrāvakas

> **In the complete liberation**
> **From the suffering of saṃsāric birth, I rejoice.**

3. Rejoicing in the virtue of Buddhas

   1. Rejoicing in the result
   2. Rejoicing in the cause

1. Rejoicing in the result

3.3
In the enlightenment of the protectors
And their sons' attainment of the bhūmis, I rejoice.

This [two line] verse is rejoicing in the result, where the first line is the ultimate result and the second line is the temporary result.

2. Rejoicing in the cause

3.4
In the ocean of virtue in generating the resolution
To bring happiness to all sentient beings,
And in the virtuous deeds for the benefit
Of sentient beings, I rejoice.

Rejoicing in the cause is two-fold: rejoicing in the generation of aspiration bodhicitta and rejoicing in the generation of application for the benefit of others, which apply to the first two and second two lines, respectively.

5. Requesting the wheel of dharma be turned

3.5
Folding my hands, I implore
The Buddhas in all directions:
Please shine the light of dharma
For sentient beings suffering in darkness.

These four lines indicate the act, the object of supplication, the dharma and the recipients, respectively.

6. Supplicating the Buddhas not to enter nirvāṇa

3.6
Folding my hands, I implore
The conquerors who wish to pass beyond torment:
Please do not leave these creatures to their blindness

But stay here for countless aeons.

These four lines indicate the act, object of supplication, purpose and duration, respectively.

7. Dedication of the roots of merit

1. General aspiration for freedom from suffering
2. Aspiration to eliminate the suffering of sickness [281]
3. Aspiration to eliminate the suffering of hunger
4. Aspiration to eliminate the suffering of poverty

1. General aspiration for freedom from suffering

> **3.7**
> **Having done all this,**
> **Whatever I may have gathered by this virtue,**
> **May it eliminate all the sufferings**
> **Of all sentient beings.**

2. Aspiration to eliminate the suffering of sickness

> **3.8**
> **Whatever sicknesses beings may have,**
> **Until they are all cured,**
> **May I be their medicine, their doctor,**
> **And may I nurse them back to health.**

3. Aspiration to eliminate the suffering of hunger

> **3.9**
> **May deluges of food and drink**
> **Eliminate the sufferings of hunger and thirst**
> **And, during ages of famine,**
> **May I become food and drink.**

4. Aspiration to eliminate the suffering of poverty

3.10
May I become an inexhaustible supply of riches
For beings in deprivation and poverty,
And may I be right there in their presence,
As all kinds of provisions and necessities.

2. The main part: the actual practice of generating bodhicitta

> Section overview: The main part: the actual practice of generating bodhicitta [v11-24]
>
> 1. Aspiration to give up everything
>   1. How to give up everything
>   2. The reason for doing so
>   3. The subsequent practice
> 2. Aspiration for inexhaustible causes
>   1. General explanation
>   2. Aspiration for their attitudes to become inexhaustible causes
>   3. Aspiration for their actions to become inexhaustible causes
> 3. Aspiration to be a cause of sustenance
>   1. Necessities
>   2. Vast worlds
>   3. Unconstrained location and duration
> 4. Reciting the words of the vow

1. Aspiration to give up everything
2. Aspiration for inexhaustible causes
3. Aspiration to be a cause of sustenance
4. Reciting the words of the vow

One can recite the words of the three aspirations once as a preparation to bring about mindfulness and then recite the words of the vow three times to actually take the vow.

1. Aspiration to give up everything

1. How to give up everything
2. The reason for doing so
3. The subsequent practice

1. How to give up everything

> **3.11**
> **In order to bring benefit to all beings,**
> **I will, without any hesitation, give up**
> **My body, its pleasures,**
> **And all my merits of the past, present and future.**

The intended purpose, aspiration to give and substances given are indicated in the first, second and last two lines, respectively.

2. The reason for doing so

> **3.12**
> **Nirvāṇa is attained by giving everything up.**
> **Nirvāṇa is my goal,**
> **And to give everything at once**
> **To sentient beings is the supreme gift.**

Nirvāṇa will be attained by giving up all. Because one's intent is to attain nirvāṇa, that is what should be done. The third line indicates sentient beings as the precious field of giving. Giving up all 'at once' means completely letting go of both that which is appropriate to be given and that which is appropriate not to be given.

3. The subsequent practice

> **3.13**
> **Since I have now given my body to embodied beings**
> **For whatever end may make them happy,**
> **Let them do with it whatever they like—**
> **Even killing, insulting or beating it.**

> **3.14**
> **Though they may treat my body as worthless,**
> **Or make it a source of ridicule or mockery,**

Since I have now given it to them,
What is the point of cherishing it?

3.15
I will put up with anything they might do to it,
As long as it will not cause them harm.

The first two verses are countering the habitual presumption of one's own autonomy, while the last two lines indicate what kinds of actions are appropriate, which applies to all the actions mentioned. What are the actions that will not cause them harm? Virtuous actions. [282]

2. Aspiration for inexhaustible causes

   1. General explanation
   2. Aspiration for their attitudes to become inexhaustible causes
   3. Aspiration for their actions to become inexhaustible causes[1]

1. General explanation

   Whenever someone sees me,
   May it not be without benefit.

2. Aspiration for their attitudes to become inexhaustible causes

   3.16
   Having seen me, regardless of whether they develop
   An angry or a respectful attitude,
   May that always become a cause
   Of fulfilling the benefit of all.

3. Aspiration for their actions to become inexhaustible causes

   3.17
   Whoever may disparage me,
   Or harm me in other ways,
   However they may insult me,
   May they all come to have the good fortune of enlightenment.

3. Aspiration to be a cause of sustenance

1. Necessities
2. Vast worlds
3. Unconstrained location and duration

1. Necessities

3.18
May I be a protector for the unprotected,
A guide for travellers on the road
And, for those who want to cross the water,
May I be a boat, a ship or a bridge.

3.19
May I be land for those who seek dry land,
A light for those who lack light,
A lodging for those who want lodging
And, for those who want a servant,
May I be the servant of them all.

3.20
May I be the wishing jewel, the wondrous vase,
The vidya-mantra, the great medicine,
The inconceivable tree of wishes,
And the cow of plenty, fulfilling the hopes of beings.

2. Vast worlds

3.21
Like the great elements—earth and so forth—
And, like space itself, remaining without end,
May I be the ground which supports
The countless lives of sentient beings.

3. Unconstrained location and duration

3.22
Similarly, in all places where sentient beings

> Dwell throughout the limits of space,
> May I be a cause of sustaining life
> Until they have all passed beyond suffering.

The first two lines indicate the unconstrained location while the second two lines indicate the unconstrained duration.

4. Reciting the words of the vow

> **3.23**
> **Just as the Sugatas of the past**
> **Generated bodhicitta,**
> **And gradually practised**
> **The bodhisattva trainings,**
>
> **3.24**
> **Likewise for the benefit of beings,**
> **I now generate bodhicitta,**
> **And likewise I, too,**
> **Will gradually practise the trainings.**

These words constitute undertaking the generation of bodhicitta:

> Just as the Sugatas of the past
> Generated bodhicitta,
> Likewise for the benefit of beings,
> I now generate bodhicitta.

These words constitute undertaking the training:

> Just as the Sugatas of the past
> Gradually practised
> The bodhisattva trainings,
> For the benefit of beings,
> Likewise I, too,
> Will gradually practise the trainings.

These two can be expressed together as they are in the root text or separated in accord with the liturgy of Ācārya Jetāri.[2] In this system, there are two main points:

> Section overview: The ritual for generating bodhicitta
>
> 1. The cause of generating bodhicitta with nothing lacking
>   1. The cause—meditation on compassion
>   2. The root—stabilizing faith
>   3. Other supports of bodhicitta
> 2. The purpose of a proper ritual
>   1. That there is a purpose to properly receiving it
>   2. The method of taking it
>   1. From whom it is received
>   2. Basis
>   3. Time
>   4. The ritual
>   5. Overcoming the objection that it is not always possible to maintain it

1. The cause of generating bodhicitta with nothing lacking
2. The purpose of a proper ritual

1. The cause of generating bodhicitta with nothing lacking

Without a proper ritual, can bodhicitta be generated or not? If not, when an attitude of wishing to attain enlightenment for the benefit of beings arises without a ritual, the essential characteristic of generating bodhicitta would nevertheless be satisfied, so it is an exaggeration to say one must receive the proper ritual. [283] If bodhicitta can be generated without the ritual, is the procedure of going through the ritual not meaningless? [This is the subject matter of 'the purpose of the proper ritual', below.]

Yet, if one does not receive the proper ritual, bodhicitta can arise from other conditions. What are those other conditions? There are three:

1. The cause—meditation on compassion
2. The root—stabilizing faith
3. Other supports of bodhicitta

1. The cause—meditation on compassion

- While having attachment to both self and others as immutable, singular sentient beings, when one wishes to free others from their suffering, this is the compassion which perceives sentient beings, held in common with tīrthikas.
- When one cognizes the emptiness of the individual self and others—that they are composed of momentary skandhas and innumerable atoms—and one wishes to free them from their suffering, this is the compassion which perceives dharmas, held in common with śrāvakas.
- When one cognizes that self and others are empty of true existence, like an illusion, and wishes to free them from their suffering, this is non-perceptual compassion, unique to bodhisattvas.

Through reliance upon whichever of these three is appropriate, one cultivates compassion, which is the perpetuating cause.

2. The root—stabilizing faith

If a compassionate person only practises such things as purification rites as the means for freeing others from suffering, like the non-Buddhists do, then bodhicitta will not arise, despite their wish to free others from their suffering. Bodhicitta requires the three kinds of faith:

- Faith in the result—perfect enlightenment
- Faith in the supports—the Three Jewels
- Faith in the cause—the bodhisattva conduct

3. Other supports of bodhicitta

One relies on the prātimokṣa vows, in which one ceases doing harm to others.

Objections: 'It is illogical for the prātimokṣa vows to be supports for the arising of bodhicitta, since hermaphrodites, eunuchs, gods, etc. [284] do not take the prātimokṣa vows but they do generate bodhicitta. It is also illogical as a basis of maintaining bodhicitta, for at the time of death, the prātimokṣa vows are relinquished but the generation of bodhicitta is not relinquished.'[3]

It is true that [the prātimokṣa vows] as they are specified in the texts of the śrāvakas are illogical as a support for either the arising or the maintenance of bodhicitta because:

- When an act is committed which constitutes a defeat in the śrāvaka tradition, if it is motivated by some opportunity to benefit others, it counts only as a resembling downfall for bodhisattvas.[4]
- Their duration, intention and so forth are incompatible.
- Although someone who offers back their vows gives up the śrāvaka prātimokṣa, he does not abandon the generation of bodhicitta.

Furthermore, the bodhisattva vow is superior to the prātimokṣa vows of the śrāvakas in respect of its continuity, its commitment to others and the practicability of its repair when it is infringed.

However, apart from these incompatibilities with the śrāvakas, both vows are pervaded by a 'bare prātimokṣa', which is a support for the arising of bodhicitta: the intention to stop harming others and instead benefit them. This satisfies the criteria for supporting and maintaining the generation of bodhicitta. It is what is held by gods, eunuchs and so forth and is not relinquished at death.

'Since this bare prātimokṣa is distinct from the final bodhisattva prātimokṣa, they are distinct as support [the prātimokṣa vows] and supported [the bodhisattva conduct], which is contradictory to the explanations that there are only three vows.'[5]

This is incorrect. That the support and supported are distinct in this way is taught in the *Ratnamegha*:

> What is perfect moral conduct? It is holding the prātimokṣa vows [support] and it is the practice of the bodhisattva trainings [supported].[6] [285]

Also in the explanations of the three vows, the bodhisattva prātimokṣa and the lower monastic observances are separately designated, or else they are explained as a graduated training. Otherwise, there would be a contradiction.

Concerning a ritual for the receipt of the bodhisattva prātimokṣa, there is no need to take additional vows. If one has formerly undertaken to hold the śrāvaka training, subsequently, when one embraces the superior attitude, it is transformed into the bodhisattva prātimokṣa because, although one relinquishes the inferior attitude, one does not give up the intention of renunciation.[7]

'If one does not abandon the intention of renunciation, is it not a contradiction to say that a śrāvaka who commits murder for the benefit of others has broken the vow, while a bodhisattva has merely committed a resembling downfall and not broken it?'

There is no contradiction. For someone who has a narrow attitude, killing to benefit others is tainted with a harmful intent, so that is to be abandoned. However, a vast attitude is not tainted by any harmful intent and is not to be abandoned. It is like someone holding the full vows of ordination becoming an elder monk: although they do not have distinct monastic observances and although they do not request or maintain any new vows, nevertheless certain distinct infringements are present and absent.[8]

2. The purpose of the proper ritual

1. That there is a purpose to properly receiving it
2. The method of taking it

1. That there is a purpose to properly receiving it

Since bodhicitta can arise even without a formal ritual, is there any purpose to receiving the ritual? There is a purpose. By generating bodhicitta oneself or in the presence of another in this way, self-respect and shame become causes of its not deteriorating and of its stability.

2. The method of taking it

1. From whom it is received
2. Basis
3. Time
4. The ritual [286]
5. Overcoming the objection that it is not always possible to maintain it

1. From whom it is received

> The spiritual friend is
> Learned in the Mahāyāna
> And supreme in the discipline of the bodhisattvas.
> I should never leave him even at the cost of my life.[9]

In this way, the one from whom it is received is someone who has attained the vow, has not violated it and is learned in the means of its restoration. He maintains the discipline of a vow-holder and has the ability to give the vow to others, by communicating the signs of the vow, etc. That is the person from whom it is received, since these are the factors of his having respect for training. However, if there are obstacles to one's life or the maintenance of one's existing vows in finding such a teacher, then one should take the vow in the presence of the Buddhas and bodhisattvas.

2. Basis of receiving

If it is possible to practise the three activities—the moral discipline of vows, gathering virtuous dharmas and benefitting sentient beings—then one should maintain all three but, if not, practise whichever of these are appropriate, or just rely on some of the rules of conduct of vows.[10] If one does not do so, the vow one has taken will be violated. In the *Foundations of Mindfulness Sutra*, it says that if one does not give what one has promised, one will be reborn in hell and if one does not give what one has dedicated, one will be reborn as a hungry ghost. What can be said therefore of someone who, having made the great commitment to accomplish the benefit of others, leaves it merely to fade away?

3. Time

Through applying one's strength, until enlightenment, and for long as one lives, and every single day, one should practise the training disciplines according to one's circumstances.

'In the vinaya of the holy dharma, it says that vows must be absent of the five exemptions, so the presence of exemptions of time[11] contradicts that. Also, since its intermittent timing is unsuitable as the cause of benefitting self and others without limitation, [287] this is in contradiction to the bodhisattva vow. Also, since the maintenance is intermittent, it will be corrupted by downfalls and the vow will become contaminated with faults which will obstruct the attainment of the bhūmis.'

Since the absence of the five exemptions is only taught in the treatises of the śrāvakas, although exemptions of time are present in this case, nevertheless there is no contradiction. There will be no incompleteness in the cause because one trains in its vastness gradually. Nor will it be corrupted by downfalls because one is not breaking a promise [to train continuously], since one cannot maintain a promise one has not made.

4. Ritual

The preliminaries, main part and conclusion, as has been explained, comprise the ritual. The ritual is for those who are strong enough to maintain the vow. For those who are weaker, they should just receive the training disciplines and maintain them according to however much time, etc., they have.

5. Overcoming the objection that it is not possible always to maintain it

Objection: 'If one promises to train until enlightenment, then at death it will be damaged by a downfall.'

Formerly, Akṣobhya prevented such damage to his vow by making aspiration prayers. Likewise, by maintaining aspiration, one will not damage the vow and it will not be forgotten in future lives.[12] As it says in the *Sutra Requested by Kāśyapa*, one should abandon the four dharmas which damage bodhicitta,[13] and it says in the *Sutra of Simha's Questions* that by giving the dharma, one will remember it and by leading the sentient beings of all directions to enlightenment, one will not give up bodhicitta even in one's dreams. Therefore one should train in these.

Some say, 'The actions of certain kinds of beings who cannot have a monastic position[14] and certain kinds of killing[15] are not defeats. Therefore, if the direct cause—the intention to engage in the training—is absent, that is not a violation by a downfall and no result will be elicited, like a fire that smoulders under ash.'

This is not the case, for the vow would have no function and a vow empty of any ability to function makes no sense. When something has a function, it is unreasonable for it to be unaffected by its opposite condition.[16] While not abiding in a certain state of mind may preclude a downfall,[17] it is not the case that lacking any intention to engage in training is not a downfall. If it were, the old monks who were deceived by Upananda due to their not knowing the training precepts would not have committed downfalls.[18]

Thus, in accord with line 3.24d, 'I will gradually practise the trainings', beginners should mainly train in [the moral discipline of][19] the vow, devoted conduct practitioners[20] should mainly train in the gathering of virtues and those who have attained the bhūmis should mainly train in benefitting sentient beings.

3. The conclusion

    1. Generating joy in the attainment of the benefit of self
    2. Generating joy in the attainment of the benefit of others

1. Generating joy in the attainment of the benefit of self

    1. Identifying the benefit established
    2. To have concern not to corrupt it with faults
    3. Identifying the difficulty of acquiring it

1. Identifying the benefit established

> **3.25**
> **Accordingly, those who with intelligence**
> **Have lucidly taken hold of bodhicitta,**
> **In order to increase it,**
> **Should praise the mind with these words:**
>
> **3.26**
> **Now, my life is fruitful.**
> **I have properly attained human existence.**
> **Today, born into the family of the Buddhas,**

I have become a Buddha's child.

The four lines of the second verse indicate, respectively, that one's life has meaning, not to waste one's freedoms and endowments, that it is possible to attain buddhahood and that one is an heir of the conquerors.

2. To have concern not to corrupt it with faults

> **3.27**
> **Whatever I undertake to do, my actions**
> **Will be consistent with this lineage.**
> **Nothing I do will corrupt**
> **This faultless, noble lineage.**

That which is consistent with the lineage is the Mahāyāna path. Not to corrupt it means not to damage the vow with downfalls.

3. Identifying the difficulty of acquiring it

> **3.28**
> **Like a blind man finding**
> **A gem in a pile of rubbish,**
> **Somehow this bodhicitta**
> **Has arisen in me.**

2. Generating joy in the attainment of the benefit of others [289]

1. The power to dispel suffering
2. The power to dispel obscurations
3. The power to establish benefit and happiness

1. The power to dispel suffering

There are five kinds of suffering to be dispelled. The suffering of death:

> **3.29**
> **This is the supreme elixir of life,**
> **Vanquishing death's sovereignty over the world.**

The suffering of poverty:

> It is an inexhaustible treasure,
> Dispelling beings' sufferings.

The suffering of sickness:

> 3.30
> It is the supreme remedy,
> Relieving the sicknesses of beings.

The suffering of fatigue:

> It is a tree to rest under for all beings
> Who are wandering and exhausted on saṃsāric paths.

The suffering of bad rebirths:

> 3.31
> It is an open bridge, leading them
> Over bad rebirths to freedom.

2. The power to dispel obscurations

> It is the shining moon of mind
> Which dispels the misery of beings' defilements.

This indicates dispelling the obscurations of the defilements.

> 3.32
> It is the great sun which brings an end
> To the gloom of beings' ignorance.

This indicates the dispelling of the obscurations of cognizables.

3. The power to establish benefit and happiness

Establishing benefit:

> It is the fresh butter extracted

From churning the milk of the holy dharma.

Churning the milk of the holy dharma indicates ascertaining the meaning of the explanans, experiencing the excellent teachings. The fresh butter indicates liberation by seeing the truth.

Establishing happiness:

> **3.33**
> **Beings wandering abroad on the paths of conditioned existence,**
> **Wishing to have happiness,**
> **Will encounter this supreme happiness,**
> **And those great wanderers will at last be contented.**

Having wandered on the paths of conditioned existence, if they desire the highest bliss, they may attain the bliss of meditation.

Developing the joy of others:

> **3.34**
> **Today, in the presence of all the protectors,**
> **Until they have attained buddhahood itself,**
> **I invite beings to every happiness.**
> **May the gods, demigods and all the rest be joyful.**

This verse constitutes an invitation. By whom is it made? By oneself. Invited to what? To the happiness of the gods for as long as they have not yet attained buddhahood itself. Who is the witness of this? It is done before all the Buddhas.

PART IV

THE COOPERATING CONDITION

PRACTISING THE TRAINING

Chapter 4
CONCERN

The training in bodhicitta, which is the cooperating condition, can be explained in relation to the six perfections. Although there is no specific chapter on giving, the first perfection, its practice is nevertheless explained throughout the text. [290] The chapter on Clear Comprehension explains the perfection of moral conduct. The following four chapters ['Patience' through to 'Wisdom'] are concerned with their eponymous perfections. The chapter on Concern is taught before these as the general cause of practice. Some other commentators have explained both Concern and Clear Comprehension as the general causes of practice, while the chapter on Patience shows how to practise the antidotes and abandon remaining obstacles [chapter 6]. This is followed by an explanation of reliance on the accompanying training [chapter 7] and then calm abiding and insight meditation [chapters 8 and 9] are the seeing of the true nature of the antidotes themselves.

The general cause of practice, concern, has two parts:

1. Briefly [v1]
2. Extensively [v2-48]

1. Briefly

4.1
Having firmly grasped bodhicitta
In this way, a conqueror's son
Should never neglect it,
But instead strive never to violate the training.

This verse indicates that one should maintain bodhicitta, i.e. that one should endeavour to prevent one's initial enthusiasm to keep the vow from dissipating. The second two lines indicate that one should take care to train by endeavouring in the training. How should one train? One should abandon downfalls and resembling non-downfalls and one should adopt the non-downfalls and resembling downfalls.

1. Downfalls and non-downfalls

Downfalls comprise the five root downfalls of kings, the five of ministers and the eight of beginners, etc.[1] Non-downfalls are the abandonment of those.

2. Resembling downfalls and resembling non-downfalls

In respect to inherent misdeeds in the moral conduct of the vow: If a person is harming the teachings of the Buddha and leading beings to the lower realms, etc. and there is a peaceful method to stop them[2] which does not involve killing them but, despite that, one kills them to stop them, [291] it would be the heavy fault[3] of practising a dispensation even though a formal rule applies.[4] In the case that one could not stop them by any other deed apart from killing them and so one kills them, it is a resembling downfall. If they are not killed, it is a resembling non-downfall.[5] By contrast, according to the texts of the śrāvakas, such a deed is never permitted even if one sees that it would benefit others.

In respect to attendant misdeeds in the moral conduct of the vow: If some insects living in grass are about to drown and there is some way to save them, one should do it. If there was a way that does not involve the monk destroying the grass but he destroys it anyway, it would be the fault of practising a dispensation even though a formal rule is present.[6] If there is no other way and the monk destroys the grass, it is a resembling downfall. But if he does not act [and the insects die], it is a resembling non-downfall.

Thus in order to alleviate the terrible sufferings of such sentient beings, one should be happy even to go to the lower realms by becoming stained with such faults. Such is the attitude of thinking only of how to benefit others. However, if one does not have this attitude, since one's motivation is tainted with the mind of the defilements, it would be an actual downfall, though one would have the conceit that it was a resembling downfall.

In respect to gathering virtuous dharmas: When engaged in yoga [i.e. a practice of gathering virtuous dharmas], seeing some external deed that would benefit beings, one accomplishes their benefit by that other means [i.e. abandons the yogic practice to do so]. If their benefit could have been accomplished by any other means without abandoning one's engagement in samādhi, it is the first misdeed [i.e. practising a dispensation even though a formal rule is present]. If there was no other way to accomplish their benefit and so one abandoned the practice of yoga in order to do it, [292] it is a resembling downfall. If one did not accomplish their benefit, it is a resembling non-downfall.[7]

In respect to benefitting sentient beings: When engaged, for example, in accomplishing the benefit of many beings, one sees among them one being harming those who are practising meditation and developing good qualities and one sees that in his future life, that harmful being will himself be harmed by his actions. For the benefit of that one being, one should accomplish the benefit of the many who have good qualities by some other means or, by another means, overcome the harm that one being is doing in this life and to his future lives. If such means are available but one simply abandons accomplishing a benefit, it is the first fault [practising the dispensation though the formal rule applies]. If it was not possible to accomplish the benefit of the many by any other means and nor was it possible to overcome both the harm done by one person to the many and to his own future life, one should abandon the benefit of the one. However, one should still try to help the many and pacify the harms done to them and the harms done to the harm-doer himself. That situation is a resembling downfall. If one does not do so, it is a resembling non-downfall.[8]

2. Extensively

1. Concern for bodhicitta
2. Concern for the training

> Section overview: Concern for bodhicitta [v2-11]
>
> 1. Reasons for not abandoning bodhicitta
> 2. The faults of abandoning it
>   1. One goes to the lower realms
>   1. Deceiving all beings
>   2. Scriptural establishment
>   3. Abandoning contradiction with other scriptures
>   2. The benefit of others is damaged
>   1. It is the most serious downfall for oneself
>   2. Interrupting the virtue of others is just as bad
>   3. The reason for these
>   3. The attainment of the bhūmis is obstructed

1. Concern for bodhicitta

1. Reasons for not abandoning bodhicitta
2. The faults of abandoning it

1. Reasons for not abandoning bodhicitta

The essential characteristics of non-abandonment, and what must cease in order to achieve that, are respectively indicated in the next two verses:

> **4.2**
> **Whatever I have undertaken rashly**
> **Or not properly thought through,**
> **Even if I have promised to do it,**
> **I should reconsider, asking myself, 'Should I stop?'**

4.3

> The Buddhas and their sons
> Examine things with their great wisdom,
> And even I can examine them,
> So why would I hesitate in doing so?

'Rashly' means without conducting analysis. 'Not properly thought through' means doing something misconceived. One should subsequently question whether such activities should be abandoned. [293] Since the Buddhas and their sons examine their activities, one should cease that which has not been properly analysed and since one can also examine it oneself, one should cease that which is rash.[9]

2. The faults of abandoning it

1. One goes to the lower realms
2. The benefit of others is damaged
3. The attainment of the bhūmis is obstructed

1. One goes to the lower realms

1. Deceiving all beings
2. Scriptural establishment
3. Abandoning contradiction with other scriptures

1. Deceiving all beings

> 4.4
> Having made this commitment,
> If I do not act to fulfil it,
> Then, since I will have deceived all sentient beings,
> What kind of rebirth will I take?

One deceived them because one promised to liberate all sentient beings but they were not liberated.

2. Scriptural establishment

> 4.5
> If it is taught that someone who intended to give
> Some slight, unremarkable thing,

But then did not do so,
Will be reborn as a hungry ghost,

4.6
Then, having sincerely intended to bring them
To unsurpassed bliss,
If I then deceive all sentient beings,
To what sort of happy rebirth shall I proceed?

The first verse is the example and the second is the application of the example. If, having had an intention, one does not fulfil it, one will be reborn as a hungry ghost. In the *Foundations of Mindfulness Sutra*, it is taught that even for something slight, one will be reborn as a ghost if, having intended to give it, one does not give it and one will be reborn in hell if, having promised to give it, one does not give it. What can one say then of someone who promises sentient beings the freedom of enlightenment but then does not free them?

3. Abandoning contradiction with other scriptures

In Ārya Śāriputra's former life as King Vinasena,[10] a demon appearing as a Brahmin asked for his right hand. Śāriputra cut off his right hand and offered it with his left but the Brahmin became angry [since it was offered with the 'unclean' hand]. Śāriputra despaired and gave up bodhicitta. Although he returned to the Hīnayāna, he was not reborn in the lower realms. Is this not a contradiction?

4.7
To give up bodhicitta
But still be liberated;
Such a thing is inconceivable.
Only the Omniscient One could comprehend it.

Although he gave up bodhicitta, he was not reborn in the lower realms but attained liberation from saṃsāra. This was due to his application of the antidote to his nonvirtue. What is that antidote? To do such a thing is inconceivable, i.e. it can be comprehended only by the Omniscient One. Others say that giving up bodhicitta does not mean giving up the enlightenment of the śrāvakas.[11] [294] However, I will not go into this point here.[12]

2. The benefit of others is damaged

   1. It is a heavy downfall for oneself
   2. Interrupting the virtue of others is just as bad
   3. The reason for these

1. It is a heavy downfall for oneself

   4.8
   This is the most serious of downfalls
   For a bodhisattva,

The abandonment of bodhicitta is, among downfalls, the most serious. Is this a serious downfall for śrāvakas? No, only for bodhisattvas. How serious is the abandonment of bodhicitta for them?

> Even if they have practised the path of the ten virtues for
>   millions of aeons,
> If the wish to become a pratyekabuddha or arhat develops,
> It is a fault for the development of bodhicitta and the
>   development of bodhicitta is lost.
> For one who was generating bodhicitta, this is more serious
>   even than a monastic defeat.[13]

That is to say, the abandonment of bodhicitta is more serious even than praising oneself and disparaging others out of desire for wealth and honour, etc.[14] Why?

For, if should it occur,
The benefit of all beings is discarded.

It is because while one is afflicted by this downfall, it is impossible to accomplish the benefit of others.

2. Interrupting the virtue of others is just as bad

   4.9
   Should someone even for a moment
   Interrupt or prevent this merit,

> Since the benefit of beings is diminished,
> Nothing can stop him going to the lower realms.

Those who interrupt another's merit create a karmic obscuration for themselves, and it is impossible to benefit others through such an obscuration. Therefore, nothing will prevent them going to the lower realms.

3. The reason for these

4.10
> If destroying the happiness of even one sentient being
> Will harm me,
> What need to mention destroying
> The happiness of all beings, as vast as space?

Destroying the happiness of one sentient being is like ending a life. To abandon bodhicitta is to destroy the happiness of all sentient beings without exception because one cuts the continuity of the aspiration and application to achieve the happiness of others.

3. The attainment of the bhūmis is obstructed

One may respond that, once it is broken, the vow can be subsequently be retaken and restored.

4.11
> Thus, when vacillating in saṃsāra,
> Sometimes with the power of downfalls,
> Sometimes with the power of bodhicitta,
> The attainment of the bhūmis will be obstructed for a long
>   time.

[295] Because the contamination of bodhicitta with downfalls creates obstacles to the accomplishment of the path, the attainment of the bhūmis will be obstructed for a long time. It is like the bodhisattva is travelling in a chariot drawn by cattle.

2. Concern for training

   1. Concern to abandon nonvirtue

2. Concern to cultivate virtue
3. Concern to abandon the defilements
4. Concluding summary

Section overview: Concern to abandon nonvirtue [v12-20]

1. Faults causing rebirth in the lower realms
    1. Again and again taking lower rebirths
    2. Not having had the circumstances of their final exhaustion
    3. The same again in the future
2. Not attaining freedom
3. The instability of freedom when it is attained
4. No virtuous deeds in the lower realms
    1. No opportunity for virtue
    2. The reason for this
    3. The inability to return from the lower realms
    4. A scriptural reference for that

---

1. Concern to abandon nonvirtue

    1. Faults causing rebirth in the lower realms
    2. Not attaining freedom
    3. The instability of freedom when it is attained
    4. No virtuous deeds in the lower realms

1. Faults causing rebirth in the lower realms

    1. Again and again taking lower rebirths
    2. Not having had the circumstances of their final exhaustion
    3. The same again in the future

1. Again and again taking lower rebirths

> **4.12**
> **Therefore, with dedication I should fulfil**
> **The promise I have made.**
> **If I do not persevere from now on,**
> **I will descend to lower and lower rebirths.**

2. Not having had the circumstances of their final exhaustion

> 4.13
> Although there have been innumerable Buddhas
> Who worked for the benefit of all beings,
> My own faults excluded me
> From their restorative reach.

3. The same again in the future

> 4.14
> Moreover, if I continue in this way,
> Again and again it will end the same way:
> Diseased and fettered in the lower realms,
> Shattered and cut apart.

2. Not attaining freedom

> 4.15
> The arising of a Tathāgata,
> Faith, obtaining a human birth
> And the conditions for cultivating virtue
> Are very rare. When will they be attained again?

The arising of a Tathāgata is the attainment of endowment based upon other. Faith in the remaining teachings and obtaining a human birth are explained as endowments of oneself, as well as freedoms. The conditions for cultivating virtue are the mental basis. They are rare, i.e. they are acquired infrequently.

3. The instability of freedom when it is attained

> 4.16
> Today, at least, I am not sick.
> I have food to eat and am not afflicted.
> But this life is fleeting and deceptive,
> And this body is on loan only for a little while.

One has obtained circumstances which are today free from contrary conditions, such as being without obstructions like sickness. One possesses harmonious conditions, as expressed in the second line. Nevertheless, this life is fleeting, i.e. unstable and deceptive, i.e. it will cease. It is on loan, i.e. possessed only temporarily. 'Today' means the time when the sun is visible, or else it means the length of a day, i.e. the duration for which one is not sick is like the length of a day. [296]

4. No virtuous deeds in the lower realms

1. No opportunity for virtue
2. The reason for this
3. The inability to return from the lower realms
4. A scriptural reference for that

1. No opportunity for virtue

4.17
My conduct being the way it is,
I will not attain a human body again
And, if I do not attain a human body,
There will be only nonvirtue and no virtue.

The first two lines indicate that there are no causes for a happy rebirth and the second two lines indicate that there is no opportunity to practise virtue for those in the lower realms.

2. The reason for this

4.18
Even when I do have the chance to practise virtue,
If I fail to do so,
What will I do when I am
Completely obscured by the sufferings of the lower realms?

What does one fail to do despite having the chance? Accomplishing virtue, the basis of the higher realms, even though there is the opportunity to do it. The lower realms in which one is consumed by sufferings are those rebirths as a hell-being, hungry ghost or animal.

3. The inability to return from the lower realms

4.19
**Not practising any virtues,
But gathering many nonvirtues,
For hundreds of millions of aeons
I will not even hear the words 'happy rebirth'.**

4. A scriptural reference for that

4.20
**It is because of this the Bhagavān said
That the difficulty of attaining a human birth
Is like a turtle putting its neck through
A wooden yoke adrift on a great ocean.**

The analogy comes from the *Ordination of Nanda Sutra*.[15]

> Section overview: Concern to cultivate virtue [v21-27b]
>
> 1. Many nonvirtues were previously gathered
> 2. They are not exhausted by themselves
> 3. Therefore, one should strive in virtue, the antidote
>   1. General explanation of the fault of not striving
>   2. The fault in this life
>   3. The fault in future lives
>   4. Advice in overcoming that with an admonition
>   1. One has attained freedom, the basis
>   2. One has clearly distinguished the good from the bad
>   3. It is only logical, therefore, to persevere

2. Concern to cultivate virtue

　1. Many nonvirtues were previously gathered
　2. They are not exhausted by themselves
　3. Therefore, one should strive in virtue, the antidote

1. Many nonvirtues were previously gathered

4.21

> If just a moment of nonvirtue
> Can lead to an aeon in the Avīci Hell,
> What need to mention my not proceeding to a happy rebirth,
> With nonvirtues collected since beginningless time in saṃsāra?

A momentary nonvirtue which leads to rebirth in the Avīci Hell is, as previously explained in verse 1.34, a malevolent intention towards a bodhisattva who is generating bodhicitta. Such nonvirtues have been collected in saṃsāra, from time without beginning, through which, while they are not purified, one will not proceed to happy birth.

2. They are not exhausted by themselves

Although there are many nonvirtues, if they have not yet ripened, might they become exhausted? No, they are not exhausted by themselves:

> 4.22
> Even after having suffered such experiences,
> I still won't be free of them
> For, even while undergoing them,
> I will commit yet more nonvirtue.

This is because nonvirtues, etc. will ripen as effects in conformity with their causes.

3. Therefore, one should strive in virtue, the antidote

1. General explanation of the fault of not striving
2. The fault in this life
3. The fault in future lives [297]
4. Advice in overcoming that with an admonition

1. General explanation of the fault of not striving

> 4.23
> Having acquired this kind of freedom,
> If I do not cultivate virtue,
> There could be no greater deception,

And no greater delusion.

The deception here is thinking of this life. The delusion is not understanding the harm for future lives.

2. The fault in this life

> **4.24**
> **So, having understood this,**
> **If later in confusion I stop trying,**
> **Then the hour of my approaching death**
> **Will stir up extreme distress.**

3. The fault in future lives

> **4.25**
> **When my body is burning**
> **For a long time in the torturous fires of hell,**
> **Without doubt, my mind will also be tormented**
> **By the unbearable fire of remorse.**

The first two lines indicate the fires that harm the body while the latter two indicate the fire that harms the mind.

4. Advice in overcoming that with an admonition

1. One has attained freedom, the basis
2. One has clearly distinguished good from bad
3. It is only logical, therefore, to persevere

1. One has attained freedom, the basis

> **4.26**
> **Having somehow attained this beneficial state,**
> **Extremely difficult to find,**

Freedom, being extremely difficult to find, is precious and is beneficial, since, being the basis of such things as moral conduct, it brings great benefit. These two lines indicate the attainment of this.

2. One has clearly distinguished good from bad

> While I have this understanding,

3. It is only logical, therefore, to persevere

> If still I am led back to the hells,

> **4.27**
> **Like someone manipulated by mantras,**
> **I must have lost my mind.**

To behave in this way is to lack autonomy, like being manipulated by an evil mantra which has destroyed one's perseverance. Thus, the benefits of perseverance are implicitly suggested. 'Manipulated by mantras' mean the loss of autonomy by mantras such as wrathful summoning mantras.

> Section overview: Concern to abandon the defilements [v27c-47]
>
> 1. Examining the contrasting attitude
>   1. Examination of the harms
>   1. Loss of autonomy
>   2. Application to suffering
>   3. Their perpetual presence
>   4. They achieve nothing
>   2. Examining impatience
>   1. Harmful to the mind
>   2. Harmful to the body
>   3. Developing pride
> 2. Rejecting the idea that application will create suffering
>   1. The faults of non-application
>   1. An example of being subject to the faults of non-application
>   2. The point of the example
>   2. The qualities of application
>   1. Benefit of self
>   2. Benefit of other
>   3. Fulfilment of vows
>   3. The means of devoting oneself to that application
>   1. Not stopping until the defilements have been abandoned
>   2. Dedication in this
>   3. Relying on antidotes for one's own impatience
>   4. Abandoning objections to that
>   5. No obedience to the defilements
> 3. Developing enthusiasm in one's ability to abandon them
>   1. They have no other basis
>   1. Presenting an example of extirpation
>   2. The related meaning
>   3. The nature of the antidotes which bring about abandonment
>   4. The essential characteristic of their not returning
>   2. They are erroneous perceptions

3. Concern to abandon the defilements

   1. Examining the contrasting attitude
   2. Rejecting the idea that application will create suffering
   3. Developing enthusiasm in one's ability to abandon them

1. Examining the contrasting attitude

   1. Examination of the harms
   2. Examining impatience
   3. Developing pride

1. Examination of the harms

   1. Loss of autonomy
   2. Application to suffering
   3. Their perpetual presence
   4. They achieve nothing

1. Loss of autonomy

> I don't even know who is manipulating me.
> Who is this inside of me?

The cause of losing autonomy is not knowing by whom one is being manipulated. To ask, 'who is inside of me?' indicates that one's mental activity is not right. [298] Concerning the characteristics of this loss of autonomy:

> **4.28**
> **Enemies like hatred and craving**
> **Don't have hands or feet,**
> **Aren't courageous or intelligent,**
> **And yet I act like their slave.**

The first two lines indicate one's loss of autonomy is not caused by a physical body. Lacking courage means weakness. Lacking intelligence means being influenced by ignorance. Although these harmful characteristics are absent, nevertheless, one acts like a slave without any autonomy.

Concerning the characteristics which establish the extent of that:

> **4.29**
> **While they remain in my mind**

> They can harm me whenever they want,
> And I patiently accept it without any resentment,
> But this is not a situation that warrants patience.

It is not logical to be patient with this enemy who is causing one harm, so one should not develop patience with it.

2. Application to suffering

There are two kinds of enemies: ordinary enemies, who are unable to create suffering for oneself, and enemy defilements who are able. These two are indicated in the next two verses, respectively:

> **4.30**
> Even if all the gods and demigods
> Stood against me as enemies,
> They could not lead me into the fires
> Of the Avīci Hell, or send me there.

> **4.31**
> But these enemies, the mighty defilements,
> Can put me there in an instant,
> Where Mount Meru and even its very ashes
> Are consumed on contact.

3. Their perpetual presence

There is the presence of ordinary enemies and the perpetual presence of the enemy defilements, indicated, respectively, in the first two and second two lines of the next verse:

> **4.32**
> What enemy is so interminable,
> Without beginning or end, as my own defilements?
> No other enemy
> Endures as long as they do.

4. They achieve nothing

> **4.33**

When treated well and respected,
Enemies are cooperative and content
But, when the defilements are respected,
They return only pain and suffering.

The first two lines indicate that ordinary enemies can become friends, while the latter two lines indicate that is not the case for the enemy defilements.

2. Examining impatience

1. Harmful to the mind
2. Harmful to the body

1. Harmful to the mind

4.34
Accordingly, these being my old, implacable enemies,
The sole cause of vastly increasing all kinds of harm,
If I make room for them in my heart,
How can I be unafraid or enjoy saṃsāra?

The aspects of harm indicated here are its examination in the first line, the greatness of the harmful effects in the second, their proximity in the third and, in the fourth, the absence of happiness and joy.

2. Harmful to the body

4.35
They are the prison guards of saṃsāra who,
In the hells and elsewhere, become my killers and
    executioners.
So, if they remain in my mind, abiding in the web of
    attachment,
How can I be happy?

The four characteristics of harm to the body here are:

1. The perpetual and temporal functions: their perpetual harm is

indicated in the first line and their temporal harms are indicated in the second. [299]
2. The proximity: their 'remaining in my mind'.
3. To be a cause of grasping: their 'abiding in the web of attachment', where attachment means the habitual imprints of grasping at substantiality.
4. The type of harm: this is indicated in the last line.

3. Developing pride

1. Meaning
2. Example

1. Meaning

4.36
Therefore, as long I have not with certainty
Vanquished this enemy, I will never stop persevering.

For how long should one persevere? For as long as this enemy has not been vanquished, i.e. until the defilements have been abandoned.

2. Example

Growing angry upon some slight, fleeting injury,
The proud and haughty will not sleep until their enemy has been vanquished.

When receiving a slight, fleeting injury, some will not sleep until that ordinary enemy has been defeated. Who does this? Those who become angry, being inflated with pride.

2. Rejecting the idea that application will create suffering

1. The faults of non-application
2. The qualities of application
3. The means of devoting oneself to that application

1. An example of the faults of non-application

4.37
On the battlefield, they are eager to vanquish
People with defilements, who would suffer an ordinary death anyway.
Disregarding the pain of being pierced by arrows or swords,
They will not retreat until their objective is won.

They may not have been killed, yet those who have defilements should be the objects of compassion, being bound by the suffering of dying naturally. Those who are eager to vanquish their ordinary enemies 'will not retreat', i.e. instead of turning to flee, they remain on the battlefield. For how long? For as long as their objective is not achieved, i.e. until they have won. What makes this difficult? They must 'disregard the pain of being pierced by arrows or swords'.

2. The point of the example

4.38
So, what need to mention that I should not be discouraged or frustrated
To be caused even one hundred thousand sufferings,
When striving to finally vanquish my true, natural enemies,
Who cause all my endless suffering?

In wishing to vanquish one's true, natural enemies—the defilements—what need is there to mention that one should not become discouraged or frustrated? What could make one discouraged? One hundred thousand sufferings. [300] Why are the defilements one's natural enemies? Because they are the cause of all one's endless suffering.

2. The qualities of application

1. Benefit of self
2. Benefit of other
3. Fulfilment of vows

1. Benefit of self

4.39

> If scars inflicted by meaningless enemies
> Can be shown off on the body like trophies,
> What trouble is suffering to me,
> When I am striving to achieve a great benefit?

The first two lines indicate that their fighting ordinary enemies is of no benefit to the veterans themselves. The second two lines indicate that sufferings which overcome the defilements benefit oneself.

2. Benefit of other

> 4.40
> If even fishermen, butchers, farmers, etc.
> Thinking only of their livelihoods,
> Put up with the discomforts of heat and cold,
> Why have I no patience for the sake of beings' happiness?

The first three lines indicate that patience with ordinary occupations such as fishing is of no benefit for others, while the last line indicates that the bodhisattva conduct is of benefit for others.

3. Fulfilment of vows

> 4.41
> To liberate from the defilements
> Beings of the ten directions, as far as the ends of space,
> Was my promise but, when I made it,
> I was not free from defilements myself.

> 4.42
> Not understanding my own limitations,
> I spoke without knowing how insane this was.

The first two lines indicate the scope of the vow to benefit others. The remaining lines indicate that the vow will not be fulfilled until the defilements have been abandoned.

3. The means of devoting oneself to that application

  1. Not stopping until the defilements have been abandoned

2. Dedication in this
3. Relying on antidotes for one's own impatience
4. Abandoning objections to that
5. No obedience to the defilements

1. Not stopping until the defilements have been abandoned

> But now I should never turn back from
> Vanquishing the defilements.

2. Dedication in this

> **4.43**
> **I will be fixated on this,**

One should have attachment to applying the antidotes.

3. Relying on antidotes to one's own impatience

> **And full of resentment, wage war**

One should regard the defilements with enmity, i.e. oppose them.

4. Abandoning objections

In that case, does this contradict the teaching that one should abandon resentment?

> **Against the defilements, except those**
> **Which destroy the other defilements.**

The resentment of regarding defilements with enmity, though it may be called a 'defilement', is not otherwise distinguishable from antidotes, so it is not included among that which is to be abandoned.

5. No obedience to the defilements

> **4.44**
> **It would be better to be burned alive**
> **Or decapitated**
> **Than to be constantly grovelling**

To the enemy defilements.

Even at the cost of one's life, [301] one should not be obedient to the defilements.

'Although one might abandon the defilements once, is this not pointless, since they will only return again?'

3. Developing enthusiasm in one's ability to abandon the defilements

   1. They have no other basis
   2. They are erroneous perceptions

1. They have no other basis

   1. Presenting an example of expulsion
   2. The related meaning
   3. The nature of the antidotes which bring about abandonment
   4. The essential characteristic of their not returning

1. Presenting an example of expulsion

> **4.45**
> **Though ordinary enemies may be driven from our homelands,**
> **They resettle elsewhere,**
> **And return when they have recovered their power,**

After expelling ordinary enemies, they may return again and again.

2. The related meaning

But the nature of the enemy defilements is not like this.

When one abandons the seeds of the defilements, they never arise again.

3. The nature of the antidotes which bring about abandonment

> **4.46**
> **These pathetic defilements, cast out by the eye of wisdom,**

The defilements are pathetic, or miserable, i.e. they have little power against being cast out by their antidote, the eye of wisdom.

4. The essential characteristic of their not returning

> And extirpated from my mind, where can they go?
> Where can they settle to hurt me again?
> And yet, weak-willed, I give up without even trying.

When their complete basis is eliminated, they have no other support.

2. They are erroneous perceptions

> **4.47**
> **The defilements are not within objects, nor within the senses,**
> **Nor in anything else, yet, wherever they are, they harm all beings.**
> **They are like illusions. So, giving up this heartfelt fear, I will cultivate the perseverance to achieve wisdom.**
> **Why should I be tormented in places like the hells for no reason?**

The first two lines indicate their having no external support. The first part of the third line indicates their basis not being real. The second part of the third line indicates the characteristics of striving in the antidotes. The last line indicates the fault of not striving in this.

4. Concluding summary of concern for training

> **4.48**
> **Having considered this, I will strive**
> **To fulfil the training as it has been explained.**
> **If he doesn't listen to the doctor's instructions,**
> **How can the patient be cured by the medicine?**

The first two lines indicate that one should endeavour consistently with the training. The second two lines give an example of the faults of not endeavouring.

Chapter 5

CLEAR COMPREHENSION

1. Guarding the mind as the means of guarding training [1-22]
2. Guarding mindfulness and clear comprehension as the means of guarding the mind [v23-33] [302]
3. How to train in the conduct of guarding the mind with mindfulness and clear comprehension [v34-97]
4. Factors which enhance the training [v98-108]
5. Applying the key point [v109]

> Section overview: Guarding the mind as the means of guarding training [v1-22]
>
> 1. By guarding the mind, one guards all
>   1. Showing this with a forward pervasion
>   2. Showing the reverse pervasion
>   3. Establishing the reverse pervasion
>   4. When one guards the mind, dangers subside
>   5. Condensed meaning
> 2. The reason everything depends upon mind
>   1. All faults depend upon mind
>   1. Presenting a scriptural gloss
>   2. Establishing that
>   3. Conclusion
>   2. All virtues depend upon mind
>   1. Giving
>   2. Moral conduct
>   3. Patience
>   1. The actual meaning
>   2. A related example
>   3. The related point
>   4. Energy
>   5. Meditation
>   6. Wisdom
> 3. Making effort to guard the mind
>   1. General explanation
>   2. Everything is accomplished by it
>   3. A perspective for guarding the mind in this way
>   4. The reason it makes sense to guard it
>   5. Properly guarding it
>   6. Conclusion to take great care in mindfulness

1. Guarding the mind as the means of guarding training

1. By guarding the mind, one guards all
2. The reason everything depends upon mind
3. Making effort to guard the mind

Clear Comprehension | 119

1. By guarding the mind, one guards all

   1. Showing this with a forward pervasion
   2. Showing the reverse pervasion
   3. Establishing the reverse pervasion
   4. When one guards the mind, dangers subside
   5. Condensed meaning

1. Showing this in a forward pervasion

   5.1
   Those who want to guard the training
   Must always carefully guard their minds.

2. Showing the reverse pervasion

   If one fails to guard the mind,
   It is impossible to guard the training.

3. Establishing the reverse pervasion

   5.2
   While the rampaging elephant of mind
   Creates the ravages of the Avīci Hell,
   An actual wild and untamed elephant
   Cannot cause anything like that destruction.

4. When one guards the mind, dangers subside

   5.3
   When the rope of constant mindfulness
   Restrains the elephant of mind,
   All troubles subside,
   And all virtues fall into my hands.

5. Condensed meaning

   5.4
   Tigers, lions, elephants, bears,

> Snakes, every kind of enemy,
> The prison guards of the hells,
> Demons and ogres,
>
> **5.5**
> Will all be restrained
> By restraining mind alone,
> And will all be subjugated
> By subjugating mind alone.

The prison guards of hell are dangers of the next life, while the others are dangers in this life. One 'restrains' them with the rope of mindfulness and one 'subjugates' them with clear comprehension.

Alternatively, the verse 5.1 is a general statement, 5.2 indicates the faults of not guarding and the following verses indicate the good qualities of guarding.

2. The reason everything depends upon mind

   1. All faults depend upon mind
   2. All virtues depend upon mind

1. All faults depend upon mind

   1. Presenting a scriptural gloss
   2. Establishing that point

1. Presenting a scriptural gloss

> **5.6**
> In this way, the teacher of perfect truth himself said
> That all dangers,
> And all the infinite sufferings
> Arise from mind.

'Dangers' means the harms of this life. 'Sufferings' means the harms of future lives. These, it is taught, arise from mind. As it says in the *Cloud of Jewels Sutra*:

Mind is the root of all dharmas. When one completely understands mind, one will completely understand all dharmas... Whether actions are virtuous or nonvirtuous is the intention of the mind.[1]

2. Establishing that [303]

> **5.7**
> **Did anyone deliberately make**
> **The weapons of the hell-beings?**
> **Who made the molten iron ground?**
> **Where did these hosts of women come from?**
>
> **5.8**
> **The Sage has taught that all these things**
> **Come from a nonvirtuous mind.**

Since the weapons of the hell-beings, etc. have no creator apart from mind, they are appearances that accord with a mind that generates nonvirtue. The Sage taught in the *Foundations of Mindfulness Sutra* that by the power of one's actions [karma], one sees the women who one formerly looked upon [with attachment].[2]

3. Conclusion

> **Thus, in the three realms,**
> **There is nothing to fear apart from mind.**

2. All virtues depend upon mind

These all depend upon mind:

1. Giving
2. Moral conduct
3. Patience
4. Energy
5. Meditation
6. Wisdom

1. Giving

5.9
'If the perfection of giving
Means dispelling the poverty of beings,
How did the earlier protectors perfect it,
When beings are still poor?'

5.10
It is taught that the perfection of giving
Is the intention to give to all beings
All of one's possessions, along with the results of doing so.
In that sense, it is mind itself.

This refutes the claim that one completes giving by external actions.

Objection: 'If one completes the perfection of giving by dispelling the poverty of beings, how was it perfected in the past? It follows that the protectors of the past did not complete giving for, at the present time, beings are still poor, so poverty still exists.'

The perfection of giving was completed by those protectors. By what cause? By fulfilling their intention to give to all beings all of their possessions, along with the results of doing that.

2. Moral conduct

5.11
'Where has the killing of fish and other creatures
Been eradicated?'
The Sage has taught that the intention to abandon this
Is the perfection of moral conduct.

This refutes the claim that one can complete moral conduct by external actions.

'If the completion of moral conduct is the complete nonexistence of harm done to sentient beings, all the places where fish and so forth are killed would have been eradicated but there has been no such eradication. It follows that the perfection of moral conduct is incomplete.'

It is taught that the protectors of the past did complete the perfection of moral conduct. By what cause? By the intention to abandon harm, as the Sage has said.

3. Patience

   1. The actual meaning
   2. A related example
   3. The related point

1. The actual meaning [304]

   5.12
   Unpleasant beings are as vast as space;
   Defeating them would take forever.
   But if I overcome this one angry mind,
   It would be like defeating all enemies.

The first line indicates enemies are never ending. The second line indicates the impossibility of completely controlling the external world. The last two lines indicate overcoming anger instead.

2. A related example

   5.13
   If I were to cover all the land with leather,
   How much leather would it take?
   But if I just put leather on my shoes,
   It is as if the whole world is covered.

3. The related point

   5.14
   Likewise I can never force
   All external things to change their course.
   But if I could turn around just this mind of mine,
   What need would there be to change anything else?

4. Energy

Here mind-dependence is demonstrated by example and then it is negated that this can be achieved by dependence upon body and speech:

> **5.15**
> While the result of just generating a clear mind
> Is rebirth in realms like that of Brahmā,
> Not even a great many results of body and mind,
> Being of lesser modes of conduct, can equal this.

The first two lines refer to the examples from the *Parinirvāṇa Sutra* of how a mother's feeling of love for her dying child and the great love of a mother and daughter swept away in a river led to their rebirth in the realm of Brahmā. The second two lines, negating the dependence upon body and speech, indicate they are 'lesser modes of conduct', i.e. they are inferior activities.

5. Meditation

> **5.16**
> All recitations and austerities,
> Even if performed extensively,
> Are useless, so the Omniscient One has taught,
> If practised with a wavering mind.

Recitations are verbal, austerities physical. If there is no meditation, i.e. if there is a wandering mind, they are useless, i.e. their results are weak.

6. Wisdom

> **5.17**
> Those who do not understand the secret of mind,
> The supreme lord of dharmas,
> May wish to have happiness and end their suffering,
> But their wishes are futile and they will wander in vain.

The 'lord of dharmas' means ultimate truth. It is also the 'secret of mind', i.e. the reality of mind, which is emptiness itself. This secret is not comprehended by those of inferior fortune. Not understanding it, their wishes are 'futile', i.e. they do not attain liberation and they 'wander in vain', i.e. they wander in saṃsāra.

3. One should make effort to guard the mind[3]

1. General explanation
2. Everything is accomplished by it
3. A perspective for guarding the mind in this way
4. The reason it makes sense to guard it
5. Properly guarding it
6. Conclusion to take great care in mindfulness

1. General explanation

> **5.18**
> **Therefore, my mind**
> **Should be skilfully held and guarded.**

'Holding skilfully' [305] means holding a virtuous intent with mindfulness. 'Guarding skilfully' means not failing to act with clear comprehension.

2. Everything is accomplished by it

> **Without the discipline of guarding the mind,**
> **What is the point of many other disciplines?**

The 'discipline of guarding the mind' means the discipline of perfectly holding the mind as opposed to unconducive conditions such as vacillating moral conduct. 'Many other disciplines' are external disciplines apart from that, such as ritual bathing and wearing a Brahmā thread.[4]

3. A perspective for guarding the mind in this way

> **5.19**
> **Like being careful to protect a wound**
> **In the midst of jostling crowd,**
> **So I will constantly guard this wound of a mind**
> **In the midst of bad people.**

When among an ordinary crowd, one would take care not to let them touch a wound. Similarly, when among nonvirtuous people, one should be careful not to let them damage one's mind.

4. The reason it makes sense to guard it

> 5.20
> If, frightened of a little pain,
> I am careful of a wound,
> Why do I not protect the wound of mind
> Out of fear of the Crushing Hell?

If one is frightened of a little bit of pain from a wound, why is one not frightened of the suffering of the hells?

5. Properly guarding it

> 5.21
> If he can keep to this conduct,
> Then whether among bad people
> Or a group of women,
> The vow-holder's stability will not be impaired.

If one can keep to the conduct of protecting the mind, then when among a group of bad people, one's stability will not be impaired, i.e. the intentions of nonvirtuous friends will not cause defilements for oneself. One's stability will also not be impaired when among a group of women, i.e. though they have thirty-two modes of deception to steal one's moral conduct,[5] one cannot be budged.

6. Conclusion to take great care in mindfulness

> 5.22
> It is better to have no money, no respect,
> And no bodily subsistence,
> And better even for every other virtue to degenerate,
> Than for the mind for degenerate.

Not having attachment to the things of this world is better than having no money or respect, or no subsistence of body or mind. Better than

Clear Comprehension | 127

the degeneration of other virtues means it is better than the degeneration of virtues conducive to merit and even those conducive to liberation. 'Mind' here refers to the mind of a Mahāyānist. [306]

Section overview: Guarding mindfulness and clear comprehension as the means of guarding the mind [v23-33]

1. Brief description
2. The faults of lacking mindfulness and clear comprehension
    1. Little power to act
    2. Wisdom will not flourish
    3. Moral conduct will not flourish
    4. Accumulated virtues are destroyed
    5. Accumulated virtues are not produced
3. Guarding mindfulness as the means of guarding clear comprehension
    1. Expressing the main point
    2. Showing its cause
        1. Keeping in mind the faults of its loss
        2. Relying on the conditions which prevent its loss
            1. The outer condition: reliance on the spiritual friend
            2. The inner condition: a proper mental attitude
            3. An additional benefit
    3. How to definitively generate clear comprehension through mindfulness

---

2. Guarding mindfulness and clear comprehension as the means of guarding the mind

1. Brief description
2. The faults of lacking mindfulness and clear comprehension
3. Guarding mindfulness as the means of guarding clear comprehension

1. Brief description

> **5.23**
> **To those of you who want to guard your mind,**

> I implore you, with folded hands:
> Protect mindfulness and clear comprehension
> With all your might!

Mindfulness is not forgetting to think of virtue. Clear comprehension is distinguishing what is to be done from what is not to be done.

2. The faults of lacking mindfulness and clear comprehension

1. Little power to act
2. Wisdom will not flourish
3. Moral conduct will not flourish
4. Accumulated virtues are destroyed
5. Accumulated virtues are not produced

1. Little power to act

> **5.24**
> **People disturbed by sickness**
> **Have no strength to do anything.**
> **Similarly, those disturbed by defilements**
> **Also have no strength to do anything.**

The first two lines are an example. The second two lines indicate the meaning of the example, i.e. one should have unwavering focus on what is to be done and what is not to be done. Doing 'anything' in this sense means doing virtuous acts.

2. Wisdom will not flourish

> **5.25**
> **Someone whose mind lacks clear comprehension**
> **May hear, reflect and meditate,**
> **But he will not keep it in his memory.**
> **It will leak like water from a vase.**

Distracted by a variety of inferior objects, the mind that cannot hold its focus on reality will not attain perfect wisdom.

3. Moral conduct will not flourish

5.26
Many who had learning, faith,
And dedicated enthusiasm,
By the fault of losing clear comprehension,
Became embroiled in downfalls.

Learning is the excellent condition, faith is the excellent cause and dedicated enthusiasm is the excellent application. Despite holding these, one can still be stained by downfalls. This is like monks who have been sick, etc. forgetting their dispensation on the permitted times of eating and thus becoming stained by downfalls.[6]

4. Accumulated virtues are destroyed

5.27
The thieves who want to steal my clear comprehension
Will show up after my loss of mindfulness.
Then, after they have stolen my merit,
I will go to the lower realms.

If one loses mindfulness of virtue, one no longer knows what to do and, in dependence upon that, anger and so forth destroy all of one's virtue and one proceeds to the lower realms as a result.

5. Accumulated virtues are not produced

5.28
This band of robbers, the defilements,
Are waiting for a good opportunity.
When they find it, they will steal all my virtues
And destroy the life of a good rebirth.

Alternatively, concerning these last two verses, since their meaning is in accord, they may both be explained under the heading '[Accumulated] virtues are destroyed'.

3. Guarding mindfulness as the means of guarding clear comprehension

  1. Expressing the main point

2. Showing its cause [307]
3. How to definitively generate clear comprehension through mindfulness

1. Expressing the main point

5.29
Consequently, I should never let mindfulness stray
Past the gateway of mind.

Mindfulness should never stray. From what? The 'gateway of mind', i.e. the intention to rely on the antidotes. Why not? Because of its being 'consequential', i.e. because of mindfulness being the root of training.

2. Showing its cause

1. Keeping in mind the faults of its loss
2. Relying on the conditions which prevent its loss

1. Keeping in mind the faults of its loss

If it ever leaves, remembering
The horrors of the lower realms, I must get it back.

If mindfulness leaves for somewhere else, i.e. if it is lost, then it must be gotten back, i.e. restored to its former condition. By what consideration? By remembering the horrors of rebirth in the lower realms.

2. Relying on the conditions which prevent its loss

1. The outer condition: reliance on the spiritual friend
2. The inner condition: a proper mental attitude
3. An additional benefit

1. The outer condition: reliance on the spiritual friend

5.30
Through associating with teachers
And attending abbots

> With fear, fortunate ones who have respect
> Easily develop mindfulness.

Through association with teachers who bestow the scriptural transmissions and with holy people, one will easily develop mindfulness. How is it developed through those two? By having fear, i.e. developing a sense of shame, toward abbots, i.e. when attending[7] the teachers and the holy persons. For whom will it develop? For fortunate ones who have respect.

2. The inner condition: a proper mental attitude

> 5.31
> At all times I am
> In the presence of
> All the Buddhas and bodhisattvas
> Whose vision is completely without obstruction.
>
> 5.32
> With this in mind, I should have
> Shame, respect and fear.

For oneself, i.e. from one's own self-perspective, one should have shame by being humble, and have respect for training and fear of downfalls. What causes that? It comes from thinking that at all times one is in the presence of all the Buddhas and bodhisattvas. How is one in their presence? In the sense that their vision is completely unobstructed.

3. Showing an additional benefit

> It will also remind me
> Again and again of the Buddha.

3. How to definitively generate clear comprehension through mindfulness [308]

> 5.33
> When mindfulness stays,
> Guarding the gateway of mind,

**Clear comprehension will come.
Then, even if it is lost, it will return.**

3. How to train in the conduct of guarding the mind with mindfulness and clear comprehension

1. Training in the conduct of vows
2. Training in the conduct of accumulating virtue
3. Training in the conduct of benefitting sentient beings

Section overview: Training in the conduct of vows [v34-58]

1. In relation to type
    1. In relation to the body
        1. Temporarily remaining at ease
        2. In relation to sight
        3. In relation to other situations
        4. Preparing and checking oneself
    2. In relation to the mind
    3. Times when there is a dispensation regardless of type
        1. Times when there is a dispensation on bodily conduct
        2. Referencing a scriptural source for that
        3. Abandoning an objection
        4. The qualities of behaving in this way
        5. The faults of not doing do
        6. Concluding summary
2. Guarding against damage
    1. Guarding against damage to vows of body
        1. Not letting the vows be stolen by distracting conditions
        2. Abandoning meaningless behaviour
        3. Examining the motivation
    2. Guarding against damage to vows of mind
        1. Types of antidote
        2. Briefly explaining how to apply them

---

1. Training in the conduct of vows

    1. In relation to type[8]

2. Guarding against damage

1. In relation to type

   1. In relation to the body
   2. In relation to the mind
   3. Times when there is a dispensation regardless of type

1. In relation to the body

   1. Temporarily remaining at ease
   2. In relation to sight
   3. In relation to other situations
   4. Preparing and checking oneself

1. Temporarily remaining at ease

> **5.34**
> **At the outset, having found a mind like this**
> **With some fault,**
> **At that time, like a block of wood,**
> **I should remain undiverted.**

'At the outset' means before one engages in an activity. 'A mind like this with some fault' means wanting to engage in negative physical activities. To remain like a block of wood at that time means, by overcoming the negative mind, one's attention does not get distracted elsewhere.

2. In relation to sight

> **5.35**
> **I should never look all around**
> **Distractedly for no reason,**
> **But rather, with a resolute mind,**
> **Look with eyes lowered.**

Unless it is necessary, in general, one should stop staring into the distance.

5.36
In order to relax my gaze,
I can from time to time look in some direction

If it is necessary to rest the gaze, one can focus one's attention in this way.

And, if someone appears in my field of vision,
I should look up and greet them.

This establishes how to look at that time.

5.37
In order to identify dangers on the road, etc.
I can repeatedly survey the area.
Pausing and having looked ahead,
I should then look behind.

5.38
Having checked both ahead and behind,
I can continue on or turn back.

One should look ahead for dangers on the ground. [309] One may perceive some danger in a particular direction by pausing. To avoid such dangers that may lie ahead, one can either continue on to where one was looking, or return to the place one saw when one looked behind.

3. In relation to other situations

Similarly, in all circumstances,
I should proceed after understanding whatever is appropriate.

4. Preparing and checking

5.39
Having prepared for some activity
With the thought, 'I will maintain such and such a position',
I should occasionally check to see

If I am remaining as intended.

The last two lines indicate that one should scrutinize the bodily conduct adopted for one's activities. When? When preparing for an activity, i.e. beforehand. How should one prepare? By deciding that one will maintain a particular physical position.

2. In relation to mind

> **5.40**
> **Tying the crazed elephant of mind**
> **To the great pillar of contemplating the dharma,**
> **I will always make an effort to check**
> **It has not escaped.**
>
> **5.41**
> **Whoever perseveres in this samādhi**
> **Will not lose control even for a moment.**
> **'Where is this mind of mine going?'**
> **In this way, I will acutely scrutinize my mind.**

The first verse indicates placing the untethered mind's attention on virtue and the second verse indicates that by doing so, the mind is stabilized. 'Persevering in this samādhi' means placing one's attention on virtue as opposed to merely practising calm abiding meditation.

3. Times when there is a dispensation regardless of type

1. Times when there is a dispensation on bodily conduct
2. Referencing a scriptural source for that
3. Abandoning an objection
4. The qualities of behaving in this way
5. The faults of not doing do
6. Concluding summary

1. Times when there is a dispensation on bodily conduct

> **5.42**
> **If, due to some danger or celebration,**
> **This is not possible, I can relax.**

When necessary, one can to some extent relax the gaze, etc.

2. Referencing a scriptural source for that

> It is taught in this regard that
> At times of giving, moral conduct can be overlooked.

It says in the *Sutra Requested by Akṣayamati*, 'One can overlook the maintenance of moral conduct at the time of giving'.[9] This applies to minor attendant misdeeds, but not to inherent misdeeds or downfalls.

3. Abandoning an objection [310]

> **5.43**
> **Whatever I have intended to do, I should undertake it**
> **And not change my mind about it.**
> **With my mind committed like this,**
> **It will be accomplished in due course.**

'Why should one overlook a more important practice—moral conduct—to practise giving?'

Whatever is most important, that is what should be practised. In this context, once something has been undertaken, it becomes more important.

4. The qualities of behaving in this way

> **5.44**
> **I will carry out everything to completion in this way,**

Having completed those tasks which were already begun, subsequently one can accomplish other things.

5. The faults of not doing so

> **Or nothing else will get done either.**

If one begins something else before the previous tasks are completed, one will not accomplish anything.

6. Concluding summary

Clear Comprehension | 137

**I will not lose clear comprehension
Nor increase the secondary defilements because of this.**

Since it is a time when one has a dispensation, there is no fault of lacking clear comprehension and no fault will occur due to one's relaxation because the intention to overlook moral conduct[10] is not a giving up of the mind of abandonment.

2. Guarding against damage

   1. Guarding against damage to vows of body
   2. Guarding against damage to vows of mind

1. Guarding against damage to vows of body

   1. Not letting the vows be stolen by distracting conditions
   2. Abandoning meaningless behaviour
   3. Examining the motivation[11]

1. Not letting the vows be stolen by distracting conditions

> **5.45
> When I come across
> The various kinds of senseless chatter
> And the many impressive entertainments,
> I should abandon my attachment to them.**

'Senseless chatter' means talk which is pointless, unnecessary and for distraction. 'Impressive entertainments' means events such as festivals.

2. Abandoning meaningless behaviour

> **5.46
> When I meaninglessly gouge at the earth,
> Pick at the grass or draw lines on the ground,
> Then, remembering the Tathāgata's training,
> I will concernedly stop right away.**

3. Examining the motivation

5.47
When I think of moving or
When I think of speaking,
Having first examined my mind,
I should, with deliberateness, act appropriately.

Ceasing activities motivated by the root defilements:

5.48
When my mind is desirous or angry
And I want to react, at that time,
I should not react and should not say anything.
Rather, I should remain like a block of wood.

Ceasing activities motivated by the secondary defilements:

5.49
When my attitude is irritated or derisive,
Proud, vain,
Cutting,
Cruel or deceptive,

'Irritated' here means not at peace, 'proud' means being puffed-up, 'vain' means attachment to one's perceptible qualities, 'cutting' means exposing their faults, [311] 'cruel' means harming someone through exposing some true situation about them and 'deceptive' means misrepresenting something.

5.50
When I am seeking praise
Or criticizing someone,
Insulting them or picking a fight,
At such times, I should remain like a block of wood.

'Insulting' means deprecating someone. 'Picking fights' means physical disputes.

5.51
When I want to profit, be respected and recognized,

When I want to have subordinates,
Or when I think I should be attended to—
At such times, I should remain like a block of wood.

'Profit' means wealth, etc. 'Respected' means having my seat prepared, etc. 'Attended to' means being served with food, etc.

5.52
When I want to give up benefitting others
To pursue my own benefit,
Or when I am about to speak out,
Then I should remain like a block of wood.

5.53
When I am about to be impatient, lazy, afraid,
Rude, stupid,
Or preferential to my own side,
That is when I should remain like a block of wood.

'Impatient' means not being able to put up with something. 'Afraid' means scared to act. 'Rude' means unrestrained conduct. 'Stupid' means spouting meaningless words.

Thus, having examined those motivations which are based on the defilements or are neutral, one can abandon them.

The concluding summary:

5.54
Examining the mind in this way for defilements
And meaningless aims,
The heroic one should hold the mind firmly
With the antidotes.

This hero never instigates negative conduct, since he has captured his enemies, such as aggression.

2. Guarding against damage to vows of mind

  1. Types of antidote

2. Briefly explaining how to apply them

1. Types of antidote

> **5.55**
> **Fully resolved, with proper faith,**
> **Steadfast, respectful, polite,**
> **With care and apprehension,**
> **And with calmness, I will strive for the happiness of others.**

'Fully resolved' means firmly applying oneself or distinguishing what to accept and reject. 'Proper faith' means the three kinds of faith. 'Steadfast' means not retreating from the antidotes. 'Respectful' means regarding one's respect and service of the Three Jewels as of great importance. 'Polite' means addressing impartially the old, the middle-aged and the young with courteous words. 'Care' means avoiding nonvirtues, whether inherent misdeeds or due to the power of dharma [i.e. attendant misdeeds]. 'Apprehension' means fearing the ripening of karma. 'Calmness' means the senses are disciplined. 'Striving for the happiness of others' means acting with great concern for the benefit of others.

> **5.56**
> **Undiscouraged by the inclinations**
> **Of bickering, childish people,**
> **I will think kindly that they are like this**
> **Because of the defilements arising in their minds.**

'The inclinations of bickering, childish people' means those whose intentions are in conflict. One should not be discouraged by them. The antidote to such discouragement is kind affection, indicated in the last two lines.

> **5.57**
> **Without propagating misdeeds,**
> **Whether acting for myself or for sentient beings,**
> **I will always keep this attitude,**
> **Acting selflessly, like an apparition.**

[312] The first line refers summarily to the antidotes which guard the mind from damage. The rest indicates abandoning conceit both in oneself and towards others.

2. Briefly explaining how to apply the antidotes

> **5.58**
> **Thinking again and again**
> **That finally I have attained this supreme freedom,**
> **I will hold on to this mind and it will stray**
> **No more than the king of mountains.**

The first two lines are a consideration of the difficulty of acquiring freedom and leisure. The latter two indicate not damaging the mind's virtue.

142 | BODHICARYĀVATĀRA WITH COMMENTARY

Section overview: Training in the conduct of accumulating virtue [v59-83]

1. Accomplishing non-attachment to the body
    1. Inanimate
    2. Impure
    3. Essenceless
    4. Useless
    5. Applying it to use
2. Training in the means of accomplishing virtue
    1. Skilful means for an ordinary person's conduct
    2. Skilful means for conduct towards agents
        1. How to respond to those who are giving advice
        2. How to respond to those who expressing the truth
        3. How to respond to those who are creating merit
        4. How to respond to descriptions
        5. The greatness of the mind that is respectful to others
    3. Skilful means for conduct of action
        1. Connected with speaking
        2. Connected with looking
        3. Connected with virtuous action
            1. Intention
            2. Fields
            3. Application
            4. Specific types

2. Training in the conduct of accumulating virtue

 1. Accomplishing non-attachment to the body
 2. Training in the means of accomplishing virtue

1. Accomplishing non-attachment to the body

 1. Inanimate
 2. Impure
 3. Essenceless
 4. Useless
 5. Applying it to use

1. Inanimate

> **5.59**
> Though vultures, wanting flesh,
> Will fight to tear it apart,
> That does not bother you, mind.
> So why cherish it so much now?
>
> **5.60**
> Having taken this body as 'mine',
> Why, mind, are you so protective of it?
> For if it is really separate from you,
> What good is it to you anyway?

The first verse indicates that it is illogical to protect something which must eventually be discarded. The second verse indicates that it is illogical to protect something distinct from mind.

2. Impure

> **5.61**
> Why, my defiled mind,
> Don't you instead take a nice, clean block of wood?
> Wouldn't that be better than trying to look after
> This contraption, which is a pile of filth, falling apart?

The first two lines indicate that it is illogical not to grasp something pure. The second two lines indicate that it is illogical to grasp something impure.

3. Essenceless

> **5.62**
> First of all, in my mind,
> I distinguish the layers of skin.
> Then, with the scalpel of discrimination,
> I separate the flesh from the skeleton.
>
> **5.63**
> Having analysed the bones as well,

Until I see their very marrow,
I look and ask myself,
'Where is the essence in this?'

5.64
If, in such a determined search,
I can see no essence,
Why go on protecting
This body with such attachment?

4. Useless

The thing is useless to oneself:

5.65
If you cannot eat this impure body,
Nor drink its blood,
Nor chew on its offal,
What actual use is it to you?

The thing is useless to others:

5.66
On the other hand, it is alright to look after it
So that the jackals and vultures have something to eat.

'On the other hand' indicates what happens if one does look after it.

5. Applying it to use

A general comment on applying it to benefitting others:

These human bodies of ours
Should be used only in service.

Giving up the body is certain:

5.67
In this way, even if you do look after it,
When the unsentimental Lord of Death

> Seizes it and gives it to the birds and dogs,
> What will you do then?

An example where one does not maintain their upkeep if there is no benefit:

> **5.68**
> If you don't give clothes, etc.
> To servants who will not work for them,

Applying the meaning of that example:

> Why do you reward this body,
> Which you are going to lose no matter what you feed it?

Summarizing the meaning of applying its use to one's own benefit:

> **5.69**
> I have already paid the body its wages,
> So now it must start working for me.
> If it is of no use,
> It should not be given anything.

Methods of reinforcing that: [313]

> **5.70**
> On account of its coming and going,
> I will think of the body as a boat.
> In order to accomplish the benefit of beings,
> I will transform it into a wish fulfilling body.

2. Training in the means of accomplishing virtue

  1. Skilful means for ordinary conduct
  2. Skilful means for conduct towards agents
  3. Skilful means for conduct of action[12]

1. Skilful means for ordinary conduct

Consideration of the motivation:

5.71
While there is the freedom to do this,

Physical conduct:

Always presenting a cheerful countenance,
I will stop scowling angrily

Verbal conduct:

And, instead, be a straightforward friend to the world.

How to interact with external objects:

5.72
I will cease moving my seat around, etc.
In an inconsiderate or noisy way,
And cease slamming doors,
Always enjoying quietness.

5.73
Cranes, cats and thieves
Move silently and undetected
And evidently get what they want.
The wise should always behave like they do.

2. Skilful means towards agents

  1. How to respond to those who are giving advice
  2. How to respond to those who expressing the truth
  3. How to respond to those who are creating merit
  4. How to respond to descriptions
  5. The greatness of the mind that is respectful to others

1. How to respond to those who are giving advice

5.74

> By accepting respectfully and with gratitude
> The unsolicited and beneficial words of others
> That admonish or advise me,
> I will always be the pupil of everyone.

This means treating detractors respectfully.

2. How to respond to those who expressing the truth

> 5.75
> For all that is well-said,
> I should call it virtuous.

3. How to respond to those who are creating merit

> When I see something meritorious being done,
> I will praise it and take delight in it.

One should praise it with words and be delighted in one's mind.

4. How to respond to descriptions

> 5.76
> I should describe good qualities that are hidden,
> And I should confirm good qualities that are expressed.
> If my own good qualities are mentioned,
> I should notice that those good qualities were recognized.

The first line indicates not disputing descriptions of others' good qualities, while the second line indicates giving confirmation of descriptions of others' good qualities. The last two lines indicate giving up conceit when one's own good qualities are described.

5. The greatness of the mind that is respectful to others

> 5.77
> Everything we do should be for the sake of joy,
> But joy is difficult to buy, even for the wealthy.
> So, I will be happy when joy
> Is brought about by the good qualities of others.

5.78
It will cost me nothing now,
And in future lives it will bring great bliss.
Otherwise I will have no joy and only suffering,
And in future lives I will have even greater suffering.

The first two lines indicate establishing the benefit of others. The next two lines indicate one's developing of joy in that benefit. The next two lines indicate the good qualities of developing joy for others. The last two lines indicate the faults of not having joy. [314]

3. Skilful means for conduct of action

   1. Connected with speaking
   2. Connected with looking
   3. Connected with virtuous action

1. Connected with speaking

5.79
When speaking, my speech should be
Authentic, consistent, clear, pleasant,
Without attachment or aversion,
Gentle and appropriate.

'Authentic' means having sincerity. 'Consistent' means what is said later should not contradict what was said before. 'Clear' means not being obscure. 'Pleasant' means pleasing. 'Without attachment or aversion' means having a virtuous intent. 'Gentle' means not being aggressive. 'Appropriate' means speaking at the right times.

2. Connected with looking

5.80
When my eyes see someone,
Thinking, 'I can attain buddhahood itself
In dependence upon this very person',
I will look at them directly and with a gentle regard.

Clear Comprehension | 149

'When my eyes see someone' is the establishing condition. 'Gentle' means pleasing.

3. Connected with virtuous action

   1. Intention
   2. Fields
   3. Application
   4. Specific types

1. Intention

> **5.81**
> **Always motivated by aspiration**
> **Or antidotes,**

'Aspiration' means increasing one's resolve. 'Antidotes' are the mental antidotes of not being greedy, avoiding negative actions, not being angry, having energy, being undistracted and recognizing the illusory nature of greed, etc.[13]

2. Fields

> **There will be great virtue**
> **In the fields of good qualities, help and suffering.**

The field of 'good qualities' is the Three Jewels, etc. The field of 'help' is parents, abbots and ācāryas. The field of 'suffering' is the poor, etc.

3. Application

> **5.82**
> **When I have the knowledge and ability,**
> **I should always do things myself.**
> **In whatever I do, I should not**
> **Be dependent on someone else.**

One should do things oneself and not depend on others.

4. Specific types

5.83
The perfections of generosity, etc.
Are each superior to the preceding one.
I should not give up the greater in favour of the lesser,
But the most important thing is to consider the benefit of others.

The first three lines indicate the causes of merit—the perfections—or the cause of giving itself, while the last line indicates the reason for doing these.

Section overview: Training in the conduct of benefitting sentient beings [v84-97]

1. Increasing activities for the benefit of others
2. The conduct of gathering sentient beings
    1. Gathering with wealth and possessions
        1. External gathering
        2. Internal gathering
    2. Gathering with dharma
        1. Vessels of its explanation
        2. Methods of its explanation
3. The subsequent conduct of protecting the minds of sentient beings

---

3. Training in the conduct of benefitting sentient beings

   1. Increasing activities for the benefit of others
   2. The conduct of gathering sentient beings
   3. The subsequent conduct of protecting the minds of sentient beings

1. Increasing activities for the benefit of others

5.84
With this in mind, I should always
Keep working to benefit others.
For this, the far-seeing Compassionate One
Permitted what is otherwise forbidden.

The most important thing is the benefit of others. [315] Can one become tainted by downfalls through this? No, since what is forbidden for śrāvakas is permitted for those whose principal intention is to benefit others. Who permitted this? It was permitted by the Buddha, whose intentions are compassionate and whose understanding is far-seeing, i.e. he perceives that which is extremely distant.

According to Ācārya Ratnākaraśānti,[14] the last two lines are,

> Though otherwise forbidden, it is permitted
> For the compassionate one who sees far.

To whom is this permitted? To one whose intention is compassionate, i.e. whose objective is to benefit others, and who is far-seeing.

2. The conduct of gathering sentient beings

1. Gathering with wealth and possessions
2. Gathering with dharma

1. Gathering with wealth and possessions

1. External gathering
2. Internal gathering

1. External gathering

5.85
Apart from consuming just enough food
And wearing the three dharma robes, I will donate the rest
To those who have fallen, those with no protector
And those maintaining discipline.

The recipients: 'those who have fallen'—hungry ghosts, hell beings etc.—'those with no protector'—the poor—and 'those maintaining discipline'—friends observing monastic rules. The substances: consuming in moderation food acquired though begging alms and donating the rest and wearing only the three dharma robes and donating the rest.

2. Internal gathering

5.86
A body being used to practise the holy dharma
Should not be harmed for the sake of something trivial.
If I act in this way, the wishes of beings
Will be fulfilled more quickly.

5.87
My compassionate intentions being impure,
I should not give away this body but,
In this and future lives,
It may be given to accomplish a great benefit.

Abandoning meaningless harm, the necessity of that, not giving the body for the time being and the correct method of giving it are indicated in each of the four pairs of lines respectively.

2. Gathering with dharma

1. Vessels of its explanation
2. Methods of its explanation

1. Vessels of its explanation

5.88
The dharma should not be explained to the disrespectful:
Those wrapping their heads in cloth like sick men,
Those carrying parasols, sticks, or weapons,
And those covering their heads.

5.89
The profound and vast should not be taught to the lesser,
Nor to an unaccompanied woman.

'Disrespectful' means lacking faith. 'The lesser' means those who are afraid of the profound doctrine and are unsuitable vessels. Being 'unaccompanied' causes others to forget their faith.[15] The implication is that one should turn these three away. [316]

2. Methods of its explanation

> **5.89**
> **I should always show equal respect**
> **To the lesser and supreme teachings.**

> **5.90**
> **I should not impart the lesser teachings**
> **To a vessel of the vast teachings.**
> **I should not abandon the conduct.**
> **I should not mislead others with sutras or mantras.**

'Equal' means holding all the teachings equally and 'respect' means holding them in the highest regard. Lines 90ab indicate matching the vessel and the teaching. 90c is a reference to the supreme path of conduct. 90d indicates not subverting the teachings, such as denying that they teach a connection between actions and effects.

3. The subsequent conduct of protecting the minds of sentient beings

In relation to effluence:

> **5.91**
> **When cleaning my teeth or spitting,**
> **I should discreetly dispose of it.**
> **To urinate, etc. in water**
> **Or places used by others is disgusting.**

In relation to eating:

> **5.92**
> **I should not eat noisily or with my mouth open,**
> **Or by cramming my mouth full.**
> **I should not sit with my feet up**
> **Or massage my shoulders with both hands at once.**[16]

In relation to company:

> **5.93**
> **I should not be alone with a woman**

When travelling, sleeping or staying somewhere.

In short, abandon all disrespectful conduct:

I should know or find out whatever
Is disrespectful to the world and avoid it.

In relation to physical movements:

5.94
I should never indicate by finger-pointing
But politely gesture towards things
With my right hand open.
This is also how I should show which way to go.

5.95
I should not gesticulate wildly,
But express my point with slight movements,
Signalling with a click of the fingers, etc.
To do otherwise would be rude.

In relation to sleep:

5.96
I should sleep like the Protector passing into nirvāṇa—
Lying in the preferred direction.
With clear comprehension, I should resolve
To promptly rise early in the morning.

In summary, practise the conduct which purifies the mind:

5.97
Though it is taught
That bodhisattva conduct is limitless,
For now, I should actually practise
As much conduct as possible that purifies the mind.

> Section overview: Factors which enhance the training [v98-108]
>
> 1. The cause of purifying faults
> 2. The basis of training
> 3. The aim
> 4. The teacher of the training
>   1. The spiritual friend
>   2. One should rely upon him
>   3. Consideration of reliance upon application
> 5. Becoming knowledgeable
> 6. Summary of the training

4. Factors which enhance the training

1. The cause of purifying faults
2. The basis of training
3. The aim
4. The teacher of the training
5. Becoming knowledgeable
6. Summary of the training

1. The cause of purifying faults

> **5.98**
> **Three times each day and night,**
> **I should recite the *Sutra of the Three Heaps* and**
> **Pacify the residual downfalls**
> **By relying upon the conquerors and bodhicitta.**

The three heaps are confession of nonvirtues, rejoicing and dedication.[17] These skilful means for swiftly attaining perfect enlightenment can be used to confess downfalls. 'Residual downfalls' means accompanying negativities released by confession, i.e. even if one's moral conduct is restored, the unripened karmic potential of the former downfall may remain. The three heaps will pacify that. [317] It says in the *Sutra of the Great Lion's Roar of Maitreya*,

Because one should exhaust nonvirtues previously committed, one should recite the dharma liturgy of the *Three Heaps*. If one does so, though there are remnant downfalls, one confesses the faults. Merely by doing so, they are purified and henceforth one will not break the vows.[18]

2. The basis of training

5.99
Regardless of whether it is one's own or another's [training],
For any particular situation,
I should train with diligence
In whatever is taught for that situation.

The trainings which relate to oneself are the bodhisattva pitakas. The trainings which relate to others are the practices of the śrāvakas. Does this mean it is necessary to undertake all of these trainings?

5.100
There is nothing that
The sons of the conquerors fail to train in.

It is necessary to become learned in every one of the vehicles which cause omniscience. One should not fail to achieve this because one must train all those to be trained.[19] The result of this:

For the wise, who always keep to this,
Nothing will fail to be meritorious.

3. The aim

5.101
Whether directly or indirectly,
I should do nothing apart from benefitting beings.
'So that this may only benefit beings,
I dedicate it all to enlightenment.'

One 'indirectly' benefits beings by dedicating one's gathering of vows and virtues for the benefit of others. Benefitting beings 'directly' is straightforward.

4. The teacher of the training

  1. The spiritual friend
  2. One should rely upon him
  3. Consideration of reliance upon application

1. The spiritual friend

> **5.102**
> **The spiritual friend is**
> **Learned in the Mahāyāna**
> **And has mastered the discipline of the bodhisattvas.**

He is learned in that the trainings he has received are undamaged and is skilled in the means of restoring them if they are damaged. He keeps the bodhisattva vow and bestows it on others, his students.

2. One should rely upon him

> **I should never discard him, even at the cost of my life.**

This is like Sadaprarudita.[20]

3. Consideration of reliance upon application

> **5.103**
> **I should train in relying upon the teacher**
> **As in the chapter of Śrisambhava.**

The boy Śrisambhava [318] served one hundred and ten spiritual friends.[21]

5. Becoming knowledgeable

The trainings are explained in the sutras, so one must learn them from there:

> **This and the other instructions given by the Buddha**

> I should understand through reading the sutras.

'This' means the bodhisattva trainings. The 'other instructions given by the Buddha' means the śrāvaka trainings and so forth. One should gradually learn these:

> 5.104
> The trainings are found in the sutras,
> So I should read the sutras.
> The *Ākāśagarbha Sutra*
> Is the one I should look at first.
>
> 5.105
> Because what is always to be practised
> Is taught there very extensively,
> I will be certain to also study
> The *Śikṣā-samuccaya*.
>
> 5.106
> Otherwise I should study
> The *Sutra-samuccaya*.
> I should also make an effort to study
> These two works composed by Ārya Nāgārjuna.

The *Ākāśagarbha Sutra* explains the root downfalls.[22] The two *Samuccayas*[23] give a general account of the main body of training.

6. Summary of the training

> 5.107
> I should practise whatever is not
> Prohibited there.
> In order to protect worldly minds
> I should fully practise what I have learnt.
>
> 5.108
> I should examine again and again
> The conditions of body and mind.
> This alone encapsulates

The key point of maintaining clear comprehension.

Practising that which one has seen, training in protecting the minds of others and training in examining one's own delusions are indicated in v107ab, v107cd and verse 108, respectively.

5. Applying the key point

> 5.109
> I should put this into practice,
> For what use are mere words?
> Are sicknesses cured
> Just by reading about the treatment?

That application will bring the result, that mere words will not bring the result and an example of that are indicated in the first, second and final two lines, respectively.

Chapter 6
PATIENCE

Chapter overview: Patience

1. Developing motivation for patience [v1-6]
    1. Invisible results
    2. Visible results
        1. Harm to the mind
        2. Harm to the body
    3. Summarizing the invisible and visible results
2. Keeping in mind the skilful means for accomplishing patience [v7-134]
    1. Preventing the characteristics of anger
        1. The nature of its cause
        2. Striving in the means of averting that cause
        3. The means of averting that cause
        4. Keeping in mind the means of averting the cause of the cause (cont.)
    2. Keeping in mind the results of patience
        1. Brief presentation
        2. An example from the perspective of the result
        3. The example is far outweighed
        4. Summary enumeration of results

1. Developing motivation for patience [v1-6]
2. Keeping in mind the skilful means for accomplishing patience [v7-134]

1. Developing motivation for patience

The problems caused by anger are set out explicitly and this establishes implicitly the results of patience. The explanation of this has three parts:

1. Invisible results
2. Visible results
3. Summarizing the invisible and visible results

1. Invisible results

> **6.1**
> **All those good actions**
> **Like giving and making offerings to the Sugatas,**
> **Accumulated over a thousand aeons,**
> **Are destroyed in an instant of anger.**

'Giving and making offerings to the Sugatas' means that giving itself is distinguished according to its recipients, which are of the inferior and superior fields. 'Like' means that what arises from moral discipline [319] and from meditation are also included. 'Good actions' means those that were meritorious but were not dedicated to liberation. 'Anger' means an aggressive attitude. 'Destroyed' means that since one is reborn into the lower realms in the next life as the result of anger, the possibility of all one's good actions ripening into experience is destroyed.

'If it is impossible to permanently destroy the seeds of past actions on worldly paths, is it not a contradiction to say here that the seeds are destroyed by anger?'

Since the possibility of their coming to fruition is postponed, their potential is suppressed but the seeds themselves are not permanently destroyed because there is no possibility to destroy seeds apart from the transcendental path.

Therefore, it is established that both anger and patience have great results:

> **6.2**
> **There is no nonvirtue like anger,**
> **And no austerity like patience.**
> **Therefore, in the various ways,**
> **I should persevere in developing patience.**

To develop patience 'in the various ways' means, from the ultimate perspective, developing certainty in the dharma and, from the relative perspective, being unconcerned by difficulties and undaunted by suffering.

2. Visible results

1. Harm to the mind
2. Harm to the body

1. Harm to the mind

> **6.3**
> **If I hold onto thoughts afflicted by anger,**
> **My mind will know no peace.**
> **Having no happiness or pleasure,**
> **I will be unsettled and unable to sleep.**

'Peace' means certainty. 'Happiness' relates to the mind. 'Pleasure' relates to the five senses. 'Settled' means the mind remains at ease.

2. Harm to the body

> **6.4**
> **Some may depend on his favour**
> **For wealth and status,**
> **But even they will turn against**
> **A hateful master and kill him.**

> **6.5**
> **Friends and relatives will become fed up with him and,**

> Though drawn by his generosity, will not want to be
> around him.

'Status' means to be served food and so forth. Such people will turn against an angry master and will kill him. Those who are his friends and relatives will not want to be around him, even though they are attracted by his giving.

3. Summarizing the invisible and visible results

> In short, someone who stays angry
> Will never be happy.

> 6.6
> It is the enemy, anger, which creates
> Sufferings like these.

The first two lines indicate non-happiness. The next two indicate the creation of suffering. Since this describes explicitly the result of anger, [320] the result of abandoning anger is implicitly established. Nevertheless, the result of abandoning anger is explicitly described in the last two lines:

> But whoever takes control and destroys anger
> Will be happy in this life and future lives.

2. Keeping in mind the skilful means for accomplishing patience

1. Preventing the characteristics of anger
2. Keeping in mind the results of patience

1. Preventing the characteristics of anger

1. The nature of its cause
2. Striving in the means of averting that cause
3. The means of averting that cause
4. Keeping in mind the means of averting the cause of the cause

1. The nature of its cause

> **6.7**
> **It arises in the production of what I wish against,**
> **And in the obstruction of what I wish for.**
> **Feeding on an unhappy mind,**
> **Aggression grows and destroys me.**

Through experiencing the production of the twelve undesirables and the twelve obstructions of desirables,[1] an unhappy mind arises and, in conjunction with that, aggression, by which one's mind is tormented and troubled.

2. Striving in the means of averting that cause

> **6.8**
> **Therefore, I should completely eliminate**
> **The sustenance of this enemy—**
> **An enemy which does nothing**
> **But harm me.**

This verse indicates the elimination of the means—an unhappy mind—and aggressive actions.

3. The means of averting the cause

> **6.9**
> **Whatever may befall me,**
> **My joyful disposition will not be disturbed.**
> **Being unhappy won't accomplish any of my wishes**
> **And my virtues will only deteriorate.**

> **6.10**
> **If something can be done,**
> **What's the point of being unhappy?**
> **If nothing can be done,**
> **What good is it to be unhappy?**

The first two lines indicate generally the abandoning of an unhappy mind; the third line indicates that an unhappy mind does not result in one's wishes being accomplished; the fourth line indicates that what one wishes against results from an unhappy mind; the second verse indicates the mental antidote for an unhappy mind.

> Section overview: Keeping in mind the means of averting the cause of the cause [v11-126]
>
> 1. General explanation distinguishing desirable and undesirable dharmas
> 2. Ceasing anger towards the production of undesirables
>   1. Stopping impatience with the production of negative actions towards oneself
>   1. Stopping impatience with the establishment of suffering for oneself
>   (cont.)
>   2. Stopping impatience with the establishment of disrespect, etc. [for oneself]
>   (cont.)
>   2. Stopping impatience with the production of negative actions towards one's own side
>   (cont.)
>   3. Stopping impatience with the production of good towards one's enemies
>   (cont.)
> 3. Ceasing anger towards those who obstruct desirable dharmas
> (cont.)

4. Keeping in mind the means of averting the cause of the cause

   1. General explanation distinguishing desirable and undesirable dharmas
   2. Ceasing anger toward the production of undesirables
   3. Ceasing anger towards those who obstruct desirable dharmas

1. General explanation distinguishing desirable and undesirable dharmas

   6.11
   For myself and my friends,

**I want no suffering, no disrespect,
No criticism and nothing unpleasant.
For my enemies, I want the opposite.**

The twelve undesirables are:

- Suffering, disrespect, criticism and displeasure for oneself
- The same four for my friends
- Happiness, respect, praise and pleasure for one's enemies

The twelve desirables are:

- Happiness, respect, praise and pleasure for oneself
- The same four for one's friends [321]
- Suffering, disrespect, verbal abuse and displeasure for one's enemies

In addition, there are obstructions to the twelve desirables, i.e. twenty-four undesirables in total. Concerning friends of enemies, if they make one unhappy and cause harm, they are essentially the same as enemies, whereas if they bring benefit and happiness, they are essentially friends. If they bring neither benefit nor harm, since they are objects neither of attachment or aversion, they are not determined one way or the other.

2. Ceasing anger toward the production of undesirables

   1. Stopping impatience with the production of negative actions towards oneself
   2. Stopping impatience with the production of negative actions towards one's own side
   3. Stopping impatience with the production of good towards one's enemies

1. Stopping impatience with the production of negative actions towards oneself

   1. Stopping impatience with the establishment of suffering for oneself

2. Stopping impatience with the establishment of disrespect, etc. [for oneself]

> Section overview: Stopping impatience with the establishment of suffering for oneself [v12-51]
>
> 1. Tolerating suffering by examining the suffering itself
>   1. Examining the nature of suffering
>   2. Examining the great benefits of suffering which is undergone for happiness
>   3. Examining that the reliance on suffering is not difficult
>   4. Examining the qualities of the practice
>   5. Examining the inherent qualities
> 2. Definitive consideration of the qualities in the discrimination
>   1. Since it depends on a cause, it does not have autonomy
>   1. Anger and the angry person do not have autonomy
>   2. Their conditions do not have autonomy
>   2. Refuting the essential characteristics of autonomy
>   1. Refuting the position of the Sāṃkhyas
>   2. Refuting the position of the Naiyāyikas
>   3. Summary
>   3. The necessity of overcoming anger
>   4. Summary
> 3. In discriminating harmful sentient beings, how to think of them as not causing the harm
>   1. One should have the characteristics of affection in one's attitude
>   2. Not dwelling on the characteristics of anger
>   3. Examination of one's own faults
>   1. The faults are one's own
>   2. The fault of grasping the body, which causes suffering
>   3. The fault of attachment, which causes suffering
>   4. The fault of activities which are of no benefit to others
>   5. The angry mind has it the wrong way round
>   6. Abandoning objections

1. Stopping impatience with the establishment of suffering for oneself

1. Tolerating suffering by examining the suffering itself
2. Definitive consideration of the qualities in the discrimination

3. In discriminating harmful sentient beings, how to think of them as not causing the harm

1. Tolerating suffering by examining the suffering itself

   1. Examining the nature of suffering
   2. Examining the great benefits of suffering which is undergone for happiness
   3. Examining that the reliance on suffering is not difficult
   4. Examining the qualities of the practice
   5. Examining the inherent qualities

1. Examining the nature of suffering

> **6.12**
> **While the causes of happiness are few,**
> **The causes of suffering are many.**

Since the former are occasional or adventitious, while the latter are ubiquitous, it makes no sense to be angry with them for their nature, for it is like being angry with a fire for being hot.

2. Examining the great benefits of suffering which is undergone for happiness

> **Without suffering, there is no renunciation.**
> **Therefore, mind, remain steady.**
>
> **6.13**
> **The devotees of Gaurī and the practitioners of Karna**
> **Undergo burns, cuts and so forth,**
> **Enduring them patiently for no benefit. Yet, for the sake**
> **Of liberation, why do I have no courage?**

The three points here are:

- The result of austerities—the first two lines
- An example of patience which has no result—beginning of verse 13

- Patience which does have a result—from 'Yet, for the sake…' [322]

Gaurī, also known as Umā, is a goddess of austerities. Those who have faith in her actually cut off their own heads. The people of the country of Karna believed they could be liberated by killing one another with weapons during a lunar eclipse.

3. Examining that reliance on suffering is not difficult

Accomplishing patience by familiarization:

> 6.14
> There is nothing that does not
> Become easier with habituation.
> Therefore, by habituation to small difficulties,
> I will have the patience for great difficulties.

Reasons for having patience:

> 6.15
> Who has not undergone the pointless sufferings
> Of snake or insect bites,
> Experiences of hunger and thirst,
> And afflictions like skin inflammations?

Objects of patience:

> 6.16
> I should not be so sensitive
> To heat, cold, rain, wind and so forth,
> To sickness, confinement, blows and so forth—
> Because that only magnifies their harm.

An example of generating the force of patience:

> 6.17
> Some, when they see their own blood,
> Develop even greater courage and resolve.
> Some, when they see the blood of another,

Feel faint and fall unconscious.

6.18
These come from having a stable
Or a weak state of mind.

Summary:

Therefore, disregarding harm,
I will be unaffected by suffering.

4. Examining the qualities of the practice

6.19
Even when suffering occurs,
The wise should not let it disturb their peace of mind.
In battles with the defilements
There will be many injuries.

6.20
Having disregarded all sufferings,
Enemies like aggression will be overcome.
Those who do so are the real conquering heroes—
The rest are just butchering corpses.

When aggression occurs, one who cultivates the antidote is a heroic warrior. But to cultivate the antidote when aggression is not occurring is like butchering corpses.

5. Examining the inherent qualities

6.21
Furthermore, suffering has good qualities:
Sadness dispels arrogance,
One feels compassion for those in saṃsāra,
Avoids nonvirtue and delights in virtue.

The four points here are that pride, the cause of suffering, is destroyed (first two lines), one has the courage to benefit others (third line), the causes of suffering are dispelled (first half of last line) and one pursues the causes of happiness (second half of last line).

2. The patience of a definitive consideration of their qualities

  1. Since it depends on a cause, it does not have autonomy
  2. Refuting the essential characteristics of autonomy
  3. The necessity of overcoming anger
  4. Summary

1. Since it depends on a cause, it does not have autonomy

  1. Anger and the angry person do not have autonomy
  2. Their conditions do not have autonomy

1. Anger and the angry person do not have autonomy

  1. Establishing the fact
  2. General explanation of the sameness of their qualities by example
  3. Connecting with the meaning
  4. Summary

1. Establishing the fact

> 6.22
> **I have no anger towards things like bile,**
> **Though they can be great sources of suffering,**
> **So why be angry with those which have a mind?**
> **They are all just responding to conditions.**

[323] One gets angry with the cause of suffering when it is sentient but not when it is insentient, yet they are similar in respect of both being causes.

2. General explanation of the sameness of their qualities by example

> 6.23
> **Though they are unwanted,**
> **Such sicknesses nevertheless occur.**

> Similarly, though they are unwanted,
> Defilements stubbornly arise.

These two are not distinct in as much as they are similarly unwanted, yet arise from causes.

3. Connecting with the meaning

> **6.24**
> They don't think, 'I'm going to get angry now',
> But people nevertheless get angry.
> Similarly, it doesn't think 'I'm going to arise now',
> But anger nevertheless arises.

The first two lines indicate ordinary people's lack of autonomy. The latter two lines indicate the lack of autonomy in anger itself.

4. Summary

> **6.25**
> All the various negative actions
> And all the many kinds of nonvirtue
> Arise through the power of conditions.
> They are not autonomous.

2. Their conditions do not have autonomy

> **6.26**
> Though there is a coming together of conditions,
> There is no thought of, 'I'm going to arise now.'
> Nor does that which is produced
> Have any thought of itself as produced.

Though they have no intentional thought of, 'We will create a cause', nor any intentional thought of, 'We will produce a result', nevertheless they naturally arise.

'Though these conditions have no autonomy, is there not some other autonomous creator?'

2. Refuting the essential characteristics of autonomy

1. Refuting the position of the Sāṃkhyas
2. Refuting the position of the Naiyāyikas
3. Summary

1. Refuting the position of the Sāṃkhyas

6.27
Some claim that there is a primal substance,

[Objection:] 'That which depends upon external conditions has no autonomy. However, we postulate a primal substance and individual consciousnesses[2] that are sempiternal and arise by their own power without dependence upon conditions. When the three material natures that comprise the primal substance are in disequilibrium, its universal flow displays manifestations,[3] all of which are pervaded by the oneness of the primal substance.'

And they designate a 'self',

'The nature of individual sentient beings is containers of cognition and awareness within the primal material substance, resting evenly within the two-sided, sempiternal mirror of mind.[4] The manifestations are classified as follows:

1. The 'Great One'
2. Pride [324]
3. The five bare elements
4. The five elements
5. The eleven organs[5]

'In the mirror of mind, happiness and so forth—the manifesting nature of the five bare elements—are resting passively. The selves—cognizing awarenesses—are also resting passively. When these two factors connect, objects arise as experiences of benefit and harm to the self. The primal nature and its manifestations are ultimately one, arising in themselves, though the primal nature is sempiternal while the manifestations are temporary. Therefore, an individual consciousness creates harm autonomously by engaging in aggressive actions such as attacking an enemy.'[6]

[Response:] Regarding this designation of a self, were the impermanent manifestations of the sempiternal primal substance existent or nonexistent before their arising? If existent:

> But it does not deliberately think,
> 'I will arise now', and then arise,

The logical subject is the manifestation. The manifestation of aggression does not have a premeditated intention[7] which deliberately thinks, 'I will arise now', because it would have to exist before it had arisen. If a manifestation existed before arising, it would follow that its arising subsequently would be meaningless. The position is untenable because you yourselves assert that manifestations are newly arisen, thus it is a contradiction. Furthermore, it violates valid cognition, since arising is established by direct perception.

If the manifestation is nonexistent before its arising:

> 6.28
> And if that which has not arisen does not yet exist,
> What in that moment wants to create itself?

[Proof:] The logical subject is the moment when the manifestation has not yet arisen. The probandum is indicated in the second line, i.e. that there is no premeditating intention at that time. The reason is indicated in the first line, i.e. because a wish to create itself cannot exist before the manifestation has arisen. Therefore, since there is no premeditating intention before the manifestation has arisen, the manifestation itself is not an autonomous creator.

'Since the sempiternal nature of the individual consciousness is sentience, [325] it is that which has the premeditated intention.'

> Since it would immutably attend to its object,
> It would never cease.

The individual consciousness exists in all circumstances, regardless of the existence or nonexistence of its objects and experiences. It follows that, though objects are temporary, its consciousness of them would be unchangeable. If that is the position, it is incompatible with direct perception.

2. Refuting the position of the Naiyāyikas

'The self is inherently insentient matter[8] but possesses all the capabilities [of an agent]. Since its mind is separate from it, the self is the autonomous producer of aggression.'

6.29
Furthermore, if the self is sempiternal,
Like space, it is clearly not an agent.

To present these lines in logical form: the sempiternal self is the logical subject. [The probandum:] it is not an agent, i.e. something which produces an effect. [The reason:] because it is empty of gradual and instantaneous functions. The pervader is not supported.[9] 'Like space' is the example confirming the pervasion.

The qualification for that[10] is established *a priori* according to the following definition of 'sempiternal': if sempiternality is the positive establishment of the absence of graduation [i.e. alteration over time], the existence of graduation is eliminated, i.e. graduation is logically exclusive with sempiternality. Since sempiternal objects are incompatible with the presence of graduation, it is established that a sempiternal object is logically exclusive from any graduation. By the logical exclusion of any graduation, it is established that the sempiternal object is completely incompatible with both instantaneous functions—those in which it produces a previously unproduced result in a single instant—and gradual functions—those in which it produces results gradually over time.

'Your pervasion[11] is not established. While the sempiternal self is not itself graduated, the result is gradually produced by the gradual introduction of conditions, so there is no contradiction.'

Even if it encountered extraneous conditions,
Being immutable, what could it do?

The logical subject is the self which is designated as 'immutable'. [326] The probandum is indicated by, 'Even if it encountered extraneous conditions, what could it do?' i.e. it could not begin to do something which it was not previously doing. The reason: 'Because it is immutable.' The pervader is not supported.[12] To establish the qualification for that:[13]

> 6.30
> During creation, if it is as it was previously,
> In what sense did it create the thing?

At the time of the creation [of anger] by conditions, the self is the same as it was before, when the conditions were absent. If it is no different at the later time, in what sense was it the creator? It did not do anything. Thus [the qualification] is established *a priori* according to the above conception of 'sempiternal'.

'Although, being sempiternal, the self does not change, it can change only in the sense that it has the ability [to produce harm] under the right conditions. In this sense, it produces a result but in another sense it does not produce the result.'

What results from conditions cannot be the result of the sempiternal object:

> 'It was produced due to this [condition].'
> Then what relation does the self have to the product?

3. Summary

> 6.31
> In this way, everything is extraneously controlled,
> And not even the controllers have any power.
> When this is recognized, I will not get angry
> At things which are like apparitions.

What depends upon conditions is extraneously controlled. 'Like apparitions' means it is a deluded perception.

Alternatively, the author of the *Great Commentary* explains it this way:

> 6.27

> Some claim that there is a primal substance,
> And they designate a 'self'.

The first line refers to the sempiternal material primal substance asserted by the Sāṃkhyas. The second line refers to the sentient mind, a premeditating intentionality comprised of matter with a separate awareness connected to it, asserted by the Naiyāyikas.[14] Having presented their doctrines, then they are refuted.

1. Refuting the position of the Sāṃkhyas

   1. Refuting the primal substance as creator
   2. Refuting the manifestations as creator
   3. Refuting the individual consciousness as creator

1. Refuting the primal substance as creator

> But it does not deliberately think,
> 'I will arise now', and then arise,

The primal substance itself cannot have the deliberate thought or premeditated intention, 'I will produce the manifestations', because it is material. Thus, the contrary pervader is supported.[15]

'The primal substance is not the creator; the manifestations are the creator.'

2. Refuting the manifestations as creator

6.28
> And if that which has not arisen does not exist,
> What in that moment wants to create itself?

[327] The state in which the manifestations have not arisen is the logical subject. 'What wants to create itself' indicates that there is no mind to think 'I want to create myself'. 'If it does not exist' indicates [the reason]: because it has no nature before it has arisen.

'The individual consciousness is the creator.'

3. Refuting the individual consciousness as creator

  1. It is contradictory to a creator
  2. Refuting its connection to temporary objects and experiences

1. It is contradictory to a creator

This also refers to the first two lines of v28. The individual consciousness is the logical subject. Line 28b is the probandum, a statement that it is not a creator. The reason: 'Because it does not exist [28a]'. If one thinks this reason is not established, [it is established]: the individual consciousness—the logical subject—has no nature because it has not arisen, like a sky flower. Thus, the pervader is not supported.[16] It has 'not arisen' even according to the opponent, whose position is that the individual consciousness is primordially without arising or destruction.

2. Refuting its connection to temporary objects and experiences

> **Since it would immutably attend to its object,**
> **It would never cease.**

The individual consciousness is the logical subject. It follows that it would never cease because of 'immutably attending to its object', i.e. its experience is sempiternal. Since objects and experiences are temporary, this position is to be rejected. Therefore, because objects and experiences are temporary, one must accept their creator [i.e. individual consciousness] is not sempiternal. The contrary pervader is supported,[17] i.e. it is proven that this is incompatible with an individual consciousness.

The refutation of the Naiyāyikas in the *Great Commentary* is the same as above.

3. The necessity of overcoming anger

'Since in reality neither the aggressor nor the one who prevents aggression is accomplished, it is not logical to practise preventing something.' This is the objection:

6.32

> 'Who prevents what?
> It is inappropriate to prevent anything.'

Although in reality there is no prevention nor anything to prevent, in dependence upon their existence in relative truth, one dispels the sufferings of others. Therefore, one should prevent them [328]:

> Through reliance on this, the stream
> Of suffering will be cut—there is nothing wrong with this.

4. Summary

> **6.33**
> Therefore, regardless of friend or enemy,
> When I see them behaving negatively,
> Thinking, 'This comes from related conditions',
> I will remain happy.
>
> **6.34**
> If it were true that we could achieve whatever we wanted,
> Then, since among all living beings,
> Nobody wants to suffer,
> There would never be any suffering.

The first verse establishes extraneous control and the second verse refutes autonomy.

3. The patience of not thinking of them as the cause of harm

1. One should have the characteristics of affection in one's attitude
2. Not dwelling on the characteristics of anger
3. Examination of one's own faults

1. One should have the characteristics of affection in one's mind

The harms of this life are created by delusion:

> **6.35**
> Those who lack concern cause harm

> Even to themselves, with weapons, etc.
> And for the sake of what they might attain, such as women,
> They go hungry, refuse food and so on.
>
> 6.36
> Some, by hanging themselves, jumping off precipices,
> Taking poisonous or harmful food,

The harms of future lives are created the same way:

> Or by unmeritorious actions,
> Do harm to themselves.

It is not illogical that they would cause harm to others:

> 6.37
> When the defilements are in control,
> Even the precious self can be killed.
> How, then, could they not
> Do harm to the bodies of others?

Therefore, focus on the characteristics of affection:

> 6.38
> Even if I do not develop vast compassion
> For those who, driven by defilements,
> Resort to killing themselves and so forth in such ways,

And cease the characteristics of anger:

> How can I become angry?

2. Not dwelling on the characteristics of anger

Anger towards an intrinsic nature is wrong:

> 6.39
> If it is in the nature of fools
> To cause harm to others,

Then it is wrong to be angry with them:
That is like getting angry with a flame for having the nature to burn.

Anger towards an accidental nature is wrong:

6.40
On the other hand, if their faults are accidental,
Occurring despite their intrinsic nature,
Then it is wrong to be angry with them:
That is like getting angry with an empty space for the presence of a cloud of incense.

Anger is wrong under examination of the direct and indirect causes:

6.41
It is their weapons and so forth that are the direct instruments of harm,
So when I get angry with someone who strikes me,
It would make more sense to be angry with their aggression,
Since they are themselves driven by aggression.

3. Examination of one's own faults

1. The faults are one's own
2. The fault of grasping the body, which causes suffering
3. The fault of attachment, which causes suffering
4. The fault of activities which are of no benefit to others
5. The angry mind has it the wrong way round
6. Abandoning objections

1. The faults are one's own

6.42
Previously, I caused sentient beings
Some similar kind of harm.
Therefore, it is only right that harm should come
To me, a doer of harm to sentient beings.

One should consider the results of harmful actions performed by oneself.

2. The fault of grasping the body, which causes suffering

> 6.43
> His weapon and my own body
> Jointly caused this suffering.
> He drew the weapon, I brought the body:
> Which of these should I be angry with?

> 6.44
> The human form is like an abscess:
> It is unbearably sensitive and painful.
> If, blinded by craving, I cling to it,
> Who should I be angry with when I am harmed?

The first verse indicates that just as one is angry with the person who strikes one with the condition of suffering—a weapon, so one should also be angry with the person who grasps the body. How to do this is indicated in the second verse.

3. The fault of attachment, which causes suffering [329]

> 6.45
> If a fool does not want to suffer
> But, nevertheless, is attached to its causes,
> It is his own negative actions that are harming him,
> So why fall out with others?

> 6.46
> It like how, for example, the guardians of hell
> Or the forest of razor leaves
> Come from my own actions.
> That, then, is who I should be angry with.

4. The fault of activities which are of no benefit to others

> 6.47
> Provoked by my own actions,

> Beings come to harm me
> But, in doing so, they fall into the hells.
> Is it not I who am destroying them?

By the cause—one's own negative actions, others have become involved in doing harm to oneself. Thus, one has involved them in the causes of rebirth in the lower realms.

5. The angry mind has it the wrong way round

> 6.48
> In dependence upon them,
> With patience, many nonvirtues are purified,
> But in dependence upon me,
> They fall into the hells for a long time.

> 6.49
> So if I am doing harm to them
> But they are bringing benefit to me,
> Do I not have it the wrong way round?
> It is wrong of you, mind, to be angry.

If someone harms himself but benefits oneself, one would not feel anger towards that person. Since he is benefitting oneself, why would one feel anger? That would be to have it the wrong way around. How does he benefit oneself? Many of one's own nonvirtues are purified in dependence upon him. By what essential cause? By patience: since he is helping one practise patience and helping purify one's nonvirtues, he is benefitting oneself. How is one doing harm to him? Since the enemy's harm is directed towards oneself, it is in dependence upon oneself that he is reborn as a hell-being for such a long time.

6. Abandoning objections

1. Abandoning the objection that it is illogical to say others benefit oneself
2. Abandoning the objection that it is illogical to say one harms others
3. Refuting instigating harm

1. Abandoning the objection that it is illogical to say others benefit oneself

'Since they will be going to a rebirth in the lower realms through me, I am supporting the nonvirtues of others. I cannot both support their nonvirtues and purify my own nonvirtues. Therefore, if I am not purifying my own nonvirtues, how can you say that their nonvirtues benefit me by supporting the purification of my own nonvirtues?'

6.50
If I have the right attitude,
I will not go to the hells.

Although the nonvirtues of others are conditional upon oneself, one's own nonvirtues will be purified and one will not be reborn in hell because of this.

'Why will I not be reborn in the hells when I am the condition for their nonvirtues?' [330]

Because of having the right attitude, i.e. patience. Therefore, when one's own nonvirtues are purified, it is established that others are the beneficial supports of that.

2. Abandoning the objection that it is illogical to say one harms others

'Since others are helping me purify my nonvirtues, they will not be reborn in the hells. Thus, I am not sending them to the hells, so it is contradictory to say that I am harming them.'

But if I only look after myself,
What does this do for them?

If one has a benevolent attitude, thinking, 'They are supporting my practice of virtue', what does this do for them? It does nothing for them. Therefore, since they will still go to the hells, it is not contradictory that one harms them, since oneself is the condition of their going there.

'If they did not intend to support my virtue, how are they supports of my virtue?'

It is 'if I only look after myself', i.e. while they can support both nonvirtue and virtue, if one protects one's own mind from nonvirtue with patience, then they are supporting only the virtue.

3. Refuting instigating harm

'If harming someone can help them, I should benefit others by actively harming them.'

> **6.51**
> **However, if I return their harm,**
> **That will not protect them either,**
> **But it would damage my conduct,**
> **And so destroy the discipline.**

It would not support virtue for someone with the right attitude [patience] to actively harm others. Rather, one would be supporting nonvirtue. Rather than protect them, since one's own conduct would be damaged, one's discipline would be destroyed.

Patience | 187

> Section overview: Stopping impatience with the establishment of disrespect, etc. for oneself [v52-63]
>
> 1. It does no harm to the body
> 2. It makes no sense to get angry in connection to the hatred of others
> 3. It makes no sense to get angry with obstacles to acquisition
>   1. The meaninglessness of the acquisitions themselves
>   2. Ceasing to create more harm
>   3. Demonstrating their meaninglessness by example
>   4. Their specific kind of meaninglessness
>   5. Objection and response
>   6. Establishing the point
> 4. Disrespectful beings are inappropriate as objects of anger

2. Stopping impatience with the establishment of disrespect, etc. [for oneself]

1. It does no harm to the body
2. It makes no sense to get angry in connection to the hatred of others
3. It makes no sense to get angry with obstacles to acquisition
4. Disrespectful beings are inappropriate as objects of anger

1. It does no harm to the body [331]

6.52
Since the mind lacks physical form,
What could destroy it?
It is by attachment to the body
That I am harmed by physical suffering.

6.53
If disrespectful words,
Harsh speech and criticism
Cannot harm the body,
Why, mind, do you fly into a rage?

The first two lines refute the idea that unpleasant words can harm the mind. The second two lines indicate that physical suffering is created not by criticism but by clinging to the body as 'mine'. The second verse indicates that disrespect and so forth do not create physical suffering.

2. It makes no sense to get angry in connection to the hatred of others

'Although disrespect may not harm my body, nevertheless someone is taking a hateful attitude towards me, so I should be angry.'

> **6.54**
> **If contempt from others**
> **Will not, in this life or future lives,**
> **Destroy me,**
> **Why am I so averse to it?**

One commentary explains this verse as a response to the objection that although it does no physical harm, nevertheless people would lose respect for oneself. But that would just be a repetition of what is stated below [verses 62-3].

3. It makes no sense to get angry with obstacles to acquisition

1. The meaninglessness of the acquisitions themselves
2. Ceasing to create more harm
3. Demonstrating their meaninglessness by example
4. Their specific kind of meaninglessness
5. Objection and response
6. Establishing the purpose[18]

1. The meaninglessness of the acquisitions themselves

> **6.55**
> **I am averse to something**
> **Because it hinders acquisition,**
> **But the acquisitions of this life will be lost,**
> **While the nonvirtues will firmly remain.**

Although acquisitions may be acquired though anger, they will be lost but one's future lives will be accompanied by the nonvirtues of anger.

2. Ceasing to create more harm

> **6.56**
> **It would be better to die today**
> **Than to live a long life badly,**
> **For although someone like me might be around for a long time,**
> **The suffering of death still awaits.**

Even though one may live a long life, the suffering of death cannot be avoided.

3. Demonstrating their meaninglessness with an example

> **6.57**
> **Someone wakes from a dream**
> **Of having a hundred years of happiness,**
> **And another awakes**
> **Having dreamt he had just a moment of happiness.**

> **6.58**
> **Though they have both awoken,**
> **The happiness of neither one will return.**
> **No matter whether life is long or short,**
> **At the moment of death, it is exhausted just the same.**

Whether life is long or short, it ends in death. At that time, the happiness one had when alive will be just a memory.

4. Their specific kind of meaninglessness

> **6.59**
> **Though I may have gotten many acquisitions**
> **And enjoyed happiness for a long time,**
> **I will nevertheless go forth naked and empty-handed,**
> **As if robbers had left me that way.**

At death, one's acquisitions will be left behind, depicted here as robbers stealing them.

5. Objection and response

> **6.60**
> **'But can't I live off these acquisitions,**
> **Exhausting nonvirtue and gathering merit?'**

Objection: 'I will attain acquisitions to practise virtue and give up nonvirtue.'

> **If I get angry over acquisitions,**
> **Won't that merit be exhausted in nonvirtue?**

Response: 'Exhausting merit' [332] is a reference to anger destroying virtues that have been gathered over thousands of aeons. 'Nonvirtue' means the nonvirtue of aggression.

6. Establishing the purpose

> **6.61**
> **What am I living for**
> **If I am violating the very point of life?**
> **Where is the meaning in living a life**
> **In which there is only nonvirtue?**

The point of life is to practise virtue, so if we damage that through aggression towards others, since there would not be any virtue in that, what would be the meaning of it?

4. Disrespectful beings are inappropriate as objects of anger

> **6.62**
> **'It is because of the damage they do**
> **By criticizing me that I get angry with beings.'**

'By criticizing me, they will damage the respect others have for me. It is for this reason that I become angry.'

**Then why do you not get angry like this
When they are criticizing others?**

And yet, when those same people criticize someone else, causing others to lose respect for him, it follows that you should also become angry with them.

'Damage done to the reputations of others by someone else criticizing them has nothing to do with me.'

**6.63
You are patient with a loss of respect
When it depends on someone else,**

Yet, when respect for oneself is damaged through the defilements of a contemptuous person, that also has nothing to do with oneself, so it is inappropriate to be angry with them:

**So why not be patient with criticisms,
Since they are dependent upon the arising of the defilements.**

Section overview: Stopping impatience with criticism, etc. towards one's own side [v64-75]

1. Properly considering those [who criticize or harm] the dharma
2. The patience of putting up with harm-doers
    1. The marks of anger are not established
    2. Examining its irrationality
    3. Examining one's own faults
    4. Consideration of the results
        1. Merit will not be diminished
        2. Suffering will be averted
        3. Great benefit will be achieved

---

2. Stopping impatience with criticism, etc. towards one's own side[19]

1. Properly considering those [who criticize or harm] the dharma
2. The patience of putting up with harm-doers

1. Properly considering those who criticize or harm the dharma

One should have patience towards those who harm the Three Jewels:

> **6.64**
> **Although they may disparage or destroy**
> **Statues, stupas or the holy dharma,**
> **It is wrong for me to be angry,**
> **For they have no power to harm the Buddhas and so forth.**

One should have patience towards those who harm one's own side:

> **6.65**
> **They may even harm my teachers,**
> **Friends or relatives but,**
> **Seeing these things arise from conditions,**
> **As explained above, anger will be averted.**

'As explained above' means, just as it was explained in the previous section on being patient towards those who do harm to oneself, consider that being aggressive or harmful are not autonomous states [333] but arise from extraneous conditions and hence one should have patience.

2. The patience of putting up with harm-doers

1. The marks of anger are not established
2. Examining its irrationality
3. Examining one's own faults
4. Consideration of the results

1. The marks of anger are not established

> **6.66**
> **If bodies with minds**
> **And bodies without minds both do harm,**
> **Why be angry only at those with minds?**
> **I should be patient with their harm either way.**

One gets angry with enemies who have a mind, like those who harm one's own side, so why not get angry with something mindless like bile?

2. Examining its irrationality

> **6.67**
> **If someone out of delusion does something wrong**
> **And someone else out of delusion gets angry,**
> **Which of them is without fault,**
> **And which of them is at fault?**

To practise negative actions out of delusion means harming one's side due to not understanding the ripening of actions. To become angry out of delusion means the anger is due to not understanding the faults of aggression. It is inappropriate for both of them to become angry.

3. Examining one's own faults

> **6.68**
> **Why did I previously commit actions**
> **That make others harm me?**
> **If it all comes down to my own actions,**
> **Why get mad at others?**

> **6.69**
> **Looking at it this way,**
> **I should concentrate on increasing merit**
> **And bringing about an attitude**
> **Of mutual love between everyone.**

It is wrong to be impatient towards those who bring harm to one's side, since one has accumulated the direct causes of that harm.

4. Consideration of the results

1. Merit will not be diminished
2. Suffering will be averted
3. Great benefit will be achieved

1. Merit will not be diminished

6.70
For example, when a fire consumes a house,
Before it spreads to another house,
One removes from it inflammables
Such as dry straw and so forth.

6.71
Similarly, if the mind is attached to something,
The fire of aggression will spread there,
So I should remove it right now
Out of fear that merit will be consumed.

Just as it is essential when a fire is spreading to remove the causes of fire from its path, so when one's merit is about to go up in the flames of aggression that feed upon attachment to one's side, one should abandon the cause of aggression—attachment to one's side.

2. Suffering will be averted

6.72
Isn't it better for a man to be freed with his hand chopped off
Than for him to be executed?
Isn't it better, then, to experience human suffering
If it spares me from the hells?

6.73
If I am unable now to bear
Even these slight sufferings,
Why do I not avert anger,
The cause of the sufferings of hell?

Like someone who receives the punishment of a severed limb and is freed from the punishment of execution, similarly, when human sufferings ripen, freeing one from the sufferings of the hells, it is a good thing. Yet, if one cannot bear even comparatively minor human suffering, what can be said about the sufferings of the hells, which are very great?

3. Great benefit will be achieved

6.74
Out of desire, I have undergone burning and so forth
In the hells, thousands upon thousands of times,
Without it doing anything meaningful for me
Or anything meaningful for others.

6.75
Now, great benefit can be achieved
For a harm that is not even a tiny fraction of that.
I should only be joyful
In sufferings that dispel the harms of beings.

The first verse is an example of having the patience to bear sufferings which have no result. [334] The first line of the second verse indicates that the sufferings which have a result are only minor, while the second line indicates the greatness of the results. The last two lines indicate that therefore it is right to have patience.

> Section overview: Stopping impatience with the production of goodness for one's enemies [v76-86]
>
> 1. Abandoning impatience with their being praised and renowned
>   1. Abandoning impatience since they cause one's own happiness
>   2. Abandoning impatience since they cause others' happiness
> 2. Abandoning impatience with their achieving happiness
> 3. Abandoning impatience with their getting acquisitions
>   1. When they get what they wish for
>   2. Not wishing for them not to have it

3. Stopping impatience with the production of goodness for one's enemies

  1. Abandoning impatience with their being praised and renowned
  2. Abandoning impatience with their achieving happiness
  3. Abandoning impatience with their getting acquisitions

1. Abandoning impatience with their being praised and renowned

1. Abandoning impatience since they cause one's own happiness
2. Abandoning impatience since they cause others' happiness

1. Abandoning impatience since they cause one's own happiness

> **6.76**
> If others take pleasure in
> Praising someone's good qualities,
> Why, mind, do you find no joy
> In praising them?

> **6.77**
> The pleasure you would have
> Would not infringe your vows but bring you happiness.
> It is permitted by excellent ones,
> And is the supreme gathering of others.

When one's enemies are made joyful by praising others, one should also praise them oneself, adding to their joy because the pleasure of benefitting others is a source of happiness, not a negative action and because it is extolled by the learned and accomplishes the benefit of others. In short, it is as joyful to join in with someone else's praise of another as when others praise oneself. So, it is right that one should also take joy in that.

2. Abandoning impatience since they cause others' happiness

'Although them praising me brings me joy, I do not want the causes of joy in certain others, such as my enemies.'

It is wrong not to want the causes of happiness for others:

> **6.78**
> 'But only others would have that happiness.'
> If the happiness of others does not matter to you,
> The visible and invisible will be lost,
> Because of not paying them their wages and so forth.

If one never cared about the happiness of others, since one would abandon paying them wages, the benefits of this life would be lost—

the loss of visible dharmas—and one would abandon giving and so forth—the loss of the invisible results.

The happiness of others is the cause of one's own happiness and if that cause does not exist, the result—one's own happiness—will not arise. [335] Therefore, work for the result by taking joy in the causes of others' happiness without taking joy in the causes of one's own happiness. Otherwise one will be endeavouring in the wrong causes:

> **6.79**
> **When they are describing my good qualities,**
> **That's when I want them to be happy, too,**
> **But, when they are describing someone else's good qualities,**
> **That's when their happiness doesn't matter.**

2. Abandoning impatience with their achieving happiness

> **6.80**
> **Having generated bodhicitta**
> **By wishing for the happiness of all sentient beings,**
> **Why do I get angry**
> **When beings find happiness by themselves?**

It is right to be joyful about benefits that one would have had to establish oneself but no longer need to.

3. Abandoning impatience with their getting acquisitions

   1. When they get what they wish for
   2. Not wishing for them not to have it

1. When they get what they wish for

> **6.81**
> **If I am claiming to want sentient beings to be**
> **Enlightened objects of veneration in the three worlds,**
> **Why, seeing them receive just some basic respect,**
> **Am I aghast at the sight of it?**

6.82

If your relative who needs looking after,
And who relies on what you can provide for him,
Becomes able to look after himself,
Wouldn't this make you joyful? Or would you get angry with him?

6.83
Why would someone want enlightenment
If they do not want what is best for beings?
How can someone have bodhicitta
Who gets angry with the acquisitions of others?

These three verses indicate, respectively, the contradiction of wishing for the enlightenment of others without wanting their lesser happiness, an example of how one should wish for others' happiness and the contradiction of generating bodhicitta while not wishing for others' happiness.

2. Not wishing for them not to have it

6.84
Regardless of whether he gets the thing
Or it stays in the donor's house,
Either way, you won't get it,
So what does it matter whether it is given away or not?

6.85
Why did I reject merit,
Faith and good qualities?
Tell me why I am not angry with the one
Who did not take the opportunities for acquisitions?

These two verses indicate, respectively, that it is equally of no use to oneself whether others get acquisitions or not and that it is one's own fault if one does not have acquisitions. 'Merit' means the accumulated actions of giving to others over a succession of lives. 'Faith' in this sense means practising giving, the skilful means of faithful people. 'Good qualities' means moral conduct and so forth. Why did one reject these in one's former lives? Therefore, as someone who rejected these

Patience | 199

in former lives, why compare oneself—someone bearing the faults of their own past nonvirtues—with others?

6.86
Not only are you not worried
About your own nonvirtues,
Do you also want to compete
With others who have gathered merit?

Section overview: Ceasing anger towards those who obstruct desirable dharmas [v87-126]

1. Abandoning impatience with those who obstruct accomplishing negative actions towards one's enemies
2. Abandoning impatience with those who obstruct good for oneself and one's own side
   1. Abandoning impatience with those who obstruct worldly dharmas
      1. Not regarding obstruction to worldly praise and reputation as harmful
         1. Praise and reputation do not bring benefit or happiness
         2. Mere joy is not meaningful
         3. Misconceived grasping for meaning
         4. Misconceived happiness
            1. The mere sound is inappropriate as a cause of joy
            2. The intention of the one giving praise is inappropriate as a cause of joy
            3. Establishing that by a counterfactual
            4. Summary
      2. Regarding the cessation of worldly dharmas as beneficial
         1. It stops rebirth in the lower realms
         2. It accomplishes liberation
   2. Abandoning impatience with those who obstruct merit
      1. It is contradictory to be angry with someone obstructing merit
      2. They are not actually an obstruction
      3. Considering them as objects of respect
      (cont.)

---

3. Ceasing anger towards those who obstruct desirable dharmas

1. Abandoning impatience with those who obstruct accomplishing negative actions towards one's enemies
2. Abandoning impatience with those who obstruct good for oneself and one's own side

1. Abandoning impatience with those who obstruct accomplishing negative actions towards one's enemies [336]

> **6.87**
> Even if an enemy is unhappy,
> What in that brings you happiness?
> Your merely hoping for it
> Cannot be a cause of his harm.
>
> **6.88**
> Even if your wishes could bring him suffering,
> What happiness is in it for you?
> 'I would be satisfied.'
> Could anything be more destructive than that?

The first two lines indicate that harm to others is of no use as an object of happiness for oneself. The second two lines indicate that the subjective malevolent mind does not harm others.[20] The second verse indicates that one's subjective malevolent mind harms oneself. One's destruction by the creation of suffering for others means that one will be reborn in the lower realms. Why?

> **6.89**
> Those caught painfully on this sharp hook,
> Cast by the angling defilements,
> Will be cooked in the pots
> Of the guardians of hell.

Caught by the hook of one's anger, one will be boiled in the pots of hell.

2. Abandoning impatience with those who obstruct good for oneself and one's own side

1. Abandoning impatience with those who obstruct worldly dharmas
2. Abandoning impatience with those who obstruct merit

1. Abandoning impatience with those who obstruct worldly dharmas

   1. Not regarding [obstruction to] worldly praise and reputation as harmful
   2. Regarding the cessation of worldly dharmas as beneficial

1. Not regarding obstruction to worldly praise and reputation as harmful

   1. Praise and reputation do not bring benefit or happiness
   2. Mere joy is not meaningful
   3. Misconceived grasping for meaning
   4. Misconceived happiness

1. Praise and reputation do not bring benefit or happiness

> 6.90
> **The prestige of praise and reputation**
> **Will bring no merit, nor extend my life,**
> **Will not make me stronger, nor free me from sickness,**
> **Nor will it bring any physical pleasure.**
>
> 6.91
> **If care about what is good for me,**
> **I should ask what use these things are.**

'Merit' is beneficial in future lives, the rest is beneficial in this life.

2. Mere joy is not meaningful

> **If it is only a happy state of mind that I want,**
> **I ought to turn to gambling, drinking, etc.**

3. Misconceived grasping for meaning

6.92
If, for the sake of reputation,
They spend all their money and even get themselves killed,
What use will mere words be to them?
If they are dead, who is going to enjoy them?

6.93
When their sandcastles collapse,
Children howl and cry.
Like them, when praise and reputation decline,
My mind is like a child's.

The first two lines indicate the loss of happiness in this life, the third line indicates the hollowness of mere words and the fourth indicates that they are useless in future lives. In the second verse, the first two lines give an example of this and the second two lines apply the meaning of the example.

4. Misconceived happiness

1. The mere sound is inappropriate as a cause of joy
2. The intention of the one giving praise is inappropriate as a cause of joy
3. Establishing that by a counterfactual
4. Summary

1. The mere sound is inappropriate as a cause of joy

6.94
Because it has no consciousness,
A fleeting sound cannot consciously praise me.

[337] The mere sound of praise, which itself has no respect, is not a cause of joy because, occurring only within a conversation, it eventually ceases.

2. The intention of the one giving praise is inappropriate as a cause of joy

'But praising me makes someone else happy.

Is that not a cause of joy?'

6.95
What difference does it make to me
Whether their joy is based on me or someone else?
The happiness and joy belongs to them alone.
I will not get even a little bit of it.

The joy that others have in oneself does not benefit oneself. That joy is merely a happy state of mind for the person who is joyful.

3. Establishing that by a counterfactual

6.96
If his happiness gives me happiness,
Then it should do so in every case.
If it did, I would not be so unhappy
When someone is made happy by their joy in others.

If the happiness of another gives oneself happiness, then when someone takes joy in someone else, one would not be impatient with their happiness.

4. Summary

6.97
Therefore, it is the thought, 'They are praising me'
That brings me joy.
This is really ridiculous.
It is the behaviour of a child.

2. Regarding the cessation of worldly dharmas as beneficial

1. It prevents rebirth in the lower realms
2. It accomplishes liberation

1. It prevents rebirth in the lower realms

6.98
Praise and so forth only distract me.

They ruin my dissatisfaction with saṃsāra.
They make me envious of those who have something good,
And destroy anything that is excellent.

6.99
Therefore, those who are at hand
To destroy my praise, etc.
Are they not in fact
Protecting me from the lower realms?

The first verse indicates that praise and so forth involve oneself in the causes of the lower realms. The second verse indicates abandoning the causes of the lower realms.

2. It accomplishes liberation

6.100
The shackles of acquisition and honour
Are not needed for the pursuit of liberation,
So how can I be angry
With someone who frees me from them?

6.101
They are like Buddhas bestowing blessings upon me—
Holding me back and bolting the door
As I try to run towards suffering.
How can I be angry with them?

The first two lines indicate that acquisition and honour are the causes of being shackled to saṃsāra. The next two lines indicate that someone who opposes them is releasing one from those shackles. The next three lines give an example of averting one's own suffering. The last line indicates that, therefore, it is wrong to be angry with them.

2. Abandoning impatience with those who obstruct merit

1. It is contradictory to be angry with someone obstructing merit
2. They are not actually an obstruction
3. Considering them as objects of respect

1. It is contradictory to be angry with someone obstructing merit

> **6.102**
> **'He is obstructing my merit.'**
> **It is not right to be angry with him either,**
> **For if there is no austerity equal to patience,**
> **Shouldn't I stick to it?**

Someone who obstructs one kind of merit helps us practise patience. Thus, when one encounters such a friend, one can impartially practise the alternative virtue, i.e. cultivate patience. [338]

'Whilst the conditions for merit may be present, the cause is absent, so how can patience arise?'

Others provide the conditions, so their contribution is complete. Since one cannot practise patience alone, it is oneself who creates the only remaining obstacle to merit:

> **6.103**
> **It is my own fault**
> **That I do not practise patience towards him**
> **When the cause of merit is at hand,**
> **So I am the only obstruction.**

2. They are not actually an obstruction

The harm-doer himself is the logical subject. The probandum is indicated by the question, 'How can I call them an obstruction? [v104d]', i.e. they are not an obstruction [to merit]. The reason is because they are a cause of virtue.[21] If one wonders whether this reason is established:

> **6.104**
> **If, without them, nothing happens but,**
> **When they are present, it happens,**
> **That person is a cause,**
> **So how can I call them an obstruction?**

The harm-doer—logical subject—is a cause of virtue because it is not possible to practise patience when harm-doers are absent. Similarly, when a beggar is absent, since it is not possible to practise giving, the beggar is a cause of giving, or when an abbot is absent, since one cannot take ordination, the abbot is a cause of ordination:

6.105
A beggar arriving during alms-giving
Is hardly an obstruction to giving,
And it would be absurd to say that an abbot
Is an obstruction to taking ordination.

The first is an example of giving and the second of moral conduct.

Section overview: Considering obstructors as objects of respect [v106-126]

1. One should respect them for their own qualities
    1. They are greatly beneficial
    2. Overlooking the factor of intention
    3. Regarding them, therefore, as like the Teacher
        1. Brief scriptural presentation
        2. Establishing the fact of that
        3. Therefore, they are equal as objects of respect
        4. Abandoning an objection
        5. Summary
            1. The same result
            2. Different qualities
            3. Summarizing the fact that sentient beings are an excellent field [of merit]
2. One should respect them out of one's faith in the Buddhas
    1. The Buddhas treat sentient beings as their own
        1. Briefly expressing this
        2. One should be patient with harm-doers
        3. Abandoning self-importance
        4. Abandoning harm
        5. Confessing needless faults before the Sage
        6. Desisting from now on
    2. The Buddhas treat sentient beings as themselves

3. Considering them as objects of respect

1. One should respect them for their own qualities
2. One should respect them out of one's faith in the Buddhas

1. One should respect them for their own qualities

1. They are greatly beneficial
2. Overlooking the factor of intention
3. Regarding them, therefore, as like the Teacher

1. They are greatly beneficial

> **6.106**
> **In this world, there are plenty of beggars,**
> **But few who do us harm,**
> **For unless I have harmed them,**
> **They will not harm me.**
>
> **6.107**
> **Therefore, like a treasure appearing**
> **In my own home without my doing anything,**
> **They help me practise the bodhisattva conduct,**
> **So I should take joy in enemies.**
>
> **6.108**
> **Both he and I are involved in this,**
> **So the results of practising patience**
> **Should be given to him first,**
> **For he was the cause.**

The first verse indicates that sources of patience are rarer than sources of giving alms. The next three lines indicate that those rare ones are helpers of enlightenment. The next line indicates that therefore, one should take joy in them. The last verse indicates that one should give them the results of patience.

2. Overlooking the factor of intention

6.109
'But he did not intend for me to practise patience.
I should not have such respect for an enemy.'
He is nevertheless a cause of practice,
And do you not respect the holy dharma for the same thing?

6.110
'But my enemy really was intending to harm me,
So I should not respect him.'
If he was working for my benefit, like a doctor,
How could I practise patience?

6.111
Therefore, since the arising of patience
Completely depends upon someone's hostility,
That person is a cause of patience,
So I should respect him like I respect the holy dharma.

The first verse indicates that someone who does not intend to benefit oneself is nevertheless an object of respect. The next two verses indicate that, when there is no intention to do harm, there is no field of patience. [339]

3. Regarding them as like the Teacher

Just as we respect the Teacher [Buddha] because he is the basis of merit, so we should equally respect sentient beings, who are also the basis of merit.

1. Brief scriptural presentation
2. Establishing the fact of that
3. Therefore, they are equal as objects of respect
4. Abandoning an objection
5. Summary

1. Brief scriptural presentation

6.112
Therefore, as the Sage has taught,
The field of sentient beings is a Buddha field.

Sentient beings are a field of patience, compassion, etc. and Buddhas are a field of respect, offerings, etc. If one wonders where the Sage taught this, it is in the *Dharmasaṃgīti*:

> Sentient beings are the bodhisattva's Buddha field, the Buddha field in which the qualities of a Buddha will be attained. To practise otherwise is wrong. One should think of them accordingly.[22]

2. Establishing the fact of that

Many have practised respect for them and,
In that way, completely crossed over.

Having practised in the field only of sentient beings, many Buddhas have crossed over and been freed from saṃsāra. Thus it is a Buddha field.

3. They are equal as objects of respect

6.113
The Buddha qualities are established
Through sentient beings and Buddhas alike,
So how can I respect the conquerors
But not also respect sentient beings?

These fields are similar in that they both establish the qualities of a Buddha. So it would be inconsistent to have respect for Buddhas but not for sentient beings.

[Objection:] 'Then they undifferentiated in every way.'

4. Abandoning an objection

6.114
It is not in their respective intentions
That they are equal but in their results.
It is in this sense that sentient beings have the qualities
Due to which they are like the Buddha.

6.115

> The greatness of sentient beings
> Is there in venerating someone who has a loving mind.
> The greatness of the Buddha
> Is there in the merit of having faith in him.

The first line indicates that there is no contradiction in their being the same as a basis of accumulation whilst not being the same in abandonment, realization and so forth. The next three lines indicate that although they are not the same in nature, they are the same in being a basis of accumulation. The second verse indicates the accomplishment of that.

It is taught that there is greater merit in venerating someone who is practising loving kindness than there is in venerating a monk [340] who is practising renunciation. Hence, the meditation of loving kindness is preeminent. Since sentient beings are the basis of that meditation, it is established that sentient beings are an excellent basis of merit. Since there is merit in having faith in the Buddha, faith in the Buddha is preeminent. Since the Buddha is the basis of that [faith], it is established that the Buddha is an excellent basis of merit.

5. Summary

1. The same result
2. Different qualities
3. Summarizing the fact that sentient beings are an excellent field [of merit]

1. The same result

6.116
It is in respect of their producing the Buddha qualities
Therefore, that we hold them equal,

The position we hold is that sentient beings and Buddhas are equal. In what respect? In respect of their both being fields from which the conditions for establishing the Buddha qualities are created. Therefore, they are equal in this regard.

2. Different qualities

But none is equal to the Buddha,
Who has limitless oceans of qualities.

3. Summarizing the fact that sentient beings are an excellent field of merit

6.117
His collection of supreme qualities is unequalled but,
If someone with just a fraction of those qualities were to appear,
Then to offer him even the three realms
Would be a small offering.

'Collection of supreme qualities' means mastery of the ten powers, etc. 'Unequalled' means the Buddha is peerless. 'Just a fraction of those qualities' means that although it is impossible for sentient beings to have all the qualities of the Buddha, nevertheless they do possess one of these, i.e. being a field of accumulation. Therefore, if one were to make offerings to someone who encompasses merely the cause of those qualities, to offer him everything in the three realms would be a small offering.

To present the conclusion that it is right to venerate someone who has the essential characteristic of being a field of accumulation:

6.118
Since sentient beings have a part in generating
The supreme Buddha qualities,
It is right to venerate them
Just for their doing this.

The first two lines present the reason and then the subsequent two lines draw the conclusion.

2. One should respect them out of one's faith in the Buddhas

  1. The Buddhas treat sentient beings as their own [341]
  2. The Buddhas treat sentient beings as themselves

1. The Buddhas treat sentient beings as their own

1. Briefly expressing this
2. One should be patient with harm-doers
3. Abandoning self-importance
4. Abandoning harm
5. Confessing needless faults before the Sage
6. Desisting from now on

1. Briefly expressing this

> 6.119
> Furthermore, apart from my dedication to sentient beings,
> How can I ever repay
> Their steadfast friendship
> And their carrying out limitless benefit?

'Steadfast friendship' refers to their aspiration, which is loving. 'Carrying out of limitless benefit' refers to their application. Similarly, one can return the benefit they give one by one's dedication to sentient beings, i.e. by treating them as one's own.

2. One should be patient with harm-doers

> 6.120
> If I am to repay the benefit
> Of those who give up their bodies to enter the Avīci Hell,
> I should do everything good for everyone,
> Even if they do me great harm.

To repay the Buddhas who, having given up their bodies to enter the Avīci Hell, work to benefit sentient beings, one should be patient with sentient beings who do one harm.

3. Abandoning self-importance

> 6.121
> If our masters sometimes act
> Without regard even for their own bodies,
> How can I, a confused person,
> Have such conceit as to not be their servant?

As the Buddhas are one's masters, it would be wrong to be filled with self-importance, as they work for the benefit of others. Rather, one should act as their servant.

4. Abandoning harm

> **6.122**
> The sages are pleased when beings are made happy,
> And displeased when they are harmed.
> By bringing beings joy, we please all the sages but,
> By harming beings, we harm the sages.
>
> **6.123**
> Just as no object of desire could delight
> Someone whose whole body is on fire,
> So when sentient beings are harmed,
> There is no way to please the great compassionate ones.

Just as if the body which one holds as 'mine' were to catch fire, food and so forth would not ease one's mind, so if sentient beings which are held as 'mine' are being harmed, it is impossible for the Buddhas to be pleased.

5. Confessing needless faults before the Sage

> **6.124**
> Therefore, since I have harmed beings,
> And displeased the great compassionate ones,
> I now confess every one of those nonvirtues,
> And ask the sages to be patient with everything I have done
>   to displease them.

6. Desisting from now on

> **6.125**
> To please the tathāgatas,
> From now on I will serve the world.
> Even if many beings kick me in the head, beat me
> And try to kill me, I will not retaliate but will please the lords
>   of the world.

2. The Buddhas treat sentient beings as themselves

> 6.126
> There is no doubt that the lords of compassion
> Treat all beings as own selves.
> I may see them as sentient beings
> But the protectors see them as self. Why then do I have no respect?

Though one may see the nature of sentient beings, the lords of the world see their similarity to themselves.

2. Keeping in mind the results of patience

   1. Brief presentation
   2. An example from the perspective of the result
   3. The example is far outweighed [342]
   4. Summary enumeration of results

1. Brief presentation

> 6.127
> This is what pleases the tathāgatas,
> And it perfectly accomplishes my own benefit.
> It even dispels the world's sufferings.
> Therefore, I should always practise this.

The first line refers to pleasing the conquerors by practising respect for sentient beings. The second line indicates that this also accomplishes one's own benefit. The last two lines indicate that sentient beings have the power of liberation.

2. An example from the perspective of the result

> 6.128
> For example, though one of the king's men
> May harm many people,
> The judicious people
> Do not retaliate, even though they could.

6.129
For he is not alone,
But his power is that of the king.
Similarly, I should not have contempt
For even the weakest of harm-doers,

6.130
For they are supported by legions
Of hell-guardians and compassionate ones.
Therefore, like the subjects of a wrathful king,
I should try to placate sentient beings.

Even though they can return the harm done to them by someone close to the king, they do not do so out of fear of the king himself. Similarly, out of fear of rebirth in hell by going against the teachings of the Buddha, one should not return harm to sentient beings even though one is able.

3. The example is far outweighed

6.131
If the king were to become angry
He could not bring the miseries of hell upon me.
Yet, that is what is brought about
By my harming sentient beings.

6.132
On the other hand, if the king were to be pleased,
He could not bestow buddhahood upon me.
Yet, that is what is brought about
By my pleasing sentient beings.

The first verse indicates that the harms of the lower realms that result from doing harm far outweigh the harms of this life. The second verse indicates that the benefits of buddhahood that result from helping others far outweigh the benefits of this life.

4. Summary enumeration of results

6.133

> Quite apart from the fact that the future achievement of buddhahood
> Comes from pleasing sentient beings,
> Can I not see that patience brings good fortune,
> Reputation and prosperity?
>
> 6.134
> In saṃsāra, patience brings beauty,
> Good health and reputation,
> A long life,
> And all the vast pleasures of a universal emperor.

The first two lines indicate the principal result. The second two lines indicate the visible results [in this life]. The second verse indicates the fully ripened result [in future lives].

Chapter 7

EFFORT

1. Developing enthusiasm for effort [v1]
2. The nature of effort [v2a]
3. Abandoning opposing factors [v2b-30]
4. Fully developing effort [v31-76]

1. Developing enthusiasm for effort

> 7.1
> With such patience, I should undertake effort,
> For there is enlightenment in effort.
> Just as there is no movement without wind,
> So there is no merit without effort.

The first two lines are presented from the perspective of effort as the indirect cause of enlightenment, while the second two lines are presented from the alternative perspective, i.e. as the direct cause of merit.

2. The nature of effort

> 7.2

What is effort? Joy in virtue.

'What is effort?' indicates the definiendum. 'Virtue' is its essential characteristic, which excludes nonvirtue and [343] mundane joy. 'Joy' is the manifest characteristic.

> Section overview: Abandoning opposing factors [v2b-30]
>
> 1. Summarizing the opposing factors
> 2. Abandoning the laziness of non-application
>   1. Examining the cause of non-application and averting it
>   2. Examining the faults of this life and averting them
>   1. Having certainty about impermanence
>   2. An example of seeing this
>   3. It will befall one
>   4. Impossible to hold back time
>   5. The time of death is too late
>   6. Explaining the impossibility of holding back time
>   7. Describing the actual kinds of suffering
>   3. Examining the sufferings of future lives and averting them
>   1. Suffering is certain to arise
>   2. A difficult consideration
>   3. A mass of contradictions
>   4. Exhortation for the means of liberation from that
> 3. Abandoning the laziness of negative behaviour
> 4. Abandoning the laziness of despondency
>   1. The antidotes and their result, briefly explained
>   2. The antidote to the despondency of thinking that one lacks the cause
>   3. The antidote to the despondency of impatience with application
>   1. The difficulties have great benefit
>   2. It is not suffering
>   3. It is actually happiness

3. Abandoning opposing factors

1. Summarizing the opposing factors
2. Abandoning the laziness of non-application

3. Abandoning the laziness of negative behaviour
4. Abandoning the laziness of despondency

1. Summarizing the opposing factors

> **Its opposing factors are**
> **Laziness, attachment to the negative**
> **And the despondency of self-loathing.**

'Laziness' means finding no joy in anything good through one's compulsion towards inferior happiness. 'Attachment to the negative' means finding joy in nonvirtue. 'The despondency of self-loathing' means giving up hope in the result.

2. Abandoning the laziness of non-application

1. Examining the cause of non-application and averting it
2. Examining the faults of this life and averting them
3. Examining the sufferings of future lives and averting them

1. Examining the cause of non-application and averting it

> **7.3**
> **With the sweet taste of inactivity**
> **And the craving of sleep,**
> **I am not yet tired of the sufferings of saṃsāra,**
> **So laziness arises.**

Laziness arises in not being tired of inactivity and saṃsāric concerns.

2. Examining the faults of this life and averting them

1. Having certainty about impermanence
2. An example of seeing this
3. It will befall one
4. Impossible to hold back time
5. The time of death is too late
6. Explaining the impossibility of holding back time
7. Describing the actual kinds of suffering

1. Having certainty about impermanence

> **7.4**
> **Hunted by the defilements,**
> **I will be caught in the trap of rebirth,**
> **And disappear into the jaws of the Lord of Death.**
> **Do I understand this at all?**

Just as there is no getting away for one caught in a hunter's trap, so, for one caught in the trap of rebirth which comes from the defilements of former lives, death is certain.

2. An example of seeing this

> **7.5**
> **Our kind are being gradually eradicated.**
> **Can you not see that?**
> **Those who go on sleeping regardless**
> **Are like cattle before their butchers.**

By seeing that oneself and those who, like oneself, are caught in the trap of rebirth, will die, it makes sense to practise effort through giving up sleep and inactivity. Regarding cattle and their butchers, although the cattle see that the butchers are slaughtering the ones before them, this does not then cause them to be afraid.

3. It will befall one

> **7.6**
> **Having blocked off all paths,**
> **The Lord of Death is now looking for you.**
> **How can you enjoy food?**
> **How can you enjoy sleep?**

There is no other path to escape death, so how can one remain inactive?

4. Impossible to hold back time

> **7.7**

> Since death is approaching fast,
> How will I be able to accumulate merit?

5. The time of death is too late [344]

> At that time, even if I did abandon laziness,
> It would be too late. What would be the point?

If one were to practise at the time of death, even though one might make an effort then, since death would have already arrived, one could not accomplish virtue.

6. Explaining the impossibility of holding back time

> 7.8
> When I haven't done this, have just started this,
> Am in the middle of this...
> Suddenly the Lord of Death will come,
> And I will cry, 'Oh please no! It's over!'

Some activity is not done at all, something is only just started, something else is half done and so on. Yet, even while it is all incomplete, the Lord of Death will come and one will fall into despair, thinking, 'I have to leave everything behind! It's all over!'

7. Describing the actual kinds of suffering

> 7.9
> Overcome with misery, their eyes swollen and red,
> Tears streaming down their faces,
> My family will have lost all hope,
> And all the while I will see the messengers from the Lord of Death.

> 7.10
> Tortured by the memories of my own nonvirtues
> And hearing the immanent sounds of hell,
> Terrified, I will clothe my body in excrement.
> What could I possibly do in such a delirious state?

The first three lines indicate leaving behind one's family of this life. The next line indicates visions of the next life arising. The next line indicates having many strong mental impressions. The last three lines indicate one's overwhelming fear.

3. Examining the sufferings of future lives and averting them

   1. Suffering is certain to arise
   2. A difficult consideration
   3. A mass of contradictions
   4. Exhortation for the means of liberation from that

1. Suffering is certain to arise

> **7.11**
> **If, in this life, you are terrified,**
> **Like a fish flipping about out of water,**
> **What can be said of the unbearable sufferings**
> **Of hell, created by your own nonvirtues?**

If one's suffering at the moment of death is unbearable, what need to mention the sufferings of hell?

2. A difficult consideration

> **7.12**
> **How can you rest content,**
> **Having done deeds which will lead to**
> **The heating hells, where your tender flesh**
> **Will be scalded by boiling water?**

3. A mass of contradictions

> **7.13**
> **Wanting the result but not wanting to make an effort,**
> **Sensitive to all kinds of harm,**
> **Like a god in the grip of death**
> **You cry out, 'I cannot stand this suffering!'**

The first line indicates wanting happiness but being distracted from its cause. The second line indicates having little fortitude but great suffering. The last two lines indicate being grasped by death just as one was enjoying a long life. 'Like a god' means that they, too, enjoy long lives.

4. Exhortation for the means of liberation from that

> **7.14**
> **Cross the great river of suffering**
> **Using the boat of human life.**
> **Since this boat will be very difficult to find again,**
> **Now is not the time for sleeping, you fool!**

3. Abandoning the laziness of negative behaviour

> **7.15**
> **Having given up the supreme joy of the holy dharma,**
> **A limitless cause of joy,**
> **How can you find joy in distractions**
> **And agitations, which are causes of suffering?**

To enjoy the taste of holy dharma is a limitless cause of joy because it establishes manifold joys for the future. Through abandoning that, one relies on the causes of suffering, with attachment to objects of desire and abandoning joy. [345]

4. Abandoning the laziness of despondency

1. The antidotes and their result briefly explained
2. The antidote to the despondency of thinking that one lacks the cause
3. The antidote to the despondency of impatience with application

1. The antidotes and their result briefly explained

> **7.16**
> **Without despondency, with the powers,**
> **With dedication and self-control,**
> **Equalizing myself and others,**

I should then exchange myself and others.

'Without despondency' means to have in one's nature the characteristics of high-mindedness with which to carry out excellent activities. The antidotes to despondency, i.e. the 'powers', are motivation for application, reliance upon the main practice, joy and subsequent abandonment. To concentrate these powers in one's mind when engaging in application is like amassing an army and then charging into battle. 'Dedication' and 'self-control' are just aspects of the foregoing. Then, one should rest the mind in equanimity, i.e. equalizing and exchanging oneself and others, which is the result.

2. The antidote to the despondency of thinking that one lacks the cause

> 7.17
> 'How can I possibly become enlightened?'
> Don't be so despondent.
> The Tathāgata,
> Whose words are true, said
>
> 7.18
> That even bees, mosquitoes,
> Wasps and worms,
> If they could develop the power of effort,
> Would attain unsurpassable enlightenment, so hard to attain.

Although animals are inferior vessels, they can attain everything up to unsurpassable enlightenment. Therefore, since one has attained the basis of freedom and can differentiate what is to be accepted and rejected, if one does not abandon the bodhisattva conduct, one will attain it:

> 7.19
> Someone like me, born into humanity,
> Recognizing what is of benefit and harm—
> As long as I do not abandon the bodhisattva conduct,
> Why would I not attain enlightenment?

If one does not abandon effort, one will attain enlightenment. In the *Ratnamegha* it says,

> The bodhisattva does not think, 'The attainment of enlightenment is difficult, my effort is weak and feeble and I am lazy. To achieve enlightenment, one must practise for many hundreds of aeons as if one's head were on fire. I do not think I can bear such a burden!' Do not develop this attitude. Rather, the bodhisattva [346] should think, 'The tathāgata, arhat, samyasambuddhas—the fully manifest Buddhas and the holy beings, who have fully manifested enlightenment, who are fully manifesting enlightenment, and who will fully manifest enlightenment—it is by that kind of moral conduct and by that kind of effort that they became fully manifest enlightened ones, are becoming fully manifest enlightened ones, and will become fully manifest enlightened ones.'[1]

3. The antidote to the despondency of impatience with application

1. The difficulties have great benefit
2. It is not suffering
3. It is actually happiness

1. The difficulties have great benefit

Comparing the sufferings of saṃsāra to a heavy burden:

7.20
If I am more frightened at the prospect
Of having to lose an arm or a leg,
I have not examined what is heavy and what is light.
That fear comes from my own confusion.

The suffering of that heavy load is meaningless:

7.21
For countless millions of aeons,
Countless times I have been cut,
Impaled, burned and torn apart,
But I did not attain enlightenment.

The suffering of that light load is meaningful:

> **7.22**
> But the suffering through which I can accomplish
> Enlightenment is limited.
> It is like the suffering of making an incision
> In order to extract something painful within.

Establishing this with the example of eliminating a great suffering with a lesser one:

> **7.23**
> All physicians use unpleasant treatments
> To cure illnesses.
> So, to overcome many sufferings,
> I can put up with a little unpleasantness.

2. It is not suffering

> **7.24**
> Yet, the supreme physician does not use
> Ordinary treatments like these.
> With his extremely gentle practice,
> He cures the limitless number of great sicknesses.

> **7.25**
> At first, the guide only has us practise
> Giving away a few vegetables, etc.
> Eventually, having gotten used to this,
> We can come to give away even our own flesh.

> **7.26**
> When I eventually come to regard my own body
> As like those vegetables, etc.
> Why would it be difficult
> To give away its flesh?

The first two lines indicate the supreme physician. The two next lines indicate accomplishment by familiarization. The next verse gives an example of that. The last verse indicates that something one is used to is not difficult.

3. It is actually happiness

7.27
There is no suffering because nonvirtue is given up.
There is no lack of joy because of wisdom.
It is wrong understanding that harms the mind
And nonvirtues that harm the body.

The first line indicates that application does not exhaust the causes of physical pleasures. The second line indicates it is the cause of a joyful mind. The last two lines indicate the true causes of physical and mental suffering.

The next verse indicates that their opposites are causes of happiness:

7.28
Merit brings physical pleasure,
And wisdom brings mental happiness.
Are the compassionate ones fed up
With remaining in saṃsāra for the benefit of others?

Praising the preeminent activity:

7.29
Their former nonvirtues are exhausted
By the force of their bodhicitta,
And they gather oceans of merit,
Due to which they surpass the śrāvakas.

Concluding what is the real foundation of happiness: [347]

7.30
Therefore, riding the chariot of bodhicitta,
Which relieves all discouragement and fatigue,
And takes one from happiness to happiness,
What thinking person would be despondent?

The body is harmed by suffering and the mind is harmed by wrong understanding. It is these which obstruct joy. Therefore, because they are their opposites, merit and becoming wise bring the happiness of body and mind.

4. Fully developing effort

1. Briefly
2. Extensively

1. Briefly

7.31
The powers that can accomplish the benefit of beings
Are motivation, steadfastness, joy and rest.

The purpose of effort is to accomplish the benefit of sentient beings. Its nature is motivation, steadfastness, joy and rest. Motivation is engaging with the armour of unshakeable aspiration. Steadfastness is unfaltering application. Joy is the enthusiasm to carry out a specific task. Rest is relaxing one's application when one becomes fatigued by it.

Motivation is developed through fear of suffering
And considering its benefits.

This indicates the cause of motivation, i.e. it is developed through fear of suffering and consideration of the benefits of virtue.

7.32
Therefore, give up the factors that oppose
Motivation, pride, joy and rest,
And with dedication and self-control,
Work to increase effort.

This indicates the result. The more these six powers are enhanced, the more one's effort will increase. This is the direct result, while the indirect result is the benefit of others.

2. Extensively

   1. Developing the array of powers
   2. Dedication
   3. Self-control

1. Developing the array of powers

   1. The power of motivation
   2. The power of steadfastness
   3. The power of joy
   4. The power of rest

Section overview: The power of motivation [v33-46b]

1. Object
   1. Abandoning the faults of oneself and others
   2. Accomplishing all good qualities
   3. Kinds of acts
2. Result
3. Cause
   1. The result of mixed actions
   2. The ripening of purely white actions
   3. The ripening of purely black actions
4. Conclusion

---

1. The power of motivation

   1. Object
   2. Result
   3. Cause
   4. Conclusion

1. Object

   1. Abandoning the faults of oneself and others
   2. Accomplishing all good qualities
   3. Kinds of acts

1. Abandoning the faults of oneself and others

> **7.33**
> I will overcome the endless faults
> Of myself and others,
> Even if each one of those faults
> Takes an ocean of aeons to wear out.
>
> **7.34**
> When I see that I have barely begun
> To exhaust my own faults,
> Why do I not have a heart attack, thinking
> I will end up in the realms of limitless suffering?

The first two lines indicate that one should abandon all faults. The second two indicate that previous bodhisattvas made all kinds of exertion. [348] The next two indicate the weakness of one's own undertaking. The last two indicate how much there is to be abandoned.

2. Accomplishing all good qualities

> **7.35**
> I will establish the many good qualities
> Of myself and others,
> Even if each one of those qualities
> Takes an ocean of aeons to cultivate.
>
> **7.36**
> Since I have never developed
> Much familiarity with even a part of those qualities,
> It is quite amazing that I, someone who has acquired
> Such a rare rebirth, should act so meaninglessly.

The first two lines indicate that one should establish all good qualities. The second two indicate that previous bodhisattvas engaged in all kinds of exertions. The next verse indicates how little effort one makes.

3. Kinds of acts

7.37
I have not made offerings to the Buddhas,
Nor provided great feasts.
I have not done anything for the teachings,
Nor fulfilled the wishes of the poor.

7.38
I have not protected the frightened from what threatens them,
Nor given comfort to the destitute.
The only thing I have done is cause
My mother the pain and suffering of carrying me in her
    womb.

The first six lines indicate the kinds of acts that one has not accomplished. The rest indicates the meaninglessness of one's birth.

2. Result of motivation

7.39
In the past, until now,
I have had no motivation for dharma,
And now I am destitute like this.
Who abandons the motivation for dharma?

7.40
Motivation is the source
Of all virtuous pursuits, as the Sage has said.

The result of motivation is virtuous dharmas, indicated here first by the reverse pervasion and then by the forward pervasion.[2]

3. Cause of motivation

The cause is conviction in actions and results [i.e. karma]:

1. The result of mixed actions
2. The ripening of purely white actions
3. The ripening of purely black actions

1. The result of mixed actions

The source of motivation is continual meditation
On the ripening of results.

7.41
Sufferings, anxieties,
All kinds of distress,
And being separated from our desires
All come from nonvirtue.

7.42
For one who keeps a virtuous intent in mind,
No matter where he goes,
His merit will present offerings to him
With the gifts of ripening results.

7.43
But one who practises nonvirtue, though he may want
    happiness,
No matter where he goes,
Will be defeated by his nonvirtues,
Bearing instruments for inflicting pain.

The first two lines are a short summary. The next verse indicates the main visible results of nonvirtue. The next verse indicates the results of virtue. The last verse indicates the visible results of nonvirtue. 'Sufferings' means physical suffering and 'distress' means fires, etc.

2. The ripening of purely white actions

7.44
In the vast, fragrant, cool heart of a lotus,
Where the sound of the Conqueror's words nurtures their
    resplendence,
The virtuous, prompted by the Sage's light, arise from a lotus
    in a supreme form
And become children of the Sugatas in the presence of the
    Conqueror.

The first line indicates the place of birth; the second, the presence of the teacher; the third, the birth itself and one's body and the fourth, the place.

3. The ripening of purely black actions

> **7.45**
> **The servants of the Lord of Death will relentlessly flail all the skin from their bodies,**
> **And pour molten copper, liquefied by ferocious furnaces, down their throats.**
> **As one hundred chunks of flesh are gouged from them with red hot swords and knives,**
> **The nonvirtuous will fall upon the fiercely blazing iron ground.**

The first line indicates one's body; the second indicates the internal experience; the third indicates the external experience; the last line indicates the place.

4. Conclusion

> **7.46**
> **Therefore, I should be motivated to virtue,**
> **And develop enthusiasm for it.**

> Section overview: The power of steadfastness [v46c-62]
>
> 1. Stable preparation
>   1. Method of not being deterred
>   2. Method of preparation
>   3. The fault of not doing it
> 2. Stable engagement
>   1. Briefly
>   2. Pride in actions
>   1. Briefly
>   2. Extensively
>   3. Benefitting others engaged in inferior actions
>   3. Pride in ability
>   1. The logic of reliance
>   1. Showing the fault by example
>   2. The cause of that arising
>   3. The greatness of that pride
>   4. Striving to rely on that
>   5. If one does not strive, one's vows will be broken
>   2. The means of reliance
>   1. The nature of antidotal pride
>   2. 'Pride' does not mean defiled pride
>   3. Developing enthusiasm by praising antidotal pride
>   4. Pride in overcoming the defilements

2. The power of steadfastness

   1. Stable preparation
   2. Stable engagement

1. Stable preparation

   1. Method of not being deterred
   2. Method of preparation
   3. The fault of not doing it

1. Method of not being deterred [349]

   I should cultivate pride from the outset

According to the practice of Vajradhvaja.

In the *Sixth Dedication of Vajradhvaja* it says,

> For example, Devaputra, when the sun rises, it is not stopped by the faults of the blind nor of the gandharvas, nor by dust, Rāhu, smoke, mist and so forth, nor by shadows, nor by the rugged mountains but shines regardless upon any objects it reaches. Similarly, bodhisattvas arising for the benefit of others are not stopped by any kind of faults of hostility or wildness but rather they strive regardless to motivate, ripen and completely liberate those sentient beings who are suitable.[3]

2. Method of preparation

7.47
I should assess my own resources
Before deciding whether or not to undertake something.
It is better not to undertake it
Than to undertake it and then stop,

If one is able to, one should undertake it. Otherwise, one should not, for not undertaking is better than undertaking and then stopping.

3. The fault of not doing it

7.48
For that habit will continue in future lives,
And increase nonvirtue and suffering.
Also, other actions and their results
Will be weakened and will not be accomplished.

The fault of undertaking and then stopping is that one becomes habituated to stopping in future lives. This is called the 'effect similar to the cause'. An increase of negative deeds in this life is called the 'proliferating effect'. An increase in suffering throughout future lives is called the 'fully ripened effect'. It diminishes other actions—i.e. since conduct ceases, it is an action diminishing the unattained. It also diminishes results—i.e. since it is impossible to attain the results themselves, it is an action diminishing the attained. Since one does not fulfil what should have been accomplished, it is an action diminishing their attainment.[4]

2. Stable engagement

   1. Briefly
   2. Pride in actions
   3. Pride in ability
   4. Pride in overcoming the defilements

1. Brief overview

   7.49
   I should take pride in three things:
   Actions, defilements and ability.

   - Considering antidotal actions as the best, to engender the thought, [350] 'There is nobody other than someone like me who can properly engage such actions' is pride in actions.
   - Considering the defilements as weak, to think, 'I can control such things' is pride in overcoming the defilements.
   - Considering oneself as superior, to engender the thought, 'Nobody else can abandon faults and accomplish good qualities' is pride in ability.

2. Pride in actions

   1. Briefly
   2. Extensively
   3. Benefitting others engaged in inferior actions

1. Briefly

   'I will do it alone.'
   This is pride in actions.

2. Extensively

   7.50

> The world is overpowered by defilements
> And cannot achieve its own benefit.
> Since beings cannot do it for themselves,
> I will do it for them.

Since others who have defilements are powerless, they are unable to accomplish virtue, so it will be done by oneself.

3. Benefitting others engaged in inferior actions

> 7.51
> How can I just sit here
> When others are performing negative actions?
> I don't act because of pride,
> But it would be better not to have such pride.

2. Pride in ability

1. The logic of reliance
2. The means of reliance[5]

1. The logic of reliance

1. Showing the fault by example
2. The cause of that arising
3. The greatness of that pride
4. Striving to rely on that
5. If one does not strive, one's vows will be broken

1. Showing the fault by example

> 7.52
> When it comes across a dying snake,
> A crow acts as if it were an eagle.
> Similarly, when I am weakened,
> Even a small downfall will harm me.

Just as when a snake is weakened, it is attacked by scavengers, so when antidotes are weak, the downfalls are heavy.

2. The cause of that arising

7.53
When I am discouraged, I give up,
So how will I ever be liberated from destitution?

Since out of discouragement one does not try, one takes no pride in one's ability and so one is not liberated from destitution.

3. The greatness of that pride

The proud, generating exertion,
Can handle difficulties, even great ones.

4. Striving to rely on that

7.54
Therefore, with a steady mind,
I will overcome all downfalls,

5. If one does not strive, one's vows will be broken

For if I am defeated by the defilements,
My wish to conquer the three realms would be a joke.

2. The means of reliance

1. The nature of antidotal pride
2. 'Pride' here does not mean defiled pride
3. Developing enthusiasm by praising antidotal pride

1. The nature of antidotal pride

7.55
'I will conquer all,
And be conquered by nothing.'
I, a child of conquering lions,
Should take pride in this.

[351] The first two lines indicate the wish to conquer all among the three worlds. The second two lines indicate the subsequent training of a child of the conquerors.

'Is this not contradictory to the teaching that pride is to be abandoned?'

2. 'Pride' here does not mean defiled pride[6]

7.56
Whoever is defeated by their pride
Does not have this pride; he has defilements.
The proud are not overpowered by their enemies;
They bring the enemy pride under their power.

7.57
Their defilements inflate them with pride,
And their pride leads them to the lower realms.
It steals the wealth of their human life,
And leaves them a slave, begging food from others,
Stupid, ugly and pathetic,

7.58
Despised wherever they go.
If these wretches, inflated with pride,
Are counted among the proud,
Who could be considered shamed?

The first two lines indicate that someone whose antidotal pride is defeated has defilements and does not take pride in his abilities. Why? Because taking pride in one's abilities acts as an antidote to the defilements and thus overpowers them (lines 56cd). The next lines indicate that taking pride in one's abilities brings happiness, while here the person attains suffering, i.e. they are led to the suffering of the lower realms (57ab) and, even while they are in the higher realms, they experience painful sufferings (57c-58b). The last two lines indicate that if such a person is proud, nobody would be shamed.

3. Developing enthusiasm by praising antidotal pride

7.59
Whoever takes pride in conquering the enemy pride
Is one of the proud and a completely victorious hero.
Whoever finally overcomes the enemy pride when it is upon him
Brings the results of his conquest to completion in accord with the wishes of beings.

'The proud' are those who take pride in conquering the enemy pride. Though the enemy pride is upon him, the one who overcomes it is a hero. If he brings the results of his conquest to completion in accord with the wishes of beings, he is completely victorious.

4. Pride in overcoming the defilements

Developing strength in dangerous conditions:[7]

7.60
Amid the amassing defilements,
I will withstand them in a thousand ways.
Like a lion among foxes,
The host of defilements will not disturb me.

One should remain focussed on not being tainted by defilements:

7.61
In a deadly situation,
People protect their eyes.
Similarly, even in a threatening situation,
I will not fall under the power of the defilements.

The actual explanation:

7.62
It would be better to be burned alive
Or decapitated
Than to be constantly grovelling
To the enemy defilements.

7.62a

Similarly, in all circumstances,
I should do nothing apart from what is appropriate.

A 'deadly situation' [v61a] means something life-threatening.

Section overview: The powers of joy and rest [v63-66]

3. Joy
   1. One should enjoy the play of good actions themselves without concern for a result
   2. Consideration of the result: enjoyment
      1. Certainty that the result will come
      2. Consideration of what is better
   3. How to apply the power of joy
4. Rest
   1. Temporary rest
   2. Finishing rest

---

3. The power of joy

1. One should enjoy the play of good actions themselves without concern for a result
2. Consideration of the result: enjoyment
3. How to apply the power of joy

1. One should enjoy the play of good actions themselves without concern for a result [352]

> 7.63
> **Whatever actions are to be done,**
> **I will carry them out**
> **Like someone who enjoys the playing of a game as its own reward;**
> **I will insatiably delight in participating.**

One should just enjoy it like playing a game of dice.

2. Consideration of the result: enjoyment

1. Certainty that the result will come
2. Consideration of what is better

1. Certainty that the result will come

> **7.64**
> **When we act for the sake of our own happiness,**
> **We do not know whether we will get it or not.**
> **But how can one for whom the action itself brings happiness**
> **Be happy without doing it?**

While the results of engaging in ordinary actions are doubtful, if one practises antidotal actions, there is no doubt that the result will come.

2. Consideration of what is better

> **7.65**
> **If I never have enough sense pleasures,**
> **Which are like honey on a razor's edge,**
> **How can I ever have enough merit,**
> **Which ripens in happiness and bliss?**

'Happiness' means attaining sense pleasures.

3. How to apply the power of joy

> **7.66**
> **Therefore, in order to carry out an action,**
> **I will engage in it**
> **Like an elephant tormented by the midday sun,**
> **Plunging into a lake.**

4. The power of rest

1. Temporary rest
2. Finishing rest

1. Temporary rest

> **7.67**

> If, after some time, my strength declines,
> I should leave it so I can return to it later.

The first line indicates the circumstance. The second line indicates the necessity and the manner of resting.

2. Finishing rest

> When I have completed something properly,
> I should leave it, wanting to get on with the next thing.

The first line indicates the circumstance. The second line indicates the necessity and the manner of resting.

2. Dedication

1. Dedication to concern
2. Dedication to mindfulness and clear comprehension
3. Not allowing circumstances to arise which oppose those two
4. Overcoming their arising
5. Subsequently accomplishing supporting actions

1. Dedication to concern

> 7.68
> Like engaging in a sword fight
> With a veteran enemy warrior,
> I will dodge the defilement weapons
> And cut down the defilement enemies.

One dodges the defilements and fights against the three poisons and laziness by maintaining their antidotes.

2. Dedication to mindfulness and clear comprehension

> 7.69
> If I dropped my sword in battle,
> I would hurriedly snatch it up, horrified.
> Likewise, if I lose the blade of mindfulness,
> I will quickly restore it, in horror of hell.

3. Not allowing circumstances to arise which oppose those two

7.70
Poison spreads throughout the body
By means of the blood.
Likewise, if they find an opportunity
Faults will spread throughout my mind.

7.71
Practitioners should be as careful
As someone carrying a pot of mustard oil,
Attended by a knifeman
Threatening to kill them if they should spill any.

The first verse indicates that faults will spread if they find an opportunity. The second verse indicates making effort in the means of not providing them with any opportunities.

4. Overcoming their arising [353]

7.72
I would hurriedly jump up
If a snake slid onto my lap.
Likewise, if I sink into sleep or lethargy,
I will quickly repel them.

7.73
Each time some fault occurs,
I should reproach myself,
Reflecting for a long time,
'I will not allow this to happen again.'

The first verse indicates repelling sleep and laziness, while the second verse indicates repelling downfalls.

5. Subsequently accomplishing supporting actions

7.74
'How can I develop mindfulness
In these particular circumstances?'

> With this in mind, I should plan for
> Occasions of meeting and practising.

To develop mindfulness, one should take up the actions of meeting with teachers and practising their meditations.

3. Self-control

The means of practising self-control:

> 7.75
> Before committing any act,
> I should be fully prepared.
> Calling to mind the advice on concern,
> I should proceed to carry it out.

The result of effort in self-control:

> 7.76
> Like cotton blown back and forth
> Under the power of the wind,
> I should accomplish everything in this way
> Under the power of enthusiasm.

Chapter 8

MEDITATION

1. Abandoning contradictory factors
2. Developing joy in solitude[1]
3. Focussing the mind on samatha

Section overview: Abandoning Contradictory Factors [v1-84]

1. Briefly
2. Abandoning the world
    1. The causes of not abandoning the world
    2. The greatness of the antidote to those causes
    3. How the antidotes are accomplished
       (cont.)
    4. The faults of worldly involvement
    5. The qualities of non-distraction
       (cont.)
3. Giving up conceptual discrimination
    1. Examining how the result is destroyed
    2. Examining the impure nature
       (cont.)
    3. Considering how harm is abandoned by its cause
       (cont.)

1. Abandoning contradictory factors

1. Briefly
2. Abandoning the world
3. Giving up conceptual discrimination

1. Briefly

8.1
Having developed effort in this way,
I should place my mind in samādhi.
Someone whose mind is distracted
Lives between the jaws of the defilements.

8.2
With the isolation of body and mind,
There are no distractions.
Therefore, I should abandon this world,
And give up all conceptual discrimination.

Why should one place the mind, as it says, in samādhi after developing effort? It is to abandon conceptual distractions. What is the problem if one does not abandon them? As explained in lines 1cd, if one is overpowered by objects, it is easy to be devoured by the defilements. How can one abandon distraction? Lines 2ab explain this. If one wonders what the method is for the isolation of body and mind, it is given in lines 2cd, i.e. to abandon craving for the causes of distraction.

2. Abandoning the world

1. The causes of not abandoning the world
2. The greatness of the antidote to those causes
3. How the antidotes are accomplished
4. The faults of worldly involvement
5. The qualities of non-distraction

1. The causes of not abandoning the world

8.3
Out of attachment and craving for possessions, etc.
I do not abandon this world.

'Attachment' means attachment to the bodies of others which are aggregations of the five perpetuating skandhas. [354] 'Craving for possessions, etc.' means attachment to external enjoyments.

2. The greatness of the antidote to those causes

Therefore, to completely abandon it,
The wise should analyse it as follows.

8.4
Understanding that insight with complete calm abiding
Will utterly destroy the defilements,
I should seek calm abiding first,
And that is achieved through the joy of having no worldly attachment.

The first two lines briefly summarize abandoning the world. The next two lines indicate that the defilements are destroyed by the unification of calm abiding and insight. The next line indicates that the cause of insight is calm abiding. The last line indicates that the cause of calm abiding is abandoning attachment to the world.

250 | BODHICARYĀVATĀRA WITH COMMENTARY

Section overview: How the antidotes are accomplished [v5-21]

1. Establishing non-attachment towards sentient beings
    1. The faults of the subject with attachment
        1. One does not attain the desired person
        2. One is disturbed when one does not see the desired person
        3. One's misery knows no end
        4. One does not attain liberation
        5. Freedom and opportunity are wasted
    2. The faults of the desired object
        1. They destroy great benefits
        2. They lead one to lower rebirths
        3. They are unreliable
        4. They are difficult to please
        5. One does not get any benefit
        6. One engages in faults
        7. Summary of faults
        8. How to abandon them
2. Establishing non-attachment towards possessions, etc.
    1. The faults of the subject with attachment
    2. The faults of the desired object
        1. Volatility
        2. Praise and criticism are neither beneficial nor harmful

---

3. How the antidotes are accomplished

   1. Establishing non-attachment towards sentient beings
   2. Establishing non-attachment towards possessions, etc.

1. Establishing non-attachment towards sentient beings

   1. The faults of the subject with attachment
   2. The faults of the desired object

1. The faults of the subject with attachment

   1. One does not attain the desired person
   2. One is disturbed when one does not see the desired person
   3. One's misery knows no end

4. One does not attain liberation
5. Freedom and opportunity are wasted

1. One does not attain the desired person

> **8.5**
> **Which impermanent person would have attachment**
> **To another impermanent person?**
> **He will not see his loved one again**
> **For thousands of lifetimes.**

Although the impermanent self has attachment to another impermanent self, it cannot attain the object of its desire.

2. One is disturbed when one does not see the desired person

> **8.6**
> **I am unhappy when I don't see them**
> **And my mind will not settle.**

When one cannot see the person to whom one is attached, one's mind is disturbed with unhappiness.

3. One's misery knows no end

> **Yet, even when I see them, I am not satisfied,**
> **But just as tormented by craving as before.**

4. One does not attain liberation

> **8.7**
> **If one is attached to sentient beings,**
> **Reality is obscured,**
> **Renunciation is forgotten,**
> **And one ends up suffering in misery.**

5. Freedom and opportunity are wasted

> **8.8**
> **Thinking solely of them,**

This life passes by without any meaning.

2. The faults of the desired object

   1. They destroy great benefits
   2. They lead one to lower rebirths
   3. They are unreliable
   4. They are difficult to please
   5. One does not get any benefit
   6. One engages in faults
   7. Summary of faults
   8. How to abandon them

1. They destroy great benefits

**The unchanging dharma
Is lost though transient friends.**

In this way, they diminish actions which lead to the great enlightenment.

2. They lead one to lower rebirths

**8.9
If I act like a fool,
I will surely go to the lower realms.
If they are leading me to that different end,
Why would I follow such fools?**

This is because they are conducive to the causes of the lower realms. [355] 'A different end' means rebirth other than a human one.

3. They are unreliable

**8.10
One second they are friends
But, in an instant, they become enemies.**

4. They are difficult to please

Since they get angry even in joyful situations,
People are very hard to please.

8.11
If I say something helpful, they get angry,
And oppose my help.
If I don't listen to them,
They get angry, and then will go to a bad rebirth.

The first two lines indicate their response to benefit is backwards. The next line indicates their response to helpful advice is backwards. The next line indicates that they involve one in nonvirtue. The last two lines indicate that when one does not comply with them, their minds become agitated.

5. One does not get any benefit

8.12
They are envious of superiors, competitive towards equals,
And arrogant towards inferiors. When praised, they become conceited.
When criticized, they get angry.
What good can ever come from such children?

The first two lines indicate that all people from superior to inferior become objects of the defilements. 'When praised...' indicates that both praise and blame become objects of defilements. The last line indicates that, therefore, they are not conducive to virtue.

6. One engages in faults

8.13
When associating with the childish,
We praise ourselves and criticize other children,
And nonvirtues, like discussing
The joys of saṃsāra, inevitably occur.

It is certain that one will engage in negative conduct.

7. Summary of faults

8.14
To associate with others like this
Only brings loss.

8. How to abandon them

Therefore, since I will not benefit them,
And they will not benefit me,

8.15
I should stay far away from childish people.
When I come across them, I should be happy to please them.
Without being very familiar,
I should treat them well just like any ordinary person.

8.16
Like a bee taking nectar from a flower,
I should accept only what is for the dharma.
I should remain unfamiliar,
As if they were someone I had never met before.

The first three lines indicate abandoning friendships with sentient beings. The next three lines indicate protecting the minds of others when one encounters them. The last verse indicates protecting one's own mind from weakening. 'What is for the dharma' means conditions which are conducive to the practice of dharma such as food, clothing and alms.

2. Establishing non-attachment towards possessions, etc.

1. The faults of the subject
2. The faults of the object

1. The faults of the subject

8.17
'I have lots of possessions and respect.
I am really popular.'
If I hold on to such thoughts,

> My death will be horrible.

> 8.18
> Therefore, whatever it is
> That this utterly confused mind desires,
> Along with it comes
> A thousand sufferings.

> 8.19
> Therefore, the wise don't have desires.
> Fear comes from desire.

The first verse indicates the faults of arrogance. The next six lines indicate the faults of desire. The combined power of the imprints of attachment result in the arising of suffering.

2. The faults of the object

1. Volatility
2. Praise and criticism are neither beneficial nor harmful

1. Volatility

> Since it is the nature of things to be let go of,
> I will be firm and recognize this well.

> 8.20
> I may have many possessions,
> And I may be famous and praised,
> But these possessions and fame—
> I don't know what will become of them.

The first two lines indicate the certainty of having to let go of possessions. The next verse indicates the impossibility of staying with one's possessions. [356]

2. Praise and criticism are neither beneficial nor harmful

> 8.21
> Why does someone's praise please me,

When there is someone else to criticize me?
Why does someone's criticism displease me,
When there is someone else to praise me?

4. The faults of worldly involvement

One does not have the power to take care of others:

> 8.22
> If even the Conqueror could not satisfy
> The various inclinations of sentient beings,
> What can one say of a wretch like me?
> Therefore, I will give up thinking about worldly people.

The reason for that:

> 8.23
> They criticize those who have no possessions,
> And complain about those who have them.
> Since they are so difficult to get along with,
> How can they bring me any joy?

The reason for not getting involved with them:

> 8.24
> The Tathāgata said,
> 'Since the childish are not happy
> Unless they are benefitting themselves,
> The childish are friends to no one.'

> Section overview: The qualities of non-distraction [v25-37]
>
> 1. Friends
> 2. Places
> 3. Livelihood
> 4. Discriminations
>   1. Impurity
>   2. The inevitability of separation from friends
>   3. They are not truly friends
>   4. They are unreliable
> 5. Non-distraction

5. The qualities of non-distraction[2]

1. Friends
2. Places
3. Livelihood
4. Discriminations
5. Non-distraction

1. Friends

8.25
In the forest, the deer, birds
And trees do not speak unpleasantly.
When will I come to live among
Such good company?

2. Places

8.26
Staying in caves or deserted shrines,
Or at the foot of a tree—
I will not look back
But will be free from attachment.

8.27
When will I come to live

> In naturally spacious places,
> Not claimed by anyone as their own,
> Free to do as I please, without attachment?

The first verse indicates not being involved in worldly activities. The second verse indicates the attainment of freedom.

3. Livelihood

> 8.28
> Having just a begging bowl and a few things,
> Wearing clothes not wanted by anyone,
> Not even having to conceal this body—
> When will I come to live without worry?

The first line indicates owning just a few possessions for day-to-day living. The second line indicates having meagre possessions. The last two lines indicate not having to look after anything.

4. Discriminations

1. Impurity
2. The inevitability of separation from friends
3. They are not truly friends
4. They are unreliable

1. Impurity

> 8.29
> When will I go to the burial ground, where,
> Between my body and those heaps of bones,
> There is no difference
> In our subjection to disintegration?

> 8.30
> That is where this body of mine will end up,
> With a stink so putrid
> That not even the wolves
> Will want to go near it.

The first verse indicates perceiving oneself as a skeleton. The second verse indicates perceiving oneself as a putrefying corpse. These reflections are antidotes to having attachment to one's body.

2. The inevitability of separation from friends

> **8.31**
> **If the very flesh and bones**
> **That comprise my body**
> **Must come apart,**
> **What can be said of friendships?**

The first three lines present the example of giving up the body and the last line indicates its meaning, i.e. separation from friends.

3. They are not truly friends

> **8.32**
> **When we are born, we are born alone.**
> **When we die, we die alone.**
> **If they cannot relieve us of our burden of suffering,**
> **What do friends do but create obstacles?**

The first two lines indicate that friends are impermanent. The third line indicates that they cannot take on one's own share of suffering. The last line indicates that they create obstacles to one's benefit.

4. They are unreliable

> **8.33**
> **As travellers on the roads**
> **Take their places to stay,**
> **So, on the paths of conditioned existence,**
> **All take their places of birth.**

Separation from friends such as these is a remedy for unhappiness.

5. Non-distraction [357]

> **8.34**
> **While everyone is completely grief-stricken,**

Four pallbearers carry someone away.
Before that time comes for me,
I will go to the forest.

8.35
I will stay alone in isolation,
Somewhere without friends or antagonists.
When I die, since they will already think of me as dead,
I won't cause them any distress.

8.36
And since they won't be around me,
Being miserable and causing problems,
Nobody will be able to distract me
From mindfulness of the Buddha and so on.

8.37
Therefore, I will go to live
In the bright, beautiful forest where,
With few problems, happy and content,
All disturbances will be pacified.

The first verse indicates resolving to live in isolation. The next two verses indicate not being distracted by either enemies or friends. The last verse summarizes the qualities of isolation.

> Section overview: Giving up conceptual discrimination [v38-84]
>
> 1. Examining how the result is destroyed
> 2. Examining the impure nature
>   1. Impurity connected with the burial ground
>   1. The result is not what one thinks
>   1. Uncleanliness
>   2. Obstructing the door to liberation
>   2. It is nothing other than what is discarded in the burial ground
>   3. It is not logical to selfishly protect that
>   4. It is not logical to attach ornaments to it
>   5. It is not logical to be so afraid of it
>   6. Adorning it with clothes does not make it desirable
>   2. Impurity connected with the living
>   1. Seeing their impurity directly
>   2. Making certain of this with reasoning
>   1. Establishing impurity by the cause which produces impurity
>   2. Analysing impurity by its impure result
>   3. It makes no sense to want impurity
>   4. Establishing the impurity of one's own body
>   5. Summarizing freedom from attachment
>   3. Negating the characteristics of purity
> 3. Considering how harm is abandoned by its cause
>   1. Explanation
>   2. Elaboration
>   1. The desirable object itself is not attained
>   2. Other faults connected with that

3. Giving up conceptual discrimination

Although there are many ways to give up conceptual discrimination in general, since the conceptual discrimination of desirable objects is particularly difficult to abandon, this section focuses specifically on the antidotes for that.

1. Examining how the result is destroyed
2. Examining the impure nature
3. Considering how harm is abandoned by its cause

1. Examining how the result is destroyed

> **8.38**
> **Giving up all other purposes,**
> **I will endeavour single-mindedly**
> **To place my mind in meditative equipoise**
> **And subdue it.**

One should make an effort to place the mind in samādhi, resting in equipoise upon wisdom and subduing it in moral conduct.

> **8.39**
> **In this world and in the next,**
> **Our desires bring us only ruin.**
> **Here, we are killed, imprisoned and broken,**
> **And in the next, we go to the hells.**

What should one contemplate? Abandoning other purposes, such as thinking about desirable objects and benefitting oneself (the first two lines). What is the antidote that one should try to apply? One should clearly understand the faults of desirable objects (the second two lines).

2. Examining our own impure nature

1. Impurity connected with the burial ground
2. Impurity connected with the living

1. Impurity connected with the burial ground

1. The result is not what one thinks
2. It is nothing other than what is discarded in the burial ground
3. It is not logical to selfishly protect that
4. It is not logical to attach ornaments to it
5. It is not logical to be so afraid of it
6. Adorning it with clothes does not make it desirable

1. The result is not what one thinks

1. Uncleanliness
2. Obstructing the door to liberation

1. Uncleanliness

> **8.40**
> **To get her, you had entreated her,**
> **With messengers, male and female,**
> **Without any thought**
> **For nonvirtue or shame.**
>
> **8.41**
> **You would do things that terrified you,**
> **Waste your wealth and,**
> **When she was finally in your arms,**
> **Were overjoyed with what was really**
>
> **8.42**
> **Nothing but a skeleton,**

The first six lines establish the difficulty of the acquisition. The next two lines indicate [358] grasping the situation as joyful. The last line indicates having nothing but a skeleton.

2. Obstructing the door to liberation

> **With neither autonomy nor self.**
> **But because of your intense desire and attraction to her,**
> **You did not go beyond suffering.**

Lacking 'autonomy' means being under the power of extraneous conditions. Lacking 'self' means being impermanent. Because of one's attraction to her, one did not travel the path to nirvāṇa.

2. It is nothing other than what is discarded in the burial ground

> **8.43**
> **At first, you tried to get her**
> **To raise her face to you but, modestly, she looked down.**
> **Whether anyone could see her or not,**

She covered her face with a veil.

> **8.44**
> That face, which so concerned you,
> Is right there before you now,
> For the vultures have stripped it bare—
> So why do you run away?

At first, when she is alive, one cannot see her even if one tries but, when she is in the burial ground, one can see her quite clearly.

3. It is not logical to selfishly protect that

> **8.45**
> When someone looked at her,
> You would completely shield her face from him,
> But now that the vultures are eating that face away,
> Why, selfish, don't you protect it?

It is contradictory to later reject what formerly one selfishly protected from others.

4. It is not logical to attach ornaments to it

> **8.46**
> Seeing this pile of flesh
> Being eaten by vultures and other creatures,
> Why don't you go and present to their food
> Those flower garlands, sandalwood and ornaments?

5. It is not logical to be so afraid of it

> **8.47**
> If you are afraid of a mere pile of bones,
> Even though it cannot possibly move,
> Why are you not frightened
> By something that stirs like a zombie?

6. Adorning it with clothes does not make it desirable

8.48
You wanted it when it was covered.
Why don't you want it now it is uncovered?
If you have no need of it now,
Why did you want it then?

2. Impurity connected with the living

   1. Seeing their impurity directly
   2. Making certain of this with reasoning
   3. Negating the characteristics of purity

1. Seeing their impurity directly

Its tactile quality is not the object of attraction:

8.49
If excrement and saliva
Come from the same source—food,
Why do you love her saliva,
But not her excrement?

Its softness is not the object of attraction:

8.50
You don't have any love for your pillow
Of soft cotton but,
Telling yourself she doesn't really stink,
Your desire confuses you about what is impure.

The copulation itself is not the object of attraction:

8.51
Those confused, desirous wretches,
Though their pillows are soft,
Get angry, saying,
'I can't copulate with this!'

Stopping the false conception of purity:

8.52
If you aren't attracted to impurity,
Why do you embrace
A cage of bones joined by ligaments,
And plastered over with flesh?

8.53
You yourself have plenty of impurity,
Which you continually have to experience,
And yet you hungrily chase after the filth of others
Though they, too, are bags of impurity.

The body and mind by themselves are not the objects of attraction:

8.54
'It's just their flesh I enjoy.'
If that is what you want to see and touch,
Do you want it in its natural state,
Devoid of a mind?

8.55
The mind that you desire
Cannot be seen or touched,
So it makes no sense to want to copulate with it.
What can be seen and touched is not conscious.

Neither self nor other is an object of attraction:

8.56
It is unremarkable to misunderstand
The impure nature of other bodies,
But it is very remarkable to misunderstand
The impurity you yourself have.

The physical appearance is not the object of attraction:

8.57
Not noticing a young lotus flower,
Spreading its petals in the sunlight on a cloudless day,

Why is the mind so attracted to impurity,
And drawn to cages of impurity?

2. Making certain of this with reasoning

   1. Establishing impurity by the cause which produces impurity
   2. Analysing impurity by its impure result [359]
   3. It makes no sense to want impurity
   4. Establishing the impurity of one's own body
   5. Summarizing freedom from attachment by applying the meditation on impurity

1. Establishing impurity by the cause which produces impurity

   8.58
   If you don't want to touch
   An area covered in excrement,
   Why do you want to touch
   The body it issued from?

If certain areas of the body produce impurity, what need is there to say the body itself is also impure?

2. Analysing impurity by its impure result

   8.59
   If you are not attracted to impurity,
   Why do you want to copulate with the body parts of others,
   Which came from an impure place,
   And developed from an impure seed.

   8.60
   You are not attracted to
   A tiny grub, born on excrement.
   Yet, you are attracted to bodies which have many natural impurities,
   And are even born from impurities.

The 'place' here is the mother's womb, while the 'seed' is the seed of the father. To 'develop' that means being developed by the mother's menstrual fluids, etc.

3. It makes no sense to want impurity

> **8.61**
> **Not only do you not mind**
> **The impurity of your own body,**
> **But, wanting even more impurity,**
> **You desire other bags of impurity, too.**

4. Establishing the impurity of one's own body

> **8.62**
> **When pleasing substances like camphor,**
> **Rice or cooked vegetables**
> **Are spat out after chewing,**
> **Even the ground is considered dirty.**

5. Summarizing freedom from attachment by applying the meditation on impurity

> **8.63**
> **Though such impurity is quite obvious,**
> **If there are any doubts about it,**
> **Take a look at the bodies in the cemetery.**
> **You can see even more impurity there.**

> **8.64**
> **If someone's skin were to be peeled away,**
> **You would be completely horrified.**
> **You know this, so how can you**
> **Ever be attracted to such a thing again?**

The first verse relates to the qualities of the body in the cemetery, while the second indicates it as an object of fear.

3. Negating the characteristics of purity

This section is for when one clings to objects of attachment due to their wearing of ornaments, etc. First, artificial scents do not make the body pure:

> 8.65
> Scents applied to the body
> Are of sandalwood and so forth, nothing else.
> Why are you attracted to things
> That smell of something else?
>
> 8.66
> The body's natural smell is awful.
> Isn't it right not to be attracted to it?

The artificial scents are not themselves the objects of attraction:

> Why do the worldly, craving something meaningless,
> Daub it with a fragrance?
>
> 8.67
> For, if the fragrance is that of sandalwood,
> How could it come from the body?
> Why are you attracted to things
> That smell of something else?

The body is naturally frightening:

> 8.68
> The body in its natural state,
> With long hair and nails,
> With stinking, grey teeth, covered with foul-smelling dirt,
> And naked, is actually frightening.
>
> 8.69
> Why make such an effort to clean up
> Something that is like a weapon for wounding me?

It is an object of revulsion:

> This world is in chaos

With lunatics, frantic in their self-centred confusion.

8.70
Having seen a few skeletons in the cemetery,
You felt revulsion.
So are you happy in this cemetery city,
Full of moving skeletons?

3. Considering how harm is abandoned by its cause

   1. Explanation
   2. Elaboration

1. Explanation

8.71
In this way, you cannot have
Such impurity without paying a price.
For those who get it, exhaustion
And agonies such as those of hell ensue.

Wealth is necessary for a wife, etc. The exhaustion of those who get it indicates the difficulties of pursuing wealth in this life. The agonies of hell, etc. indicates the harms of next life.

2. Elaboration

   1. The desirable object itself is not attained
   2. Other faults are associated with that

1. The desirable object itself is not attained

There is no opportunity to enjoy one's desires in this life [360]:

8.72
Children cannot amass any wealth,
And the young cannot enjoy it.
When life is wasted chasing them,
What use are those desires to the old?

It is impossible to enjoy one's desires due to fatigue:

8.73
Some miserable people, full of desire,
Are completely worn out at the end of a long day.
They come home and collapse,
Their lifeless bodies sleeping like the dead.

One cannot be with loved ones for a very long time:

8.74
Some are afflicted by travelling,
And have to suffer being far from home.
Though they miss their families,
They will not see them for years on end.

One cannot attain what one desires due to coming under the control of others:

8.75
Some confused ones, wanting to help themselves,
Sell whatever they have but,
Without getting what they wanted, are driven aimlessly
By the winds of others' karma.

2. Other faults connected with that

No autonomy:

8.76
Some sell their own bodies,
And are helplessly exploited by others.
If his wife should give birth, she must do so
At the foot of a tree or in whatever remote place she finds
    herself.

Suffering due to the fear of loss of life:

8.77

> Fools, deceived by their desire,
> Want a livelihood and, thinking they will make a living,
> Join the army, though they are afraid of dying,

Coming under the control of others:

> Or enter into servitude for money.

Experiencing various physical sufferings:

> 8.78
> Some desirous people can be seen with broken bodies,
> Or impaled upon stakes,
> Or pierced by blades,
> Or even burned.

Sufferings amassed in the three times:

> 8.79
> Due to the anxieties of getting, keeping and losing wealth,
> Understand that its problems are endless.

Obstructing liberation:

> Those who become distracted by attachment to wealth
> Have no opportunity for liberation from the sufferings of saṃsāra.

Summary of faults:

> 8.80
> Those who have desire for such things
> Will have many problems and little satisfaction.
> They are like beasts pulling a wagon,
> Able to eat just a few mouthfuls of grass.

Wasting their freedom:

> 8.81

> For the sake of something that gives little satisfaction
> And which is so common that even animals can get it,
> Those tormented by their karma waste the magnificent freedoms and endowments
> That they had acquired with such difficulty.

Comparing such faults with striving in the means of liberation:

> 8.82
> The objects of desire will inevitably perish,
> But I will fall into the hells and so forth.
> For the sake of something not very important,
> I have been wearing myself out.

> 8.83
> If buddhahood itself can be attained
> With just a millionth of that difficulty,
> Having desire is much more suffering
> Than practising the bodhisattva conduct but without any enlightenment.

It is the foremost among all the sources of faults:

> 8.84
> If one thinks about the sufferings of the hells,
> Weapons, poisoning, fires, ravines
> And enemies are nothing
> Compared to the objects of desire.

'Beasts pulling a wagon, able to eat a few mouthfuls of grass' means that the sufferings they experience are much greater than the happiness they get from eating. 'So common that even animals can get it' refers to sexual intercourse. 'Been wearing myself out' means from beginningless time until now. 'Buddhahood itself can be attained with just a millionth of the difficulty' refers to the three incalculable aeons.[3] To 'think about the sufferings of the hells' means that the sufferings of poisoning, etc. are not even a fraction of that because they are just human sufferings.

2. Developing joy in solitude

1. [361] Its unique preeminence
2. Its unique happiness

1. Its unique preeminence

1. Explanation
2. No opposing conditions
3. Supporting conditions

1. Explanation

8.85
Disillusioned with the objects of desire,
I will develop joy in solitude.

2. No opposing conditions

In peaceful forests,
With no conflict or defilements,

'Conflict' refers to outer distractions. 'Defilements' refers to inner distractions.

3. Supporting conditions

8.86
Fortunate ones, cooled by sandalwood moonlight,
Stroll and contemplate the benefit of others,
Among wondrous palaces of immense rocks,
As a silent, soothing forest breeze blows.

One is cooled by moonlight, like the cooling sandalwood water of a king's palace. The vast slabs of rock are like a king's palace. A gentle forest breeze blows, like wafting fans cooling a king. One is free to focus on the benefit of others and carry out one's daily activities, just as a king considers the affairs of his realm and carries them out.

2. Its unique happiness

> **8.87**
> **In an empty hut, at the foot of a tree or in a cave,**
> **They stay as long they want.**
> **They have left behind the sufferings of masters and protection and,**
> **Not reliant on anyone, live carefree.**
>
> **8.88**
> **Free and without attachment,**
> **Not tied to anyone,**
> **They live with a contentment and happiness**
> **That even Indra would have difficulty finding.**

Since they are free, they can do as they please. They are their own masters. They are protected from enemies and need nothing from friends. Since their contentment is not worldly, it is difficult for Indra to find it.

3. Focussing the mind on samatha

1. Equalizing self and others
2. Exchanging self and others

Section overview: Equalizing self and others [v89-112]

1. Brief explanation
2. Equality of subjection to suffering from self-grasping
   1. Explanation
   2. Accomplishing it
3. Equality in suffering as the object of abandonment
   1. Brief presentation of the proof
   2. Establishing the pervasion of that
   3. Establishing the necessary criterion of the pervasion
      1. The error that follows from the different times
      2. Establishing that grasping the self as singular is error
      3. The error that follows from the parts of the body
      4. Abandoning the consequence that the example is not established
   4. Abandoning objections
   5. Summarizing the definitive meaning of valid cognition
   6. Abandoning objections that it is not definitive
4. The qualities of meditating on equality
   1. Undertaking the benefit of others with happiness
   2. Establishing that to accomplish the benefit of others is the supreme happiness
   3. Pacifying one's own arrogance
   4. Disregarding the results
   5. Advice to strive in practising this
5. The possibility of meditating on equality

---

1. Equalizing self and others

1. Brief explanation
2. Equality of subjection to suffering from self-grasping
3. Equality in suffering as the object of abandonment
4. The qualities of meditating on equality

5. The possibility of meditating on equality

1. Brief explanation

What is the cause of meditating on equalizing self and others?

> **8.89**
> **Having considered how solitude**
> **Has such good qualities,**

What is its purpose?

> **I should pacify conceptual discrimination**
> **And meditate on bodhicitta.**
>
> **8.90**
> **Equalizing self and others**
> **Is the first thing to try and cultivate.**

In other words, it is in order to give up improper mental activity. How should one practise this?

> **Since everyone is the same when it comes to happiness**
> **And suffering, I should look after them as I do myself.**

Due to the equality between oneself and others in wanting to have happiness, [362] one should protect their virtues from decline. Due to the equality in wanting to abandon suffering, one should abandon their nonvirtues as if they were one's own.

2. Equality of subjection to suffering from self-grasping

   1. Explanation
   2. Accomplishing it

1. Explanation

> **8.91**
> **Just as the whole body should be protected,**
> **Though it has many different parts—hands and so on,**

So different beings, whether happy or suffering,
All want to be happy, just as I do.

The substantial parts of the body, such as the hands, are equal in that they should all be protected even though they are distinct, since they are pervaded by the same self-clinging. Similarly, individual streams of being should be protected even though they are distinct, since they are likewise pervaded by the same self-clinging.

2. Accomplishing it

> 8.92
> Though my suffering doesn't harm
> The bodies of others,
> Nevertheless, it is my suffering,
> And clinging to it as 'mine' makes it intolerable to me.
>
> 8.93
> Similarly, though the suffering of others
> Does not befall me,
> Nevertheless, it is my suffering,
> And clinging to it as 'mine' will make it hard for me to tolerate.

The first two lines establish the reverse pervasion, i.e. if there is no self-clinging, [sufferings] do not arise as unbearable. The second two lines establish the forward pervasion, i.e. if there is self-clinging, [sufferings] arise as intolerable [i.e. to be dispelled]. The second verse concludes from this that if one grasps the streams of being of others as one's own, [sufferings] will arise as hard to tolerate.

3. Equality in suffering as the object of abandonment

   1. Brief presentation of the proof
   2. Establishing the pervasion of that
   3. Establishing the necessary criterion of the pervasion
   4. Abandoning objections
   5. Summarizing the definitive meaning of valid cognition
   6. Abandoning objections that it is not definitive

1. Brief presentation of the proof

> **8.94**
> **I should expel the suffering of others**
> **Because it is suffering, like my own suffering,**
> **And I should benefit others**
> **Because they are sentient beings, like I am.**

The suffering of others is the logical subject. This term is related to 'I should' and 'expel', i.e. to form the proposition, 'I should expel that'. [The reason:] because it is suffering, like one's own suffering. Next, taking the benefit of others as the logical subject, the probandum is, 'I should perform that'. [The reason:] because it is the happiness of a sentient being, which is like one's own physical happiness.

2. Establishing the pervasion[4] of that

> **8.95**
> **When you and I**
> **Are the same in wanting to be happy,**
> **What is so special about me**
> **That I work only for myself?**

> **8.96**
> **When you and I**
> **Are the same in not wanting to suffer,**
> **What is so special about me**
> **That I look after myself and not you?**

'Such suffering does not warrant abandonment. Where is the contradiction?'

What is the criterion for regarding the sufferings of one's own stream of being as warranting abandonment? [363]

'The criterion is not wanting them for oneself.'

In that case, the sufferings of others are the same in also not being wanted. Since the criterion for warranting abandonment is satisfied, all sufferings should be abandoned. This is the pervasion. Hence, why would one look after oneself but not others?

This logic is now repeated in relation to establishing happiness:

'The happiness [of others] is not an object to be established. Where is the contradiction? The pervasion[5] is not established.'

What is the criterion for regarding one's own happiness as an object to be established?

'It is an object to be established because I want it.'

If that is so, since the happiness of others also has that criterion, it is also pervaded by being an object to be established. Therefore, all happiness is to be established—the pervasion. When oneself and another are the same in wanting happiness, why work for oneself alone and not for the other? Here, lines 96cd repeat the point of 95cd.

3. Establishing the criterion of the pervasion

'The criterion for something to warrant my protection against is its doing harm to myself. Something that is unwanted only by others does not satisfy that criterion. Therefore, since the sufferings of others do me no harm, they do not warrant protection against.'

The explicit refutation presented here is of doing no harm to oneself alone as the criterion for not warranting protection against. This will implicitly establish that being unwanted *per se* is the criterion for warranting protection against. This has four parts:

1. The error that follows from the different times
2. Establishing that grasping the self as singular is error
3. The error that follows from the parts of the body
4. Abandoning the consequence that the example is not established

1. The error that follows from the different times

> **8.97**
> 'Their suffering doesn't hurt me,
> So why should I care about them?'
> Future sufferings don't hurt you either,
> So why protect yourself from them?

The first two lines are the objection and the second two are the response. If non-harm to oneself is pervaded by not needing protection against and the logical subject is the sufferings of future lives, one's old age, etc., it follows that there is no need to protect oneself from them because right now there is no physical harm. So it is for the sufferings of others. Yet, one protects the body even though there is no harm to it right now. Thus, non-harm to oneself is not pervaded by not needing protection, i.e. the pervasion is not established.

2. Establishing that grasping the self as singular is error

'There is harm to the present body because the self of present and future are one. Therefore, I should protect it from such experiences.'

8.98
To think, 'I'm the one who will experience it',
Is a mistake.

The oneness of the self is not established. Concerning this supposed oneness:

It is someone else who dies after this,
And someone else again who is born.

The momentary mind ceases and its continuity ceases. Therefore, it is an error to think that harm will be experienced by oneself.

3. The error that follows from the parts of the body

8.99
'The ones with the suffering
Should look after themselves.'
The suffering of the feet is not that of the hands,
So why should the hands protect them?

If the experiencer of suffering is pervaded by not warranting the protection of one who is not experiencing suffering, since the suffering of the feet is not experienced by the hands, it follows that the hands should not protect them. Yet, in that case, the unharmed one protects the one warranting protection from harm.

4. Abandoning the consequence that the example is not established

> 8.100
> 'It may not be right,
> But I do it out of self-clinging.'
> Neither self nor other is right:
> You should try to give them both up.

'Since the sufferings of others do not harm me, it is not right to protect others from them. It is not right to protect myself from experiencing the sufferings of the future either but, nevertheless, I do it out of self-clinging.'

If self-clinging is not right, one should try to give it up. [365]

'Self-clinging is right, even though the self is momentary and with distinct parts.'

In that case, it is right to have self-clinging towards the distinct streams of being of others, too, so one should protect them from suffering.

'Self-clinging is right, but that is other-clinging.'

Other-clinging is not right either; one should try to abandon it.

4. Abandoning objections

'Self-clinging to the future self is right because, despite being in a different time, there is a single cause. Clinging to other sentient beings is not right because they have distinct causes. Self-clinging is right because, despite having separate parts, the body is a unified composite. Clinging to the bodies of others is not right because they are distinct composites. Therefore it is not true that "neither self nor other is right".'

> 8.101
> A 'stream' and a 'composite' are false,
> Like a string of beads or an army.

The so-called 'stream of being' of self is the logical subject. That it is false is the probandum. [Reason:] because it is a sequential multiplicity grasped as singular, like grasping a string of beads as singular. Next, the so-called 'composite' is the logical subject. It is false because it is a multiplicity of moments grasped as singular, like grasping a manifold army as singular.

5. Summarizing the consistency with valid cognition

> **Suffering is not owned by anyone,**
> **So, who should be the one to remove it?**

Since the bodies of others and one's own body are distinct, one's mind is not the owner of the sufferings of the bodies of others. Similarly, though each particle and moment of those others are distinct, each one has the nature of suffering but none of them is the owner of that suffering, i.e. nothing constitutes an experiencer. So who is it that is subjected to that suffering? There is no self that is subjected to suffering.

> **8.102**
> **Sufferings have no owner:**
> **None of them is unique.**
> **If it is suffering, it should be eradicated.**
> **Why be inconsistent about this?**
>
> **8.103**
> **There is no disagreement about the reason**
> **For preventing everyone's suffering.**

Therefore, [366] just as one's own stream of being is not the owner of others' sufferings, neither is there an experiencer of the sufferings of one's own stream of being. Therefore, sufferings have no owner, i.e. 'none of them is unique'.

Therefore, the criterion for warranting abandonment is not that it harms one's own stream of being but simply that it is suffering—i.e. if it is suffering, it should be abandoned. So why inconsistently abandon one's own suffering but not the suffering of others? This establishes the sufferings of others as warranting abandonment.

The summary:

> If you prevent it at all, prevent it for all.
> Otherwise, don't do it for yourself or others, either.

6. Abandoning objections

> **8.104**
> 'Compassion will bring me a lot of suffering,
> So why should I develop it?'
> If you think about the sufferings of living beings,
> How can compassion be considered a lot of suffering?

'If suffering is pervaded by warranting abandonment, it follows that suffering undertaken for the sake of others warrants abandonment. If it did not warrant abandonment, there would be the error of the pervasion not being established.'

Although the practices to be undertaken for others are difficult, they do not satisfy the criterion for being abandoned as it is presented here. Here, the reason for abandonment is 'because it is endowed with suffering', but these difficulties are not suffering, so compassion is not suffering.

'How can the difficulties not be suffering?'

They are not suffering if one 'thinks of the sufferings of living beings', i.e. having considered how one should prevent the sufferings of sentient beings, one will not grasp the suffering of benefitting others as suffering. Even if one were to enter the Avīci Hell for the benefit of others, one would take joy in it as if one were diving into a lotus pool. Or, having considered how great the sufferings of the lower realms and the sufferings of conditionality are, the suffering one has from such difficulties will seem comparatively minor. Or, just because the difficulties are suffering, their nature does satisfy the general reason for abandonment; nevertheless, it is a suffering which has a result, [367] i.e. since it is not a suffering which does not have a result, it does not satisfy the more specific reason for abandonment:

8.105

> If one person's suffering
> Can stop many sufferings,
> A kind-hearted person would take on that suffering
> For his own sake and the sake of others.

Presentation of an instance of this:

> **8.106**
> **It was for this reason that Supuṣpacandra,**
> **Though he knew the king would harm him,**
> **Did not evade his own suffering**
> **In order to exhaust many sufferings.**

According to the *Sutra Requested by Candrapradipa*,[6] the dharma teacher Supuṣpacandra, in the forest of Samantabhadra, perceived that if he were to go alone, he would subdue King Vīradatta,[7] but the king would kill him. Despite knowing this, without any fear, he proceeded to the king's palace, where he proclaimed the dharma. Why did he disregard his own suffering? In order to exhaust many sufferings.

4. The qualities of meditating on equality

1. Undertaking the benefit of others with happiness
2. Establishing that to accomplish the benefit of others is the supreme happiness
3. Pacifying one's own arrogance
4. Disregarding the results
5. Advice to strive in practising this

1. Undertaking the benefit of others with happiness

> **8.107**
> **One who cultivates this in their being,**
> **With the joy of pacifying the suffering of others,**
> **Would enter the Avīci Hell**
> **As if they were diving into a lotus pool.**

The first line indicates the cause of grasping the benefit of others as happiness. The second line indicates the intent and the last two lines give an example.

2. Establishing that to accomplish the benefit of others is the supreme happiness

> 8.108
> **When sentient beings are completely liberated,**
> **It is an ocean of joy.**
> **Is that not enough?**
> **What use is it wanting my own liberation?**

For someone accomplishing the benefit of others, that is enough. Mere individual liberation is not a cause of joy.

3. Pacifying one's own arrogance

> 8.109
> **In this respect, though I am benefitting others,**
> **I will do it without conceit or thinking it is a big deal.**

Without the conception that they are other, one will not develop the arrogance of thinking, 'I am benefitting others'.

4. Disregarding the results

> **By taking joy solely in their benefit,**
> **I will not expect the ripening of any results.**

5. Advice to strive in practising this

> 8.110
> **Therefore, just as I protect myself**
> **From the slightest criticism,**
> **So I should have a protective attitude towards others,**
> **And a compassionate intent.**

5. The possibility of meditating on equality

> 8.111

Just as out of habit I regard
The drops of semen and blood
Of others as 'myself',
Even though they have no substance,

8.112
Why don't I regard the bodies of others
As 'myself' in the same way, too?
Nor should it be hard to see
My own body as theirs, too.

The body one now clings to was previously the semen and blood of one's parents [368] and one's mind was distinct from it. Through habituation, conceptual thought which clings to it as self was developed. Similarly, though one's mind is separate from them, why, through habituation, would one not be able to come to regard the streams of being of others as self?

2. Exchanging oneself and others

1. Brief description of the essential characteristics
2. Detailed explanation of the essential characteristics
3. Detailed explanation of the practices related to aspiration
4. Detailed explanation of the practices related to application

1. Brief description of the essential characteristics

1. Establishing the aspiration
2. Establishing the application

1. Establishing the aspiration

> **8.113**
> **Having recognized that self is defective,**
> **While others are an ocean of good qualities,**
> **I should completely abandon self-clinging**
> **And practise embracing others.**

One should regard the self as defective and others as an ocean of good qualities, regarding them as inferior and superior. Self-clinging is to be completely abandoned and others are to be regarded as one's own stream of being. To 'embrace others' means having the perception in which the streams of being of others are accepted and self-grasping is rejected, i.e. thinking that they come first and oneself comes after.

2. Establishing the application

> **8.114**
> **Just as I regard my hands, etc.**
> **As parts of my body,**
> **Why don't I regard embodied beings**
> **As limbs of one life?**

Just as through habituation, the hands and so forth are protected and grasped as one's own, even though they are distinct, so the streams of being of others should be treated in application with self-clinging and protected.

Section overview: Detailed explanation of the essential characteristics of exchanging self and others [v115-139]

1. Accepting others
    1. The possibility of exchanging oneself and others
    2. Pacifying arrogance
    3. Disregarding the results
    4. Advice to strive in practising this
    5. A particular practice for the benefit of others
    6. Accomplishing by habituation
    7. Liberation of self and others from suffering
2. Abandoning clinging to 'I'
    1. Out of attachment to one's body, one is afraid of things which are not frightening
    2. Getting involved in all kinds of nonvirtue
3. The faults of putting oneself first and qualities of putting others first
    1. Various faults and qualities
    2. The faults of self-cherishing
        1. Invisible faults
        2. Visible faults
        3. Summary
        4. Abandoning the cause of fear—self-grasping
4. Summary
    1. The purpose of exchanging
    2. Nature
    3. Specific intention
    4. Stopping incorrect application distinct from the correct application
    5. Establishing the correct application

2. Detailed explanation of the essential characteristics

1. Accepting others
2. Abandoning clinging to 'I'
3. The faults of putting oneself first and qualities of putting others first
4. Summary

1. Accepting others

The explanation of this section has seven parts, some of which repeat the headings of the commentary on v107-112 ['The qualities of meditating on equality']:

1. The possibility of exchanging oneself and others
2. Pacifying arrogance
3. Disregarding the results
4. Advice to strive in practising this
5. A particular practice for the benefit of others
6. Accomplishing by habituation
7. Liberation of self and others from suffering [369]

1. The possibility of exchanging oneself and others

> **8.115**
> **Just as habituation has brought about**
> **The idea of self for this selfless body,**
> **Why should habituation not create**
> **The same idea about sentient beings?**

Though body and mind are distinct, they can be grasped as self through habituation. Similarly, though the streams of being of others are distinct, if one becomes habituated, it is possible to grasp them as self.

2. Pacifying arrogance

> **8.116**
> **Though I might benefit others in this way,**
> **I will not have conceit or think it is a big deal,**

Just as one does not have a conceited attitude when benefitting oneself, similarly, when others are grasped as self, one should not have a conceited attitude in carrying out their benefit.

3. Disregarding the results

> **Like not expecting a reward**

After eating my own food.

4. Advice to strive in practising this

> **8.117**
> **Therefore, just as I protect myself**
> **From the slightest criticism,**
> **So I should have a protective attitude towards beings,**
> **And cultivate a compassionate intent.**

5. A particular practice for the benefit of others

> **8.118**
> **The protector Avalokiteśvara,**
> **Out of great compassion**
> **Blessed even his own name**
> **To dispel the fear of crowds.**

Because everything he did was only for the benefit of others, the protector Avalokiteśvara blessed his own name, such that simply by remembering it, beings would be freed from fears such as enemies and fire and freed from anxiety among crowds. Fear of enemies and fire is what crowds are afraid of. Anxiety among crowds is the fear of being among crowds.

6. Accomplishing by habituation

> **8.119**
> **I shouldn't turn away from difficulty.**
> **Just hearing someone's name might have once frightened me but,**
> **By the power of habituation,**
> **I will come to be disappointed at their absence.**

By facing difficulty directly, one will become habituated to it in the same way that habituating to a person of whom one was once afraid leads to familiarity.

7. Liberation of self and others from suffering

8.120
Whoever wants quickly
To protect himself and others
Should practise the holy secret:
Exchanging self and others.

It is the 'holy secret' because someone who has this attitude can liberate themselves and others, but an inferior person cannot, even if they wanted to do so.

2. Abandoning clinging to 'I'

  1. Out of attachment to one's body, one is afraid of things which are not frightening
  2. Getting involved in all kinds of nonvirtue

1. Out of attachment to one's body, one is afraid of things which are not frightening

8.121
Out of attachment to my body,
I am frightened by the slightest threat.
Who would not resent as an enemy
A body which creates so much fear?

If one does not have self-cherishing, one will not be afraid of such things but, if one does, one will be afraid of even little things. Therefore, since it is the source of such fears, it is like an enemy. [370]

2. Getting involved in all kinds of nonvirtue

Involvement in nonvirtue:

8.122
Wanting to alleviate the body's
Hunger and thirst, or its sickness,
Someone kills a bird, fish or deer,
Or lies in ambush by the roadside.

8.123

> For the sake of wealth and status,
> Someone kills his father and mother,
> Or steals the offerings made to the Three Jewels and,
> Because of this, burns in the Avīci Hell.

Therefore, resentment is good:

> **8.124**
> **Who, then, would be wise**
> **To cherish, protect and lavish gifts upon that body?**

Protection is wrong:

> **Who would not see it as their enemy,**
> **And regard with contempt?**

3. The faults of putting oneself first and qualities of putting others first

1. Various faults and qualities
2. The faults of self-cherishing

1. Various faults and qualities

In relation to giving:

> **8.125**
> **'If I give this, what will I have?'**
> **Thinking of one's own benefit is the way of demons.**
> **'If I keep this, what will I give?'**
> **Thinking of the benefit of others is dharma of the gods.**

In relation to harm:

> **8.126**
> **If I harm others for my own sake,**
> **I will be tormented in the hells and so forth but,**
> **If I am harmed for the sake of others,**
> **I will attain everything I could possibly want.**

In relation to praise:

> **8.127**
> If I desire a high status for myself,
> I will go to the lower realms, lowly and stupid but,
> If I wish it for others,
> I will obtain a happy rebirth and every honour.

In relation to the employment of the body:

> **8.128**
> If I use others for my own sake,
> I will come to know servitude and so forth myself but,
> If I work for the sake of others,
> I will come to experience a high status and so forth.

In relation to benefit:

> **8.129**
> Whatever happiness there is in this world
> All comes from wanting others to be happy.
> Whatever suffering there is in this world
> All comes from wanting one's own happiness.

Summary:

> **8.130**
> Does this need to be explained any further?
> Just look at the difference between
> The childish, who pursue their own benefit,
> And the Buddhas, who carry out the benefit of others.

2. The faults of self-cherishing

   1. Invisible faults
   2. Visible faults
   3. Summary
   4. Abandoning the cause of fear—self-grasping

1. Invisible faults

> 8.131
> If I do not actually exchange
> My happiness for the suffering of others
> Not only will I not attain buddhahood but,
> Even in saṃsāra, I will find no happiness.

One will not attain liberation and even in saṃsāra one will not find happiness, i.e. one will not proceed to a happy rebirth.

2. Visible faults

> 8.132
> Even apart from my future lives,
> Nothing would get done in this life:
> Servants would fail to do their work
> And masters would refuse to pay them.

3. Summary

> 8.133
> Completely discarding the abundant joy and contentment
> Of achieving both visible and invisible happiness
> And, instead, being a cause of suffering for others,
> In confusion, I am bringing unbearable suffering upon myself.

4. Abandoning the cause of fear—self-grasping

> 8.134
> All the dangerous forces in the world
> And as much fear and suffering as there is,
> Come from self-grasping,
> So what good is this great demon to me?

> 8.135
> If I don't give it up completely,
> I cannot avoid suffering,

> Just as if I don't put out a fire,
> I cannot avoid being burnt.

The first verse establishes the forward pervasion that self-grasping is the basis of fear, which is exemplified in the second verse.

4. Summary

   1. The purpose of exchanging
   2. Nature
   3. Specific intention
   4. Stopping incorrect application distinct from the correct application
   5. Establishing the correct application

1. The purpose of exchanging

   8.136
   Because it will, in this way, pacify harm to myself
   And pacify the sufferings of others,

2. Nature

   I will give myself up for others,
   And embrace others as I did the self.

3. Specific intention

   8.137
   'I am under the control of others.'
   With this conviction, mind,
   You will now have no thought
   Other than benefitting all sentient beings.

[371] One should give one's own body to others and abandon the intention to accomplish self-benefit.

4. Stopping incorrect application distinct from the correct application

   8.138

**Since my eyes, etc. are controlled by others,
It is not right for them to accomplish my benefit.
Since my eyes, etc. are for their benefit,
It is not right for them to do any harm.**

Since one's own body, with eyes and so forth under the control of other people, must accomplish only the benefit of others, it is not right for it to accomplish self-benefit. If this body, which is for benefitting others and which has eyes and so forth for accomplishing the benefit of others, does something wrong to them, i.e. if it harms them and diminishes their virtues, that is inappropriate.

5. Establishing the correct application

**8.139
Therefore, I should put sentient beings first.
Anything I see on my body
Should be taken away from it
And used to help others.**

Even the good qualities of one's own body should be taken away and given to others.

> Section overview: Detailed explanation of the practices related to aspiration [v140-158]
>
> 1. Brief explanation
> 2. Meditation on envy
>   1. Meditating on envy of worldly dharmas
>   2. Meditating on envy of good qualities
>   3. The outcome of meditating like this
>   1. Developing the perspective of the assumed self
>   2. Having patience with the harm they may cause
>   3. Disregarding one's good qualities which are unhelpful
>   4. Having sympathy for those beings who are destined for rebirth in the lower realms
>   5. Abandoning conceit and giving up aggression towards the learned
> 3. Meditation on competitiveness
> 4. Meditation on pride
>   1. Types of pride
>   2. The goodness of thinking about that
>   3. Having so meditated, the practice to be relied on
>   4. Faults unrelated to pride
> 5. The results of the meditations
>   1. The fault of looking after the unexchanged self
>   2. The qualities of exchanging self and other
>   3. Experiencing the results
>   4. Making an effort to meditate for the sake of the results

3. Detailed explanation of the practices related to aspiration

1. Brief explanation
2. Meditation on envy
3. Meditation on competitiveness
4. Meditation on pride
5. The results of the meditations

1. Brief explanation

> **8.140**
> **Taking my inferiors, etc. as self;**

And taking self as other,
With a disinterested mind,
I will meditate on envy, competitiveness and pride.

If one classifies sentient beings, there are three kinds: one's inferiors, equals and superiors. To treat these three as self means taking one's own body as if it were someone else and regarding it vicariously, meditating that the 'self' as someone inferior has envy, the 'self' as someone equal has competitiveness and the 'self' as someone superior has pride. 'Disinterested' means not discriminating between the streams of being of self and other as one had before.

2. Meditation on envy

  1. Meditating on envy of worldly dharmas
  2. Meditating on envy of good qualities
  3. The outcome of meditating like this

1. Meditating on envy of worldly dharmas

> 8.141
> He gets respect, but I don't.
> I don't have any wealth like his.
> He is praised while I am criticized.
> He is happy while I am suffering.

One should be envious of the person with respect, acquisitions and a high position. 'He' refers to one's own stream of being which is now taken as other. 'I' refers to the inferior person now taken as self. [372]

2. Meditating on envy of good qualities

> 8.142
> I have to work
> While he sits back comfortably.
> He is renowned in the world as great,
> While I am his inferior, with no good qualities.

> 8.143
> How can I have no good qualities?

> **Everyone has good qualities.**
> **Compared to some, he is inferior.**
> **Compared to some, I am superior.**

If he (one's own stream of being taken as other) is thought of as having great qualities while I (the inferior person taken as self) am thought of as having no good qualities, I dispute this: how can someone have no good qualities? In other words, the inferior person (taken as self) must have good qualities. This thought constitutes envy.

Next, if he (one's own stream of being taken as other) has pride towards me (the inferior person taken as self), since higher and lower are relative, everyone has someone higher than them, compared to whom they are inferior. Since he (one's own stream of being taken as other) is inferior to some, it is inappropriate for him (one's own stream of being taken as other) to have pride just because I (the one taken as self) am his inferior.

Also, concerning my (the inferior person taken as self) being an object of contempt from his (one's own stream of being taken as other) perspective, that contempt is also inappropriate. Since someone's inferiority is relative to someone's superiority, I (the inferior one taken as self) am superior compared to someone inferior to me. Therefore since superiority is also relative, contempt is inappropriate.

However, it is inappropriate to then think that the inferior one taken as self is contemptible since he has a degenerate view, moral conduct, etc.

8.144
> **My degenerate view, moral conduct and so on**
> **Are not my fault but are due to the power of the defilements.**

They are not his fault; he is not autonomous. Why not? Because he is under the power of the defilements.

3. The outcome of meditating like this

1. Developing the perspective of the assumed self
2. Having patience with the harm they may cause
3. Disregarding one's good qualities which are unhelpful [373]

4. Having sympathy for those beings who are destined for rebirth in the lower realms
5. Abandoning conceit and giving up aggression towards the learned

1. Developing the perspective of the assumed self

He should do whatever he can to help me;

2. Having patience with the harm they may cause

I accept this may cause some pain.

Even if taking the inferior one as self causes pain to one's own stream of being (taken as other), this is acceptable. Alternatively, this means that although I (the inferior one taken as self) cause pain which establishes good qualities, I will accept this and will establish those good qualities.

3. Disregarding one's good qualities which are unhelpful

8.145
Why does he not help me,
But only criticize me?
What use are his qualities to me,
When he keeps them for himself?

'If you have compassion, why do you not help me (the inferior one taken as self)? Why do you instead criticize me?'

Because he (one's own stream of being taken as other) has all the good qualities.

'What good to me (the inferior one taken as self) are qualities which don't help me?' In other words, his (one's own stream of being taken as other) qualities are useless.

4. Having sympathy for those beings who are destined for rebirth in the lower realms

8.146

He has no compassion for beings
Living precariously at the mouth of the lower realms.

5. Abandoning conceit and giving up aggression towards the learned

Conceited in how his own qualities compare to others,
He wants to outrival the learned.

3. Meditation on competitiveness

Competitiveness with the assumed self's wealth and respect:

8.147
Though he is regarded as my equal,
I should be his superior,
So I will acquire wealth and respect
Even if it brings conflict.

Competitiveness with his qualities:

8.148
I will do what I can to make my own good qualities
Apparent to the whole world,
And make sure nobody has heard of
His good qualities.

Competitiveness in other ways:

8.149
I will hide my own faults
And everyone will praise me instead of him.
From now on, I will get all the wealth,
And they will respect me instead of him.

8.150
I will happily watch for a long time,
As he is unfairly treated.
Everyone will laugh at him
And we will all agree he is contemptible.

4. Meditation on pride

1. Types of pride
2. The goodness of thinking about that
3. Having so meditated, the practice to be relied on
4. Faults unrelated to pride

1. Types of pride

> 8.151
> I hear this miserable wretch
> Is trying to compete with me.
> How can he equal me in learning, wisdom,
> Looks, intelligence or wealth?

Taking someone of a high status as oneself, one looks at one's former self from his perspective in these regards.

2. The goodness of thinking about that

> 8.152
> When they hear of my good qualities,
> Which everyone talks about,
> I will enjoy the pleasant feeling
> Of a tingling sensation.

Considered from the perspective of the assumed self, [374] one will experience in one's own mind a blissful feeling that one has such good qualities.

3. Having so meditated, the practice to be relied on

> 8.153
> In case he has something of his own,
> As long as he works for me,
> I will force him to give it to me,
> And he will get just enough to live on.

Regarding one's former stream of being (taken as other) as like a servant, one takes the perspective of the other's stream of being (taken as self) and practises stealing his possessions and so forth.

4. Faults unrelated to pride

> 8.154
> I will constantly deprive him of happiness
> And inflict harm upon him.
> While I have been wandering in saṃsāra,
> He has hurt me hundreds of times.

The first two lines indicate applying the harm of others to oneself from their perspective, while the second two lines indicate holding resentment from their perspective.

5. The results of the meditations on exchanging self and other

1. The fault of looking after the unexchanged self
2. The qualities of exchanging self and other[8]
3. Experiencing the results
4. Making an effort to meditate for the sake of the results

1. The fault of looking after the unexchanged self

> 8.155
> Wanting to benefit yourself, mind,
> Countless aeons have been wasted.
> Now you are exhausted,
> And you have achieved only suffering.

2. The qualities of exchanging self and other

> 8.156
> Those who decisively engage
> In truly benefitting others,
> In future will, as the Sage has incontrovertibly said,
> Know the excellence of doing so.

The first two lines urge one to exert oneself, the third line is the scriptural establishment of the result and the last line indicates the experiential establishment of the result.

3. Experiencing the results

> **8.157**
> **If, in the past, you had acted this way,**
> **Your current predicament,**
> **Devoid of the magnificent bliss of buddhahood,**
> **Would not have come about.**

If one had previously exchanged self and other, one would have attained the bliss of buddhahood.

4. Making an effort to meditate for the sake of the results

> **8.158**
> **Therefore, just as you grasp as self**
> **The drops of semen and blood from others,**
> **So you should regard all others as self**
> **Through habitual practice.**

Just as one grasps the semen and blood of others as self, so one should practise grasping others as oneself.

306 | BODHICARYĀVATĀRA WITH COMMENTARY

Section overview: Detailed explanation of the practices related to application [v159-187]

1. How to accomplish the practice
    1. General statement
    2. The practice for the benefit and happiness of others
    3. Taking on all faults
    4. Completely taking a lowly status for the benefit of others
    5. Concise summary of the practice: accepting harm
    6. Correctly protecting the mind
2. Controlling the mind for practice
    1. In respect of subjugating the mind
    2. The faults of activities for one's own sake
        1. Recalling the meaningless actions of the past
        2. Not giving away any control
        3. The practice of abandonment
        4. The fault of not abandoning
        5. Contemplating the faults of that
    3. The faults of taking the body as an object of grasping
        1. Dissatisfaction
            1. The faults of dissatisfaction
            2. The qualities of satisfaction
        2. Immobility
        3. Confusion
            1. Confusion over good and bad
            2. Confusion over praise and blame
            3. Abandoning an objection to this
            4. The necessity of a faulty support
    4. The practice of controlling the mind

---

4. Detailed explanation of the practices related to application

   1. How to accomplish the practice
   2. Controlling the mind for practice

1. How to accomplish the practice

   1. General statement
   2. The practice for the benefit and happiness of others

3. Taking on all faults
4. Completely taking a lowly status for the benefit of others
5. Concise summary of the practice: accepting harm
6. Correctly protecting the mind[9]

1. General statement

> 8.159
> On the lookout for others,
> If you see something on the self's body,
> Steal it from him
> And use it to benefit others.

The practice for one's own stream of being is to give to others whatever makes them happy. [375]

2. The practice for the benefit and happiness of others

> 8.160
> 'I am happy but others are unhappy.
> I have a high status but others are low.
> I help myself but never others.'
> Why am I not envious of myself?

One cannot bear to have respect or happiness for oneself, so one practises giving help and happiness to others.

3. Taking on all faults

> 8.161
> I will go without my own happiness,
> And instead take on the sufferings of others.
> I will examine my own faults, thinking,
> 'What should I do here?'

> 8.162
> Although others have their faults,
> I will treat them as my own faults but,
> When I do something even slightly at fault,
> I will admit it openly.

These verses taken in pairs of two lines indicate taking sufferings onto oneself, examining one's own faults, seeing the faults of others but treating them as one's own and confessing one's own faults.

4. Completely taking a lowly status for the benefit of others

> 8.163
> Letting the reputations of others
> Eclipse my own,
> I will work for the benefit of all
> Like the lowliest servant.

> 8.164
> Imperfection is in my nature,
> So don't praise me for some accidental quality.
> Should I even have such a quality,
> Nobody needs to know about it.

These verses taken in pairs of two lines indicate drawing attention to the reputation of others, working for others, giving up conceit in one's own qualities and not drawing attention to one's own qualities.

5. Concise summary of the practice: accepting harm

> 8.165
> In short, let whatever harm
> You have selfishly inflicted on others
> Fall upon yourself
> For the sake of sentient beings.

The one who has harmed others for his own benefit in the past should take harm onto himself for the benefit of others.

6. Correctly protecting the mind

> 8.166
> Don't be overbearing,
> With an arrogant manner.
> Have manners like a new bride:
> Be modest, apprehensive and restrained.

Develop the antidotes to an unrestrained and overbearing attitude, like that of a mighty ruler. Completely subdue the mind with such antidotes.

2. Controlling the mind for practice

1. In respect of subjugating the mind
2. The faults of activities for one's own sake
3. The faults of taking the body as an object of grasping
4. The practice of controlling the mind

1. In respect of subjugating the mind

> 8.167
> That which is to be kept
> And that which is to be avoided
> Should be under your control.
> Transgressions should be subjugated.

If the mind is resistant to the practice, it should be subjugated. The first line indicates that one should practise establishing virtuous dharmas and benefitting sentient beings and the mind is to be under one's control in accord with this. The second line indicates abandoning nonvirtue in respect of the morality of vows, which should also be under control. The third line indicates establishing these three trainings and [376] maintaining conditions which are physically conducive [to the trainings], etc.[10] Transgressions of the three trainings should be subjugated. How will they be subjugated?

> 8.168
> Despite being given such advice,
> If you, mind, do not practise accordingly,
> You will be the source of the faults,
> So it is you who will be subjugated.

Having been given such advice, one should maintain control over the mind. If you, mind, do not practise accordingly, you will be subjugated, i.e. your compliance will be compelled by antidotes. Why? Because it is you who are the source of the faults. In what way?

2. The faults of activities for one's sake

   1. Recalling the meaningless actions of the past
   2. Not giving away any control
   3. The practice of abandonment
   4. The fault of not abandoning
   5. Contemplating the faults of that

1. Recalling the meaningless actions of the past

> **8.169**
> **Though you have destroyed me,**
> **That is in the past. That time is over.**
> **Now I have seen you,**

In the past, self-grasping ('you') has led one to destruction in places such as the hells, but now that time is over, for now one can see the faults of such destruction.

2. Not giving away any control

> **…where can you go?**
> **I am going to completely crush your arrogance.**

'Where can you go' means to be given no chances. The second line indicates the manner of being giving no chances.

3. The practice of abandonment

> **8.170**
> **Also, give up any idea**
> **Of benefitting yourself.**
> **Since I have handed you over to others,**
> **Stop complaining and get to work.**

The first two lines indicate giving up self-benefit. The second two lines indicate applying oneself to the benefit of others.

4. The fault of not abandoning

8.171
In case I lose concern
And fail to hand you over to sentient beings,
Then no doubt you will hand me over
To the guardians of hell.

To lose concern means not to control the mind with the antidotes.

5. Contemplating the faults of that, i.e. applying the conditions for subjugation

8.172
That is how you have betrayed me before:
Handing me over to long-lasting misery.
Recalling my past resentments,
I will crush you, selfish mind.

8.173
If I want joy,
I should not pursue my own joy.
If I want protection,
I should always protect others.

The first two lines indicate the faults of self-grasping; the second two indicate the outlook which is incompatible with that; the next two are a reflection on abandoning joy for oneself; the last two summarize the application of practising for others.

2. The fault of taking the body as an object of such grasping in order to establish that selfish conduct is illogical

1. Dissatisfaction
2. Immobility
3. Confusion

1. Dissatisfaction [377]

1. The faults of dissatisfaction, the principal point
2. The qualities of satisfaction, the secondary point

1. The faults of dissatisfaction

Sensitivity to harm increases:

> 8.174
> The more I look after
> This body,
> The more sensitive
> It becomes.

There is no satisfaction of desires:

> 8.175
> Having become so sensitive,
> The whole world will not be enough
> To fulfil its wishes,
> So who could give it what it wants?

By pursuing one's desires, the mind deteriorates:

> 8.176
> Unable to get what it wants,
> The defilements grow and the mind deteriorates

2. The qualities of satisfaction

> But, for someone who does not need anything,
> There is no end to his riches.
>
> 8.177
> Therefore, I should not allow opportunities
> For the body's desires to grow.
> Not grasping attractive objects—
> That is the best possession to have.

2. Immobility

> 8.178
> In the end, this unclean form

> Cannot prevent itself turning to dust.
> Unable to move and moved only by others—
> Why grasp that as 'me'?
>
> 8.179
> What use is this contraption to me,
> Living or dead?
> What is special about this particular lump?
> Why don't I overcome pride?

Turning to dust in the end is impermanence. 'Unclean' means emitting a foul smell. The inability to move means being material. Being moved by others means being intentionally moved. 'Living or dead' means the material substance is separate from mind. 'Pride' means having conceit in self and not holding onto that.

3. Confusion

   1. Confusion over good and bad
   2. Confusion over praise and blame
   3. Abandoning an objection to this
   4. The necessity of a faulty support

1. Confusion over good and bad

> 8.180
> By cherishing the body,
> I have gathered suffering for no purpose,
> So why have attachment and aggression
> Over something indistinguishable from a block of wood?

'For no purpose' means that although one maintains the body, it is not a source of happiness.

> 8.181
> Whether I am attending to its needs
> Or it is being eaten by the vultures, etc.
> It feels neither attachment nor anger,
> And yet I have attachment to it.

Though one attends to its needs, it has no attachment and yet one has attachment oneself. Attachment to what? To this material that is no different to a block of wood, except for being fit to be eaten by vultures. If it has no anger about that, why does one get angry by its being harmed? Therefore, it is the same as a block of wood.

2. Confusion over praise and blame

> **8.182**
> **If it feels no**
> **Anger when criticized**
> **Nor happiness when praised,**
> **What am I tiring myself out for?**

If something feels no anger when criticized, nor feels happiness when praised, what purpose does it serve to tire oneself out for that?

3. Abandoning an objection to this

'Although the body itself has neither happiness nor unhappiness, [378] it is the mind that creates the thought of self which has happiness. Therefore, praising the body makes the mind happy.'

> **8.183**
> **'I am attached to this body**
> **Because I am close to it.'**

Response: If that is the case, one's enemies having attachment to their bodies also satisfies this criterion, so one should also be joyful when they are praised:

> **Since everyone is attached to their own body,**
> **Why have I no joy for them?**

4. The necessity of a faulty support

> **8.184**
> **Therefore, I will give up this body**
> **Without any attachment for the benefit of beings.**
> **Therefore, though it has many faults,**

> I will keep it for use in this work.

'For use in this work' means that just as a farmer uses base substances in order to complete his work, so one keeps the body for use in one's work.

4. The practice of controlling the mind

Abandoning incompatible factors:

> **8.185**
> **Therefore, no more childish behaviour.**
> **I will follow the wise—**
> **Remembering their words on concern,**
> **I will fight off sleep and lethargy.**

Relying on conducive factors:

> **8.186**
> **Like the great, compassionate sons of the conquerors,**
> **I will bear whatever must be done.**
> **If I don't work at this night and day,**
> **When will my suffering ever end?**

Focussing on meditation:

> **8.187**
> **Therefore, in order to dispel the obscurations,**
> **I will withdraw my mind from its mistaken ways,**
> **And continually rest in equipoise**
> **Upon the perfect object.**

Chapter 9
WISDOM

1. Explaining that wisdom is the principal [v1]
2. It is the wisdom of the emptiness of intrinsic nature [v2-56]
3. How to engage in meditation on emptiness [v57-110]
4. Ceasing to grasp at true existence [v111-150]
5. The result of meditation on emptiness [v151-167]

1. Explaining that wisdom is the principal

1. The reason wisdom is the principal
2. Advice to strive in this

1. The reason wisdom is the principal

> **9.1**
> **All of these factors were taught**
> **By the Sage for the sake of wisdom.**

The other five perfections, or five aspects of skilful means, have now been presented. They are called here 'factors', i.e. causes of wisdom, since wisdom develops by meditating on the first five perfections. Or, whilst wisdom is the antidote to saṃsāra and the defilements, the other perfections act as helpers. 'For the sake of wisdom' means in order to develop it. [379]

2. Advice to strive in this

> **Therefore, those who wish to pacify sufferings**
> **Should develop wisdom.**

Since only wisdom can overcome attachment to existence, the root of suffering, it should be developed.

2. It is the wisdom of the emptiness of intrinsic nature

1. Establishing the object as empty
2. Establishing the subject as the path

1. Establishing the object as empty

1. The nature of the two truths in our tradition
2. Abandoning objections[1]

Section overview: The nature of the two truths in our tradition [v2-5]

1. Distinguishing the two truths
    1. Basis of the distinction
    2. Meaning of the distinction
    3. Ascertaining the number
    4. Definitions
2. Their characteristics
3. The valid cognitions which ascertain those characteristics
    1. Distinguishing the types of conceptual thought
    2. The graduations of refuter
    3. Abandoning objections about these [graduations]
        1. Abandoning the objection that practice is meaningless
        2. Abandoning the objection that there are no distinctions in understanding

---

1. The nature of the two truths in our tradition

1. Distinguishing the two truths
2. Their characteristics
3. The valid cognitions which correctly ascertain those characteristics

1. Distinguishing the two truths

1. Basis of the distinction
2. Meaning of the distinction

3. Ascertaining the number
4. Definitions

9.2
Relative and ultimate:
These are asserted as the two truths.

1. Basis of the distinction

The basis is mere cognoscibility. Since the ultimate is how cognizables really are and the relative is how they seem to be, both are pervaded by mere cognoscibility.

2. Meaning of the distinction

The two truths are not distinct entities because, if they were:

- The two truths would not be dharma-possessors [*chos can*] and the true nature of dharmas themselves [*chos nyid*].
- Deluded perceptual attributes would not be overcome by the ultimate realization of emptiness.
- The complete non-establishment of the relative would not be ultimate.
- The defilements and their complete purification could be simultaneous.

Yet, they are not completely indistinct because, if they were:

- In seeing the relative, one would see truth.
- Likewise for the ultimate: the relative would be inseparable from it.
- Just as the relative is obscured perception, so the ultimate would also be obscured perception.
- Just as the relative is not to be found anywhere other than in seeing and hearing, likewise the ultimate would also not be found anywhere else. [380]

Nor are they distinct dharmas which have an identical nature or substance, like the impermanence and composition of a vase, because the ultimate is not established as a substance. What are they then?

They are like hairs appearing to pass across the sky and one thinking they are external. In this way, one cannot express the meaning of the distinction between the two truths as either identity or complete difference.[2]

3. Ascertaining the number

It is certain that truth and falsity are mutually exclusive. It is false that one can establish the existence of objects of conceptual discrimination with valid cognition. This is the relative. It is true that one can negate the existence of objects of conceptual discrimination with valid cognition. This is ultimate truth. Therefore, there are only two truths.

4. Definitions

- 'Relative': the obscured objects of deluded conceptual thought.
- 'Relative truth': the deluded perspective which takes those objects as true.[3]
- 'Ultimate': a sought after and undeceiving pure cognition.
- 'Ultimate truth': the unelaborated dharmadhātu, which is true from the perspective of realization.

2. Their essential characteristics

Ultimate truth is completely empty of deluded perceptions. Any kind of positive claim about it as existent, nonexistent, both, or neither, is a perception of deluded conceptual thought. Being completely distinct from that, it is unelaborated. The relative, appearing but untrue from the perspective of realization, is the perception of erroneous conceptual thought.

3. The valid cognitions which ascertain those characteristics

The unelaborated ultimate is a cognition that sees reality with yogic direct perception by not seeing anything. It is ascertained by the elimination of objects to be negated with inferential reasoning cutting off elaborations. [381] The illusion-like relative is ascertained by conventional valid cognition in mere appearances and by the negation of untrue appearances with inferential reasoning that cuts off elaborations upon truth.[4] These characteristics are explained in the root text as follows:

> The ultimate is not within the domain of conceptual thought.
> Conceptual thought is said to be relative.

This section is explained by some[5] as follows:

1. Distinguishing the types of conceptual thought
2. The graduations of refuter
3. Abandoning objections about these graduations

1. Distinguishing the types of conceptual thought

> 9.3
> We can see two types of people:
> Yogins and ordinary people.

'Yogins' are stream-entrants and those on the first bhūmi and above, who have achieved transcendental wisdom. 'Ordinary people' are those who have not seen reality—both the non-Buddhists, such as the followers of Kapila,[6] and ordinary Buddhists.

2. The graduations of refuter

> Ordinary, worldly people
> Are opposed by worldly yogins.

Worldly ones, such as those who hold the view of self, are opposed by those who, with the direct perception which sees non-self, cognize it is not true. Among these, ordinary worldly people are opposed by 'worldly yogins', i.e. śrāvaka yogins who see the self of dharmas. They in turn are opposed by the insight of yogins who see the non-self of subject and object—those who have the vision of mere discriminating awareness. They are opposed in turn by those [Madhyamaka yogins] who have the wisdom without dualistic appearances.[7]

> 9.4
> Yogins, too, have distinct conceptual thought,
> With higher and higher objectors,

Why are ordinary people, who do not see reality, opposed by those with higher minds? It is because of the ascertainments of inferential reasoning made with those higher minds. Their inferential reasoning which refutes the self of the individual ascertains that the self and so forth, conceived of as objects by ordinary minds, are not established and their inferential reasoning which refutes the self of dharmas ascertains that there is no subject, object, nor mere discriminating awareness. How are these refutations made?

Both agreeing upon examples,

[382] An agreement is established for both the proponent and the objector that reflections, etc. are free from singularity and multiplicity. For freedom from singularity and multiplicity, the pervasion by essencelessness[8] is ascertained to establish their essencelessness and thus agree on this. By the positive establishment that appearances possess different parts, a partless singularity and multiplicity are eliminated. Thus, freedom from singularity and multiplicity is established. Thus, the qualification[9] and pervasion are ascertained. As it is said:

> It is because of their freedom from singularity and multiplicity
> That they are without intrinsic nature, like reflections.[10]

In this way, objections are based on inferential reasoning in dependence upon an example.[11]

3. Abandoning objections

'It is established that all conceptual thought—that of yogins and that of ordinary people—is deluded in regard to the nature of the relative and that there are objections between them. But if it established that all conceptual thought is deluded, those yogins who have exhausted delusion must have abandoned all conceptual thought by their ultimate realization of reality.'

And not analysing for the sake of the result.

They do not abandon conceptual thought because they do not analyse, i.e. if one does not examine the conceptual thought, one will not abandon pleasant appearances. Why do they not analyse? To achieve results such as the perfection of the accumulations and the benefit of others.

'Is it not a contradiction to say one can comprehend deluded appearances?'

There is no contradiction, for there are 'agreed upon examples', i.e. just as the proponent and objector are not in contradiction that reflections are the comprehension of untrue appearances, similarly, for the yogin, there is the comprehension of appearances as untrue.

'In that case, it follows that yogins and ordinary people are undifferentiated in their understanding. That is to say, do deluded appearances not exist equally for both?'

There is a difference regarding the existence and nonexistence of attachment to their reality [383]:

> 9.5
> Worldly people see existent objects
> And discriminate them as reality,
> Not as illusion-like. Therefore, on this,
> Yogins and worldly people are in dispute.

This is how verses 3-5 are explained by some.[12] However, it is not correct. It suggests that yogins see truth but ordinary people do not see truth[13] but that is inconsistent with line 5d, which refers to a proponent and objector being in dispute, i.e. the objections between them are not direct perceptions but are inferential.

There are no inferential objections regarding the 'examples accepted by both', for how could there be any such objections, either between the conceptual thought of yogins and ordinary beings, or between the conceptual thought of superior yogins and ordinary yogins? They are both in agreement on the examples, so there are no differences in this regard.

The objections of the conceptual thought of superior yogins are not direct perceptions, either. If they were, it would be unreasonable for proponents of wisdom without dualistic appearances [i.e. Mādhyamikas] to express any objections towards those who see subject and object as mere discriminating awareness [i.e.

Vijñaptimātrins] because, concerning the distinction between Mahāyāna Mādhyamikas and proponents of mere discriminating awareness, for those who have newly entered the vehicle, there are no differences amongst them in terms of their seeing truth, so a disputer and the disputee cannot be distinguished.[14]

Verses 3-5 are correctly explained this way:

1. Distinguishing the types of conceptual thought
2. The graduations of refuter
3. Abandoning objections about these graduations

1. Distinguishing the types of conceptual thought

> **9.3**
> **We can see two types of people:**
> **Yogins and ordinary people.**

Yogins are those who accept the textual tradition sealed by the words of the Sugata. Ordinary people are tīrthikas, who assert the doctrine of self, and other ordinary people. [384]

2. The graduations of refuter

> **Ordinary, worldly people**
> **Are opposed by worldly yogins.**

Worldly people and non-Buddhists grasp many tiny atoms as a composite whole and take the stream of instants of cognition as a unified continuity. Since they are grasping at permanence, worldly yogins are opposed to them. These are śrāvakas who, with lower conceptual thought, have established tiny atoms and momentary instants of grasping. Furthermore, if one wonders whether there are objections among the conceptual thoughts of yogins, such as the śrāvakas:

> **9.4**
> **Yogins, too, have distinct conceptual thought,**
> **With higher and higher objectors,**

The Vaibhāṣikas hold the position that in the appearance of a blue object, cognition and object are connected without an intervening representation. They are opposed by the Sautrāntika yogins with arguments such as the ascertainment of simultaneous perception.[15]

The Sautrāntikas hold that all appearances are mental representations and so they are representationalists, asserting that representations take on the shape of outer objects like reflections within a mirror. These proponents of the reality of external perceptual objects are opposed by Cittamātrin yogins who argue that if atoms were partless, they would all be combined with a central atom, so it would follow that the edges of the atoms would form a whole unified mass. Since this would constitute an agglomeration extending in all directions, there can be no partless atoms. Thus, they refute the possibility of subtle particles forming gross substances. They also object to the Sautrāntikas with a refutation of the essential characteristics of the object resembling its product.[16]

The True Representationalists[17] claim that the true nature of everything is mind. The proponents of the doctrine of the reality of individual moments of cognition like a pure crystal [i.e. False Representationalists] object to them by saying that since there are many connected representations, there cannot be a single, partless cognition of them. [385]

The Madhyamaka yogins object to them, arguing if each moment of cognition were not comprised of many parts, it would follow that its earlier and later instants would be one, such that even an aeon would be indistinguishable from an instant. Seeing the relation between many such instants, they argue that there cannot be an indivisible moment.

Who is it that understands arguments such as these?

Both agreeing upon examples,

Both proponent and objector accept examples such as reflections in a mirror.

An extensive explanation of the differences among the conceptual thought of the [Buddhist] yogins will be given below [v6-56]. The objections to ordinary ones [i.e. non-Buddhists] will be taught in detail in the sections on the non-self of the individual [v57-110] and on the ceasing of grasping at existence [v111-150].[18]

'Are these refutations true in the Madhyamaka tradition or not? If the refutations are true, there is an infinite regress. If the refutations are not true, the Madhyamaka arguments would then be established as true, so there would be no delusion in such conceptual thought, and yet your position is that all conceptual thought is established as relative. This is a fault.'

For Mādhyamikas, although for any assertion put forth, there is a refutation, nevertheless, it is not correct to assert emptiness. As it says,

> If the empty slightly existed,
> The non-empty would have to slightly exist.
> If the non-empty slightly existed,
> Emptiness would also exist.
>
> The emptiness of the conquerors
> Truly delivers one from all views.
> Whoever holds a view of emptiness
> Will not attain accomplishment.[19]

Therefore, in the Madhyamaka, since no assertion is made, there are no refutations and therefore no infinite regress. There being no assertions, no objects of conceptual thought are established and therefore there is no erroneous consequence [386] that there could be a position with no refutation. Furthermore:

> Not establishing any side as existent,
> Nonexistent, or both,
> Although they may try,
> It is not possible to be disputed in any way.[20]

3. Abandoning objections about these graduations

1. Abandoning the objection that practice is meaningless
2. Abandoning the objection that there are no distinctions in understanding

1. Practice is meaningless

'If all conceptual thought is deluded, the continuity of bodhisattva conduct such as giving by yogins who are free from conceptual elaborations would cease, because for one who makes no assertions whatsoever, all conceptual engagements are delusions.'

And not analysing for the sake of the result.

Although practising the completion of the accumulations in order to attain the result—buddhahood—is an untrue cognition, appearances are left unexamined, i.e. they are not analysed.

'If the accumulations are made for the sake of untrue appearances, why gather them?'

For example, just as one would manifest an illusory army for the sake of those who are to be freed from external objects, likewise for the sake of benefitting sentient beings, one does not reject appearances:

> For example, like destroying illusory demons,
> One should work with apparitions for the sake of liberation.[21]

There are similar teachings in the *Mahāyānasūtrālaṃkāra*.

Is it not a contradiction for an appearance to be untrue? There is no contradiction, for the appearances are like illusions, i.e. examples accepted by both [proponent and objector].

2. Abandoning the objection that there are no distinctions in understanding

'It follows that since they have not abandoned the conceptual thought which has appearances, even the higher yogins are not different to worldly ones.'

There is a difference:

9.5
Worldly people see existent objects
And discriminate them as reality,
Not as illusion-like. Therefore, on this,

Yogins and worldly people are in dispute.

Worldly people see existent objects with a non-comprehending cognition. Those who have such conceptual discrimination [387] conceptualize reality without understanding it as illusion-like. Yogins are distinct from this because they have such illusion-like understanding. Therefore, yogins and worldly people are in dispute, since the worldly cling to reality while yogins inferentially refute truly existent objects.

2. Abandoning objections by those who cling to reality

Most of the Tibetan Geshes, such as Geshe [Ngok] Lotsawa, explain this in two sections:

1. Abandoning objections from the relative perspective
2. Abandoning objections from the ultimate perspective

However, this is not correct. If the 'relative perspective' is what Mādhyamikas mean by 'relative', then the second section also concerns the relative, so it would be part of the same section. If realists accepted this as relative, they would be in agreement with Madhyamaka and there would be no objections. Similarly with the latter section: if the 'ultimate perspective' is what realists mean by 'ultimate', then the first section is also ultimate. If Mādhyamikas accepted this as ultimate, there would be no objections. Therefore, this whole section takes the perspective of what is relative for Mādhyamikas and ultimate for realists. Thus, it simply concerns the objections raised by realists and the abandoning of them:

> Section overview: Abandoning objections [v6-29]
>
> 1. Abandoning the objections of Vaibhāṣikas
>   1. Abandoning arguments of contradiction with valid cognition
>   2. Abandoning objections of contradiction with the textual tradition of the Bhagavān
> 2. Abandoning objections of Sautrāntikas
>   1. To do with the bases of accumulation
>   2. To do with rebirth
>   3. To do with karma
>   4. To do with the distinction between saṃsāra and nirvāṇa
> 3. Abandoning objections of the Vijñaptimātrins
>   (cont.)

1. Abandoning the objections of Vaibhāṣikas
2. Abandoning the objections of Sautrāntikas
3. Abandoning the objections of the Vijñaptimātrins

1. Abandoning the objections of Vaibhāṣikas

The Vaibhāṣikas assert there are five bases of cognizables such as form, which are established as ultimate with valid cognition.

1. Abandoning objections of contradiction with valid cognition [388]
2. Abandoning objections of contradiction with the textual tradition of the Bhagavān

1. Abandoning objections of contradiction with valid cognition

9.6
**Although there is direct perception of forms and so forth,
That is a consensus, not a valid cognition.
It is a delusion to accord with a consensus
Such as that something unclean is clean.**

'You claim existent objects are not truly established, but we establish by direct perception the ultimate existence of the five bases, such as forms.'

This is existence by consensus, not by valid cognition. Although forms and so forth appear to be direct perceptions, such direct perceptions are designated by conceptual discrimination, just as appearances are only established by relative consensus and not by valid cognition of the ultimate. How so? In the direct perception of a vase, one cannot see the vase without seeing its interior or exterior etc. These conditions for what counts as 'seeing a vase' are a consensus in the world. It is similar with forms such as the so-called 'silent subtle atoms of the eight substances': we accept them, yet they are colourless and are not seen with the eyes. They only appear to the understanding and are established by consensus.

Is this consensus ultimate reality? No, it is a delusion. For example, it is according to consensus that something unclean is clean and so forth.

2. Abandoning contradiction with the textual tradition of the Bhagavān

9.7
For the sake of introducing the worldly,
The protector taught in terms of existence. In suchness,
There is no momentariness.

'If everything is without reality, this would contradict the Bhagavān's teachings that the skandhas and so forth exist.'

This is an intentional teaching. 'Intentional' means it has three factors: an intention, an intentional basis and a valid cognition which refutes the literal meaning.[22] What is the intention? The Protector taught existence to allow worldly people to enter into the teachings. What is the intentional basis? [389] Relative existence. What is the valid cognition which refutes the literal meaning? [The following syllogism:]

The skandhas and so forth are the logical subject. The probandum: they are 'not really existent' and are 'not ultimate'. The reason: there is no momentariness, so what need to mention a corporeal existence? That is to say, there is not even an infinitesimal moment, so there cannot be something which is a composition of many of them. There is no single instant because it would comprise three parts—beginning, middle and end. If there were not these three parts, earlier and later would occur at the same instant and it would follow that even an aeon could be called an 'instant'. As it says in the *Ratnāvali*,

> Since an instant ends,
> It must have a beginning and a middle.
> Because of this triple nature of each instant,
> The world never abides for an instant.[23]

'If momentariness is not ultimate, it must be completely nonexistent, for it is neither of the two truths: you Mādhyamikas do not allow moments as ultimate, for you do not allow an aggregate of past, present and future as ultimate, i.e. you do not allow a three-fold reality. Nor do you allow momentariness to be relative, for the relative appears even to the worldly and the worldly do not see the appearance of momentariness.'

'This is incompatible with relative truth.'

An aggregate of past, present and future is not ultimate but it is relative. There are two relatives: this is not the relative which is the conceptual thought of ordinary people, so there is no error. It is the relative of yogins. Since it is an object of the direct perception of yogins who see the truth and an object of analytical inference, it exists in the sense of appearing in that conceptual thought and hence there is no contradiction:

9.8
There is no error, for it is the yogin's relative.

'There is a contradiction because śrāvakas who see momentariness are taught to be seeing truth.'

In comparison to the worldly, it is seeing reality.

The claim that to see momentariness is to see reality means to see how things are in comparison to the deluded conceptual thought of worldly people.

'The only relative is the worldly relative, for the ultimate is the only object of yogins. You cannot say there is a "yogin's relative".'

> Otherwise, the ascertainment that women are impure
> Would be refuted by the worldly.

We assert that there is a yogin's relative. If one asserted the alternative position—that 'relative' means only the relative of worldly people—then the yogin's conception of the impurity of women as relative would be refuted by the relative of those worldly people.

2. Abandoning the objections of Sautrāntikas

According to the explanations of the learned commentators, the Vaibhāṣikas believe that the Buddha has cognition of the relative, since he has mastered the ten knowledges which are relative, while the Sautrāntikas assert that all nirvāṇic perceptions are ultimate. However, they both hold the position that all perceptions based on defilements are relative and therefore they both accept the following objections of the Sautrāntikas.

1. To do with the bases of accumulation
2. To do with rebirth
3. To do with karma [391]
4. To do with the distinction between saṃsāra and nirvāṇa

1. To do with the bases of accumulation

'If everything is only a falsity, like an illusion, then making offerings to the Conqueror would not be meritorious, for the Conqueror would also be illusion-like.'

9.9
> The merit in relation to the illusion-like Conqueror
> Is just as if he really existed.

The cause of the arising of merit in relation to your real Buddha is the power of your faith in him. Just as faith arises for your truly existent Conqueror, so it also arises for the illusion-like one. It follows that his true existence is not the basis of merit.

2. To do with rebirth

Objection:

> 'If sentient beings are illusory,
> How are they reborn after death?'

'Sentient beings are the logical subject. If they were illusion-like, it would follow that there is no inner self to connect present and future lives, like illusionists conjuring up illusory snakes, etc.'

Response:

> **9.10**
> **For as long as the conditions are assembled,**
> **Even an illusion will continue to arise.**

When the conditions are assembled, there is no contradiction to something arising, even if it is illusion-like. That which is illusion-like is not pervaded by non-rebirth. Therefore, the pervasion[24] is not established.

'Since they persist for as long as the conditions exist and these conditions have existed for a long time, it follows that sentient beings must exist in truth.'

> **How could sentient beings really be existent**
> **Just because their continuity lasts for a long time?**

A stream of being that persists from birth for a long time is not pervaded by being existent. Truth and falsity are not determined by a length of time because a year-old illusion can be designated as false while a day-old sentient being [392] can be designated as true. Therefore, future lives, etc. can be connected without being pervaded by existence. The pervasion[25] is not established.

3. To do with karma

'If everything were illusion-like, it would follow that there would be no nonvirtue, such as killing, nor any virtue in doing good. If nonvirtue or virtue existed in illusions, then it would be nonvirtuous to kill a person conjured by an illusionist and virtuous to give him food.'

9.11
When illusory beings are killed,
There is no nonvirtue because they do not have minds.
Merit and nonvirtue originate
With those who possess an illusory mind.

You accept that it is not nonvirtuous to destroy a heap of stones, while it is nonvirtuous to kill a person, for there is a difference in the existence or nonexistence of a mind. Similarly, though we assert that everything is like an illusion, when there is the illusion of mind-possession, we say that there is merit in the giving of food and nonvirtue in killing. If there is no mind, there is no nonvirtue or virtue in such things.

'It is illogical to differentiate those which have a mind from those which do not among illusion-like objects.'

According to the proponents of realism, there are distinct causes for having a mind and not having a mind. Similarly, we also distinguish their distinct causes, only both are illusions:

9.12
Since mantras and so on do not have that power,
Illusory minds do not arise from them.

The implication here is that it is only actions and defilements which have the power to create a mind.

'If mind and non-mind are both illusions, it would contradict the principle that different effects must have different causes.'

In that case, if both are existent, that would also contradict it.

'But one can see their non-contradiction.'

Within illusoriness, too, one can see different effects such as horses and elephants coming from different conditions, so the differentiation of causes and their various effects is not contradicted:

> Having arisen from a variety of conditions,
> Illusions are varied too,

However, whether illusory or real [393], the arising of different effects from unvarying causes is denied:

> **9.13**
> **But nowhere is there a single condition**
> **With the ability to create them all.**

4. Abandoning the objection that it contradicts the presentation of the distinction between saṃsāra and nirvāṇa

> 'The ultimate, nirvāṇa,
> Is saṃsāra in relative truth. In this way,

> **9.14**
> **If he is in saṃsāra despite being a Buddha,**
> **What is the point of the bodhisattva conduct?'**

The following explanation is based on that of Ngok Lotsawa.

The objection: 'The reality of one's own mind is ultimate, which is naturally nirvāṇa even though one has not abandoned relative saṃsāra. If saṃsāra and nirvāṇa are therefore not mutually exclusive, although the Buddha's attainment of buddhahood is nirvāṇa, it follows that it is also saṃsāra because saṃsāra is not distinct from the completely pure nature. According to this position, since the Buddha is in saṃsāra, practising the bodhisattva conduct is meaningless.'

The response: although not distinct from the completely pure nature, in relative truth, saṃsāra and nirvāṇa are distinct. Thus, where is the contradiction? The pervasion[26] is not established. How are they distinguished in relative truth? They are distinguished according to whether or not the adventitious causes of the arising of the defilements have been exhausted:

> If the continuity of conditions is not interrupted,
> Even an illusion will not be dispelled.

This explains how saṃsāra is instigated.

9.15
If the continuity of conditions is interrupted,
It will not arise, even as relative.

This explains how it is reversed. However, this explanation is not very thorough. Now to explain it in accordance with the author of the *Great Commentary*:[27]

The objection: 'Our Sautrāntika school holds that nirvāṇic perception is ultimate and that defiled perception is relative.'

'The ultimate, nirvāṇa,
Is saṃsāra in relative truth. In this way,

9.14
If he is in saṃsāra despite being a Buddha,
What is the point of the bodhisattva conduct?'

'Thus, if nirvāṇa is ultimate and saṃsāra is the elaborations of the relative, [394] are dualistic appearances existent or nonexistent for the Buddha? If nonexistent, it would follow that the Buddha is nonexistent or an inanimate object.[28] If existent, he is either relative or ultimate. If ultimate, it would contradict your previously stated position that "conceptual thought is said to be relative". If relative, by the existence of the defilements in that relative, it would follow that Buddha is in saṃsāra. Therefore, what would be the point of the bodhisattva conduct?'

The Prāsaṅgika Mādhyamikas claim that the characteristics of relative and ultimate correspond with saṃsāra and nirvāṇa, respectively. Hence, their response is to say that the opponent's premise—that the Buddha has conceptual thought with appearances—is not established in ultimate truth.

If the continuity of conditions is not interrupted,
Even an illusion will not be dispelled.

For example, an illusory snake conjured by an illusionist will last as long as its causes and conditions exist. Similarly, for as long as the causes of perceiving appearances exist, illusion-like conceptual thought has not been abandoned, so saṃsāra exists. However:

9.15
If the continuity of conditions is interrupted,
It will not arise, even as relative.

With the signs of the vajra-like samādhi and the severance of the continuity of all conceptual discrimination, the continuity of the defilements is severed. By that severance, the continuity of actions is severed. By that severance, the continuity of conceptual thought with dualistic appearances is severed, so saṃsāra 'will not arise, even as relative'.

This response is not logical because it would follow that arhats, pratyekabuddhas and bodhisattvas who have attained realization [but not the vajra-like samādhi] remain in saṃsāra. There are other problems, too, and these should be understood in more detail from elsewhere.[29]

How then should this be explained? The objection is the same as above but the response is different.

We[30] do not assert that everything relative is saṃsāra, [395] nor do we assert that all of nirvāṇa is ultimate. Something is classified as ultimate or relative according to whether or not it is immune to analysis. What then is the distinction between saṃsāra and nirvāṇa?

> **If the continuity of conditions is not interrupted,**
> **Even an illusion will not be dispelled.**

9.15
If the continuity of conditions is interrupted,
It will not arise, even as relative.

Though it is illusory, an illusion is not dispelled while the causes and conditions exist. Similarly, saṃsāra is not dispelled while actions and defilements exist. When the continuity of those conditions—actions and the defilements—is cut, saṃsāra will not arise, 'even as relative'—

i.e. even though the Buddha has relative wisdom. This is the explanation of the Svātantrika Mādhyamikas.[31]

3. Abandoning objections of the Vijñaptimātrins[32]

  1. Non-establishment of the subject
  2. Non-establishment of the basis

Section overview: Non-establishment of the subject [v15c-27b]

1. Abandoning objections of the False Representationalists
2. Abandoning objections of the True Representationalists
    1. Objecting that mind is an appearance
        1. Presenting the objection in brief
        2. Establishing pervasion though scriptures
            1. Scriptural reference
            2. An example of the agency of cognition
            3. Conclusion
        3. Settling that with reasoning
            1. Abandoning uncertainty with the illumination of a lamp
            2. Abandoning uncertainty with the spontaneous arising of blue
    2. Rejecting arguments that mind is self-aware
        1. The nonexistence of the general concept
        2. Rejecting the perception of its existence
        3. There is no inference to the conclusion
            1. The error in the reason of the effect
            2. The error in the reason of its intrinsic nature
3. Abandoning objections

---

1. Non-establishment of the subject

  1. Abandoning objections of the False Representationalists
  2. Abandoning objections of the True Representationalists
  3. Abandoning objections

1. Abandoning objections of the False Representationalists

Objection:

'If even delusion does not exist,
What perceives the illusion?'

'You Mādhyamikas say that all dharmas are emptiness. If there is no deluded cognition, there is no perception of the arising of a perceived object. Perception is pervaded by a perceiver but, if for you there is no perceiving mind, what is there to perceive the representations of perceptual objects?'

Response:

**9.16
Since for you the illusion does not exist either,
What do you perceive?**

The False Representationalist denies the illusions exist. Since, for them, mental representations are completely nonexistent and, since perception is pervaded by a perceptual object, it follows that there is no perception, for the perceptual object—the illusion—does not exist. Therefore, their objection is answered with the question, 'Since for you there is no perceptual object—the illusion—what do you perceive?'

2. Abandoning objections of the True Representationalists [396]

1. Objecting that mind is an appearance
2. Rejecting arguments that mind is self-aware

1. Objecting that mind is an appearance

1. Presenting the objection in brief
2. Establishing pervasion though scriptures
3. Settling that with reasoning

1. Presenting the objection in brief

'They exist as if they were external,
But they are representations, which are mind itself.'

'Reality is mind itself.'

Then what is perceived?

'Representations. A representation appears as something distinct but it is mind itself. Thus the perceptual object and the perceiver are not distinct and both exist [as mind itself]. Thus the response that applied to the False Representationalist objection does not apply here.'

The response:

9.17
If the illusion is mind itself,
Then what is seen by what?

If in this way they are not distinct, then what is seen—the object of awareness—and what is the seeing subject—that which has awareness?

The founding lamas have demonstrated this point with proof by svātantras. Though these svātantras are certainly flawless, svātantras, being proofs by the inerrant application of pervasion and qualification, are excessive for the purpose of refutation. Therefore, I shall apply the inerrant deduction by prasaṅga to a 'self-cognizing awareness'.

The Cittamātrin says, 'The cognition of non-dual experience is aware of itself.' From this, it follows that either the cognition is dualistic because it is aware of itself, or it follows that it is not aware of itself because of its non-duality. Both positions [mind is dualistic, mind is not aware of itself] are untenable, for they violate the Cittamātrin's own premises. It is also not possible for the inferences to be unestablished, for both reasons [mind is aware of itself, mind is non-dual] are their own theses.

'The second pervasion[33] is not established.'

Can something be non-dual yet also self-aware? 'Awareness' is essentially characterized by the duality of agent and patient.[34] It is pervaded by these two, like, for example, the chopping of wood with an axe. [397] If mind is non-dual, since there is no agent, the pervasion is established, just as, for example, a sword's blade is unable to cut itself.

2. Showing through the scriptures that the pervasion is established

1. Scriptural reference
2. An example of the agency of cognition
3. Conclusion

1. Scriptural reference

The protector of the world has taught
That mind does not see mind.

This is a reference to the reasoning in the teachings of the protector of the world. What did he teach? In the *Sutra of Ratnacūḍa's Questions* it says,

> When looking for mind, one does not fully see it internally and one does not fully see it externally.[35]

And:

> Is perception something separate from mind? What is perception? It is itself just mind. If a perception was perceived by another mind, there would be two minds. Therefore, if perception is mind itself, how can mind see mind? It is illogical to say that mind sees mind. For example, just as the blade of a sword cannot cut itself and a fingertip cannot touch itself, so mind cannot see itself.[36]

2. An example of the agency of cognition

9.18
Just as the blade of a sword
Cannot cut itself...

3. Conclusion

... so it is with the mind.

3. Settling that with reasoning

  1. Abandoning uncertainty with the illumination of a lamp

2. Abandoning uncertainty with the spontaneous arising of blue [398]

1. Abandoning uncertainty with the illumination of a lamp

> 'It is like a lamp—
> Self-illuminating.'

'You Mādhyamikas have not established with certainty that when there is no duality of agent and patient, there is no awareness. In general, there are many examples where, although there is no agent-patient duality, it appears as if there is agent-patient duality and we refer to it as having such. For example, in a lamp, although there is no duality of agent and patient, its illumination exists. Similarly, in cognition, although there is no duality of agent and patient, awareness exists. Where is the contradiction?'

The response:

> 9.19
> **That lamp could never be illuminated,**
> **For it was never cloaked in darkness.**

Since the lamp is not both the agent and patient of illumination, it is not pervaded by both. While the lamp is an agent of illumination, it is not the patient. Similarly, cognition is pervaded by both agent and patient —that which is aware and that of which it is aware, which cannot be the same thing. If the lamp were itself the illuminated patient, it would have to have been originally pervaded by darkness. It could not then also be the illuminating agent, which was never originally in darkness.

2. Abandoning uncertainty with the spontaneous arising of blue

> 'The blue of a crystal, etc. depends on something external,
> While naturally blue objects do not depend on anything.
>
> 9.20
> Similarly, seeing is in some cases other-dependent,
> And in other cases, independent.'

'Although duality of agent and patient generally exists, there is a counterexample in which there is non-duality. The blueness in something [translucent] like a crystal is seen in dependence on something blue external to it. This is a confirming example in which there is an appearance of duality in something non-dual. Blueness such as that of a lapis lazuli, however, does not depend on anything else. Similarly, in some cases, the object of awareness is something external, upon which the agent awareness depends, while in other cases, it is like the blue object and there is no dependence on an external agent awareness. Thus, not all awareness by seeing is pervaded by a separate agent awareness. By negating that an agent is aware of something external, the pervasion in your refutation of mere awareness is not established.' [399]

The response:

> **Something already blue**
> **Cannot make itself blue.**

A blue object is not pervaded by a distinct agent and patient, for it does not have agent and patient in its intrinsic nature. Why not? If it had agent and patient, it would be necessary for it to be non-blue at first and then subsequently become blue, but that is not the case here. Therefore, by negating a distinct agent and patient, blue [as a counterexample] is refuted. The presentation of a mere object is not the same as something having the characteristics of agent and patient.

2. Rejecting arguments that mind is self-aware of its own stream of being

  1. The nonexistence of the general concept
  2. Rejecting the perception of its existence
  3. There is no inference to the conclusion

1. The nonexistence of the general concept

> **9.21**
> **A lamp, when cognized by cognition,**
> **May be designated 'the illuminator',**
> **But what do you claim cognizes**

The mind as 'self-luminous?'

It is reasonable to say that a lamp, as an object of awareness, is established as illuminated by the direct perception of someone possessing a discriminating mind, who can designate it as such. But this is incompatible with the self-knowing illuminating cognition mentioned above. That is knowledge by awareness of other, from which it follows that there would be both subject and object. By this error, the conclusion of self-awareness is not warranted and is incompatible. Thus, it is illogical to designate such knowledge 'self-cognizing awareness'.

2. Rejecting the perception of its existence

> **9.22**
> **If it is not seen by anyone,**
> **Then whether it is luminous or not**
> **Is like the looks of a barren woman's daughter—**
> **Discussing it is meaningless.**

In particular, it is meaningless to discuss whether it is luminous or not, for there can be no ascertainment of it in anyone's understanding. Why? Because the general concept of 'self-awareness' lacks an intrinsic nature from which to draw the conclusion. An example of this is the looks of the daughter of a barren woman.

3. There is no inference to the conclusion

  1. The error in the reason of the effect
  2. The error in the reason of its intrinsic nature[37]

1. The error in the reason of the effect

Objection: 'Self-experience is established by inference from its effect. [400] Memory is pervaded by having an experience similar to the remembered object, like remembering an earlier cognition of a blue object. By having a memory of, e.g. one's earlier consciousness of blue, one experiences self-consciousness. This establishes self-consciousness by inference from the effect.'

The reverse pervasion[38] of that is:

9.23
'If self-awareness did not exist,
How could consciousness be remembered?'

'If the cause—self-awareness—did not exist, how could there be the result? Thus, from the reason of the effect—memory—self-awareness is inferred by the reverse pervasion.'

The response: while memory is pervaded merely by having a preceding experience, it is not pervaded by self-experience, i.e. a memory comes from a separate experience connected with it. It is connected but is a separate experience.

> Memory comes from its connection to another experience,
> Like deducing a rat bite from an infection.

An example is the poison of rat. Although one may not notice a rat bite which leads to an infection, one experiences a sensation of burning and, by connecting that to a rat's poison, one becomes aware of the cause. Similarly, in remembering one's earlier consciousness, although that consciousness itself is not experienced again, one experiences an object connected with it, and the memory arises in one's cognition. Where is the contradiction? Thus, the pervasion[39] is not established.

2. The error in the reason of its intrinsic nature

Some explain the objection this way: 'Through having cultivated the conditions of meditation, some are able to see the existence of distant objects, such as the minds of others who are far away. Therefore one may illuminate one's own cognition, which is very near.'

9.24
'Since under the right conditions the mind can see
That of others, how can it not see itself?'

This logic is not certain, for it may be criticized as follows: if seeing something far were pervaded by seeing what is near, then if one saw a vase deep beneath the ground with an eye to which a magical eye lotion had been applied, it would follow that the eye, which is near, would also be seen. Yet, although one may see distant objects, one will not see the eye itself, smeared with eye lotion. Seeing far is not pervaded by seeing self and [401] so the reason is not certain:

> **Through applying the eye lotion of accomplishment,**
> **One will see a vase and not the eye lotion itself.**

Others explain this verse as follows: 'The logical subject is a manifest object such as a blue object. This manifestation has the nature of cognition because the condition for such manifestations is either a cognitive condition, such as a sense power, or a mental condition, such as an inferential faculty. The pervasion is established, i.e. whatever arises merely from a cognitive condition is pervaded by the nature of cognition. Therefore, manifest objects are established as self-illuminated.' Thus, it is objected:

9.24
'Since under the right conditions the mind can see
That of others, how can it not see itself?'

In that case, it would follow that when the eye is smeared with magical eye lotion, the manifestation of the underground vase would also have the nature of an eye smeared with magical eye lotion because of its arising as a manifestation from that optical condition. If arising as a manifestation from an optical condition is not pervaded by the nature of the eye, arising as a manifestation from a cognitive condition is not pervaded by the nature of cognition, so the pervasion is not established:

> **Through applying the eye lotion of accomplishment,**
> **One will see a vase and not the eye lotion itself.**

We may add that if the object—the blue manifestation—is established as having the nature of cognition by its manifestation from a cognitive condition, then the underground vase, being a manifestation from an eye lotion-condition, would also have the nature of eye lotion. If the vase does not have the same nature as eye lotion even though it is a manifestation from an eye lotion-condition, then likewise, the manifesting blue object would not have the nature of cognition even though it is a manifestation from the occurrence of a cognitive condition. Thus, self-awareness is not established.

3. Abandoning objections

'If cognitions were not real, there would be no direct perceptions such as seeing, hearing and so forth.'

That is referring to the relative, which we do not deny: [402]

9.25
Cognitions of seeing and hearing
Are not the objects of negation here.

What is it then that is negated? If it is claimed to exist ultimately, that is negated:

Here, we are preventing
The cause of suffering: their discrimination as real.

If seeing and hearing are not negated, how does one cease to grasp them as real?

9.26
Illusions are not other than mind

The proposition that dharmas of sight and sound have a reality distinct from mind is rejected by you Cittamātrins and we agree with you in this.

But you do not think of them as not other.

Yet you do not think of them as 'not other' or as identical, i.e. for you, the position that sights and sounds are identical to mind is an error [because you say representations are truly existent and there is no subject mind]. If you did not think of them as such, you would not grasp them as either true or nonexistent, because of not grasping them dualistically.

If they were real, they would be other than mind but,

If they are not other, they cannot be real.

Your position [that representations are real] is not established. In as far as they are real, they are other than mind. If they are not other, then necessarily they are mind. Since both positions are negated, appearances are established as neither real nor true.

'We assert the False Representationalist Cittamātrin doctrine of the unreality of appearances.'

Showing the error in that doctrine was already completed above.

'If you negate the true existence of mind, you are negating seeing and hearing.'

Although mind is not existent, we do not negate appearances. For example:

9.27
An illusion is not true, yet it is seen.
So it is for the mind which sees.

Just as it is with illusions, so it is for appearances which, when unexamined, are accepted as true.

Some have said that v26-27b is a refutation of the Jaina but this is incorrect. [403] It would be out of context for such a refutation and, moreover, the position refuted does not accord with that of the Jaina.

2. Non-establishment of the basis

1. Presenting the objection
2. The logic which refutes the objection
3. A counter objection
4. Establishing the pervasion for the counter objection

1. Presenting the objection

'Saṃsāra must have an existent basis.

'Just as a pile of stones is the basis for mistakenly thinking there is a person, delusion is pervaded by a basis of delusion. Therefore, because of the existence of the delusion of dual appearances, their non-dual basis—self-awareness—must exist.' This is Ācārya Sthiramati's objection, given as the reason clause of a svātantra.

Otherwise, it would be like space.'

'If there were no basis, it would follow that there would be no deluded appearances.' This is the objection given as a prasaṅga.

2. The logic which refutes the objection

9.28
If the nonexistent were to rest on the existent,
Could it then start to function?

The logical subject is deluded perception, which is nonexistent. By depending on something external which is its existent basis, how can the nonexistent thing have its own function? It follows that it has no function because what is nonexistent is established as having no nature. For example, by the resting of a rabbit's horn on a vase, it would be erroneous to say that the horn could perform functions such as piercing and so on.

It is untenable to say the reason[40] is not established because it is accepted by both of us that the sights and sounds are nonexistent. It is untenable to say that the pervasion[41] is not established, for if it were able to perform a function despite its being nonexistent, it would violate the premise [v27c] 'saṃsāra must have an existent basis', and its functioning would be indistinguishable from that basis.

'The nonexistent thing does not perform any function.'

3. A counter objection

Your mind would be unaided
And completely solitary.

It is illogical that the basis mind is true while the dualistic appearances resting on it are false, for it would follow that this mind of yours is an isolated, non-dual cognition [404] unconnected to the dualistic appearances. If this position is accepted, the objection can be made:

9.29
Being free from dualistic perception,
All would be the Tathāgata.

Since it is free from the impurities of dualistic appearances and the subject-object mind, it would follow that all there would be is buddhahood.

'Although mind is free from the dualistic appearance of subject and object, it has not attained buddhahood. Where is the contradiction? The pervasion[42] is not established.'

4. Establishing the pervasion for the counter objection

So what is achieved
By designating it mind only?

Although everything may be conceived as mere discriminating awareness, if one is not free from the obscurations, it follows that the designations of mind only and freedom from duality would be unnecessary to achieve liberation from saṃsāra. If such designations were necessary, liberation would occur when one conceived of freedom from duality. Therefore, there is no need for the conceptual discrimination of freedom from duality.

Or, these lines may be understood as a response to the opponent saying, 'We accept the consequence that saṃsāra is completely nonexistent.' The designation of mere discriminating awareness was supposed to show the true basis of saṃsāric delusion. If it does not help you establish saṃsāra after all, of what advantage is it to make that designation?

Or, if mind is the Tathāgata from the very beginning, it is meaningless to accomplish buddhahood.

> Chapter overview (recap):
>
> 1. Explaining that wisdom is the principal
> 2. It is the wisdom of the emptiness of intrinsic nature
>   1. Establishing the object as empty
>   1. The nature of the two truths
>   2. Abandoning objections
>   2. Establishing the subject as the path
> 3. How to engage in meditation on emptiness
> 4. Ceasing to grasp at true existence
> 5. The result of meditation on emptiness

2. Establishing the subject as the path

It has been taught elsewhere that this section has the following three parts:

1. Establishing the relative subject as the path
2. Establishing the ultimate subject as the path
3. Conclusion: the function of the two cognitions

However, the first part does not concern establishing the relative subject as the path, [405] for verses 32-34 are not about the relative. If they were, the subsequent verses would also be about the relative and so would not be a distinct section. Therefore:

1. Establishment of subject cognition as the path (the main part)
2. Abandoning the objections of śrāvakas
3. Conclusion: the function of the two cognitions

> Section overview: Establishing subject cognition as the path [v30-39]
>
> 1. Objection
> 2. Response
>   1. A partial knowledge of illusion is not the antidote
>   2. Knowledge that everything is illusion is the antidote
>   1. Abandoning clinging to existence
>   2. Abandoning clinging to nonexistence
>   3. The reason for these
>   3. How that is the arising of the wisdom without dualistic appearances
>   4. Engaging in activity does not depend on effort
>   1. The appearance of the Conqueror's kāya to trainees who have purified their streams of being
>   2. Those appearances engage in benefit
>   3. Abandoning an objection
>   1. Presenting the objection
>   2. Presenting the reason of scriptural citation
>   3. Establishing the pervasion of that

1. Establishing subject cognition as the path

    1. Objection
    2. Response

1. Objection

> **9.30**
> **'How will your illusion-like understanding**
> **End the defilements?**
> **When an apparitional woman is conjured,**
> **Desire for her arises even in her creator.'**

'The knowledge that defiled perceptions are like illusions is not itself an antidote to the defilements. Just as an illusionist knows that the apparitional woman is his own conjuration, nevertheless this knowledge does not function as an antidote to his desire for her.'

2. Response

1. A partial knowledge of illusion is not the antidote
2. Knowledge that everything is illusion is the antidote
3. How that is the arising of the wisdom without dualistic appearances
4. Engaging in activity does not depend on effort

1. A partial knowledge of illusion is not an antidote

If the causes of the defilements—imprints—are not overcome, objects are not overcome. If the causes of the defilements are overcome, objects are overcome. The former occurs when the seeds of the defilements are not abandoned, even though defilements towards objects may not be arising. The latter occurs when the defilements are abandoned by abandoning their seeds.

When it is understood that all objects are illusory, the seeds of the defilements—attachment to reality—are abandoned and the defilements are abandoned. But, if objects are only partially understood as illusory, one has not completely abandoned attachment to their reality and so one has not abandoned the seeds of the defilements. Therefore, the defilements continue to arise:

9.31
That creator has not abandoned the imprints
Of the defilements in her appearance.
Thus, when he sees her,
The imprints of emptiness are weak.

[406] When the creator of the illusion—the illusionist—sees the woman, desire for her arises. Why? Because he has not abandoned clinging to the reality of cognizables. Why not? The imprints of emptiness are weak because karmic formations of perceptual objectification remain. Therefore, a partial understanding of illusion is not the path.

2. Knowledge that everything is illusion is the antidote

1. Abandoning clinging to existence
2. Abandoning clinging to nonexistence
3. The reason for these

1. Abandoning clinging to existence

> **9.32**
> **By meditating on the imprints of emptiness,**
> **The imprints of reality will be abandoned.**

If one meditates on the general concept[43] of emptiness, by the force of its opposition to clinging to existence, clinging to reality ceases.

2. Abandoning clinging to nonexistence

> **By meditating it is nothing whatsoever,**
> **That, too, will then be abandoned,**

The positive determination that something is empty is subsequently abandoned. How? By meditating with no positive or negative determination whatsoever.

How does one abandon the imputation of the positive determination that something is empty?

3. The reason for these

> **9.33**
> **For when one thinks, 'It does not exist',**
> **There is no conception of an analysandum.**
> **Then, its unreality has lost its basis,**
> **So how can it remain before the conceptual mind?**

When their unreality is before the conceptual mind, how can the objects of awareness remain? They cannot. Why? Because they have lost their basis, i.e. the conception of something to be negated, which is the basis of the conception of their negation. With no thought of something to negate, there is no thought of their negation.

If one asks, 'What is it that is nonexistent?', it should be answered, 'This is nonexistent.' But, when no object of negation is identified, one is negating without any qualities to negate, so the negation is not determined. An object to be negated must be identified. But here, no basis—an object to be negated—is conceived. When does this occur?

When one thinks, 'It does not exist', i.e. when the unreality of the analysandum is conceived.[44]

3. How that is the arising of the wisdom without dualistic appearances [407]

> 9.34
> **When neither existence nor nonexistence**
> **Remain before the mind,**
> **Since there is no other category at that time,**
> **There is a complete non-conceptual pacification.**

When existents no longer remain before the mind, the path of realization has not yet been established. It is established only when nonexistents also no longer remain before the mind and there is no establishment of a positive affirmation of nonexistence as an object of understanding. The general concepts of existence and nonexistence do not arise and since there is no attachment to their externality, there is complete pacification in non-conceptualization. With no conceptual imputation, the wisdom without dualistic appearances which cuts the continuity of conceptual discrimination arises.

'Is there not some other kind of imputation, apart from the concepts of existence and nonexistence, that pervades appearances?'

There is no other category because there is no alternative apart from these two—existence and nonexistence.[45]

4. Engaging in activity does not depend on effort

  1. The appearance of the Conqueror's kāya to trainees who have purified their streams of being
  2. Those appearances engage in benefit
  3. Abandoning an objection

1. The appearance of the Conqueror's kāya to trainees who have purified their streams of being

'How is the benefit of others enacted when the wisdom without dualistic appearances is always in equanimity in the emptiness of all dharmas?'

9.35
Just as wish granting jewels and wish fulfilling trees
Fulfil hopes,
So, too, the conquerors appear
By the power of trainees and aspiration prayers.

The saṃbhogakāya appears to those who have mastered the tenth bhūmi and the nirmāṇakāya appears to ordinary individuals. What causes them to arise? They arise by the power of trainees and by the power of former aspiration prayers. How can they appear when they have no conceptual discrimination? In the same way that wish granting jewels and wish fulfilling trees fulfil hopes.

2. Those appearances engage in benefit

9.36
For example, when the creator
Of a shrine of Garuḍa had passed away,
The shrine still pacified poisons and so on,
Long after his death.

9.37
By holding the bodhisattva conduct,
The shrine of the Conqueror is built,
So even after the bodhisattva's nirvāṇa,
The benefit of others continues.

Long ago, when the people of a certain place were afflicted by nāgas, Samgu,[46] who had heard there was a woman in the land of Oḍḍiyāna with mastery of vidya-mantra, set out to visit her. He saw her collecting wood and, doubting her, respectfully asked her [408] about a method to control the nāgas. She proceeded to bless eight handfuls of milk from a black bitch with the vidya-mantra of Garuḍa. Samgu drank seven handfuls of milk but was unable to drink the last handful. Thus, seven of the eight nāgas were controlled but Ananta was not controlled. Although the people were then restored to health, Samgu later died from the afflictions of Ananta. Yet, a shrine he had consecrated with the vidya-mantra continued to pacify afflictions. Thus, just as illnesses, etc. were pacified by the shrine, following the bodhisattva's nirvāṇa, even though his conceptual discrimination has ended, all benefits continue to be performed. If one asks why, it is because by following the bodhisattva conduct—the path of establishing the benefit of others—the shrine of the Conqueror is established.[47]

3. Abandoning an objection

1. Presenting the objection
2. Presenting the reason of scriptural citation
3. Establishing the pervasion of that

1. Presenting the objection

9.38
'How could making offerings to
Someone without a mind have any result?'

'If the Buddha does not have any conceptual discrimination, it follows that the act of presenting offerings to him is without merit because he does not discriminate it.'

2. Presenting the reason of scriptural citation

Although he does not have the discrimination of being pleased by offerings, this does not conflict with the existence of merit, just as there is merit in making offerings to his physical remains after his attainment of complete nirvāṇa, which also have no thoughts. How can this be?

Remaining in the world and passing into nirvāṇa
Were taught to be equivalent.

As it says in the *Affectionate Lion Sutra*,[48]

> Therefore, whether one makes offerings to
> The Buddha who remains in the world
> Or his mortal remains and relics,
> If the intention is the same, the results will be the same.

If one argues that even though this is taught in this scripture, nevertheless, the result is not the same: [409]

3. Establishing the pervasion[49] of that

> **9.39**
> **Whether relative or in suchness,**
> **According to the scriptures, there is a result,**
> **Just as, for example, there is a result**
> **In offering to a real Buddha.**

Our position is that merit is relative, while your position is that it is ultimate. Since we both hold the position that it is established in the scriptures that merit exists, it is true for both of us and thus there is the pervasion.

360 | BODHICARYĀVATĀRA WITH COMMENTARY

> Section overview: Abandoning the objections of śrāvakas [v40-51]
>
> 1. Presenting the objection
> 2. The scriptural criterion for the path
> 3. Establishing the [Mahāyāna] scriptures as Buddha's word
>   1. We have the same criteria for accepting [texts as scriptures]
>   2. We have the same criteria for rejecting [texts as scriptures]
> 4. Establishing them as definitive meaning
>   1. The error for the śrāvaka tradition in the monk who has abandoned defilements
>   2. The error for the śrāvaka tradition in a nirvāṇa in which suffering is abandoned
>   3. Overcoming objections to that
>   1. The existence of the suffering of this life
>   1. Objection
>   2. Response
>   3. Response to a counter objection
>   2. The existence of the suffering of future lives
>   1. Presenting the objection
>   2. The existence of craving itself
>   3. The existence of its cause, sensation
>   4. The logical conclusion
> 5. Summarizing the meaning of this section
> 6. Explaining extensively the criteria for establishing the Mahāyāna scriptures as Buddha's word
>   1. We have the same criteria
>   2. To abandon it because of not understanding it is an error

2. Abandoning the objections of śrāvakas

1. Presenting the objection
2. The scriptural criterion for the path
3. Establishing the [Mahāyāna] scriptures as Buddha's word
4. Establishing them as definitive meaning
5. Summarizing the meaning of this section
6. Explaining extensively the criteria for establishing the Mahāyāna scriptures as Buddha's word[50]

1. Presenting the objection

9.40
**'You will be liberated by seeing truth,
But what is the point of seeing emptiness?'**

Śrāvakas assert the Four Truths:

1. The fourfold truth of suffering: suffering, impermanence, emptiness and non-self
2. The fourfold truth of its origin: origin, cause, arising and conditionality
3. The fourfold truth of cessation: cessation, pacification, joy and renunciation
4. The fourfold truth of the path: path, establishment, reason and certainty

'If one understands the Four Truths of the path and their sixteen aspects, emptiness is already included. Non-self, pacification and cessation are also included. Through cultivating these, nirvāṇa with remainder can be attained. Through cultivating that, nirvāṇa without remainder can be attained. Therefore, this being the path, what is the use of claiming that everything is like an illusion, or that everything in truth is without intrinsic nature, or understanding emptiness without conceptualization or discrimination? That is not the path.'

2. The scriptural criterion for the path

The scriptures teach the path of cultivating an understanding of emptiness:

**The scriptures teach
No enlightenment without this path.**

In the *Perfection of Wisdom* it says, [410] 'If one has a conception of reality, one does not have patience, let alone unsurpassable enlightenment.' It also says, 'Even those who accept the training of the śrāvakas should train in this very *Perfection of Wisdom*', and so forth.[51]

'But the Mahāyāna is not the Buddha's word. It was invented after the Tathāgata's parinirvāṇa. Therefore, the criterion is unsuitable.'

3. Establishing the Mahāyāna scriptures as Buddha's word

1. We have the same criteria for accepting [texts as scriptures]
2. We have the same criteria for rejecting [texts as scriptures]

1. We have the same criteria for accepting [texts as scriptures]

9.41
'The Mahāyāna is not established.'
Why are your scriptures established?
'Because they are established for both.'

How, if the Mahāyāna is not established as the Buddha's word, are your śrāvaka scriptures established as the Buddha's word?

'They are established as the Buddha's word for both the disputer and the respondent.'

In that case, either a) they are established as the Buddha's word for both this disputer and this respondent or else b) they are established as the Buddha's word by the agreement of any two individuals.

If the former, then either a1) they are established as scriptural for you because they have been known as such from the outset or a2) you accepted them as scriptural through logical proof. The first of these is unacceptable:

They were not established for you at first,

Your texts are not automatically known to be scriptural.

If you assert [a2], 'I accepted them through reasoning':

9.42
And whatever conditions gave you confidence in them,
We have them in the Mahāyāna, too.

What are the criteria for accepting something as Buddha's word? If one says it is 'what is included in the sutras, what appears in vinaya and what does not contradict the truth',[52] then that is the same for the Mahāyāna because that also meets these conditions. [411] Therefore, you have no criteria that distinguish only your own texts as the

Buddha's word and which are not met for both the disputer and the respondent.

If you assert [b] that they are the Buddha's word because they are accepted as such by agreement between any two people, then:

> **If truth is the belief of two others,**
> **The Vedas and so forth would also be true.**

In accord with this, since the Vedas and so forth are accepted by two tīrthikas, it would follow that they are also proven to be scriptural.

2. We have the same criteria for rejecting [texts as scriptures]

> **9.43**
> **'But the Mahāyāna is disputed.'**
> **Your scriptures are also in dispute—with those of the tīrthikas,**
> **As well as with the other [śrāvaka] scriptures.**
> **Therefore, you should abandon them.**

Whether or not the Mahāyāna is the Buddha's word, if it should be rejected because it is disputed, other scriptures even among the baskets of the śrāvakas should also be rejected because they are disputed, too. How are they are disputed? For tīrthikas, there is a dispute as to whether or not they are scriptures. Furthermore, disputations exist within the different śrāvaka schools.

4. Establishing [the Mahāyāna scriptures] as definitive meaning

Objection: 'Even if they are Buddha's word, the Mahāyāna is of provisional meaning.'

This is incorrect; the Mahāyāna is of definitive meaning. Conversely, the śrāvaka [vehicle] is of provisional meaning. How so?

1. The error for the śrāvaka tradition in the monk who has abandoned defilements
2. The error for the śrāvaka tradition in a nirvāṇa in which suffering is abandoned
3. Overcoming objections

4. The logical conclusion

1. The error for the śrāvaka tradition in the monk who has abandoned defilements

9.44
'The root of the doctrine is monasticism.'
It is difficult to be such a monk.

There are five classifications of monk:

1. Monk in name only
2. Monk who has taken vows
3. Monk who has taken full ordination
4. Begging monk
5. Arhat

The first four are not what is referred to here; rather, it is the arhat which is referred to, i.e. a monk who has abandoned the defilements. Why is the arhat the root of the doctrine? Because the arhat collects the doctrine, upholds the doctrine, disseminates it and so forth.

Why is this 'difficult' in the śrāvaka tradition? [412] Some say that if they do not meditate upon the emptiness which is the non-self of dharmas, then although there may be no direct causes of the defilements, their seeds still exist, since they still have incorrect mental activity. However, this is not the intended meaning of these lines. Śrāvaka arhats have not merely abandoned the direct causes [but have fully abandoned the defilements]. Otherwise they would not be distinct from the states of freedom from desire attainable on the higher worldly paths.[53] They still have attachment to reality through the obscuration of cognizables, not of defilements. Therefore, since there is no possibility for the defilements to arise, they do not have the seeds of the defilements. Furthermore, if fully abandoning the defilements through the tradition of the śrāvakas were not possible, it would contradict v45d below which states that they do abandon the defilements.

From the point of view of the bodhisattva vehicle, the monk who has abandoned the defilements has exhausted all that is to be abandoned, i.e. all conceptual discrimination. He is the 'root of the doctrine' which the Buddha alone has demonstrated to others out of his own profound, complete enlightenment. In the śrāvaka tradition, it is difficult to attain liberation from the self-clinging to dharmas, without which one cannot attain buddhahood and so, lacking the cause of the final result, the śrāvaka tradition is of provisional meaning and not of definitive meaning.

Furthermore, briefly, someone might say that monasticism is extremely important as the root of the doctrine because the other scriptures are in dispute. That should be rejected because there exist disputations regarding monastic discipline.

Concerning whether v44c onwards is part of this section on establishing the Mahāyāna as definitive meaning, according to Dānaśrī,[54] it is part of it.

2. The error for the śrāvaka tradition in a nirvāṇa in which suffering is abandoned

> **A nirvāṇa for the perceptual mind**
> **Is also difficult to attain.**

[413] For the śrāvaka tradition, a nirvāṇa in which suffering is abandoned is not logical because the perceptual mind still has self-clinging towards dharmas. The existence of such a nirvāṇa is difficult for them to attain because their nirvāṇa is not free from the sufferings of a mind-made body. They assert a non-final nirvāṇa that is free only from the suffering in which the skandhas are still established but the nirvāṇa being referred to here [in the root text] is final.

3. Overcoming objections to that

   1. The existence of the suffering of this life
   2. The existence of the suffering of future lives

1. The existence of the suffering of this life

   1. Objection
   2. Response
   3. Response to a counter objection

1. Objection

> **9.45**
> **'One is liberated by abandoning the defilements.'**

'By the cause—the defilements, there is the result—sufferings, from which ārya śrāvakas are liberated. Similarly by the cause—no defilements, there is the result—nirvāṇa, in which suffering has been abandoned.'

2. Response

> **Then it would happen immediately,**

The moment the defilements are abandoned, the level of an arhat would be attained. It follows that suffering has been exhausted.

'This is our position [i.e. śrāvakas exhaust suffering by abandoning defilements].'

3. Response to a counter objection

> **Yet one sees the power of karma**
> **Even though there are no defilements.**

In the nirvāṇa in which the skandhas remain, one can see the power of karma even though there are no defilements. One can see arhats such as Vibhudatta, for example, who experienced suffering.[55]

'Although they have not exhausted the sufferings of this life, they have exhausted the sufferings of clinging to rebirth.'

Although for them, the sufferings which are directly established in the skandhas are exhausted, the sufferings of the mind-made body are not exhausted, so the sufferings of future lives still exist. There are three parts to the explanation of this:

2. The existence of the suffering of future lives

    1. Presenting the objection
    2. The existence of craving itself
    3. The existence of its cause, sensation [414]

1. Presenting the objection

> **9.46**
> **'That is only temporary,**
> **For there is no direct cause—craving.'**

'Without the causes of future lives—craving and clinging—there are no sufferings of future rebirths and no clinging.'

2. The existence of craving itself

Why do you say they have no craving?

'Because they have no defilements.'

Although they have no defilements, they have craving which is without defilements. How so?

> **They do have craving, though it is without defilements,**
> **For don't they still have fundamental delusion?**

They may have no defilements due to not grasping the self of the individual but, through the imprints of unawareness, they still grasp the self of dharmas. Therefore, they are still subject to nescience. Without the craving of attachment to the self among the skandhas, they have no defilements, but they still have the craving of direct attachment to mere dharmas. Thus, they still have the condition for the attainment of a mind-made body in future lives.

3. The existence of its cause, sensation

> **9.47**
> **By the condition of sensation, there is craving,**
> **And they still have sensation.**

If the skandhas remain because one has not abandoned their basis, then five poisons are still present and wherever they arise, it is certain that sensation exists. Therefore, craving will arise because its basis is present.

4. The logical conclusion

The objectifying mind
For such people, still remains.

5. Summary of this section

9.48
Minds without emptiness
May cease, but they will arise again,
Like even settling without formations.
Therefore, meditate on emptiness.

One who has direct attachment to reality, even though their defilements may have ceased, will be reborn again. This is like entering into even settling without karmic formations, where even though the six groupings[56] cease, their seeds are not overcome, so they likewise arise again.

6. Explaining extensively the criteria for establishing the Mahāyāna scriptures as Buddha's word

  1. We have the same criteria
  2. To abandon it because of not understanding it is an error

1. We have the same criteria

'That which is included in the sutra collection, appears in the vinaya and does not contradict the truth is pervaded by being the Buddha's word. [415] This is how we establish the śrāvaka scriptural collections.'

9.49
If you accept the words included in the sutra collection
As the Buddha's teachings,
Why do you not accept the majority of the Mahāyāna
Which is the same as your sutras?

These criteria also apply to the bodhisattva collections, the Mahāyāna. Although your collections do not include the teachings on emptiness, etc., they are otherwise the same as the Mahāyāna. Therefore, the majority of the Mahāyāna is included.

Objection: 'Although some of the Mahāyāna meets our criteria, the teachings of emptiness do not meet our criteria, so the entire category is not the Buddha's word.'

Since it is established that some of the Mahāyāna teachings were taught by the Conqueror in the śrāvaka sutras, then it would follow that all the sutras in that category are established as the Conqueror's teaching:

9.50
If all are flawed
Due to a single point not being included,
Why would all not be accepted as the Conqueror's teachings
Due to a single point corresponding to your sutras?

By teaching that emptiness is ultimate truth, one is certainly not denigrating the relative truth teachings. Though there may be a defect, it does not follow there are other defects.

2. To abandon it because of not understanding it is an error

9.51
If the depths of these words were not fathomed
Even by someone like Mahākāśyapa,
Who should reject them
For not being understood by you?

According to the author of the *Great Commentary*, verses 49-51 were not originally part of the text but were later inserted.[57] However, since they have been explained thoroughly by the masters, it is not a fault to elaborate on them here.

3. The function of the two cognitions

 1. Generating the result which will become supreme
 2. Therefore you have no objections to our position
 3. Meditation on emptiness functions as an antidote
 4. It is not something to be afraid of

1. Generating the result which will become supreme

9.52
For the sake of those suffering due to confusion,
One remains in saṃsāra,
But is freed from the extremes of desire and fear:
This is the result of emptiness.

By the cause—the delusion of confused ones—there is the result—suffering. Thus, one benefits others by remaining in saṃsāra for the sake of those tormented by these sufferings. This is the result which is the cognition of compassion and the illusion-like affirming negation. [416] Freedom from direct attachment towards the reality of things (desire) and being afraid of emptiness (fear) is the result which is the cognition of the non-affirming negation emptiness.

2. Therefore, you have no objections to our position

9.53
Thus, it is incorrect to so criticize
The doctrine of emptiness.
Therefore, you should meditate on emptiness
Without entertaining doubts.

3. Meditation on emptiness functions as an antidote

9.54
Emptiness is the antidote to the darkness
Of the obscurations of defilements and cognizables.
How can those who wish to attain omniscience
Not hurry to meditate on it?

4. It is not something to be afraid of

   1. It is not a cause of suffering
   2. Having no fear

1. It is not a cause of suffering

9.55
Something that produces suffering

> Should produce fear,
> But emptiness pacifies suffering,
> So why should it produce fear?

If it is logical to be afraid of something that is a basis for suffering, such as clinging to self, or sickness, how can one be afraid of the antidote to suffering, emptiness?

2. Having no fear

> **9.56**
> **If there were something that was 'I',**
> **You would be right to be afraid.**
> **But since there is no such thing as 'I',**
> **What is there to be afraid of?**

3. How to engage in meditation on emptiness

Geshe Ngok Lotsawa and others have explained this as follows:

1. How to engage in meditation on the non-self of the individual [v57-77]
2. How to engage in meditation on the non-self of dharmas [v78-110]

However, this is not correct. If one says that the foundations of mindfulness [v78-110] comprise the non-self of dharmas, it would contradict the *Śikṣā-samuccaya*, which says,

> This completes the full explanation of the foundations of mindfulness. Having taught the non-self of the individual in that way...[58]

Therefore, both sections [i.e. v57-110] explain the non-self of the individual, while the previous section [v2-56] explains the non-self of dharmas. This is also how Ācārya Candrakīrti arranges the *Madhyamakāvatāra*.[59] First, by a complete presentation of the two truths, one gains certainty concerning the true nature of cognizables in general, which is called the 'non-self of dharmas'. After that, there remains a conception of an 'individual self' which is the cognizor of this. [417] In order for that to cease, the non-self of the individual is subsequently taught.

'If the self of the individual is grasping the coarse as singular, while the self of dharmas is grasping the subtle as singular, why is the non-self of dharmas taught first?'

It is nowhere taught that the individual is coarse and dharmas are subtle. Although nowadays there are many explanations that make this claim, they are erroneous. As it says in the *Abhidharmakośa*,

> The stream of being is called 'the individual'.
> Grasping at characteristics is called 'dharmas'.[60]

Therefore, up to this point, the non-self of dharmas has been taught by gaining certainty in all cognizables grasped as mine through the two truths. Now, the non-self of the individual is to be explained. This has four parts.

1. The general explanation of individual non-self in the six elements [v57 - 59]
2. Refuting the self of the skandhas and elements, etc. as designated by tīrthikas [v60 - 69]
3. Abandoning objections to non-self [v70 - 77]
4. Refuting the understanding of the skandhas and elements as self with the four foundations of mindfulness [v78 - 110]

1. The general explanation of individual non-self in the six elements

Non-self in the earth and water elements:

> **9.57**
> **Self is not the teeth, hair or nails.**
> **It is neither the bones nor blood.**
> **It is neither the mucus nor phlegm,**
> **Nor is it the lymph or pus.**
>
> **9.58**
> **Self is neither the fat nor sweat.**
> **Neither the lungs nor liver are the self,**
> **Nor are any of the other inner organs.**
> **Self is neither the excrement nor urine.**
>
> **9.59**
> **Neither the flesh nor skin are the self,**

Non-self in the fire, wind and consciousness elements:

> **Nor are warmth or respiration the self.**
> **The orifices are not the self,**
> **And none of the six consciousnesses are the self either.**

It has been said by some earlier masters that the first eleven lines teach the non-self of the skandha of form and the final line teaches the non-

374 | BODHICARYĀVATĀRA WITH COMMENTARY

self of the other skandhas. However, since this is not how it appears in the root text, [418] it is not the intended meaning.

> Section overview: Refuting the self of the skandhas and elements, etc. as designated by tīrthikas [v60-69]
>
> 1. Refuting Sāṃkhyas
>   1. General refutation of the individual consciousness
>   1. The consequence of its permanence
>   2. Establishing the pervasion
>   1. The violation of its intrinsic nature
>   2. The absurd consequence
>   3. Conclusion
>   3. Abandoning objections
>   1. It is unreasonable for cognition of form to perceive sounds
>   2. This has the same fault that was previously explained
>   3. It is unreasonable to call it the same thing
>   4. The example is not established
>   5. Not conceivable as a singularity
>   2. Refuting temporary multiplicity
>   3. Refuting its single nature
>   1. Question
>   2. Answer
>   1. The consequence that all beings are one
>   2. The consequence that the mirror of mind and individual consciousnesses are one
>   3. The general case is not established
> 2. Refuting Naiyāyikas
>   1. Showing the consequence which refutes a self with a material nature
>   2. Establishing the pervasion for sentience
>   3. Summarized meaning

2. Refuting the self of the skandhas and elements, etc. as designated by tīrthikas

1. Refuting Sāṃkhyas
2. Refuting Naiyāyikas

1. Refuting Sāṃkhyas

The Sāṃkhyas assert that a primal matter exists universally in all beings. Containers of self-cognition and awareness exist within it as individual consciousnesses. Each of these has the inherent nature of a sempiternal, cognizing and aware self. When it has no appearances, representations [i.e. forms, sounds, etc.] remain within the mirror of mind.[61] When it temporarily connects with manifesting representations such as the bare element of sound,[62] it temporarily experiences objects.

1. General refutation of the individual consciousness
2. Refuting temporary multiplicity
3. Refuting its single nature

1. General refutation of the individual consciousness

1. The consequence of its permanence
2. Establishing the pervasion
3. Abandoning objections

1. The consequence of its permanence

9.60
If the cognition of sound were immutable
The sound would always be perceived.

The logical subject is the individual consciousness. It must experience sound as immutable because it is a sempiternal sound-perceiving cognition. This position is untenable. By directly perceiving a single sound, it cannot perceive any other sound. It is untenable to say the reason[63] is not established, for that would contradict the Sāṃkhya's own proposition that the individual consciousness is sempiternal.

'Your pervasion[64] is not established. The sempiternal nature of self-awareness is not pervaded by an immutable experience of sound, for it can have a nature of mere cognition without depending upon any object. The experience of sound depends upon a sound, so when there is no sound, there is no experience, but the mere cognition nevertheless remains. Therefore, the immutable experience of sound is negated and the pervasion for your refutation of a sempiternal individual consciousness is not established.'

2. Establishing the pervasion

   1. The violation of its intrinsic nature
   2. The absurd consequence [419]
   3. Conclusion

1. The violation of its intrinsic nature

> **If there is no cognizable, how is that awareness?**
> **Why call this 'cognition?'**

The first line is a question and the second is the response. The establishment of a sound cognition depends upon there being a sound. If there is no sound, there is no sound cognition. Similarly, since the nature of a sound cognition depends upon its cognizable, without a cognizable, there is no subjective cognition. Therefore, without a perception of sound, cognition is negated. Thus, our pervasion is established.

2. The absurd consequence

'The experience of sound may depend upon a sound, but mere cognition does not. Therefore, the experience of sound is refuted, but mere cognition is not refuted. Therefore, your pervasion is not established.'

If it were the case that the establishment of a cognition did not depend upon a cognizable, it would follow that even wood would count as cognition:

> **9.61**
> **If cognition does not cognize,**
> **It would follow that even wood is a cognition.**

3. Conclusion

> **Without a nearby cognizable,**
> **I would definitely call that 'not cognizing'.**

Cognition is the presence of a cognizor in proximity to the cognizable which qualifies[65] it. Without that, there is definitely no cognition.

3. Abandoning objections

1. It is unreasonable for cognition of form to perceive sound
2. This has the same fault that was previously explained
3. It is unreasonable to call it the same thing
4. The example is not established
5. Not conceivable as a singularity

1. It is unreasonable for cognition of form to perceive sound

> **9.62**
> **'It is the same thing that cognizes form.'**

'Although cognition without a cognizable is impossible, when the sound is no longer in proximity, that very same cognition now cognizes forms. Since at that time the form cognizable exists, we maintain that cognition exists sempiternally.'

Either the previous cognition of sound has ceased and subsequently forms are cognized, or else the previous cognition of sound has not ceased. If the former, then although it remains the same in as much as it is designated 'mere cognition', its former nature in fact has ceased. This is a fault, since a sempiternal individual consciousness is unceasing.

> **Then why would it not also hear at the same time?**

If the sound has not ceased, then, at that time, since sound cognition [420] is pervaded by its cognizable and by self-awareness, when the forms are cognized, it follows that it would still be an awareness of sound because the grasping of the sound would not have ceased.

2. This has the same fault that was previously explained

> **If it is because no sound is nearby**
> **Then there is also no cognition of it.**

Since sound awareness depends upon a sound, the pervasion of a sempiternal sound awareness is not established. When there is no sound there is also no cognition. Since sound cognition is qualified by its sound, when there is no sound, there is pervasion by no sound cognition, as was previously shown, i.e. if cognition did not depend upon its cognizable, there would be the fault of the consequence that even wood would count as cognition.

3. It is unreasonable to call it the same thing

'The sound cognition and form cognition have one nature, but the former cognition ceases.'

The response:

> **9.63**
> **How can that which has the nature**
> **Of sound perception perceive forms?**

It is unreasonable to designate incompatible representations as having a single nature. The establishment of a cognition of form in dependence upon a form cognizable has one nature and the establishment of a cognition of sound in dependence upon sound has another.

'An example of such a single nature that is non-contradictory is someone being established as a son in dependence upon his own father and the same person being established as a father in dependence upon having a son.'

4. The example is not established

> **A single person might be called father and son,**
> **But his intrinsic nature is neither,**
>
> **9.64**
> **Just as lightness, activity and darkness**
> **Are neither father nor son.**

To call a single person a father and a son is a worldly convention. Similarly, lightness, activity and darkness—the three ultimate natures [as posited by the Sāṃkhyas]—do not have the nature of either father or son.

5. Not conceivable as a singularity

**Nobody has ever seen
Visual perception with the nature of sound perception.**

If sound cognition and visual cognition existed as a singular self, it should be apparent but, since it has never been seen, it is negated.

Having refuted the individual consciousness in general:

2. Refuting temporary multiplicity

Objection:

**9.65
'Like an actor, it assumes different characteristics.'**

'The individual consciousness has a single nature, like an actor wearing masks at different times—sometimes Indra, [421] sometimes a monkey. Although it has various characters, there is one nature without any incompatibility. Although temporarily there are representations such as a perception of sound, consciousness is free from multiplicity and has a single nature.'

The response:

If it sees, it is not immutable.

In that case, its freedom from multiplicity is also temporary, for the previous perception ceases when the subsequent one arises and thus it has a new nature. Thus, it is not immutable.

'It just appears differently.'

'The representations are dissimilar but have a single nature.'

If the representations are dissimilar but have one nature, the attribution to them of 'singularity' is the introduction of a singularity previously unknown to the world:

Such singularity is something unprecedented.

3. Refuting its single nature

   1. Question
   2. Answer

1. Question

   9.66
   'Its different characteristics are not real.'
   Then describe its true nature.

'Its multiple temporary characteristics are not real. Among these untrue characteristics, there is one nature.'

In that case, what is that nature? What kind of essential characteristics does it have?

   'It is cognition itself.'

'Although temporarily it is designated as a sound cognition or a form cognition, it has one nature, since these both qualify as mere cognition.'

2. Answer

   1. The consequence that all beings are one
   2. The consequence that the mirror of mind and individual consciousnesses are one
   3. The general case is not established

1. The consequence that all beings are one

   Then it would follow that all beings are one.

If whatever is qualified by mere awareness is pervaded by a single nature, then, taking individual beings as the logical subject, it would follow that they are all one in nature because they all have mere awareness. [422] This consequence is erroneous.

2. The consequence that the mirror of mind and individual consciousnesses are one

9.67
Sentient and insentient would also be one
Because they are equal merely in being existent.

If whatever shares the same qualification is pervaded by a single nature, then it would follow that the sentient—the individual consciousness, a cognizing awareness—and the insentient—primal matter and the mirror of mind[66]—have the same nature because they have the same qualification, being merely existent.

3. The general case is not established

> **If the instances are delusions,**
> **What common basis could they have?**

If all instances, such as sound cognitions and form cognitions, are untrue, then it is established that the general case—mere cognition as a singular self—is also untrue. If the instances such as pale blue are untrue, the universal [blue] is also not established, like the only son of a barren woman.

2. Refuting Naiyāyikas

1. Showing the consequence which refutes a self with a material nature
2. Since pervasion by possession of a separate mind has not been established, establishing that pervasion for sentience
3. Summarized meaning

1. Showing the consequence which refutes a self with a material nature

9.68
Something insentient is not the self,
Because of its very insentience, like a vase.

The Naiyāyikas assert that the self is insentient matter which becomes connected to an external mind,[67] and in this way it is an agent.

The self is the logical subject. [Contradiction:] your position is that it is an agent but it follows that it is not an agent because of its being matter, which is insentient. It is not tenable to deny that either the position [the self is an agent] or the reason [the self is insentient matter] are established, for that would contradict your own premise. If the pervasion[68] were not established, then such things as vases would be indistinct [from agents].

'It owns a separate mind.[69] Therefore, the pervasion is not established.'

2. Establishing the pervasion

Because of its possession of a mind,

'Although the self is insentient matter, since it owns a separate mind, it has the sentience of premeditating intentionality.[70] You have not shown a contradiction, since the pervasion is not established.'

[423] By owning a separate mind, either its material nature has changed or it has not changed. If it has changed, then having previously been material in nature, later it becomes an agent with intentionality. Thus, its previous material nature was impermanent:

If it then cognizes, it follows that its non-cognition has been eliminated.

If it does not change:

9.69
'The self has not changed.'
Then how did it become sentient?

'There was no change when its material nature was eliminated because the sempiternal self is immutable.'

If the former matter was insentient then, being mutually exclusive with sentience, it is not a sentient being with intentionality. Matter is pervaded by not being an agent—a sentient being with intentionality.

3. Summarized meaning

> **Thus, being non-cognizing and free from activity,**
> **Space would also be such a 'self'.**

If the self has no nature of cognition nor is an agent, it follows that space is also a self.

Section overview: Abandoning objections to non-self [v70-77]

1. Abandoning the objection that the connection of actions and effects is not logical
   1. Presenting the objection
   2. Our positions are the same
   3. Actual response
   4. Abandoning contradiction to scripture
   5. Abandoning another objection
   6. Summarized meaning
2. Abandoning the objection of objects of cultivating compassion being illogical
   1. Objection
   2. Response
      1. Establishing that sentient beings are designated
      2. Abandoning this objection
         1. The independence of the substantially established individual
         2. The mere designation is not to be abandoned
         3. Abandoning a contradiction in our own words
         4. Abandoning that they are the same

---

3. Abandoning objections to non-self

   1. Abandoning the objection that the connection of actions and effects is not logical
   2. Abandoning the objection of objects of cultivating compassion being illogical

1. Abandoning the objection that the connection of actions and effects is not logical

   1. Presenting the objection

2. Our positions are the same
3. Actual response
4. Abandoning contradiction to scripture
5. Abandoning another objection
6. Summarized meaning

1. Presenting the objection

9.70
'If the self does not exist,
A connection between actions and results is illogical.
After performing an action, it is gone,
So, for whom could there be karma?'

'If the nature of self were not the same between this life and future lives, when the skandhas of this life and its karmic deeds are destroyed, the deeds would dissipate. Since the skandhas of the next life are newly arisen, they would not have any connection with the previous actions. Therefore, for whom could there be karma?'

2. Our positions are the same

9.71
It is established for both of us
That action and result have different bases
And that a self does not have any role in this.

The basis of action—the individual of this life who is the agent—and basis of the result—the experiences of a future life [424]—are distinct. All its actions are temporary manifestations, with a completely passive sempiternal self performing no function. If this is a fault, the same fault exists equally for both of us:

So, is your objection here not pointless?

3. Actual response

9.72
'The causal agent is the recipient of its result.'

If effects were experienced by the karmic causal agents themselves, then the causal agent and the effect would have to exist at the same time, however:

No one ever sees this happen.

Therefore, the karmic agent is the body of the causal agent and the experiencer of the result is the body of another person and these are distinct.

4. Abandoning contradiction to scripture

'According to the Buddhist scriptures, the ripened results such as the result of maturation[71] do not ripen for anyone other than the karmic agent.'

**It is just in dependence upon a single stream of being
That the so-called 'agent' and 'experiencer' are taught.**

Although the karmic agent and the experiencer of the result are temporally distinct, consciousness is a changing stream of moments and in this way the result ripens for the karmic agent. Therefore, there is no contradiction to the scriptures.

5. Abandoning another objection

'That causal stream is the self.'

**9.73
The past and future minds are not the self,
Because they do not exist.
If the arising mind were the self,
Then when it ceased, there would be no more self.**

Past and future minds are not the self because the former has ceased and the latter has not yet arisen. Mind in the present moment, which has arisen but not yet ceased, is also not the self because it will cease to be. Since it becomes nonexistent, it does not have a sempiternal nature. The stream of being is nothing but a succession of many individual moments and has no real existence apart from this.

6. Summarized meaning

> **9.74**
> **For example, if you split apart**
> **The trunks of banana trees, nothing is found.**
> **Similarly, if you search for it thoroughly,**
> **You will find the self to be no more real than this.**

2. Abandoning the objection that the objects of cultivating compassion are not established

1. Objection [425]
2. Response

1. Objection

> **9.75**
> **'If sentient beings do not exist,**
> **For whom should we have compassion?'**

'If sentient beings, the objects of compassion, do not exist, it is unreasonable to cultivate compassion for them. Therefore, the Mahāyāna path is flawed.'

2. Response

1. Establishing that sentient beings are designated
2. Abandoning an objection to that

1. Establishing that sentient beings are designated

> **Compassion is for those imputed by confusion:**
> **They are accepted for the sake of the result.**

'Confusion' means grasping the illusion-like relative that a stream of many moments is a sentient being. Relative sentient beings and compassion are not incompatible. What sort of relative is this? It is an unabandoned relative acceptance of conduct for the benefit of others.

Why accept this delusion? It is for the sake of the result, i.e. we do not abandon others for the sake of benefitting them and attaining buddhahood, in accord with the earlier teaching on not abandoning conceptual thought with appearances.

2. Abandoning an objection to that

1. The independence of the substantially established individual
2. The mere designation is not to be abandoned
3. Abandoning a contradiction in our own words
4. Abandoning that they are the same

1. The independence of the substantially established individual

> 9.76
> **'If there are no sentient beings, who gets the result?'**
> **This is true but, nevertheless, they are accepted out of confusion.**

'If even sentient beings are not established, how can there be any results from benefitting them?'

It is true that in reality there are no sentient beings, i.e. the objects to be benefitted are not pervaded by being real sentient beings. Yet, while they are illusion-like and agglomerations of many moments, it is reasonable to treat these so-called 'sentient beings' as objects and to fulfil their benefit.

Objection: 'The conception of the reality of sentient beings is to be abandoned and one must abandon grasping at designations of sentient beings because they are perceptions of mistaken conceptual thought.'

2. The mere designation is not to be abandoned

> **For the sake of fully pacifying suffering,**
> **One should not oppose the delusion of this result.**

Since practice requires a variety of skilful methods, [426] those wise in such methods should rely upon the deluded relative.

3. Abandoning a contradiction in our own words

'Earlier, you said,

> Neither self nor other is right:
> You should try to give them both up. [v8.100cd]

Are you not now contradicting yourself?'

No: that self is the self which exists as a real substance. This one exists as a designation.

'Why should the first kind of self be abandoned?'

Because clinging to self as ultimate creates pride, which causes suffering:

> **9.77**
> **Confusion about the self increases**
> **Pride, the cause of suffering.**

4. Abandoning the objection that they are the same

'The conceptual thought with appearances in which there is clinging to the existence of the designated self should be abandoned, for suffering increases as a consequence of clinging to the existence of real substance.'

This kind of conceptual thought with appearances does not increase self-clinging, the cause of suffering. Why not? Because there is an antidote which destroys the seeds of clinging to self—meditating upon non-self:

> **'There is no way to resolve this [contradiction].'**
> **The meditation on non-self is supreme.**

Alternatively, the objection and response can be understood as follows: 'Clinging to the self as ultimate is not to be abandoned because, by doing so, one will attain the result, buddhahood.'

This is not established because the supreme means for the attainment of buddhahood is meditation upon non-self. This is how Dānaśrī[72] explains lines 77cd.

Having refuted the erroneous conception the non-Buddhists have of a seeing and sensing self, now to present the refutation of the idea that those sights and sensations are selves.

4. Refuting the understanding of the skandhas and elements as self with the four foundations of mindfulness

1. Mindfulness of the body
2. Mindfulness of sensations
3. Mindfulness of mind
4. Mindfulness of dharmas [427]

This section is not a teaching on the four foundations of mindfulness taught elsewhere as the impurity of the body, the suffering of sensations, the impermanence of mind and the non-self of dharmas. However, one need not think there is any contradiction here to that teaching, only a different purpose. In our bodhisattva tradition, the purpose is to analyse the individual self for which grasping arises under the power of wrong views, by developing the characteristics of non-self in the meditative objects [i.e. the four foundations] to purify defilements. In the other tradition, since conduct degenerates under the influence of defilements such as attachment, one develops in one's stream of being the characteristics of abandonment of the four wrong views[73] as meditative objects to purify conduct.[74]

Section overview: Mindfulness of the body [v78-87]

1. The individual parts are not the body
2. An existent body which possesses the parts is not established
    1. Refuting that each part is connected to it
    2. Refuting a connection throughout the entire self
    3. Summarizing the logic of that
    4. The body is deluded conception
    5. Establishing the delusion
        1. The cause of the delusion
        2. The deluded cognition
3. General summary

---

1. Mindfulness of the body

    1. The individual parts are not the body
    2. An existent body which possesses the parts is not established
    3. General summary

1. The individual parts are not the body

> **9.78**
> **The body is neither the feet nor calves,**
> **Nor is it the thighs or waist,**
> **Abdomen or back,**
> **Chest or shoulders,**
>
> **9.79**
> **Ribs or hands,**
> **Joints or cavities,**
> **Internal organs,**
> **Head or neck.**
> **What is this body then?**

2. An existent body which possesses the parts is not established

Objection: 'Although these parts are not the body, there exists a single owner of the parts.'

   1. Refuting that each part is connected to it
   2. Refuting a connection throughout the entire self
   3. Summarizing the logic of that
   4. The body is deluded conception
   5. Establishing the delusion

1. Refuting that each part is connected to it

> **9.80**
> **If this body is present as a whole**
> **Among its individual parts**
> **Then part of it consists in each part,**

If the so-called 'body' were a generality present in the individual parts, then either it consists partly in each part or else it is complete in each part. If the first, a single generality present within many parts is not established:

> But where is the thing itself?

2. Refuting a connection throughout the entire self [428]

Regarding the second position, if in each individual part there is an individual complete body, it follows that there are many complete bodies:

> 9.81
> If the body consists of a complete whole
> In the hands and so forth,
> There would be as many bodies
> As there are hands and so forth.

3. Summarizing the logic of that

> 9.82
> If the body is neither inside nor out,
> Neither within the hands and so forth,
> Nor apart from the hands and so forth,
> How does it exist at all?

The first two lines indicate that the body is not within the parts themselves. The second two lines indicate that the body is not in something else.

4. The body is deluded conception

> 9.83
> Therefore, out of confusion, we think there is a body
> Where there is none.
> It is like thinking a heap of stones is a person
> By some particularity of its arrangement.

Like the delusion that a heap of stones is a person, it is a delusion that within many parts there is a single generality which is the body.

5. Establishing the delusion

  1. The cause of the delusion
  2. The deluded cognition

1. The cause of the delusion

> **9.84**
> While the conditions are assembled,
> The body will continue to appear as a person.
> So, while the hands and so forth exist,
> A body continues to appear.

Just as the particularity of its shape is the cause of the delusion that a heap of stones is a person, so the assemblage of the hands and so forth cause the delusion that the so-called body is a single thing.

2. The deluded cognition

> **9.85**
> Similarly, what more is a hand
> Than a collection of fingers?
> These, too, are collections of joints,
> Which have their own distinct parts.
>
> **9.86**
> Even parts have distinct particles,
> And those particles have distinct areas.
> Even these distinct areas are not without parts;
> They are like space. Therefore, not even particles exist.

The first verse indicates the non-establishment of the coarse and the second verse indicates the non-establishment of the subtle.

3. General summary of the non-establishment of a body in the body

> **9.87**

> Accordingly, who could make this analysis,
> And still have attachment to dreamlike forms?
> When there is no existent body,
> What is a man and what is a woman?

The non-establishment of the body generally is indicated in the first two lines and the non-establishment of particular bodies is indicated in the second two lines.

Section overview: Mindfulness of sensations [v88-101]

1. The non-establishment of the intrinsic nature of sensations
    1. The non-establishment of suffering as ultimate
    2. The non-establishment of happiness as ultimate
    3. Abandoning objections
        1. The consequence that sensations would be experienced
        2. If that reason were not established, it would be no different to happiness
    4. Conditionality
    5. Connecting with the yogic activity of analysis
2. The non-establishment of its cause: contact
    1. Objects not meeting with sense organs
        1. There is no contact with the coarse
        2. There is no contact with the subtle
            1. Stating the consequence
            2. Establishing the reasons
            3. Establishing the pervasion
            4. Conclusion
    2. Not meeting with consciousness
    3. A composite completely refuted
    4. Summary conclusion
    5. The point of establishing that
3. The non-establishment of the object
4. The non-establishment of the subject
    1. No experiencing mind
    2. Self is not the experiencer
    3. No experiencer apart from those
    4. Concluding summary

2. Mindfulness of sensations

1. The non-establishment of the intrinsic nature of sensations
2. The non-establishment of its cause: contact

1. The non-establishment of the intrinsic nature of sensations

1. The non-establishment of suffering as ultimate
2. The non-establishment of happiness as ultimate
3. Abandoning objections
4. Conditionality
5. Connecting with the yogic activity of analysis

1. The non-establishment of suffering as ultimate

9.88
If suffering exists in reality,
Why does it not prevent joyfulness?

'Suffering' is the logical subject and 'exists in reality' is the reason. Since the nature of fire is to heat, [429] it cannot become cold. Similarly, beings' minds abide in the nature of suffering, so it follows that there should not be even an instant of unadulterated happiness. But that is not the case; it is untenable, for it is contrary to direct experience. It is untenable for the reason not to be established, for it would contradict the proposition that suffering is existent. It is untenable for pervasion[75] not to be established, for it would contradict valid cognition, just as fire cannot be cold.

2. The non-establishment of happiness as ultimate

If there is happiness, why are those afflicted by pain and so forth
Not made joyful by sweetness and so forth?

The Sāṃkhyas claim, 'Sweetness, which is of the bare element of taste,[76] has the nature of happiness.'

The bare element of the taste of sweetness is the logical subject. [Proposition:] It does not make those afflicted by pain joyful.

[Contradiction:] It follows that they should be joyful because [Reason:] it has the inherent nature of happiness. The non-establishment of the reason, pervasion and proposition are all untenable, as in the previous section.

3. Abandoning objections

   1. The consequence that sensations would be experienced
   2. If that reason were not established, it would be no different to happiness

1. The consequence that sensations would be experienced

> **9.89**
> **'It is not experienced because**
> **It is overridden by the stronger force.'**
> **If something is not experienced,**
> **How can it be a sensation?**

'Since the sensation of suffering is ultimately existent, it follows that the suffering is sempiternal—we accept this proposition. But if you claim that therefore happiness is nonexistent, that pervasion is not established.'

If suffering is sempiternal and existent, why is it not perceived?

'It is not experienced because of being overridden by the stronger force, like a daytime star.'

The logical subject is this overridden experience. It follows that it is not a sensation because if something is not experienced, there is no experience. Since the experience is negated, the sensation has ceased. The proposition [that suffering is overridden] is untenable for it contradicts your premise [that suffering is sempiternal]. If the pervasion[77] were not established, it would contradict valid cognition.

2. If that reason were not established, [the sensation] would be no different to happiness [430]

'The reason—"[because] it is not experienced"—is not established, for it is a subtle experience.'

9.90
'The suffering exists as a subtlety
When its coarseness has been removed.'
If this implies it is something other than suffering,

Is the experience of that subtlety suffering or happiness? The first is negated since it is not perceived. If you say, 'It is something other[78] than suffering', i.e. if you propose the second alternative, that is also incorrect. Just as light is incompatible with subtle darkness, so happiness is incompatible with subtle suffering. Since the experience is one of happiness, it cannot be suffering:

Then, whatever that is, that is what this 'subtlety' is.

One should also understand the corollary to this:

'Due to the intrinsic nature of happiness, even if one is afflicted by torment, although the happiness still exists, it is not experienced.'

If it is not experienced, it is not appropriate to call it a sensation.

'It is a subtle experience.'

Happiness experienced subtly but not perceived as an appearance has been refuted, i.e. if there is a subtle experience of suffering, it is incompatible with happiness and vice versa.

4. Conditionality

Sensations are not ultimate but are connected to conditions:

9.91
If suffering cannot occur
Due to the arising of its contrary condition,
Shouldn't suffering be considered
Merely the attachment to a concept?

'By the arising of suffering, its contrary condition—happiness —ceases.'

Since a fleeting happiness is established as a temporary artifice, it has no intrinsic nature. Therefore, sensation is fully established as the mere clinging to a discrimination.

5. Connecting with the yogic activity of analysis

> **9.92**
> **Because of this, meditate upon**
> **This analysis as the antidote.**
> **The meditation arising from**
> **This field of examination is the food of yogins.**

'This field of examination' means meditative wisdom which analyses the stream of being. Samādhi arises from the cause, meditation. The 'food of yogins' means the content of these teachings.

2. The non-establishment of its cause: contact

1. Objects not meeting with sense organs
2. Not meeting with consciousness
3. A composite completely refuted
4. Summary conclusion
5. The point of establishing that

1. Objects not meeting with sense organs

Contact is the cause of sensation. From the connection of three things —object, sense organ and consciousness [431]—a perceptual object is classified as pleasant, unpleasant or neutral. This causes happiness and so forth to arise. However, it is not logical that external objects make contact with sense organs:

1. There is no contact with the coarse
2. There is no contact with the subtle [particles]

1. No contact with the coarse

Is the gap between sense organ and object an existent thing or nonexistent? If existent:

> **9.93**
> **If an intermediary connects sense organ and object,**

Where do they make contact?

The logical subject is sense organ and object. [Proposition:] These have an intermediary object. The reason is because something exists between them. [Contradiction:] Although the proposition is that they have contact, it follows that they do not have contact.

If there is no intermediary object then it also follows that they do not have contact because that which has no intermediary is unified:

**If there is no intermediary, they are unified.
So, what has contact with what?**

If both positions [intermediary or no intermediary] and their reasons [something exists between them or they are unified] were not established, it would contradict the premise [that sense organ meets object]. If the pervasions[79] were not established, it would contradict valid cognition.

2. No contact with subtle particles

   1. Stating the consequence
   2. Establishing the reason
   3. Establishing the pervasion[80]
   4. Conclusion

1. Stating the consequence

**9.94
Particles do not impose upon other particles,**

Two particles are the logical subject. [Contradiction:] Although the proposition is that they are in contact, it follows that they are not in contact because [Reason:] there is no imposition of either particle, i.e. one cannot impose itself upon the other.

'This reason is not established.'

2. Establishing the reason

For they are identical in having no capacity.

Although your position is that the particles—the logical subjects—make contact, it follows that one cannot impose upon the other because it has no interior capacity.

'Although one does not impose upon the other, they do make contact. Where is the contradiction? The pervasion[81] is not established.'

3. Establishing the pervasion

> Without imposition, they cannot combine.
> Without combining, they cannot make contact.

4. Conclusion

> 9.95
> 'They make contact despite being partless.'
> How does this make any sense?
> Making contact with something partless:
> When you see it, will you show me?

If they were in contact along their entire surfaces, they would be one. If they were in contact along a single part of their surfaces, it would contradict their being partless.

2. Not meeting with consciousness

> 9.96
> It is illogical to make contact with
> Consciousness, which is bodiless,

Consciousness, the logical subject [432], cannot be in contact with anything because it is bodiless, i.e. it does not have a body.

3. A composite completely refuted

> And likewise for anything composite, because it is
>   nonexistent,
> As was analysed previously.

'"Contact" does not mean being in physical contact with a form. Contact is an effect, of which the cause is a grouping [of consciousness, sense base and object]. Thus, the faults of having contact between the surface of partless particles do not apply.'

The logical subject is the causal collection. [Contradiction:] Although your position is that it is truly existent, it follows that it is not existent because it is a multiplicity imputed as a singularity. The establishment of that pervasion[82] was explained earlier.

'Although the causal collection is relative, its effects—contact and sensation—are ultimately existent. Where is the contradiction?'

If an ultimately existent effect from a deluded relative cause is not a contradiction, then an existent effect from a cause unable to perform any function would also not be a contradiction [v9.28].

4. Summary conclusion

> 9.97
> **If there is no real contact,**
> **What are these sensations arising from?**

Because there is no contact, there is no sensation. The cause being absent:

> **Why go to all this trouble?**

All this trouble for the sake of happiness is not sensible.

> **What is harmed by what?**

One is not harmed by suffering.

5. The point of establishing that

> 9.98
> **If the one who senses**
> **And the sensations themselves are nonexistent,**
> **Once this has been seen,**
> **How could craving not be dispelled?**

If the one who senses—the self—and the cause—sensations—are

negated, then the effect—the craving of attachment to that—will be reversed.

3. The non-establishment of the object of sensation

> **9.99**
> **Even what is seen or touched**
> **Is itself dreamlike and illusion-like.**

That which is seen and touched are the first and last kinds of the five sense objects, indicating all five kinds of object. Since those objects do not ultimately exist, it is established *a priori* that the sensations of the subject relating to them also do not exist. Concerning these objects, they have already been refuted above by the negation of the body, subtle particles and so forth.

4. The non-establishment of the subject

1. No experiencing mind
2. No self-experience [433]
3. No experiencer apart from those
4. Concluding summary

1. No experiencing mind

> **Sensations are not perceived by mind,**
> **Because they arise simultaneously with it.**

Do sensations and their experiencing mind occur in the same moment, or do the sensations arise first and are experienced after?

If the former: the logical subject is the mind at the moment of the sensation. [Contradiction:] Although the proposition is that it experiences the sensation, it follows that it does not have the experience because they arise simultaneously. If one denies the establishment of the pervasion,[83] it would contradict valid cognition because a perceived object must cause the perception. But here the pervasion of cause and effect is contradicted because the perceived object and perception occur in the same moment.[84]

'The sensation arises first and the experience after. Since the sensation arises first, it is the cause. Since the consciousness arises subsequently, it is the effect. These are the object and subject.'

9.100
Although something from before may be remembered after,
That is not experiencing it.

The previous [sensation] is the logical subject. [Contradiction:] Although the proposition is that it is experienced, it follows that it is an object of subsequent remembering, not an object of present experience because its intrinsic nature has ended. If one doubts the establishment of the pervasion,[85] it would contradict valid cognition because that which is an object of present experience is pervaded by a nature which has not ended.

2. No self-experience

A sensation cannot experience itself,

This is because of the previous refutation of self-experience.

3. No experiencer apart from those

Nor does anything else experience it.

This is because, apart from consciousness and the sensation itself, there is nothing else to have the experience.

4. Concluding summary

9.101
There is nothing existent that experiences sensations.
Therefore, there are no sensations.
Therefore, what could ever harm
This selfless composite?

> Section overview: Mindfulness of mind and dharmas [v102-110]
>
> 3. Mindfulness of mind
>   1. The nature of mind is not established
>   2. Perception of the five consciousnesses is not established
> 4. Mindfulness of dharmas
>   1. Establishing all as non-arising
>   2. Abandoning objections
>   1. Abandoning the objection that there is no relative
>   2. Abandoning the objection that this ascertainment entails an infinite regress
>   1. A general comment on the division of object and subject
>   2. If the non-arising of the subject depends upon a further understanding, there is an infinite regress
>   3. Our position does not have that fault

3. Mindfulness of mind

   1. The nature of mind is not established
   2. Perceptions of the five consciousnesses are not established

1. The nature of mind is not established

> **9.102**
> **Mind does not dwell in the senses,**
> **Nor in forms, etc., nor somewhere between these.**

Mind is not in the senses because it can exist even without the senses. It is not in the object because it can exist without an object. Nor is it somewhere between these because there would be no perception. [434] This shows that its basis is not established. To show that its nature is not established:

> **Mind is neither the inner nor outer,**
> **Nor is it found anywhere else.**
>
> **9.103**
> **It is neither within the body, nor apart from it.**

> **It is not combined, nor is it something distinct.**
> **Because such a thing does not even slightly exist,**
> **Sentient beings are by nature nirvāṇa.**

The sixth mind is not an inner sense organ, for it does not possess form. Nor it is an outer sense object, for it does not have a body, so it is not one of the five kinds of objects. Since it is not instantly ceasing, it is not a momentary dharma. It is not the physical basis of the outer or inner, since it does not have a body. It is not a combination of outer and inner, since they are mutually exclusive. It is not something distinct from these, since then there would be no perception. Therefore, it is inherently nirvāṇa.

2. Perception of the five consciousnesses is not established

'The sixth mind, although not established as having an intrinsic cognizing nature, exists as nothing but the five consciousnesses themselves.'

> **9.104**
> **If the cognition exists before cognizable,**
> **What does it arise from?**

Does cognition exist a) before its cause, the cognizable, b) simultaneously with its cognizable or c) after the cognizable?

a) If consciousness existed before its cognizable, the following consequence would result. The logical subject is the cognition. It has no producer because a cognition before its cognizable has no preceding cause. It is untenable to say that the proposition and reason[86] are not established, for that would violate your own premises. It is impossible that the pervasion[87] is not established, for it would contradict valid cognition, as there is no effect without a cause.

> **If cognition is co-emergent with cognizable,**
> **What does it arise from?**

b) If they were simultaneous, one could not say the cognition arose from its object because cognition and cognizable would occur simultaneously. Thus, the previous three faults would apply.

9.105
If it exists after the cognizable,
In that moment, what does it arise from?

c) If the cognition arises after the cognizable, in the moment of cognizing, cognition and object are either temporally separated or temporally unseparated. If the former, because of their temporal separation, it follows that there is no product.[88] If the latter, then either they are completely temporally unseparated or they are partially unseparated [435]. If the former, it follows that they are arising simultaneously, which is the same faulty position as b). If the latter, the cause is a composite being taken as singular and the effect is a composite being taken as singular, like a string of beads or an army taken as singular, in which case neither has an intrinsic nature, as was explained earlier.

4. Mindfulness of dharmas

   1. Establishing all as non-arising
   2. Abandoning objections

1. Establishing all as non-arising

Accordingly, all dharmas
Should be understood as non-arising.

'All dharmas' is the logical subject. That they are completely non-arising is the probandum. 'Accordingly' indicates the reason by which the arising of all dharmas is not ultimately established. Why are they not established? It is due to the faults of an effect arising before, after and at the same time as its cause, which was explained in the previous section on refuting the perception of the five consciousnesses.

2. Abandoning objections

   1. Abandoning the objection that there is no relative
   2. Abandoning the objection that this ascertainment entails an infinite regress

1. Abandoning the objection that there is no relative

9.106
'In that case, there is not really any relative arising,
So how can there be two truths?

'If it is illogical for something ultimate to arise before its cause, at the same time as it, or after it and hence ultimate arising is illogical, then it is also illogical for something relative to arise before its cause, at the same time as it, or after it. Therefore, it follows that relative arising is also illogical. If this is your position, since there is nothing but ultimate truth, there cannot be two truths.'

It might be responded that although the relative does not exist in someone's undeluded conceptual thought, it does exist in someone's deluded conceptual thought. [436] Therefore, it is logical to assert two truths when specified as such. But this is not the correct response. If it were, although the Buddha has no obscurations, it would follow that he still has obscurations due to anyone clinging to the existence of the appearance of obscurations in their deluded conceptual thought:

If the relative exists [for the Buddha] due to others,
How can sentient beings transcend suffering?'

The correct response is as follows:

9.107
It is just the discrimination of those other minds.
The relative is not [the Buddha's] perspective.

There are no defilements in the stream of being of the Buddha. The designation of his having obscurations is a designation from the perspective of someone's conceptual discrimination. It is not the relative of one who has attained nirvāṇa, for whom there are no obscurations.

'Although it exists only from the perspective of someone's delusion, that relative depends upon conceptual thought, which is not logical, for it is negated from the perspective of one who perceives its reality. Hence, there remains the error that two truths do not exist.'

From the perspective of perceiving reality, when the logic that refutes ultimate arising is applied to relative arising, the error that the relative does not exist does not follow. We do not assert that there is arising before or at the same time as the cause, but we allow that there is arising after the cause. Likewise, we do not assert arising from a temporal separation of cause and effect, but we allow that there is arising from their non-separation. Likewise, we do not assert cause and effect are wholly unseparated, but we allow that they are partially unseparated, i.e. it is taking something composite as singular. This is a relative designation:

> **If it is ascertained as arising after, it exists.**
> **If not, it does not have even relative existence.**

Therefore, 'arising after' means if an arising is ascertained as coming after its cause, the effect exists. An effect that does not occur before its cause is the deluded relative. We do not refute relative arising when the forward and reverse functions of cause and effect are established in this way.[89] [437]

2. Abandoning the objection that this ascertainment entails an infinite regress

1. A general comment on the division of object and subject
2. If the non-arising of the subject depends upon a further understanding, there is an infinite regress
3. Our position does not have that fault

1. A general comment on the division of object and subject

'The non-arising of all dharmas could never be realized because, even if it were understood with conceptual thought, the subject itself would not have been understood as non-arising. In that case, there must be another understanding of that non-arising and so there would be an infinite regress.'

> **9.108**
> **The understanding and its analysandum**
> **Are mutually dependent.**
> **All analysis is expressed**
> **In dependence upon accord with consensus.**

The understanding of the nature of the subject and that of the object is a single understanding.

'Then what ascertains, with valid cognition, that both have no intrinsic nature?'

2. If the non-arising of the subject depends upon a further understanding, there is an infinite regress

> 9.109
> If at that time there were an analyst
> Analysing the analysis
> Then there would be an infinite regress
> Because that analysis, too, would have to be analyzed.

If the inference that all dharmas are non-arising itself required another inference, then that, too, would also require yet another conclusion and thus there would be an infinite regress.

3. Our position does not have that fault

> 9.110
> However, when the analysandum has been analyzed
> Then that analysis has no basis.
> Because it has no basis, it is non-arising.
> This is also called 'nirvāṇa'.

The inferential analytic ascertainment that the analysandum—all dharmas—has no intrinsic nature itself has no basis. Since that inference is itself included among all dharmas, it has no pervader which is a second inference. Just as when firewood is exhausted, the fire dies, so when objects have been negated, the subject is also negated *a priori*. Thus, the analysis itself has no basis and, with no basis, it is non-arising, which is also called 'nirvāṇa'.

This explanation is not very thorough, however. Now to explain in more detail in accordance with the ṭīkā:[90] [438]

'If you assert that ultimately nothing whatsoever is established, since the valid cognition that infers no intrinsic nature is itself also not established, what makes the inference?'

Although, since it is relative, it is not a valid cognition of reality, there is no contradiction in ascertaining an analysandum, as explained in lines 108cd.

'But then the existence of the subject's valid cognition is in accord with the relative [i.e. is a delusion].'

We do not deny all relative existence, such as the analysanda of conceptual thought which, with inferential reasoning, grasps the essential characteristics of conceptual objects, and general concepts. Thus, it is in dependence upon an analysandum that the conception of dharmas and dharma-possessors arises, as is explained in v108ab.

'In addition to that inferential reasoning of a relative existence without existence in reality, there must be a second analysis. What is it that makes this latter inferential analysis?' Thus, the objection is that there would be an infinite regress, as presented in v109.

When it is directly ascertained that universally all dharmas have no intrinsic nature, that ascertainment is contrary to any individual case of an inferentially known intrinsic nature. Thus, it is ascertained *a priori* that no intrinsic nature is known inferentially. In other words, if it is understood that objects—the analysanda—are not established, then it is understood *a priori* that the analyst also has no intrinsic nature. Thus, it is not necessary to form this conclusion again with another inference, so there is no fault of an infinite regress, as presented in v110. The analysis has 'no basis' [v110c], i.e. the pervader is not supported. 'It is non-arising' [v110c] means that inferentially known existence is not ultimate. Being naturally 'nirvāṇa' [v110d] means that the obscurations of reality are not ultimate.[91]

4. Ceasing to grasp at true existence

[439] This is explained by Ngok Lotsawa and others as:

1. Verses 111-115: There is no reason that establishes all dharmas as having inherent nature [v111-115]
2. Verses 116-150: Refuting tīrthikas

According to the commentary by Ācārya Vairocanarakṣita:

1. Verses 104–105ab is a joint explanation of the foundations of mind and dharmas.
2. Verse 105cd concerns the foundation of mindfulness of dharmas, presenting in general the 'non-arising of all dharmas'.
3. Verses 106-110 are the abandoning of objections to this.
4. Verses 111-115 show that an inherent nature of all cognizing and cognized dharmas cannot be proven.
5. Verses 116-150, the section on showing the errors in the tīrthika accounts of arising, is a continuation of the explanation of the foundation of mindfulness of dharmas, showing that all dharmas are without arising, ceasing, intrinsic nature or self.

Other commentaries have also explained v105cd onwards as part of the foundation of mindfulness of dharmas and I accept these explanations of the root text.[92]

Section overview: There is no reason that establishes all dharmas as having inherent nature [v111-115]

1. General presentation
2. Extensive explanation
    1. Refuting the reason of mutual dependence
        1. There is neither one
        2. The reason applied with an example
    2. Refuting the reason of cognition of the effect

Wisdom

1. There is no reason that establishes all dharmas as having inherent nature

   1. General presentation
   2. Extensive explanation

1. General presentation

   9.111
   In that case, the existence of this pair
   Is a reality that is extremely difficult to maintain.

What is asserted by realists—that both cognizable and cognition are true—is held as true without a valid proof. It is a designation of a reality that is extremely difficult to maintain. [440]

2. Extensive explanation

   1. Refuting the reason of mutual dependence
   2. Refuting the reason of cognition of the effect

1. Refuting the reason of mutual dependence

   1. There is neither one
   2. Applying the reason with an example[93]

1. There is neither one

   If objects are established from the sense powers,
   What supports the existence of cognition?

   9.112
   'Cognition is established from the cognizable.'
   Then what supports the existence of the cognizable?
   If they are in mutual dependence,
   Then neither one exists.

If the display of objects of subjective comprehension is established by valid cognition, by what valid cognition is the subject itself established? Establishment by self-cognition was shown above to be erroneous, i.e. it is contradiction for it to function like an awareness of external objects.

'Cognition is established by the power of the external object.'

Since they would be established by mutual dependence, neither of the two would exist.

2. Applying the reason with an example

> 9.113
> **If there is no father without a son,**
> **Where does the son come from?**
> **There is no father without a son.**
> **Accordingly, neither of them exist.**

If a designated son is not established, then his designated father is also not established. When no product is ascertained, it is contradictory to the ascertainment of its corollary—its producer. Thus, their mutual dependence is proven.

'But the producer is not in mutual dependence because, although the arising of the son depended upon the father, the father's arising did not depend upon the son.'

2. Refuting the reason of cognition of the effect

> 9.114
> **'When a sprout comes from a seed,**
> **We acknowledge the existence of the seed.**
> **Since cognition arises from a cognizable,**
> **Why do you not acknowledge the cognizable's existence?'**

'In the case of a sprout arising from a seed, the seed is established by its logical relation to the sprout. Similarly, in the case of cognition arising from its cognizable, the cause—the cognizable—is established from the effect—the cognition. Thus, there is no contradiction.'

This is erroneous:

> 9.115

> When it is acknowledged the seed exists,
> That cognition is independent of the sprout,
> But what independently acknowledges the cognition
> Comprehending the cognizable?

When the seed is established through its logical relation to the sprout, that establishment is comprehended by a consciousness which sees the sprout and which is independent of the sprout. If a cognizable is established by its cognition, it cannot be established until the cognition is established. What establishes that cognition? As shown above, a cognition that is aware of itself is illogical. A cognition established by the power of the established cognizable is also erroneous because they would be mutually dependent. [441]

2. Refutation of the tīrthikas' position that the arising of the inherent nature of all dharmas is established

1. The analysis of cause: the vajra slivers
2. The analysis of self-essence: dependent origination
3. The analysis of the effect: arising and ceasing of existence and nonexistence

1. The analysis of cause: the vajra slivers

The establishment of the main syllogism[94] and the establishment of its pervasion are supplemental [i.e. not in the root text]. Only the establishment of the qualification for the main syllogism is given in the root text.[95]

The main syllogism: the logical subject is mere appearances. They are without true inherent nature because they do not arise from self, other, both, nor without cause. The pervader is not supported.[96]

Establishing the reverse pervasion:[97] Whatever has mere existence must either (a) have no cause or have a cause. If it has a cause, that cause must either be (b) a composite of self and other, or else it must be non-composite. If non-composite, *a priori* it must either be (c) self or (d) other. Hence, an arising which is not included among these four extremes is refuted. Hence, it is certain that arising is pervaded by the four extremes.

414 | BODHICARYĀVATĀRA WITH COMMENTARY

Establishing the qualification:

1. The main establishment of qualification [v116-137]
2. Without making a positive affirmation, the analysis is not contrary to valid cognition [v138-140]
3. Showing the certainty of the syllogism [v141-142b]

Section overview: 9.4 Ceasing to grasp at true existence (according to the Svātantrika presentation) [v111-150]

1. There is no reason that establishes all dharmas as having inherent nature [v111-115]
2. The refutation of the tīrthikas' position on the arising of the inherent nature of all dharmas
    1. The analysis of cause: the vajra slivers [v116-140]
        1. The main establishment of qualification
        2. Although no positive affirmation is established, analysis is not contrary to valid cognition
        3. Showing the certainty of the syllogism
    2. The analysis of self-essence: dependent origination [v141-144]
    3. The analysis of the effect: the arising and ceasing of existence and nonexistence [v145-150]

The explanation of the qualification is taught by the Svātantrika founding fathers through the application of further syllogisms.[98] Although their proofs by svatantra are indeed inerrant, establishing their pervasions, qualifications and so forth is very difficult, so those establishments will not be presented here. But if they are not established, are the syllogisms not incomplete? That may be so, but the three root syllogisms [not arising from self, other or without cause] do not actually appear in the root text, [442] so it was not the intention of the Ācārya to present the non-arising of dharmas in this way. Furthermore, if they were to be established, the appropriate place for that would be before lines 105cd: 'Accordingly, all dharmas / Are not to be understood as arising...', rather than here.[99]

Therefore, in this section, verses 116–137 [do not prove syllogistically the non-arising of all dharmas but] show the errors in the tīrthikas' positions on the arising of an intrinsic nature, with verses 138-140 explaining the abandonment of objections to the teaching of emptiness as the non-arising of all dharmas. Verses 141-150 show that all dharmas arise through dependent origination:

- Verses 141-142b are a summary of the non-arising and non-ceasing of all dharmas by showing their dependent origination.
- Verses 142c-144 show the relative arising of all dharmas in dependent origination to be illusion-like.
- Verses 145-148 show the refutation of the proposition that mere dependent origination itself has its own intrinsic nature.
- Verse 149-150 are an abbreviated showing of the sameness of existence and pacification.

> Section overview: 9.4 Ceasing to grasp at true existence (revised) [v111-150]
>
> 1. There is no reason that establishes all dharmas as having inherent nature [v111-115]
> 2. Refuting the tīrthikas' positions on the arising of an inherent nature of all dharmas [v116-140]
>   1. The main teaching on refuting arising by intrinsic nature
>   2. Abandoning objections to the middle way
> 3. Showing that all dharmas arise through dependent origination [v141-150]

2. Refuting the tīrthikas' positions of arising with an intrinsic nature

   1. The main teaching on refuting an arising with intrinsic nature
   2. Abandoning objections to the middle way

1. The main teaching on refuting an arising with intrinsic nature

   1. Refuting arising from no cause
   2. Refuting arising from other
   3. Refuting arising from self

Concerning an arising from both self and other, it is refuted implicitly by the refutations of arising from self and from other.

1. Refuting arising from no cause

   1. General explanation
   2. Differences of effect in relation to cause
   3. Differences of cause in relation to cause
   4. Differences of power in relation to cause

1. General explanation

> **9.116**
> **Ordinary people can directly see**
> **Everything temporal has causes.**

The proponents of things being caused by their own intrinsic nature assert arising from no [external] cause. [443] Those who accept this tradition say,

> The roundness of a pea, the sharpness of a thorn,
> The rising of the sun, the movement of water downstream,
> The pattern of a peacock's feather and so on, whatever it
>   may be,
> It was not created by anyone. Its cause is its own nature.

The error in this is that ordinary people can directly see that everything has causes. Since such appearances as the arising of a shoot from a seed can be directly seen, merely to be is to be pervaded by having a cause. Therefore, existence without a cause is negated both ultimately and relatively.

2. Differences of effect in relation to cause

'Concerning conventional designations such as the many colours in the segments of a lotus and the colourful patterns of a peacock feather, what is the cause of their creation and their being the way they are?'

To understand this, one must analyse their specific causes:

> **Differences such as in the segments of a lotus**

Are produced by different causes.

3. Differences of cause in relation to cause

'If different effects are created by different causes, what creates the different causes?'

They are created by previous different causes:

> **9.117**
> **'What creates different causes?'**
> **They come from previous different causes.**

4. Differences of power in relation to cause

'Why do specific causes have the power to create only certain effects and not the power to create others?'

> **'Why is a cause able to produce its effect?'**
> **It comes from the power of a previous cause.**

> Section overview: Refuting arising from other [v118-126b]
>
> 1. Refuting arising from an impermanent other
>   1. Effect before the cause
>   2. Effect simultaneous with the cause
>   3. Effect after the cause
> 2. Refuting arising from a permanent other
>   1. Refuting arising from Īśvara
>   1. Īśvara is not established
>   1. Refuting Īśvara as the elements
>   2. Refuting Īśvara as space
>   3. Refuting Īśvara as self
>   4. Refuting Īśvara as inconceivable
>   2. Effects are impossible
>   1. Refuting a permanent effect
>   2. Refuting an impermanent effect
>   3. Contradictions in his being a creator
>   1. Contradictory to a temporary effect
>   2. Establishing the pervasion by Īśvara's independence
>   3. Refuting his dependence
>   1. Everything being an effect of Īśvara contradicts his dependence
>   2. Dependence is contrary to Īśvara
>   1. Establishing the concurrence of conditions as the cause
>   2. Autonomy is violated
>   3. He would be under the power of desire
>   2. Refuting the Vaiśeṣika tradition of arising from sempiternal particles

2. Refuting arising from other

1. Refuting arising from an impermanent other
2. Refuting arising from a permanent other

1. Refuting arising from an impermanent other

This section is not in the root text but is presented here as a supplement.

'Is the effect before, at the same time as, or after the cause?'

1. Effect before the cause
2. Effect simultaneous with the cause
3. Effect after the cause

1. Effect before cause

The logical subject is the effect arising in a different moment. [Contradiction:] Although the proposition is that it exists before the cause, it follows that it does not exist before the cause because its cause does not yet exist. It is not tenable to say the proposition and the reason are not established, for it would contradict your own premise.[100] [444] It is not possible for the pervasion[101] to be unestablished: an effect without a cause cannot occur, for it would contradict valid cognition.

This proof has been presented as a prasaṅga and the other two alternatives will be presented in the same way.

2. Effect simultaneous with cause

[Contradiction: Although the proposition is that the effect arises from the cause,] it follows that it does not arise from the cause because of being simultaneous with the cause. This is because at any moment when neither of them exist, since no nature is established, a producer is negated.

3. Effect after cause

[Contradiction:] If the proposition is that the effect exists after the cause, [it follows that it does not arise from the cause,] because of being temporally separated from the cause.

'Then they are not temporally separated.'

If this means there is no temporal separation whatsoever, then from the moment of the arising of the cause to the moment of the ceasing of the effect, there would be no separation, so it would follow that they would be simultaneous, and the designations of producer and produced are contrary *a priori* to their being simultaneous [as in point 2]. Since they cannot be simultaneous, it follows that they cannot be completely temporally unseparated.

If they are unseparated only partially, they are not truly existent causes and effects because of their multiplicity. These are grasped as a unity but this is like grasping something white as golden. The objects to be refuted [i.e. a truly existent cause and effect] must not be mere conceptual designations. Existence is incompatible with the grasping of a multiplicity as a singularity.

Therefore, there is no arising from an impermanent other. Since this refutation accords with the logical subject of the earlier explanation of cognition arising before its cognizable [v104-105b], it is also established there and it is not necessary to further elaborate on it here.

2. Refuting arising from a permanent other

  1. Refuting arising from Īśvara
  2. Refuting the Vaiśeṣika tradition of arising from sempiternal particles

1. Refuting arising from Īśvara

  1. Īśvara is not established
  2. Effects are impossible
  3. Contradictions in his being a creator

1. Īśvara is not established

  1. Refuting Īśvara as the elements
  2. Refuting Īśvara as space [445]
  3. Refuting Īśvara as self
  4. Refuting Īśvara as inconceivable

1. Refuting Īśvara as the elements

>9.118
>If Īśvara is the cause of beings,
>Please explain what the temporal Īśvara is.
>If you say, 'the elements', that is fine,
>But why trouble yourself over a mere name?

>9.119
>Furthermore, since the earth and so forth are multiple,

> **Impermanent, inanimate, not deities,**
> **Suitable to be trodden on and impure,**
> **They are not Īśvara.**

When asked, 'What is Īśvara?', it is claimed Īśvara is the elements, such as earth, fire, etc. The elements are the logical subject. The probandum: whatever name they are called by, that is not what is meant by the term 'Īśvara'. The reason: because of being multiple, impermanent, lacking the sentience of premeditating intentionality,[102] mundane, contemptible and impure. These are the opposites of Īśvara, who is pervaded by singularity, permanence, divinity, sentience, worthiness of worship and purity.

2. Refuting Īśvara as space

9.120
Space is not Īśvara because it is inanimate.

The logical subject is space. That is not Īśvara because it does not have the sentience of intentionality. The reason here can be proven with the well-known inferences from other sources.

3. Refuting Īśvara as self

> **He is not the self because that was refuted previously.**

4. Refuting Īśvara as inconceivable

> **Since it is inconceivable to describe**
> **A creator who is inconceivable, what would be the point of**
>   **trying?**

If he is not pervaded by conceivability, were someone to describe him, they would be describing something they cannot comprehend.

2. Effects are impossible

Showing that it is not logical for effects to be created by Īśvara comprises a question and an answer. The question:

9.121

What could he want to create anyway?

The response has two parts:

1. Refuting a permanent effect
2. Refuting an impermanent effect

1. Refuting a permanent effect

'Īśvara created himself. He and his other creations, such as the four elements, are sempiternal.'

**Do you not claim that the self, the earth, etc.
And even Īśvara's own nature are sempiternal?**

Is Īśvara's nature not sempiternal? Therefore, because both creator and creation are sempiternal, [446] it follows that all the effects created by him are contemporaneous with him. Yet, this proposition is refuted by direct perception. If the reason[103] were not established, it would contradict your premise.

Or, the logical subject is the sempiternal objects. [Contradiction:] although the proposition is that it is possible for them be created, it follows that they cannot be created because of their being sempiternal. If the proposition and the reason[104] were not established, it would contradict your premise.

'The pervasion in these two [reasons] is not established.'[105]

If a sempiternal self creates effects, it is not logical for them to have a beginning. If it does not create effects, then it is not logical for those effects to arise. This is because in neither case is there any change.

2. Refuting an impermanent effect

'The effects [creations] of Īśvara—the five consciousnesses, sensations, happiness and suffering and so forth—are impermanent objects.'

Cognitions arise from cognizables

9.122

> And beginningless happiness and suffering come from
> actions.
> So, what is it you say he has created?

It is established by direct perception that impermanent objects arise from causes other than Īśvara. It is also established by direct perception that cognitions arise from their cognizables. It is established from both our scriptures that happiness and suffering arise from actions without beginning. Therefore, these all being the effects of Īśvara is negated.

3. Contradictions in his being a creator

This section also establishes the pervasion of the previous prasaṅgas.[106]

1. Contradictory to a temporary effect
2. Establishing the pervasion by Īśvara's independence
3. Refuting his dependence

1. Contradictory to a temporary effect

> If the cause has no beginning,
> How can the effect begin?

The logical subject is the effects of Īśvara, such as happiness and suffering. It follows that they sempiternally exist without any beginning because of their arising from a sempiternal, beginningless causal power. This proposition is untenable, for it contradicts your premise that the effects are temporary. It is untenable for the reason[107] not to be established: if you say the cause is sempiternal, its power to create cannot later increase because, by your own claim, it is a primordial, beginningless causal power, as asserted in the qualification statement.[108]

2. Establishing the pervasion by [Īśvara's] independence [447]

'Even though the cause abides sempiternally, that is not contradictory to temporary effects. The pervasion is not established.'

9.123

> How could his creations not be sempiternal,
> When he depends upon nothing external?

The sempiternal cause is the logical subject. The probandum: 'How could his creations not be sempiternal?', i.e. he cannot create something temporal: because he does not depend upon external conditions, it follows that Īśvara's state of creating is immutable. Therefore, being immutable, mutability is negated and hence the creations are contemporaneous with Īśvara. Thus, the pervasion is established.

3. Refuting his dependence

'The reason, "because of his independence from external conditions", is not established.'

Here we refute Īśvara's dependence:

1. Everything being an effect of Īśvara contradicts his dependence
2. Dependence is contrary to Īśvara

1. Everything being an effect of Īśvara contradicts his dependence

> If there is nothing that was not created by him,
> What could he depend upon?

If you claim that everything was created by Īśvara and that there is nothing which he did not create, then for their cause—Īśvara—to depend on his own effect is a contradiction.

2. Dependence is contrary to Īśvara

1. Establishing the concurrence of conditions as the cause
2. Autonomy is violated
3. He would be under the power of desire

1. Establishing the concurrence of conditions as the cause

9.124
> If he were dependent, the concurrence itself

Would be the cause, not Īśvara.

If there is a concurrence of conditions, either it is an effect of Īśvara or it is not. If it is not, it would be the concurrence and not Īśvara's causal powers which would be the cause. Thus, it would not be established that Īśvara is the cause but rather that the concurrence is the cause.

2. Autonomy is violated

> **When assembled, he is powerless not to create,**
> **When absent, he is powerless to create.**

The possessor of autonomy subject to conditions is the logical subject. [Contradiction]: it follows that it is not autonomous because of coming under the power of the concurrence of conditions. Through this prasaṅga, it is established *a priori* that Īśvara is not autonomous, yet your position is that he is autonomous.

3. He would be under the power of desire

> **9.125**
> **If Īśvara creates without wanting to,**
> **He is affected by an external power.**
> **If he creates when he wants to, the effect depends on his**
>   **wishes.**
> **How then is he 'The Almighty' [Īśvara]?**

'The creation of an effect [448] does not depend upon the concurrence of conditions. Rather, the effects arise from Īśvara. He creates the effects when he wishes to.'

It follows then that his wishes arise from an external power. Being subject to such wishes, his autonomy is violated, which is inappropriate for your Īśvara.

2. Refuting [the Vaiśeṣika tradition of arising from] sempiternal particles

> **9.126**
> **For those who assert sempiternal particles,**
> **The refutation was completed previously.**

The assertion of particles referred to here is the proposal of a substance as the ultimate cause by certain non-Buddhists, such as the Vaiśeṣikas. The refutation was previously completed in the section concerning the foundation of mindfulness of the body [v86], i.e. [they are not ultimate] because they are refuted by their decomposition into parts.

Section overview: Refuting arising from self [126c-137]

1. Formulating the position of the other [i.e. Sāṃkhya] tradition
    1. A general explanation
    2. The nature of the primal substance
    3. The nature of its effects
2. The error in that
    1. A general expression of the objection
        1. Refuting the primal substance
        2. Refuting its qualities
        3. Refuting its effects
    2. Refuting pleasure and so forth being external
        1. Refuting an unperceived appearance
        2. Refuting an external cause of pleasure and so forth
            1. Recalling the logic that was already completed
            2. The idea contradicts your own words
            3. Not preexisting in its basis
            4. Not existing in reality
    3. The permanent primal substance is unreasonable
        1. Refuting by not perceiving the appearance
        2. Gross and subtle are contradictory
        3. Establishing its contingent states as impermanent
        4. Establishing the primal substance as impermanent
    4. Contradictions in an existent arising
        1. Presenting the position to be refuted
        2. The position's uncertainty
        3. Mixing up the roles
        4. Abandoning objections
            1. The roles are the same
            2. Contradictory to worldly confusion
            3. The consequence that the role of the effect is a delusion

---

3. Refuting arising from self

1. Formulating the position of the other [i.e. Sāṃkhya] tradition
2. The error in that

1. Formulating the position of the other tradition

   1. A general explanation
   2. The nature of the primal substance
   3. The nature of its effects

1. A general explanation

> **The position of the Sāṃkhyas is that**
> **The cause of beings is a permanent, primal substance.**

'The primal substance [1] is the sempiternal intrinsic nature. It is in a universal flow in which previously hidden manifestations can become manifest.[109] This intrinsic nature is unseen due to obscurations. When manifestations arise from their previous state of non-manifestation, temporal objects are seen. Their cause is the intrinsic nature. Since both the intrinsic nature and what arises from it are in reality one, the primal substance is both cause and effect, but the arising of the manifestations is a relative [delusion].'

2. The nature of the primal substance

> **9.127**
> **Its qualities are 'purity', 'activity' and 'darkness'.**
> **While they remain in equilibrium,**
> **They are called the 'primal substance'.**

'The manifestations and sempiternal matter are pervaded by a oneness of the three qualities of the primal substance in equilibrium. This is the ultimate cause of all things. Individual consciousnesses [2] exist within that as containers of cognition and awareness. Each one is a sentient being experiencing objects. The individual consciousnesses are neither causes nor effects. [449] Since both the primal substance and the individual consciousnesses are ultimate, they are unseen, and are difficult to perceive.'

3. The nature of its effects

Manifestations are said to be their disequilibrium.

'When there is disequilibrium, happiness, suffering and so forth manifest within the 'Great One' [3] by its evolution into 'pride' [4]. From pride arise:

- The five sense faculties of the eye, ear, nose, tongue and body [5-9]
- The five physical action organs which activate speech, arm movement, walking, digestion and reproduction [10-14]
- The conceptual mind [15]
- The five elements of space, earth, water, wind and fire [16-20]
- The five bare elements of sounds, smells, tastes, touchables and colours [21-25]

When there is equilibrium, happiness and so forth remain unmanifest within the primal substance. When there is disequilibrium, they become manifest. The five bare elements are then perceived as pleasant, unpleasant or neutral. Therefore, happiness and so forth are comprised of the material primal substance. When manifestations form in the mirror of mind [3], experiences arise through the combination of the inner cognizing awareness with those manifestations.'

2. The error in that

1. A general expression of the objection
2. Refuting pleasure and so forth being external
3. A permanent primal substance is unreasonable
4. Contradictions in an existent arising

1. A general expression of the objection

1. Refuting the primal substance
2. Refuting its qualities
3. Refuting its effects

1. Refuting the primal substance

The primal substance is the logical subject. [Contradiction:] although the proposition is that its nature is singular, it follows that it is not singular because it has three qualities.

The pervasion for this inference[110] is expressed in the root text:

9.128
A triple nature that is also singular
Is illogical. There is no such thing.

2. Refuting its qualities

'Nevertheless, the three qualities exist.'

The three qualities also do not exist
Because each of them would also have three parts.

The three qualities are also not real, [450] because there would have to be three parts to each of them, such as a purity of the purity and so forth.

3. Refuting its effects

9.129
Without the qualities, the existence of sound
And so forth also becomes extremely implausible.

Without the qualities, it follows that the elements such as sound would not exist because it is illogical to have the effect without the cause.

2. Refuting pleasure and so forth being external [to consciousness]

  1. Refuting by not perceiving its appearance
  2. Refuting an external cause of pleasure and so forth

1. Refuting by not perceiving its appearance

Nor can the insentient, such as cloth,
Contain pleasure and so forth.

Material objects such as cloth, comprised of the five bare elements, are established by external perception, whereas pleasure and so forth are established by one's inner awareness. That these are mutually exclusive is established by direct perception. Thus, the Sāṃkhya position is refuted for the wise by direct perception and refuted for the deluded by their never perceiving such an appearance [of e.g. cloth as containing pleasure].

2. Refuting an external cause of pleasure and so forth

'When pleasure and so forth arise in the mirror of mind, it has a cause external [to the individual consciousness], such as the bare element of sound.'

Refuting this has four parts:

1. Recalling the logic that was already completed
2. The idea contradicts your own words
3. Not preexisting in its basis
4. Not existing in reality

1. Recalling the logic that was already completed

> **9.130**
> **'They are caused by the substantial [bare elements].'**
> **Wasn't the analysis of such substances already completed?**

If you propose that the five bare elements such as sound are the causes of pleasure and so forth, this would be a cognizable as the cause of cognition and the refutation for this was completed in the section on cognizable arising before cognition. According to the author of the *Great Commentary*, 'completed' here refers to the refutation of existence as atoms, as a composite and as a threefold nature.[111]

2. The idea contradicts your own words [451]

'You may have refuted cognizable and cognition as ultimate cause and effect but you did not refute them as relative.'

Nevertheless, if you claim that the cause is the five bare elements and the effect is pleasure and so forth, you contradict your previous position that the primal substance with a threefold nature of pleasure, etc.[112] is the cause and the five bare elements are the effect:

Also, the pleasure and so forth [in the primal substance] were your causes, [not the bare elements].[113]

3. Not preexisting in its basis

'We do not assert that the five bare elements are the causes of pleasure and so forth. The proposition is that the primal substance with the intrinsic nature of pleasure and so forth creates the five bare elements.'

Cloth and so forth do not arise from pleasure and so forth.

9.131
Rather, pleasure and so forth arise from cloth and so forth.

It is established by its incompatibility with direct perception that cloth and so forth do not arise from pleasure and so forth. Direct perception does not establish that cloth, etc. and the five bare elements arise from pleasure or the rest of the three qualities; rather, direct perception establishes the non-perception of pleasure and so forth arising from the five bare elements.[114]

4. Not existing in reality

Apart from this, there is no pleasure and so forth.

'We assert that the five bare elements are the causes and pleasure and so forth are the effects.'

The five bare elements have been refuted as a reality. Pleasure, etc. do not exist as a reality because they are relative.

4. The refutation of a permanent primal substance

1. Refuting by not perceiving the appearance
2. Gross and subtle are contradictory
3. Establishing its contingent states as impermanent
4. Establishing the primal substance as impermanent

1. Refuting by not perceiving the appearance

Sempiternal pleasure and so forth

Have never been perceived.

Pleasure and so forth are the logical subject. They are not sempiternal because they are essentially apparent yet are not always perceived.

'They are not essentially apparent, so, when their appearance is not perceived, that does not refute their being sempiternal.'

At the time of pleasure manifesting, it is established with direct perception that it essentially appears. When it is unmanifest, its intrinsic nature has either been eliminated or has not been eliminated. If eliminated, you are asserting its impermanence. If not eliminated, [452] its essential appearance remains in its nature, so it is established as essentially apparent:

9.132
If pleasure and so forth are essentially manifest,
Why are they not experienced?

2. Gross and subtle are contradictory

'The pleasure is not felt since previously it was gross and subsequently it becomes subtle.'

Either subtle and gross are of one intrinsic nature or distinct intrinsic natures. If not distinct, their inherent nature abides with contradictory dharmas, which is illogical:

'They become subtle.'
How can something gross also be subtle?

3. Establishing its contingent states as impermanent

9.133
'It becomes subtle by the elimination of the gross.'
Then the gross and subtle states are both impermanent.

'Gross and subtle are contingent states and the intrinsic nature of each state is distinct.'

If the gross state is eliminated, since it possesses arising and ceasing, that contingent state is impermanent.

4. Establishing the primal substance as impermanent[115]

'The contingent states are impermanent, but the primal substance is permanent.'

> In this way, why not accept
> That all such things are impermanent?
>
> 9.134
> If the gross state is nothing other than pleasure,
> The impermanence of pleasure is evident.

The primal substance of the three qualities (pleasure and so forth) is the logical subject. 'Its impermanence is evident' [in 134b] is the probandum. [The reason:] line 134a, i.e. because it is identified by its gross and subtle impermanent states, like a vase being identified by its blueness. Therefore, if it is established that the primal substance has impermanent states and that these are the intrinsic nature of everything, it is established that all dharmas are impermanent.

4. Contradictions in an existent arising

1. Presenting the position to be refuted
2. The position's uncertainty
3. Mixing up the roles
4. Abandoning objections

1. Presenting the position to be refuted

'At the earlier time when the Sāṃkhyas' five bare elements are not manifesting, their subsequent state still exists within the primal substance, and later manifests. When there is a lump of clay, the pot is contained within that substance but is not manifest. It is later made to manifest by the potter and so forth. Therefore, only its nature as an effect arises but nothing arises which was not previously present. It does not newly arise.'

> 'Whatever does not already exist

Cannot arise because of its not existing.'

'The formerly nonexistent thing is the logical subject. It cannot arise subsequently, [453] because the former does not exist, just like, for example, the horns of a hare not existing in the clay cannot arise. The former thing is nonexistent, so if it could arise, the horns of a hare also could arise from clay, but they cannot arise.'

2. The position's uncertainty

By the reason '[because of] its former nonexistence', you establish that there is no subsequent arising. Therefore, when your contingent state of pleasure and so forth manifests, that is also a latter arising from a nonexistent former, which you say is not established:

9.135
Although you deny that manifestations can arise
From their nonexistence, you also assert it.

3. Mixing up the roles

It also follows that to experience the cause would be to experience the effect and, therefore, the effect is mixed up with the role of the cause:

If effects abide in their causes,
To eat food would be to eat excrement.

9.136
For the money you spent on cotton, you should have instead
Bought cotton seeds and worn them.

4. Abandoning objections

   1. The roles are the same
   2. Contradictory to worldly confusion
   3. The consequence that the role of the effect is a delusion

1. The roles [of cause and effect] are the same

'The worldly fail to see it due to delusion.'

'Although cotton exists in cotton seeds, it is not possible for the worldly to experience it, due to their non-realization, which is based on delusion.'

Even if the worldly do not experience it due to delusion, for the non-deluded who cognize the truth, such as Kapila, it is a contradiction to wear cotton, but not to wear cotton seeds:

> Yet, someone who knows the reality is in the same predicament

The first line is the objection and the second line is the response.

2. Contradictory to worldly confusion

> **9.137**
> **And, since that knowledge of reality exists even for**
> **The worldly, why do they not see it?**

Taking someone who has worldly delusion as the cause and an omniscient teacher who cognizes the twenty-five basic elements as the effect, since the effect abides within the cause, omniscient cognition already exists for that worldly person; in which case, how come he does not cognize the existence of cotton in cotton seeds?

3. The consequence that the role of the effect is a delusion

> **'The worldly do not have valid cognition.'**
> **Then seeing manifestations would also be untrue.**

If the worldly person does not have valid cognition, he could not experience [454] any manifest effects. If he did see them, they would be false.

2. Abandoning objections to the middle way

According to the Svātantrika perspective, first one must establish the logic that proves there is no ultimate intrinsic nature. Then, in order to abandon the error of inferential valid cognition, it is shown that no positive affirmations are established, and this analysis does not contradict valid cognition. According to the Prāsaṅgika perspective, one simply abandons objections to the teaching that all dharmas have no intrinsic nature.

1. Setting out the objections
2. Response to the first prasaṅga: our position is not a valid cognition with a positive affirmation
3. Response to the second prasaṅga: showing that the pervasion is not established, for even though there is an analysis, it is not contrary to valid cognition

1. Setting out the objections

> **9.138**
> **'If valid cognition is not valid,**
> **Are its analyses not false?**

1) 'You Mādhyamikas hold that conceptual thought is relative. If this thought is deluded, it follows that even inferential valid cognition which cuts off elaborations is delusion.'

2) 'If the primal substance etc. were not real, since a refutation depends upon something to be refuted and since the object of refutation is not real, it follows that emptiness, which refutes it, is also not real.'

> **If reality is emptiness,**
> **Meditation for the sake of it is unreasonable.'**

'Therefore, it follows that meditation on emptiness is meaningless.'[116]

2. Response to the first prasaṅga

> **9.139**
> **With no connection to an object of examination**
> **There is no grasping of its nonexistence.**
> **Therefore, whatever the false object may be,**
> **Its nonexistence is clearly false.**

Since all conceptual thought is in error, it is not valid cognition. Nor are its objects—the objects to be refuted—established. Therefore, the emptiness which negates them—the emptiness being affirmed—is itself an untrue analysandum and is also not a valid cognition. This is the meaning of 'its nonexistence is clearly false'. Grasping the negation of the object of negation is false. Why? That conceptual thought [455] has no connection to an analysandum—the object to be examined, i.e. in not fabricating an analysandum as an object of conceptual thought, there is no grasping of its nonexistence. No conceptual thought of the negation arises.

If one asks, 'What is it that is nonexistent?', it should be answered, 'This is nonexistent.' But if no object to be negated is identified, there is no instance to negate because there is only a general concept of negation.[117] Therefore, if the object to be negated is false, its negation is also false. This is like saying, 'If the child of a barren woman is false, its death is also false.'

Concerning the second prasaṅga, 'It follows that the cultivation of emptiness would be meaningless', the response is to explain that its pervasion[118] is not established:

3. Response to the second prasaṅga

> **9.140**
> **When the son dies in a dream,**
> **The discrimination that 'he does not exist'**
> **Counters the discrimination that he exists,**
> **Even though it is false.**

If the son within a dream is false, the discrimination that, 'Now he has died, so he does not exist' is also false. Nevertheless, it counters the discrimination that he exists. It functions as an antidote to the imputation that grasps him as existent, in respect of which it is not a delusion. In the same way, the explicit predicate '[it] is empty' negates the object to be negated. Although that positive affirmation of the emptiness of the external object of attachment is itself false, it overcomes the possibility for imputations to arise which could be grasped as existent. In respect of its eliminating imputations grasped as existent, there is no contradiction with the merely analytical aspect of valid cognition. This is the Svātantrika Madhyamaka argument.[119] If one applies the Prāsaṅgika Madhyamaka explanation, 'it is false' means it is the yogic relative, by which the erroneous understandings of others are refuted.

> Section overview: Showing that all dharmas arise merely through dependent origination [v141-150]
>
> 1. A summary of the refutation of the four [kinds of] arising
> 2. Showing that there is no arising or ceasing, coming or going
> 3. The implication of that: that which is dependently originated is mere illusion
>   1. Showing that dependent origination is like an illusion
>   2. Showing dependent origination
>   1. Presenting the reason
>   2. Showing the forward pervasion
>   3. The example of that
>   4. The logical consequence
>   3. Establishing the pervasion of dependent origination
>   1. The logic
>   1. Refuting existent arising
>   2. Refuting nonexistent arising
>   1. Presenting the logic in brief
>   2. The contradiction in the possibility of nonexistence being the cause for an object
>   3. Refuting [the cessation of] object itself
>   2. Making certain of the logic
>   1. Freedom from the two extremes
>   2. Abiding is like an illusion
>   3. The sameness of existence and pacification

3. Showing that all dharmas arise merely through dependent origination

   1. A summary of the refutation of the four kinds of arising
   2. Showing that there is no arising or ceasing, coming or going
   3. The implication of that: that which is dependently originated is mere illusion

1. A summary of the refutation of the four kinds of arising

9.141
Therefore, on this analysis,
Nothing exists without a cause,
Nor abides in its conditions,
Whether individually or combined.

'Without a cause' means existing without a cause. [456] 'Individually' means either self or other. 'Combined'[120] means both self and other.

2. Showing that there is no arising or ceasing, coming or going

9.142
Nor does it come from other,
Nor stay, nor go.

To 'not come from other' is to be without arising. To 'not stay' is to be free from abiding. To 'not go' is to be free from cessation. This is precisely to be free from the three characteristics of the composite.

3. The implication of this: that which is dependently originated is mere illusion

1. Showing that dependent origination is like an illusion
2. Showing dependent origination
3. Showing that dependent origination is not an intrinsic nature by establishing the pervasion of dependent origination

1. Showing that dependent origination is like an illusion

This is what deluded ones take as real,
But how is it different from an illusion?

When an analytical cognition negates true existence, appearances are established as being like illusions.

2. Showing dependent origination

9.143
Whatever manifests by illusion
And whatever manifests by causes,

Examine from where it could come
And to where it could go.

9.144
Whatever it is, it is seen in relation to something else.
Otherwise, it is not seen.
It is fabricated, like a reflection.
How can there be reality in that?

Here I shall present the so-called 'dependent origination analysis of inherent nature' according to the Svātantrika treatises:[121]

1. Presenting the reason
2. Showing the forward pervasion
3. The example of that
4. The logical outcome

[Proof: Appearances (the logical subject) have no intrinsic nature because of being dependently originated, like illusions.]

1. Presenting the reason: ['Because of being dependently originated']

In line 144d, 'in that' refers to 'these appearances', the logical subject. Questioning how they could have reality is the probandum to be established, i.e. 'they are empty of a real intrinsic nature'. Any effect whatsoever is seen to have a productive cause. If there is no such cause, there is no effect. Thus, the reason is: 'Because of having the nature of dependent origination in their forward [causative] and reverse [caused] functions.'

2. Showing the forward pervasion: ['Whatever is dependently originated (fabricated) has no intrinsic nature.']

'It is fabricated, like a reflection' [144c] indicates that if something has an intrinsic nature, then it is illogical for it to be fabricated by causes and conditions, since what arises from causes and conditions is pervaded by fabrication. Since that is contrary to its reality, it negates its reality. Thus, the negandum—its reality—is pervaded by non-fabrication. Since the contrary—fabrication by conditions—is supported by the logical subject, the contrary pervader is supported. [457]

3. The example of that: ['Like an illusion']

Line 143a gives an example of something fabricated by conditions being pervaded by the exclusion [of reality]—the manifestation of an illusion. To ask from where it comes [143c] means the arising of its reality is excluded. To ask where it could go to [143d] means the cessation of its reality is excluded. That its remaining is also excluded is implicit in this.

4. The logical outcome: ['They do not arise, cease, or persist.']

In general, whatever is a mere fabrication is pervaded by the exclusion of a true intrinsic nature. If one has doubts about this, the refutation [of the contrary] is implicit in these lines:

- 'Whatever manifests by causes, from where could it come?' [143bc], i.e. what is it that arises?
- 'Whatever manifests by causes, to where could it go?' [143bd], i.e. what is it that ceases?
- Therefore, there is also no abiding.

'Although they are dependent originations, dependent origination is their ultimate intrinsic nature. Where is the contraction? The pervasion is not established.'

One can establish the reverse pervasion[122] by the so-called 'analysis of the effect: the arising and ceasing of its existence or nonexistence'.

3. Showing that dependent origination is not an intrinsic nature by establishing the pervasion of dependent origination

[Proof:] An ultimate intrinsic nature is the logical subject. It is not a dependent origination because it is illogical for an existent or nonexistent effect to arise. This refutation of the ultimate intrinsic nature as a dependent origination establishes that dependent origination is not pervaded by an ultimate intrinsic nature and is pervaded by relative delusion.

1. The logic
2. Making certain of the reason

1. The logic

1. Refuting something existent arising as an effect
2. Refuting something nonexistent arising as an effect

1. Refuting something existent arising as an effect

9.145
For something that already exists,
What cause does it require?

That which is possible to be created by causes is pervaded by the necessary conditions for its creation. Grasping something as already existent is incompatible with grasping the necessary conditions for its creation. Since the certainty of this is established *a priori*, anything existent necessarily has no conditions for its creation.

2. Refuting something nonexistent arising as an effect

1. Presenting the logic in brief [458]
2. The contradiction in the possibility of something nonexistent being the cause for an object
3. Refuting [the cessation of] the object itself

1. Presenting the logic in brief

And if it does not exist,
What cause does it require?

That which has been created is pervaded by particular existent qualities. The existence of those qualities is incompatible with the non-establishment of its substantial intrinsic nature. Therefore, a nonexistent object does not require a cause to create it, so it is not something that can be created.

2. The contradiction in the possibility of something nonexistent being the cause for an object

'A nonexistent object cannot be created but subsequently attains a self-nature. Since this requires a cause, why do you claim it is not necessary?'

The fact that there is no such requirement is established as follows:

9.146
Even a billion causes
Cannot alter nonexistence.

A nonexistent object might have a billion causes but it is still not something that can be created because there is nothing to transform. The pervader is not supported.[123]

'An already existent object cannot transform into something else, but a previously nonexistent thing can subsequently attain a substantial intrinsic nature. Therefore, it transforms from nonexistent into existent.'

In subsequently becoming existent, does it do so without abandoning its previous nonexistence or not? If it does not abandon its nonexistence:

How can a state of nonexistence be existent,
Or become existent?

Since its existence and nonexistence are mutually exclusive, an intrinsic nature of nonexistence is contradictory to one of existence:

9.147
If its existence is impossible during its nonexistence,
When could it ever become something existent?

If it abandons its nonexistence: the contingent state of nonexistence is the logical subject. It cannot become existent through subsequently abandoning its nonexistence because its nonexistence cannot be negated. That is because becoming existent is pervaded by the cessation of nonexistence and nonexistent objects have no cessation.

'That reason is not established.'

[Contradiction:] If nonexistent objects could cease, they would be impermanent and thus would be pervaded by becoming existent, i.e. the object would be both nonexistent and existent. Therefore, because of being nonexistent, [459] it is not impermanent. Since the pervader is not supported,[124] the cessation of a nonexistent state is negated, by which the qualification[125] is established. This explains line 146d, as well as:

> While its existence has not yet begun,
> Its nonexistence has not yet been lost.

9.148
If its nonexistence has not been lost,
It is impossible for it to exist.

3. Refuting the cessation of the object itself

Having shown that a nonexistent object cannot become existent, it is next shown that an existent object cannot change into a state of nonexistence:

> **Nor can the existent become nonexistent,**
> **Because it would follow that it would have two intrinsic natures.**

The nonexistent object is the logical subject:

- The prasaṅga from the reason based on intrinsic nature: [Contradiction: you claim that the object is non-dual but] it follows that it is dual because of its transformation [from existent to nonexistent].
- The svātantra from the pervader not being supported:[126] because of being non-dual, there is no transformation.

2. Making certain of the reason

1. Freedom from the two extremes
2. Abiding is like an illusion
3. The sameness of existence and pacification

1. Freedom from the two extremes

9.149
In this way, there is no cessation.

**Nor is there any existence. Because of this,
All these beings
Are forever neither arising nor ceasing.**

Since beings have no cessation, all sentient beings are called 'always non-ceasing'. Since they have no existence, they are called 'always non-arising'.

2. Abiding is like an illusion

**9.150
Dreamlike beings,
When analysed, are like banana trees.**

The first line establishes they are deluded perceptions and the second line indicates the essence of the truth is emptiness.

3. The sameness of existence and pacification

**In suchness, there is no distinction
Between nirvāṇa and non-nirvāṇa.**

There is no distinction between saṃsāra and nirvāṇa. In every sense? Only in suchness, i.e. ultimately, they have the single taste of emptiness.

> Section overview: The result of meditation on emptiness [v151-167]
>
> 1. Benefit of self
>   1. Pacifying attachment
>   1. The non-establishment of the eight worldly dharmas, the objects of attachment
>   2. Ending conditioned existence, which depends upon these
>   2. Pacifying suffering
>   1. A summary of visible sufferings
>   2. The sufferings of other lives
>   1. The sufferings of the lower realms
>   2. Continuously experiencing suffering
>   1. The roots of suffering have not been pacified
>   2. One does not have the means to dispel it
>   3. There are many obstacles
>   1. Outer obstacles
>   2. Inner obstacles
>   4. It is difficult to rely on the supports
>   5. It is difficult to abandon its causes
>   3. Not knowing that one is suffering
>   4. The kinds of suffering which will be experienced
> 2. Benefit of others
>   1. Pacifying suffering
>   2. Pacifying attachment

5. The result of meditation on emptiness

This is explained by some[127] as follows:

1. Benefit of self
2. Benefit of others

1. Benefit of self

1. Pacifying attachment
2. Pacifying suffering

1. Pacifying attachment

1. The non-establishment of the eight worldly dharmas, the objects of attachment
2. Ending conditioned existence, which depends upon these

1. The non-establishment of the eight worldly dharmas, the objects of attachment [460]

> **9.151**
> **What is there to gain and what is there to lose**
> **Of things which are, in this way, empty?**
> **Who exists to respect me,**
> **Or to despise me?**
>
> **9.152**
> **Where do happiness and suffering come from?**
> **What is there to be joyful or miserable about?**

In relation to the eight worldly dharmas:

- Not being gained or lost corresponds to the emptiness of gain and loss.
- Not being respected or despised corresponds to not being praised or criticized.
- Happiness and suffering are named explicitly.
- Joy and misery corresponds to being famous or infamous.

2. Ending conditioned existence, which depends upon these

> **When I try to find reality itself,**
> **Who has craving and what is there to crave?**

This is a general point that ultimately the one who has attachment and the object of attachment itself are not established.

Without going into a detailed explanation, the next lines explain that the span of life, with its happiness and unhappiness, is not established:

> **9.153**
> **When analysed, what lives in this world**

And what can die in it?

The objects of direct happiness in the future are not established:

What can arise ...

The objects of intense attachment right now and those in the past which are subsequently recollected are not established:

... and what has ever arisen?

Loved ones are not established:

What friends or relatives are there?

In summary:

**9.154
All is like space.
May we come to fully understand this.**

Being empty, may one understand this and may people who are like oneself also understand this.

This concludes the analytical instructions. The next verses concern instructions on unification with compassion.

2. Abandoning suffering

Here it will be shown explicitly that if emptiness is not realized, suffering arises and hence it is implicit that when emptiness is realized, suffering is ended. The suffering from the non-realization of emptiness has two parts:

1. An introductory summary of the visible sufferings
2. The invisible sufferings of other lives

1. An introductory summary of visible sufferings

For those who want happiness,

The causes of conflict and excitement

9.155
Create intense disturbance and hysteria.
We are tormenting, fighting and arguing with one another,
Cutting and stabbing one another.
By such nonvirtues, we endure great difficulties.

Those who have not realized emptiness but want happiness have great difficulties in just getting by, with terrible sufferings in this very life. Why are virtuous actions so difficult? Because of nonvirtue. In what way? [461] By the cause of conflict with enemies, anger and intense malice are created. From that comes fighting, arguing and cutting and stabbing one another. Thus, nonvirtues arising from anger are accumulated. By the cause of excitement towards friends, when one is with them, hysteria, fighting and arguing develop and when one is not with them, misery develops. Thus, the nonvirtues which arise from these are accumulated.

2. The invisible sufferings

1. The sufferings of the lower realms
2. Continuously experiencing suffering
3. Not knowing that one is suffering
4. The kinds of suffering which will be experienced

1. The sufferings of the lower realms

9.156
Having enjoyed so much happiness,
In happy rebirths again and again,
After death, it ends, and one suffers,
Falling into torment for a long time.

Having had happy rebirths again and again, one falls from them. When? At death. Where does one fall to? To the unbearable sufferings of the lower realms, which are difficult even to think about. For how long? For a long time.

2. Continuously experiencing suffering

After escaping that suffering, will there be no more suffering? Alas! One will continue to experience suffering. In dependence upon the five types of rebirth, one will constantly experience attachment to saṃsāra. Why? There are five main causes:

1. The roots of suffering have not been pacified
2. One does not have the means to dispel it
3. There are many obstacles
4. It is difficult to rely on the supports
5. It is difficult to abandon its causes

1. The roots of suffering have not been pacified

9.157
Within conditioned existence, there are many precipices,
For there is no truth in it.
Where there is conditioned existence, there is no reality,
For they are incompatible.

There being no reality means that, since there is no wisdom of realizing suchness, grasping at existence is not pacified, so the root of suffering is not pacified. Why is there no wisdom of realizing suchness? Because of its incompatible condition, i.e. the existence of its opposite. What is that? The many precipices of affliction by suffering. They are the effects, while non-truth—the obscuration of ignorance—is the cause. [462]

2. One does not have the means to dispel it

9.158
There is no way to truly exemplify
This unending ocean of unbearable suffering.
It is where we lack strength.
It is where life is short.

9.159
It is where we are worn out, striving to live and get by,
Where we are exhausted by hunger and sickness,
Where we sleep and where we cause harm,

And where we meaninglessly associate with the childish and
with friends.

9.160
So life swiftly passes by without any meaning,
And a remedy is extremely difficult to find.
How can we find a way
To dispel habitual distraction?

Why can we not dispel it? Because the remedy—the antidote—is extremely difficult to find and because of disturbing and mistaken habitual distractions. Why is the remedy difficult to find? Because our exertion for it is weak, so we are lacking in strength, and this opportunity is unstable, so life is short. Why are there habitual distractions? Because we are worn out by striving to live and get by, exhausted by hunger and sickness and because we pass our time meaninglessly with sleep and harmful things and are occupied meaninglessly with childish people and friends, so this life passes by without meaning.

3. There are many obstacles

   1. Outer obstacles
   2. Inner obstacles

1. Outer obstacles

9.161
It is where demons are striving to cast us
Into the great lower realms.

In conditioned existence, demons are striving. For what purpose? To cast us into the lower realms. [For example], the demon Kāmadeva fired his flower-arrow at Queen Padmavati and so forth.[128]

2. Inner obstacles

It is where overcoming doubts is hard
Among its many mistaken paths.

With incorrect views and doubts, one clings to one's doubts about the paths of perfection.

4. It is difficult to rely on the supports

**9.162
An opportunity like this will be difficult to find again,**

After transmigration from this life, such an opportunity will be difficult to find again. There will be no return of the eight freedoms and the five endowments of oneself will be difficult to find.

And the presence of Buddhas will be extremely difficult to find.

The five endowments of others will also be difficult to find.

5. It is difficult to abandon its causes

It is difficult to escape the river of defilements.

It is difficult to escape the river of attachment, craving, views and unawareness. Therefore: [463]

Alas! The suffering just goes on and on.

3. Not knowing that one is suffering

The point here is that the childish are suffering but they do not know they are suffering. This main point is followed by an example. The main point:

**9.163
Although the sufferings are intense,
Some cannot recognize their own misery.
Alas! It is only right to feel pity
For those who dwell in the rivers of suffering.**

Suffering without knowing that one is suffering is the suffering of karmic formations, in which one does not know one is suffering. The example:

> **9.164**
> **This is like, for example, bathing again and again,**
> **And then stepping into a fire again and again,**
> **Proclaiming one's happiness,**
> **While being in immense pain.**

Bathing and then entering a fire is explained by the author of the *Great Commentary* as someone being submerged in painfully cold water and then, wishing to be warm, stepping into a fire.[129] Others say it is a reference to an actual yogic practice of certain tīrthikas.

4. The kinds of suffering which will be experienced

> **9.165**
> **So, carrying on as if**
> **There were no old age or death,**
> **They are first subjected to death**
> **And then fall into the unbearable lower realms.**

Those who assume they will not grow old or die will die and be reborn in the lower realms. Thus, if one has not realized emptiness, those sufferings will arise but, if one realizes it, they will be prevented.

2. Benefit of others

1. Pacifying suffering
2. Pacifying attachment

1. Pacifying suffering

> **9.166**
> **When will I be able to pacify**
> **These unbearable fires of suffering**
> **With a rain of accumulated happiness**
> **Falling from clouds of stored up merit?**

What is the means to pacify suffering? It is the rain of one's amassed happiness. From where will that rain of happiness fall? From the clouds of merit that one has well created.

2. Pacifying attachment

**9.167
Having fostered the non-conceptual
And devotedly accumulated merits,
When will I show emptiness
To those lost in conceptualization?**

Who does one do this for? For those who are lost in conceptualization. From what cause will their benefit come? From reliance upon the non-conceptual—the accumulation of primordial wisdom—and from devotion to the gathering of merit—the accumulation of merit.

According to this explanation, the dispelling of the sufferings mentioned above [v154c-165] refers to the benefit of self. This explanation does not fit the root text in one respect. [464] For one who has not realized emptiness, does the 'suffering' refer to suffering experienced by self or by others? If the former, verses 166-7 also refer to one's own suffering, so they are part of the section on the benefit of self. If the latter, even if dispelled, v154c-165 refer to the suffering of others, so should not be included in the benefit of self. Therefore, the sections on the non-establishment of the worldly dharmas and ending conditioned existence together comprise the result of realizing emptiness and what follows concerns the benefit of others, which goes from v154c through to v165 in accord with the previous explanation, then dispelling suffering is v166 and the means to dispel it is v167.

Revised structure of verses 151-167:

1. The result of realization of emptiness
    1. The non-establishment of the eight worldly dharmas, the objects of attachment [v151-152b]
    2. Ending conditioned existence, which depends upon these [v152c-154b]
2. The benefit of others
    1. Visible sufferings [v154c-155]
    2. Invisible sufferings [v156-165]
       (cont., see previous explanation, above)
    3. Dispelling the sufferings [v166]
    4. The means to dispel them [v167]

PART V
THE SUBSEQUENT RESULTS

Chapter 10

DEDICATION

To realize the results attained from practising the bodhisattva conduct in this way, one must perfect the benefit of self and others. The means for doing so is to take that benefit as the object of one's virtuous intention and dedicate it as follows:

1. Dedication related to the means
2. Dedication for the benefit of others
3. Dedication for the benefit of self
4. Dedication for the teachings to remain as a source of happiness
5. Homage of remembrance of kind ones

1. Dedication related to the means

> 10.1
> By whatever virtue there is
> In my undertaking
> To enter the bodhisattva conduct,
> May all beings enter the bodhisattva conduct.

The first three lines indicate the object to be dedicated. 'All beings' indicates to whom it is dedicated. The result is their becoming bodhisattvas.

> Section overview: Dedication for the benefit of others
>
> 1. Dedication for worldly benefit
>   1. General dedication
>   2. Dedication for the benefit of specific lower realms
>   1. Dedication for the benefit of hell-beings
>   1. Dedication for their own pacification of suffering
>   1. Dedication for general pacification
>   2. Dedication for pacifying the cold hells
>   3. Dedication for pacifying the hot hells
>   1. Dedication for pacifying the suffering of the main hells
>   2. Dedication for pacifying the neighbouring hells
>   2. Dedication for their pacification by others
>   1. Pacification by Vajrapāṇi's power
>   2. Pacification by Padmapāṇi's compassion
>   3. Pacification by Mañjughoṣa's emanation
>   4. Pacification by the force of the other bodhisattvas' proximity
>   2. Dedication for the benefit of animals
>   3. Dedication for the benefit of ghosts
>   3. Dedication for the benefit of the higher realms
>   1. Freedom from suffering
>   2. Attaining wishes
>   1. General dedication
>   1. Attaining wealth and possessions
>   2. Entering the path of perfection
>   3. Attaining worldly happiness
>   2. Dedication specific to monastics
> 2. Dedication for transcendental benefit

2. Dedication for the benefit of others

1. Dedication for worldly benefit
2. Dedication for transcendental benefit

1. Dedication for worldly benefit

1. General dedication
2. Dedication for the benefit of specific lower realms
3. Dedication for the benefit of the higher realms

1. General dedication [465]

> **10.2**
> **By my merit,**
> **May all those in all directions**
> **Afflicted with physical and mental suffering**
> **Attain oceans of happiness and joy.**
>
> **10.3**
> **As long as they remain in saṃsāra,**
> **May their happiness never fail.**
> **May beings attain the uninterrupted**
> **Happiness of a bodhisattva.**

The first verse is a dedication for them to be free from suffering and to attain happiness—the aspects of compassion and loving kindness, respectively. The next two lines are a dedication for them never to be separated from happiness—the aspect of joy. The last two lines are a dedication for them to attain benefit—the aspect of equanimity.

2. Dedication for the benefit of specific lower realms

1. Dedication for the benefit of hell-beings
2. Dedication for the benefit of animals
3. Dedication for the benefit of ghosts

1. Dedication for the benefit of hell-beings

1. Dedication for their own pacification of suffering
2. Dedication for their pacification by others

1. Dedication for their own pacification of suffering

1. Dedication for general pacification
2. Dedication for pacifying the cold hells

3. Dedication for pacifying the hot hells

1. Dedication for general pacification

> **10.4**
> **In however many hells**
> **There may be in existence,**
> **May all those living creatures**
> **Have the bliss and joy of Sukhāvatī.**

2. Dedication for pacifying the cold hells

> **10.5**
> **May those tormented by the cold find warmth,**

3. Dedication for pacifying the hot hells

   1. Dedication for pacifying the suffering of the main hells
   2. Dedication for pacifying the neighbouring hells

1. Dedication for pacifying the suffering of the main hells

> **And may boundless waters pour**
> **From the clouds of bodhisattvas,**
> **Cooling those tormented by the heat.**

2. Dedication for pacifying the neighbouring hells

The harms of the hell-forests:

> **10.6**
> **May the forests of razors**
> **Become divine groves.**
> **May the trees of Śālmari**
> **Grow into wish fulfilling trees.**

The harms of the hell-realms:

> **10.7**

> May the realms of hell become places of joy,
> Covered with vast pools, fragrant with lotus flowers,
> With calls of wild ducks, geese and swans
> Resounding gently in the air.
>
> 10.8
> May its burning pyres become heaps of jewels.
> May its molten earth become a clear, crystal floor.
> May its crushing mountains become
> Celestial palaces of worship, filled with Buddhas.
>
> 10.9
> May its showers of embers, burning rocks and fiery razors
> From now on be a rain of flowers.

The harms of internal conflict in hell:

> May the conflict of armed violence
> From now on be a casting of flowers.

The harms of the hell-rivers:

> 10.10
> May those submerged in the torrents of hell,
> Their flesh completely incinerated from their lily-white bones,
> Attain, from this virtue, the bodies of gods,
> And dwell among goddesses in gentle, divine rivers.

2. Dedication for their pacification by others

   1. Pacification by Vajrapāṇi's power
   2. Pacification by Padmapāṇi's compassion
   3. Pacification by Mañjughoṣa's emanation
   4. Pacification by the force of the other bodhisattvas' proximity [466]

1. Pacification by Vajrapāṇi's power

10.11
'Why are the servants of the Lord of Death and his dreadful
crows and vultures suddenly afraid?
Whose power clears away the enveloping darkness, bringing
joy and happiness?'
When they look up, may they see the blazing form of
Vajrapāṇi in the sky,
And the power of their intense joy clearing away all
negativities, may they go to join him.

The first line indicates the terrors of hell; the second, being filled with joy; and the last two lines indicate seeing one's protector and overcoming negative actions.

2. Pacification by Padmapāṇi's compassion

10.12
Seeing the glittering fires of hell
Extinguished by rains of flowers mixed with scented water,
May they wonder what could have brought such happiness,
And may these denizens of hell see Padmapāṇi himself.

The first two lines indicate pacifying the harms of fires. The next line indicates attaining happiness and the last line indicates finding refuge.

3. Pacification by Mañjughoṣa's emanation

10.13
'Friends, come here quickly. Don't be afraid.
He forcefully dispels all our suffering and brings the power
of joy!
A protector of all beings, who has generated bodhicitta and
kindness,
A blazing youth with hair in knotted locks delivers us from
these horrors.

10.14
'See one hundred gods offer their crowns at his lotus feet.
A rain of flowers falls upon his head, his eyes moist with
compassion.

Thousands of goddesses sing his praises atop magnificent
pavilions.'
Upon seeing Mañjughoṣa, may the denizens of hell cry out
in joy.

There are two points here—finding hope and being held by the protector. The first is indicated in 13a, comprising assembling friends and abandoning fear. This is what is cried out by the denizens of hell, indicated in 14d. The second point connects 'our' [13b] with 'delivers' [13d].[1] How are beings delivered? Through the destruction of the horrors of hell. How are they destroyed? By forcefully dispelling suffering and bringing the power of joy, thus protecting beings. With what intention does he protect them? With the generation of bodhicitta and kind affection. In what form does he deliver this? As the blazing youth with hair in knotted locks. To whom does this emanation appear? To those who 'see' [14a] him. What is his emanation like? There are four aspects: 'One hundred gods…' indicates the array of gods worshipping him; 'a rain…' indicates a rain of flowers descending upon him; 'singing his praises…' indicates music; and 'magnificent pavilions' indicates his lavish surrounds.

4. Pacification by the force of the other bodhisattvas' proximity

10.15
By the roots of my virtue, may the denizens of hell,
Seeing the cooling, fragrant rains of happiness fall
From the stainless clouds of the bodhisattvas such as
    Samantabhadra,
Be filled with joy.

May the cooling and scented rain from the unobscured clouds of the tenth bhūmi bodhisattvas bring joy to the denizens of hell. [467]

2. Dedication for the benefit of animals

10.16
May animals be freed
From the horrors of preying upon one another.

3. Dedication for the benefit of ghosts

> May ghosts have happiness
> Like that of the Northern Continent.

> **10.17**
> May their hunger be sated,
> And may they always be bathed and refreshed
> By streams of milk
> Flowing from the hands of Avalokiteśvara.

3. Dedication for the benefit of the higher realms

   1. Freedom from suffering
   2. Attaining wishes

1. Freedom from suffering

Impaired senses:

> **10.18**
> May the blind see
> And may the deaf hear.

Painful childbirth:

> May mothers give birth without any pain
> Like Māyādevī herself.

Poverty:

> **10.19**
> May the naked find clothes,
> The hungry find food,
> And the thirsty find water
> And delightful, refreshing drinks.

> **10.20**
> May the poor acquire wealth.

Discontent:

May the unhappy and miserable find joy.
May the distressed be placated,
And may they have confidence and stability.

Sickness:

10.21
Wherever sentient beings are unwell,
May their sicknesses quickly disappear.
May the diseases affecting every living creature
Cease and never occur again.

Unseen sufferings:

10.22
May those who are afraid be without fear.
May those who are bound be freed.
May the weak find strength
And may their minds be calmed.

The sufferings of travellers:

10.23
May all those travelling abroad
Be happy wherever they may go and,
For whatever purpose they are travelling,
May they achieve it without any difficulties.

10.24
May all those aboard boats and ships
Achieve whatever they set out to do and,
Having happily returned to their own shores,
May they be reunited with their loved ones.

10.25
May those who have lost their paths
Encounter fellow travellers,
And proceed to their destinations with ease,
Unmolested by bandits, wild animals and so on.

Harm from spirits:

> **10.26**
> **May those who are lost and alone in wildernesses,**
> **Children and the elderly without any protector,**
> **Those who are unconscious, mentally disturbed or insane,**
> **Be protected by the gods.**

2. Attaining wishes

   1. General dedication
   2. Dedication specific to monastics

1. General dedication

   1. Attaining wealth and possessions
   2. Entering the path of perfection
   3. Attaining worldly happiness

1. Attaining wealth and possessions

Wealth of the basis:

> **10.27**
> **May they never lack the eight freedoms.**
> **May they have faith, wisdom and kindness,**
> **Eat appropriate food, have good conduct,**
> **And remember their former rebirths.**

Material wealth:

> **10.28**
> **May they have inexhaustible wealth**
> **Like that of the bodhisattva Gaganagañja.**[2]

Non-violence:

> **May they be able to do as they please,**
> **Without conflict or violence.**

Perfect splendour:

> **10.29**
> **May beings with little splendour**
> **Come to have magnificent glory.**

Perfect form:

> **May those who are emaciated or ugly**
> **Come to have radiant beauty.**

Inferior becoming superior:

> **10.30**
> **May women everywhere in the world**
> **Be reborn as men.**
> **May the lowly achieve highness**
> **And crush any arrogance.**

Perfect virtue:

> **10.31**
> **By my merit,**
> **May all sentient beings without exception**
> **Abandon all nonvirtue**
> **And always practise virtue.**

2. Entering the path of perfection

> **10.32**
> **May they never be separated from bodhicitta**
> **And may they practise the bodhisattva conduct.**
> **May they be supported by the Buddhas**
> **And abandon the actions of Māra.**

These four lines indicate respectively the intention, practice, presence of harmonious conditions and absence of opposing conditions. [468]

3. Attaining worldly happiness

Long life:

> 10.33
> May all sentient beings
> Have immeasurably long lives.
> May they live in constant happiness
> Where the word 'death' is never even heard.

Perfect abode:

> 10.34
> Everywhere may there be
> Gardens of wish fulfilling trees
> Filled with Buddhas and bodhisattvas
> And resounding with the delightful sounds of dharma.

> 10.35
> Everywhere may the land be
> Without stones, etc.,
> Smooth like the palm of a hand,
> And even like a lapis lazuli.

Being populated by the beneficent:

> 10.36
> May many mandala circles
> Of many bodhisattvas
> Adorn the face of the earth,
> Beautifying it with their natural radiance.

Virtuous conduct:

> 10.37
> May all embodied beings
> Continuously hear sounds of dharma
> From all the birds, trees,
> Rays of light and even space itself.

> 10.38

> May they always meet
> With the Buddhas and their sons,
> And with limitless clouds of offerings
> May they pay homage to the supreme ones among all beings.

Good fortune in abundance:

> 10.39
> May the gods bring timely rains,
> And may crops be abundant.
> May kings reign in accord with dharma,
> And may the people prosper.
>
> 10.40
> May medicines be effective
> And may mantra recitation bring accomplishment.

Pacifying harms:

> May ḍākinīs and ogres
> Have compassionate minds.
>
> 10.41
> May no sentient being ever
> Be in pain, practise nonvirtue,
> Be afraid or abused.
> May they never be unhappy.

2. Dedication specific to monastics

> 10.42
> In the monasteries, may reading
> And recitation flourish and endure.
> May the saṅgha always be harmonious,
> And may they be firmly established.

For the benefit of monks:

> 10.43

May monks who wish to train
Find places of solitude and,
Abandoning all distraction,
May they meditate with peace of mind.

For the benefit of nuns:

10.44
May nuns have material support,
And may they be free from conflict or danger.

For perfecting moral conduct:

May all monastics
Never let their moral conduct be damaged.

10.45
May the immoral tire of their ways
And may their nonvirtues come to an end.
Attaining a happy rebirth,
May their conduct never be damaged.

For perfecting wisdom:

10.46
May the learned be respected
And find the support they need.
May their minds be pure
And may they be renowned in every direction.

For fruition of freedom from suffering:

10.47
In future lives may nobody experience suffering,
And may whatever they do be without difficulties.
May they quickly achieve buddhahood
With a physical form surpassing that of a god.

10.48

May all sentient beings
Make many offerings to all the Buddhas.
May their happiness
Be the inconceivable bliss of a Buddha.

2. Dedication for transcendental benefit

Dedication for the intentions of bodhisattvas:

10.49
May the wishes of bodhisattvas
For the benefit of beings be accomplished,

Dedication for the intentions of Buddhas:

And may all beings have everything
The Protectors wish for them.

Dedication for the intentions of śrāvakas:

10.50
Similarly, may all śrāvakas
And pratyekabuddhas have happiness.

3. Dedication for the benefit of self

Temporal results:

10.51
Until I have reached the 'Joyous' bhūmi,
Through the kindness of Mañjughoṣa,
May I remember my previous lives
And attain ordination.

10.52
May I live with simple food
And have simple needs,
And throughout all my lives
May I find perfect solitude.

The vision of Mañjughoṣa:

10.53
If I ever wish to look upon him
Or ask him the slightest question,
May I see the protector
Mañjughoṣa himself, without any hindrance.

Practising the bodhisattva conduct:

10.54
In order to accomplish the benefit
Of all sentient beings, as limitless as space,
May my conduct
Be like that of Mañjughoṣa.

Accomplishing the benefit of others:

10.55
As long as space endures
There will be living beings.
For that long may I remain
To dispel their suffering.

10.56
However they may be suffering,
May all their suffering ripen in me.
May the bodhisattva saṅgha
Bring happiness to the world.

4. Dedication for the teachings to remain as a source of happiness

10.57
May the teachings, which are the only
Medicine for suffering and which are the source of all
    happiness,
Be honoured and respected,
And may they long remain.

5. Homage of remembrance of kind ones

10.58
I prostrate to Mañjughoṣa,
By whose kindness my mind turned to virtue,
And I prostrate to my spiritual masters,
By whose kindness I matured.

COLOPHON

Thinking respectfully of the dust beneath the feet
Of the teacher of dharma, the monk Loden Zangpo [Ngok
　　Lotsawa], upholder of the tripitaka,
I composed this aid for illuminating the meaning
Of these words on the conduct of the conquerors' sons.
By the light rays of teaching and explanation
May it light up the bodhisattva path,
And seeing the way with the eye of wisdom,
May all beings travel this path.

Although there were already very clear explanations written by
　　learned ones,
Nevertheless, I wanted to make some minor corrections and
　　propagate this teaching.
Though it would not be of interest to ordinary people,
Nevertheless, I wrote it for my own understanding and for
　　those like me.

Being just a synopsis, certain sections of the ninth chapter [of the root text] from the explanation of the *Bodhicaryāvatāra* composed by the monk [Chapa] Chokyi Sengge remained hard to understand. To make them easier, this detailed guide was composed by the layman Sonam

Tsemo.[1] May it bring vast benefit to the precious doctrine and to many sentient beings.

TRANSLATOR'S AFTERWORD: LOGIC

The use of logic in the Buddhist tradition is dealt with authoritatively in classic works on the topic by such scholars as Dharmakīrti and Sakya Pandita. What follows is a limited attempt to help the lay reader unfamiliar with such works get the gist of the logical terminology used in the present text. Familiarity with the basics of first order predicate logic in the Western tradition would be an advantage in some of what follows, for there are instructive parallels.

Inferences can be presented either as svātantras—the establishment of a proposition's truth or falsity by proof from a given premise—or prasaṅgas—the refutation of a proposition by demonstrating an internal contradiction. Svātantras prove or disprove a proposition (*'dod pa*) or premise (*dam bca'*)—typically, the existence or nonexistence of some metaphysical type, such as a creator deity or a partless atom. In their disproving or negating mode, svātantras are used to establish the emptiness of all dharmas by arguments such as 'the refutation from existence or nonexistence'.[1] The term 'svātantra' means 'autonomous' (*rang rgyud*) in the sense of independently establishing a position from a given premise. Prasaṅgas prove that a proposition or premise asserted by a philosophical opponent leads to a contradiction and so is to be rejected. The term 'prasaṅga' means 'consequential' (*thal ba*) in the sense of making explicit the internal consequences of a proposition or premise. Sonam Tsemo uses both svātantras and prasaṅgas in the present text.² Svātantras and prasaṅgas share certain formal elements:

- A 'logical subject' (*chos can*—more literally, 'dharma possessor', i.e. something which bears properties): the subject of the inference, e.g. 'the self'.
- A 'reason' or antecedent (probans) predicate (*gtan tshigs, rtags,* or *sgrub byed,* all synonymous): a property to be attributed to the logical subject antecedent to the conclusion. It is typically suffixed to a 'because' clause, e.g. 'because it (the logical subject) is matter, which is insentient'.
- A consequent (probandum) predicate (*bsgrubs pa'i chos*): a property attributed to the logical subject as a consequence of the reason. The probandum or conclusion itself (*bsgrubs bya*) is the proposition to be established as the conclusion of the inference, e.g. 'it (the logical subject) is not an agent'.

Such inferences must satisfy the 'three forms' (trairūpya) of logical felicity:

1. Qualification: the logical subject must satisfy the reason predicate (*phyogs chos*, Skt. pakṣadharma)³
2. Forward pervasion: satisfaction of the reason predicate must imply satisfaction of the consequent predicate (*rjes khyab*, Skt. anvayavyāpti)
3. Reverse pervasion: the lack of the consequent predicate must imply the lack of the antecedent predicate (*ldog khyab*, Skt. vyatirekavyāpti)

The two key terms to be elaborated here are 'pervasion' (*khyab pa,* Skt. vyapti) and 'qualification'. A pervasion is an inferential relation between the antecedent and consequent predicates. To give an example in the form of a prasaṅga:

> The causal collection is the logical subject. Contradiction: although your proposition is that it is truly existent, it follows that it is not truly existent (the consequent predicate) because of singularity being imputed onto a multiplicity (the antecedent predicate). (See commentary to v9.96)

The pervasion here is the conditional relation between being 'a merely imputed singularity' and being 'nonexistent (dngos med)', i.e. if something is a merely imputed reality, it is nonexistent. This pervasion must be 'established', i.e. demonstrated as true.[4]

A pervasion can be a relation of cause and effect (e.g. 'where there is fire there is smoke') or a 'natural' relation between two associated properties (e.g. 'what is a merely imputed singularity is nonexistent'). There is also a third, negative case of pervasion in which the absence of one quality implies the absence of a corresponding quality (e.g. 'a non-substance is non-transforming and therefore it cannot be created'). This is called the 'non-supporting of the pervader' (khyab byed dmigs med, Skt. vyapaka-anupalabdhi, see below).

As a general relation between two predicates, a pervasion can be expressed as a universally quantified statement or conditional in accord with familiar grammatical forms. For example, these are all logically equivalent expressions of the above pervasion:

- Everything multiple onto which singularity is imputed is nonexistent
- Whatever is multiple but is imputed as singular, is nonexistent
- If something is multiple but is imputed as singular, then it is nonexistent
- (x) (x is multiple but imputed as singular $\rightarrow$ ~x is existent)

The latter representation of pervasion using the quantificational operator (x) and the material implication sign $\rightarrow$ has been highlighted by Matilal and I will continue to use it here.[5]

A pervasion involves a 'pervader' (khyab byed, Skt. vyapaka)—the antecedent predicate F in (x) $(Fx \rightarrow Gx)$—and a 'pervaded' (khyab bya, Skt. vyāpya)—the consequent predicate G. In the case of 'the pervader is not supported'—the third of the three kinds of pervasion mentioned above—the 'pervader' is a quality which the logical subjects lacks. 'The pervader is not supported' refutes an opponent's claim Gx by demonstrating (x) $(\sim Fx \rightarrow \sim Gx)$ & $\sim Fx$. For example:

> The logical subject is mere appearances. They are without true inherent

nature because they do not arise from self, other, both, nor without cause. The pervader is not supported. (See commentary above v9.116.)

Here, 'arising from self, other, both, nor without cause' is the composite pervader, F, and 'true inherent nature' is the pervaded, G. 'The pervader is not supported' means that mere appearances lack F and hence also lack G.[6]

Establishing that the logical subject has a particular property is called 'qualification'. Qualification obtains when it is established that the logical subject 'supports' or has the property attributed to it in a reason clause, i.e. it satisfies the antecedent predicate. A qualification may need to be established by introducing further antecedent premises. This implies a possible infinite regress of premises also requiring establishment, but the chain of argument typically terminates when it reaches a premise that can be seen to be true by direct perception (e.g. 'It is established by direct perception that impermanent objects arise from causes other than Īśvara', see commentary to v9.122) or which the opponent must accept or has already accepted as true, or which he cannot deny without contradicting his overall thesis, position or world view (e.g. 'It is untenable for you to deny consciousness abides sempiternally, for that would contradict the Sāṃkhya's own proposition that the individual consciousness is sempiternal', see commentary to v9.60).

In simple cases, pervasion and qualification play similar roles to the Aristotelian major and minor premise, respectively:

- Major premise (pervasion): Everything multiple that is imputed as singular is not truly existent.
- Minor premise (qualification): A causal collection is a multiplicity imputed as singular.
- Conclusion: A causal collection is not truly existent.

Formally, the forward and reverse modes of pervasion are as follows:

- Forward pervasion (*rjes khyab*) is the inference from antecedent to consequent, i.e. $(Fx \rightarrow Gx)$
- Reverse pervasion (*ldog khyab*) is the pervasion in the contrapositive form: $(\sim Gx \rightarrow \sim Fx)$.

Since establishing or proving the contrapositive of an inference is logically equivalent to establishing the original (positive) inference itself (and vice versa), to establish the reverse pervasion is sufficient to establish the forward pervasion and we see examples of this method of proof in the text. Similarly, refuting the reverse pervasion is equivalent to refuting the forward pervasion. In short, forward and reverse pervasion stand or fall together as an incontrovertible rule of logic.

A third kind of pervasion is its general negation:

- Counter pervasion (*'gal khyab*) is the negation of the pervasion:
  $\sim(Fx \rightarrow Gx)$

Establishing the counter pervasion is equivalent to refuting the forward (and reverse) pervasion and hence rejecting the inference.

GLOSSARY
ENGLISH TRANSLATIONS OF KEY TIBETAN TERMS

kun rdzob: Relative
bka': Buddha's words
bkag pa: Negate
skyes bu: Sāṃkhya philosophy: individual consciousness
kha na ma tho ba: Misdeed
khas len: Assert, claim
'khrul pa: Error, delusion, confusion
'gal ba: Logic: Contradiction, incompatibility
grangs can: Sāṃkhya
gus pa: 1. Respect 2. Faith
dgag pa: Refute
dge ba'i bshes gnyen: Spiritual friend
rgol ba: Dispute, disputant
rgyu mtshan: Essential characteristic, criterion
rgyud: Stream of being, stream
sgrib pa: Obscuration
sgro 'dogs: Imputation
bsgom pa: Cultivation, meditation
bsgrubs bya: Logic: probandum
nges pa: Ascertainment, certainty
ngo bo,
rang bzhin: Intrinsic nature, nature
dngos med: 1. nonexistent 2. Insubstantial

dngos po: 1. Existent 2. Substantial
mngon sum: Direct perception, juxtaposed with inference (*rjes drag*)
mngon zhen: Attachment
chags pa: Attachment, desire
ched du bya ba: Object of intention
mchod pa: Esteem, worship, make offerings, venerate, homage
rjes dpag: Inference, juxtaposed with direct perception (*mngon sum*)
brjod pa: Claim, say
nyams: Damage
nyes pa: Negative action, fault, evil
nyon mongs: Defilements
snyan: Praise, pleasant speech
gtan med: Nonexistent
gti mug: Ignorance, stupidity
rtag pa: Permanent, sempiternal, immutable
rtogs pa: Conception, understanding
ltung ba: Downfall
'thad pa: Logical, reasonable
dam bca': Premise, thesis
de kho na: Reality
dom dam: Ultimate
don: 1. Perceptual object 2. Meaning, purpose
don spyi: Predicate, universal
bden pa: True, real
ldog pa: Reversed, prevented, stopped, ended
sdig pa: Nonvirtue
'dod chags: Attachment
'dod pa: Proposition, belief
'du shes: Karmic formations
'dzin pa: 1. Grasping 2. (Perceptual) subject
gnod pa: 1. Harm, problem 2. Logic: opposition, objection
rnam pa: 1. Representation 2. Type, kind
rnam pa 'jog pa po: Representationalist
rnam par gcod: Logic: Elimination
rnam par shes pa,
rnam shes: Consciousness
rnam rtog: Discrimination, conceptual discrimination
snang ba: (Dualistic) appearance
spro ba: Enthusiasm, excitement, elaboration

phas pham,
pham pa: (Monastic) defeat
phyi: Outer, external
phyi rol pa: Non-Buddhist
bag yod: Concern
dben pa: 1. Solitude 2. Logic: incompatibility, exclusion
sbyor: Practice, application
mi snyan: Complain, unpleasant speech
mi 'thad: Unreasonable
mi nus pa: Untenable, impossible, unable
mi rigs pa: Illogical, not sensible
mu stegs pa: Tīrthika
dmigs pa: 1. Perception 2. Logic: predicate support (see appendix)
smod: Criticize
smra ba: Assert, say, claim
rtsod pa: Disagreement, disputation, objection
gtso bo: Sāṃkhya philosophy: primal substance
tshad ma: Valid cognition
tshor ba: Sensation
mtshan nyid: Essential (as opposed to accidental) characteristic
rdzas yod: Substance
brdzun pa: False
zhi gnas: Calm abiding
zhugs: 1. Enter, engage 2. Logic: (predicate) satisfaction
yid: Conceptual mind
ye shes: Wisdom
yongs su bcad: Positive establishment
rang bzhin: Intrinsic nature (syn. *ngo bo*)
rang rig pa'i shug las,
rig pa'i shugs,
shugs las: Implicit, *a priori*
rig pa,
rigs pa: 1. Awareness, realization 2. Logic, logical, making sense, reasonable
srid pa: Conditioned existence
sred pa: Craving
las kyi sgrib: Karmic obscuration
len pa: Clinging
blo: 1. Conceptual thought 2. Sāṃkhya philosophy: Mirror of Mind

sems pa: Mind, attitude, intention, sentient
sems med: Insentient
bsam gten: Meditation
bsrung: Look after, protect, guard, maintain
shes pa: Understanding, cognizing
shes rab: Wisdom
lhag mthong: Insight

BIBLIOGRAPHY

Abbreviations

D: *Bka' 'gyur* and *bstan 'gyur* (Derge edition)
H: *Bka' 'gyur* (Lhasa edition)
W: Buddhist Digital Resource Center (tbrc.org)

Tibetan Works

Scriptures referenced in the root text and commentary

Ākāśagarbha Sutra, *ārya-ākāśagarbha-nāma-mahāyāna-sūtra, 'phags pa nam mkha'i snying po zhes bya ba theg pa chen po'i mdo*, D260

Avataṃsaka Sutra, *buddha-avataṃsaka-nāma-mahāvaipūlya-sūtra, sangs rgyas phal po che zhes bya ba shin tu rgyas pa chen pa'i mdo*, D44, H94

Bodhisattva Piṭaka Sutra, *ārya-bodhisattva-piṭaka-nāma-mahāyāna-sūtra, 'phags pa byang chub sems dpa'i sde snod ces bya ba theg pa chen po'i mdo*, H56

Cloud of Jewels Sutra, *ārya-ratnamegha-nāma-mahāyāna-sūtra 'phags pa dkon mchog sprin ces bya ba theg pa chen po'i mdo*, H232

Dharmasaṃgīti Sutra, *ārya-dharmasaṃgīti-nāma-mahāyāna-sūtra, 'phags pa chos yang dag par sdud pa zhes bya ba theg pa chen po'i mdo*, H239

Display of Completely Definitive Pacification Sutra, *ārya-praśānta-viniścaya-prātihārya-samādhi-nāma-mahāyāna-sūtra*, 'phags pa rab tu zhi ba rnam par nges pa'i cho 'phrul gyi ting nge 'dzin zhes bya ba theg pa chen po'i mdo, H131

Eight Thousand Verse Perfection of Wisdom Sutra, *ārya-aṣṭādaśasāhasrikā-prajñāpāramitā-nāma-mahāyāna-sūtra*, 'phags pa shes rab kyi pha rol tu phyin pa khri brgyad stong pa zhes bya ba theg pa chen po'i mdo, H12

Foundations of Mindfulness Sutra, *ārya-saddharmasmṛty-upasthāna*, 'phags pa dam pa'i chos dran pa nye bar gzhag pa, D287

Mahaparinirvāṇa Sutra, *ārya-mahāparinirvāṇa-mahāsūtra*, 'phags pa yongs su mya ngan las 'das pa chen po'i mdo, H368

Ordination of Nanda Sutra, *nandapravrajyā-sūtra*, dga' bo rab tu byung ba'i mdo, H322

Perfection of Wisdom in Eight Thousand Lines, *śatasāhasrikā-prajñāpāramitā*, shes rab kyi pha rol tu phyin pa stong phrag brgya pa, H9

Samādhirāja Sutra, *ārya-sarvadharma-svabhāva-samatā-vipañcita-samādhirāja-nāma-mahāyāna-sūtra*, 'phags pa chos thams cad kyi rang bzhin mnyam pa nyid rnam par spros pa ting nge 'dzin gyi rgyal po zhes bya ba theg pa chen po'i mdo, H129

Sutra of the Great Lion's Roar of Maitreya, *ārya-maitreya-mahāsiṃhanāda-nāma-mahāyāna-sūtra*, 'phags pa byams pa'i seng ge'i sgra chen po zhes bya ba theg pa chen po'i mdo, H67

Sutra Requested by Akṣayamati, *ārya-akṣayamati-nirdeśa-nāma-mahāyāna-sūtra*, 'phags pa blo gros mi zad pas bstan pa zhes bya ba theg pa chen po'i mdo, H176

Sutra Requested by Kāśyapa, *ārya-kāśyapa-parivarta-nāma-mahāyāna-sūtra*, 'phags pa 'od srung gi le'u zhes bya ba theg pa chen po'i mdo, D87

Sutra of Simha's Questions, *ārya-siṃha-paripṛcchā-nāma-mahāyāna-sūtra*, 'phags pa seng ges zhus pa zhes bya ba theg pa chen po'i mdo, D81

Sutra of Ratnacūḍa's Questions, *ārya-ratnacūḍa-paripṛcchā-nāma-mahāyāna-sūtra*, 'phags pa gtsug na rin po ches zhus pa zhes bya pa theg pa chen po'i mdo, H91

Sutra of the Three Heaps, *ārya-triskandhaka-nāma-mahāyāna-sūtra*, *'phags pa phung po gsum pa zhes bya ba theg pa chen po'i mdo*, D284

Sutra Vīradatta's Questions, *ārya-vīradatta-gṛhapati-paripṛcchā-nāma-mahāyāna-sūtra*, *'phags pa khyim bdag dpas byin gyis zhus pa zhes bya ba theg pa chen po'i mdo*, H72

White Lotus of Holy Dharma Sutra, *saddharmapuṇḍarīka-nāma-mahāyāna-sūtra*, *dam pa'i chos pad ma dkar po zhes bya ba theg pa chen po'i mdo*, H116

Authored works referenced in the root text and commentary

Asaṅga, *yogācārabhūmi-bhūmivastu*, *rnal 'byor spyod pa'i sa las, dngos gzhi sa mang po*, D4035

——— *yogācārabhūmi viniścayasaṃgrahaṇī*, *rnal 'byor spyod pa'i sa rnam par gtan la dbab pa bsdu ba*, W1PD95844

Candrakīrti, Entering the Middle Way, *madhyamakāvatāra*, *dbu ma la 'jug pa*, D3861

Chapa Chokyi Senge, A Synopsis of the Caryāvatāra, *spyod 'jug bsdus don* in *bka' gdams gsung 'bum phyogs bsgrigs thengs dang po*, W1PD89051

Jetāri, A Ritual for Generating Bodhicitta and Receiving the Commitments, *bodhicittotpādasamādānavidhi*, *byang chub kyi sems bskyed pa dang yi dam blang ba'i cho ga*, D3968

Kamalaśīla, Stages of Meditation, *bhāvanākrama*, *bsgom pa'i rim pa*, D3916

Nāgārjuna, Root Verses on the Middle Way, *prajñā-nāma-mūlamadhyamakakārikā*, *dbu ma rtsa ba'i tshig le'ur byas pa shes rab ces bya ba*, D3824

——— Jewel Garland, *ratnāvali*, *rgyal po la gtam bya ba rin po che'i phreng ba*, D4158

——— Compendium of Sutras, *sūtrasamuccaya*, *mdo kun las btus pa*, D3934

Śāntarakṣita, Root Verses of the Adornment of the Middle Way, *madhyamakālaṃkārakārikā*, *dbu ma rgyan gyi tshig le'ur byas pa*, D3884

Śāntideva, *Compendium of Training, śikṣāsamuccaya, bslab pa kun las btus pa*, D3940

Prajñākaramati, *Commentary on the Difficult Points of the Bodhicaryāvatāra (a.k.a. Great Commentary), bodhicaryāvatārapañjikā, byang chub sems dpa'i spyod pa la 'jug pa'i dka' 'grel*, W21708

Vairocanarakṣita, *Commentary on the Difficult Points of the Bodhisattvacaryāvatāra, bodhisattvacaryāvatārapañjikā, byang chub sems dpa' spyod pa la 'jug pa'i dka' 'grel*, D3875

Tibetan works referenced in notes and supplementary material

Buton Rinchen Drup, *Rays of the Moon: A Commentary on the Caryāvatāra, spyod 'jug gi 'grel pa zla ba'i 'od zer*, W1904

Candrakīrti, *Commentary on Entering the Middle Way, madhyamakāvatāra-bhasya, dbu ma la 'jug pa'i bshad pa*, W1KG3407

Dharmamitra, *Commentary on the Vinayasutra, vinayasūtraṭīkā, 'dul ba'i mdo rgya cher 'grel pa*, D4120

Dignāga, *Praise of Ārya Mañjughoṣa, āryamañjughoṣastotra, 'phags pa 'jam pa'i dbyangs kyi bstod pa*, D2712

Lhopa Kunkhyen Rinchen Pal, *The Oral Instructions of Mañjuśrī: Notes on the Caryāvatāra, spyod 'jug zin bris 'jam dpal zhal lung*, W23697

Maitreya, *Root Verses of the Ornament of Mahāyāna Sutras, mahāyānasūtrālaṃkārakārikā, theg pa chen po mdo sde'i rgyan zhes bya ba'i tshig le'ur byas pa*, D4020

Pawo Tsuglag Trengwa, *Essence of the Limitless Vast and Profound Ocean of Mahāyāna Dharma: A Commentary on the Bodhisattvacaryāvatāra, byang chub sems dpa'i spyod pa la 'jug pa'i rnam par bshad pa theg chen chos kyi rgya mtsho zab rgyas mtha' yas pa'i snying po*, W7500

Prajñākaramati, *Commentary on the Difficult Points of the Bodhisattvacaryāvatāra (a.k.a. Great Commentary), bodhicaryāvatārapañjikā, byang chub sems dpa'i spyod pa la 'jug pa'i dka' 'grel*, W21708

Sakya Pandita Kunga Gyaltsen, *Clarifying the Sage's Intent, thub pa dgongs gsal*, in *bstan rim gces btus*, W4CZ2193

Śāntarakṣita, *Root Verses of the Adornment of the Middle Way, madhyamakālaṃkārakārikā, dbu ma rgyan gyi tshig le'ur byas pa,* D3884

Śāntideva, *Compendium of Training, śikṣā-samuccaya, bslab pa kun las btus pa,* D3940

Thokme Zangpo, *Ocean of Good Explanation: A Commentary on the Caryāvatāra, spyod 'jug gi 'grel pa legs par bshad pa'i rgya mtsho,* W1KG1795

Translations and other English language sources

Asaṅga, *The Bodhisattva Path to Unsurpassed Enlightenment: A Complete Translation of the Bodhisattvabhūmi,* trans. Artemus B. Engle, Snow Lion 2016

—— *Abhidharmasamuccaya: The Compendium of the Higher Teaching,* trans. Walpola Rahula and Sara Boin-Webb, Jain Publishing 2001

Brunnhölzl, Karl, *The Center of the Sunlit Sky: Madhyamaka in the Kagyu Tradition,* Snow Lion 2004

Cleary, Thomas (trans.), *The Flower Ornament Scripture: A Translation of the Avatamsaka Sutra,* Shambhala 1993

Davidson, Ronald M., *Tibetan Renaissance: Tantric Buddhism in the Rebirth of Tibetan Culture,* Columbia University Press 2005

Dhongthog Rinpoche, *The Sakya School of Tibetan Buddhism: A History,* trans. Sam van Schaik, Wisdom Publications 2016

Go Lotsawa, *The Blue Annals,* trans. George N. Roerich, Motilal Banarsidass 1949 [1996]

Gampopa, *Ornament of Precious Liberation,* trans. Ken Holmes, in *Stages of the Buddha's Teachings: Three Key Texts,* Wisdom Publications 2015

Hacker, P.M.S., *The Passions: A Study of Human Nature,* Wiley Blackwell 2018

Jackson, David P., *Madhyamaka Studies Among the Early Sa-skya-pas,* in *The Tibet Journal,* vol. 10, No. 2 (Summer 1985), pp. 20-34, Library of Tibetan Works and Archives 1985

Kongtrul, Jamgon, *The Treasury of Knowledge: Book Five: Buddhist Ethics*, trans. Kalu Rinpoche Translation Group, Snow Lion 2003

Kunzang Pelden, *The Nectar of Manjushri's Speech: A Detailed Commentary on Shantideva's Way of the Bodhisattva*, trans. Padmakara Translation Group, Shambhala Publications 2010

Maitreya, *Ornament of the Great Vehicle Sutras: Maitreya's Mahāyānasūtrālaṃkāra with Commentaries by Khenpo Shenga and Ju Mipham*, trans. Dharmachakra Translation Committee, Snow Lion 2014

Mathes, Klaus-Dieter, *A Direct Path to the Buddha Within: Go Lotsawa's Mahamudra Interpretation of the Ratnagotravibhaga*, Wisdom Publications 2008

Matilal, Bimal Krishna, *The Character of Logic in India*, SUNY 1998

Mipham, Jamgon Ju, *The Adornment of the Middle Way, Śāntarakṣita's Mahāyānasūtrālaṃkāra with commentary by Jamgon Mipham*, trans. Padmakara Translation Group, Shambhala Publications 2005

——— *The Wisdom Chapter: Jamgon Mipham's Commentary on the Ninth Chapter of The Way of the Bodhisattva*, trans. Padmakara Translation Group, Shambhala Publications 2017

——— *Introduction to the Middle Way: Chandrakirti's Madhyamakāvatāra with Commentary by Jamgon Mipham*, trans. Padmakara Translation Group, Shambhala Publications 2002

——— *Gateway to Knowledge: A Condensation of the Tripitaka, Vol. 1*, Rangjung Yeshe Publications, 2004

Obermiller E., *The History of Buddhism (chos hbyung) by Bu-ston. 1: The Jewelry of Scripture*, Heidelberg 1931

Patrul Rinpoche, *Words of My Perfect Teacher: A Complete Translation of a Classic Introduction to Tibetan Buddhism*, Yale University Press 2010

Sakya Pandita, Kunga Gyaltsen (Sapan), *A Clear Differentiation of the Three Codes: Essential Distinctions among the Individual Liberation, Great Vehicle, and Tantric Systems*, trans. Jared Douglas Rhoton, SUNY 2002

——— *Clarifying the Sage's Intent*, trans. David Jackson, in *Stages of the Buddha's Teachings: Three Key Texts*, Wisdom Publications 2015

Śāntideva, *A Guide of the Bodhisattva Way of Life*, trans. Vesna Wallace and B. Alan Wallace, Snow Lion Publications 1997

―――― *A Guide of the Bodhisattva's Way of Life*, trans. Stephen Batchelor, Library of Tibetan Works and Archives 1979

―――― *The Bodhicaryāvatāra*, trans. Kate Crosby and Andrew Skilton, Oxford University Press, 1995

―――― *Siksa Samuccaya: A Compendium of Buddhist Doctrine*, trans. Cecil Bendall and W.H.D. Rouse, Motilal Banarsidass 1922 [2006]

―――― *The Training Anthology of Śāntideva: A Translation of the Śikṣā-samuccaya*, trans. Charles Goodman, Oxford University Press 2016

Tāranātha, *Tāranātha's History of Buddhism in India*, trans. Lama Chimpa and Alaka Chattopadhyaya, Motilala Banarsidass, 2004

Tauscher, Helmut, *Phya pa chos kyi seng ge as a Svātantrika*, in *The Svātantrika-Prāsangika Distinction: What Difference Does a Difference Make?* Edited by Sara McClintock, Georges Dreyfus, Wisdom Publications 2003

Thaye, Jampa, *Rain of Clarity: The Stages of the Path in the Sakya Tradition*, Ganesha Press 2006

Tillemans, Tom, *Scripture, Logic, Language: Essays on Dharmakīrti and his Tibetan Successors*, Wisdom Publications 1999

―――― *Some Reflections on R.S.Y Chi's Buddhist Formal Logic*, in *The Journal of the International Association of Buddhist Studies*, vol. 11, 1988

Vasubandhu, *Abhidharmakosabhasyam*, 4 volumes, trans. Louis de la Vallee Poussin (French) and Leo M. Pruden (English), Asian Humanities Press, 1991

Wangchuk Dorje, Karmapa, *The Karmapa's Middle Way: Feast for the Fortunate*, trans. Tyler Dewar, Snow Lion 2008

Vose, Kevin A, *Resurrecting Candrakirti: Disputes in the Tibetan Creation of Prāsangika*, Wisdom Publications 2009a

―――― *Making and remaking the ultimate in early Tibetan readings of Śāntideva*, in *The Journal of the International Association of Buddhist Studies*, vol. 32, 2009b

NOTES

Introduction

1. *Byang chub kyi sems dpa' spyod pa la 'jug pa'i 'grel ba*. Adding an ornamental or poetic title later became customary in the Tibetan tradition, but the title used here follows the extant Indian commentaries, such as that of Prajñākaramati and Vairocanarakṣita, which are styled simply as 'Commentary on the Difficult Points (*dka' 'grel*) of *Caryāvatāra*'. The early Kadampa commentaries found in the *bka' gdams gsung 'bum*, such as that of Chapa Chokyi Sengge and Tsangnakpa Tsondru Sengge (*gtsang nag pa brtson 'grus sengge*), likewise have no ornamental title.
2. Tāranātha, 2004 edition, pp. 214-220.
3. For further biographical details, see Ronald M. Davidson, *Tibetan Renaissance: Tantric Buddhism in the Rebirth of Tibetan Culture*, 2005, pp. 338-343 and 359-369.
4. See Dhongthog Rinpoche, 2016, p. 103.
5. Brunnhölzl (2004, p. 855, n.47) notes that the original meaning of the Sanskrit term kleśa is 'defilement', 'pollution' or 'impurity', while its interpretation as 'affliction' is a later development from which the Tibetan translation *nyon mongs* comes. However, I will offer a few points here concerning the common translation of kleśa and *nyon mongs* as kinds of 'emotion'.

   The anglophonic conception of emotion has evolved through the Western literary canon, from dramatic and biblical origins through Shakespeare and the 19th-20th century novelists, to present day forms of secular drama and entertainment, as well having a long and rich history in art, poetry and music. Emotions in this tradition are related conceptually to expressions of the things we care about. Emotions include jealousy (Othello), pride (Coriolanus), rage and bitterness (Lear), humiliation and shamelessness (Falstaff), guilt (Henry IV) and romantic love (Romeo and Juliet), to name but a few. There are many more. The limits of what counts as an emotion are not definitively circumscribed. The Buddhist term 'kleśa' has had a variety of uses and formulations throughout the two and a half millennia of the Hīnayāna and Mahāyāna traditions, but is usually circumscribed to a specific number (e.g. the 'three poisons' or 'five poisons', the 'six root and twenty subsidiary' kleśas) and is always grounded in a soteriological context. Perhaps the lack of circumscription among the emotions provides the motivation for sometimes translating 'kleśa' as a specific *kind* of emotion, such as '*disturbing* emotion' or '*negative* emotion'. Nevertheless, certain kleśas are not any kind of emotion. If the kleśas are specified as including attachment and aversion, these are not emotions in the ordinary sense of the English word, but attitudes or prejudices. If the kleśas include desire, then this may include sexual desire, hunger, ambition, thirst, greed, avarice, covetousness etc., some of which are not emotions. Of the six root and twenty secondary kleśas, several are not emotions, such as ignorance, doubts, wrong views, laziness, unalertness, lack of faith, heedlessness and forgetfulness (for a full list of these kleśas in English, see Jamgon Mipham Rinpoche, 2004, p. 25 - 29). There is something awry, it seems, in calling ignorance or laziness a 'disturbing emotion'.

   It is because there is an important logical or conceptual difference between 'kleśa' and 'emotion' that we should keep these two concepts apart and not conflate them, even metaphorically or metonymically. Etymologically, the English word 'emotion' is related to motion, being *moved* to feel something or *motivated* to act. Motion is not a truly distinctive characteristic of the emotions, however, for intellectual and cognitive capacities such as knowledge, belief and perception—which are in no sense emotions—are also conceptually related to motivation and action: emotional, intellectual and cognitive capacities are all *reasons* for action. However, while actions based on intellectual and cognitive capacities (as well as their opposites or absences, such as ignorance, disbelief and misperception) can be carried out with indifference, casualness and disinterest, actions based on emotions cannot. Emotions and their related actions *express what we care about* and are conceptually coupled to personal interest and intensity of feeling. It is because of this distinctive characteristic that the emotions conceptually exclude certain kleśas. For, unlike the emotions, the kleśas express not only what we care about (hence attachment, craving, desire, aversion, hatred, anger, jealousy, pride and so forth) but also, and essentially, they express what we do *not* care about and what we are unmoved, unmotivated, unconcerned and unaffected by. This is our unawareness, ignorance, unconcern, indifference, lack of compassion and so forth towards certain (most) objects and beings. The English term 'emotion' logically excludes all these but they comprise an essential part of the kleśas. Indeed it is clear that the kleśas comprise not only many emotions but also many unemotional capacities and dispositions, intellectual, cognitive and otherwise. To think of the kleśas as 'emotions' of any kind is to obfuscate or exclude these, which are some of the most important and powerful kleśas.

Nevertheless, certain kleśas, such as anger, pride and jealousy, are emotions. There is also a functional sense in which the emotions and kleśas overlap, and it is particularly well evidenced in the *Bodhicaryāvatāra*. Emotions express what we care about but allow a normative gap to exist between what we *actually* care about and what we *ought to* care about. We are taught from an early age to refine and improve the things we care about and thus to handle our emotions properly and with appropriate maturity. For example, when a child refuses to share its toys or throws a tantrum over some slight proscription, or is aggressive towards another child, we correct this behaviour and the child matures. As adults, we often criticize and justify the feeling of certain emotions, including negative emotions such as anger and pride, to ourselves and to others according to circumstances. Feeling a certain emotion is often answerable to reasons—we are responsible, to a degree, for our emotions, and we can give reasons for feeling certain emotions, positive or negative. Emotions ought to be felt for the right reasons towards the right objects on the right occasions to the right degree. (This way of putting it has its origins in Aristotle, but acceptance of the connection between the emotions and reasons has been obscured in modernity by the persistent influence of empiricism, rationalism and neo-Stoicism, all of which have characterized the relationship between reason and emotion primarily as one of opposition.) To fail in any these can make us subject to criticism or censure but, when maintained properly, our emotions are *reasonable*, even though we cannot feel emotions at will. This is not true of all emotions: romantic love, for example, is licensed liberally in societies influenced by the Western canon. On the other hand, anger and pride, which are concerns of chapters 6 and 7 respectively in the present text, are usually treated, in the canon as in ordinary life, as being supported by good or bad reasons. Equally, *lacking* the proper emotions makes one liable to criticism. Emotional underreaction, lack of compassion, pity or sympathy makes one 'unfeeling' or 'heartless', even 'sociopathic', even outside of the Mahāyāna. In the *Bodhicaryāvatāra* we see an emotional education in pride, anger, desire, selfishness and ignorance, and the inculcation of mindfulness, patience, compassion and bodhicitta, all based on justification and criticism—*reasonableness*, as before but now from the Mahāyāna perspective. The warrants and justifications are being changed to a higher set of norms than those applied outside of the Mahāyāna. The usual reasons we give for, say, getting angry ('I don't deserve to be treated this way') or acting selfishly ('I deserve to have this'), or lacking compassion ('he deserves what he's got coming to him, why should I care?') or feeling proud ('I really am very clever') are no longer deemed reasonable or justifiable. For bodhisattvas, there is *no* excuse, reason or justification for anger, pride or selfishness, and no excuse for lacking compassion. Therefore, the emotions, as feelings for which it is possible, by the application of reasons, to bridge the gap between what we do feel and what we ought to feel, are similar to the kleśas. Nevertheless, the kleśas ought to be distinguished from the emotions, which are more numerous and more various, and yet which lack part of what is essential—the indifferent and unmotivated responses of ignorance and unawareness. These reflections on the nature of the emotions are informed by Peter Hacker's thorough analysis of them in *The Passions: A Study of Human Nature* (2018).

1. In Praise of Bodhicitta

1. *Dgos 'brel yan lag bzhi*, Skt. anubandha-catuṣṭaya: an explanatory system from the Sanskrit literary tradition concerning the purpose of a textual composition. The four branches are the explanandum (*brjod bya*) or topic to be explained, the immediate purpose (*dgos pa*) or reason for explaining, the metapurpose (*dgos pa'i dgos pa*) or reason why the immediate purpose is sought and the relation (*'brel ba*), i.e. how the explanans (*rab tu byed* or *rjod byed*) relates to or brings about the immediate purpose. These 'implicit' points are set out by Sonam Tsemo after the explaining the first three 'explicit' points.
2. These three points are based on Vasubandhu's *Vyākhyāyukti* (D406, pp.30-31), a system widely followed in explanatory texts, e.g. in Haribhadra's *Ābhisamayālaṃkārāloka*. See Buton's description of this system in Obermiller, 1931, pp. 71-2. Vasubandhu also adds 'connections between sections' (*mtshams sbyar*) and 'objections and replies' (*brgal ba dang lan*) to these three points. All five are present throughout the text, though these three are emphasized in the introductory section.
3. Lhopa Rinchen Pal expands on this topic in some detail (pp. 23-26). Here I have slightly elaborated the outline given by Sonam Tsemo based on these comments.
4. Lhopa Rinchen Pal (p. 26) notes the standard (*sor bzhag*) Tibetan translation of 'Sugata' is *bde gshegs*, i.e. 'one gone to bliss', which treats the syllable 'su' of 'Sugata' as signifying 'sukha' (bliss, Tib. *bde ba*). However, he gives examples where Tibetans translate 'su' not as *bde ba* but as *legs pa* (excellence, beauty, goodness) and thus explains the meaning of 'Sugata' as 'those who have gone (to abandonment and realization) excellently'. In the extant Tibetan editions of Sonam Tsemo's text, this point is not clear; rather the three terms 'excellent', 'without exception' and 'irreversible' all seem related to 'su'. This is probably a typographical error caused by a subsequent repetition of *legs pa* in relation to 'gata', omission of repetition being the most common detectable typographical error throughout the present text. Hence, I have altered this passage slightly in light of Lhopa Rinchen Pal's explanation.
5. According to certain śrāvaka doctrines, continuity of their vows has a subtle physical form while maintained. See Sapan, *A Clear Differentiation of the Three Codes*, trans. Rhoton, p. 73 n.1. Note the Tibetan text has *spong ba* here, a misprint for *sbyong ba*.
6. See note 1 in this chapter.
7. The three aspirations of the main part of the bodhisattva vow—the aspiration to

give up all, to be an inexhaustible source of goodness and to be the causes of enjoyment. See chapter 3.
8. This verse in Śāntideva's text is a quote from the *Samādhirāja Sutra*. See also *The Training Anthology of Śāntideva: A Translation of the Śikṣā-samuccaya*, pp. 329-330.
9. Ibid., appearing as the last of the text's twenty-seven root verses.

In Praise of Bodhicitta (2)

1. *Bram ze rgyal ba'i drod kyi skye mched kyi rnam par thar pa'i gzhung*, found in the *Avataṃsaka Sutra*, wherein the bodhisattva Sudhana receives instruction from over fifty teachers, including Brahmin Jayosmayatana, a non-Buddhist ascetic practising heat endurance by sitting among four large fires. The sutra provides a list of eight difficulties (the difficulties of acquiring the opposite of the eight non-freedoms, of acquiring human birth itself, of acquiring pure and abundant freedoms, of the Buddha appearing, of unimpaired senses, of hearing the Buddhadharma, of associating with holy persons and of meeting pure spiritual friends), of which the first and third are referred to here. See *The Flower Ornament Scripture: A Translation of the Avatamsaka Sutra*, p. 1218.
2. *Chos 'dir gtogs pa la 'jug pa*, c.f. Lhopa Rinchen Pal, *rnam gzhag 'dir la 'jug pa* (p. 40)

In Praise of Bodhicitta (3)

1. *Gzung ba'i cho ga*—later this section is styled more generally as 'Generating bodhicitta in one's stream of being'.
2. To kill one's father, mother, or an arhat, to maliciously shed the blood of a Buddha, or to cause a schism in the saṅgha.
3. H94, p. 248b
4. See *The Training Anthology of Śāntideva: A Translation of the Śikṣā-samuccaya*, pp. 10-12.
5. This is a reference to Jetāri's text, *A Ritual for Generating Bodhicitta and Receiving the Commitments* (D3968). In Jetāri's liturgy (p. 243a), one first vows three times to 'take hold of the mind of aspiration and application', and then vows three times to undertake the bodhisattva training:
   ' "Just as the Sugatas of the past
   Generated bodhicitta,
   And maintained bodhicitta,
   At all times,
   Likewise for the benefit of beings,
   I will generate bodhicitta,
   And likewise at all times,
   I will maintain bodhicitta."
   'Recite this three times to take hold of the bodhicittas of aspiration and application. When one has the stability in holding this bodhisattva vow, this vow is given:
   ' "Just as the Sugatas of the past
   Held the bodhisattva trainings—
   Gradually practising
   Training in bodhicitta,
   Likewise for the benefit of beings,
   I, too, will hold the vow of enlightenment
   And likewise I will gradually
   Practise the trainings."

'Recite this three times to take the vow.'
Jetāri's ritual is based on v3.23-24 of the *Bodhicaryāvatāra* and Jetāri himself is considered a lineage holder of Śāntideva's vow (see e.g. Lhopa Rinchen Pal, p. 76) but, nevertheless, differs slightly from Sonam Tsemo on treating application bodhicitta as protection from decline rather than the latter's 'pursuit of the means to achieve the result'.

6. The practice of generating application bodhicitta, as distinct from undertaking the bodhisattva training, is not emphasised in the present text. However it is taught elsewhere, just as the practice of generating aspiration bodhicitta is often taught separately. See Sapan, *Clarifying the Sage's Intent*, trans. David Jackson (2015), pp. 412-413. Lhopa Rinchen Pal concurs that application bodhicitta is not the training itself and cites Sapan:

'My own lama said, "For the Ācārya [Śāntideva], the vow of aspiration is the promise to complete the bodhisattva training [*bslabs pa mtha' dag gzung ba*] and the vow of application is the promise to practise in accord with that undertaking [*ji ltar gzung ba ltar spyad pa*]." Some say that application is the training itself, however that is not correct. That is taught separately, as Ācārya Asaṅga explains [in the *Bodhisattvabhūmi*]... Therefore, aspiration and application bodhicitta are the pursuit [*don du gnyer*] of the result and pursuit of the conduct which is the means for the result.' (p.51-52)

Lhopa Rinchen Pal adds that according to Sapan, it is not merely that the intention of aspiration bodhicitta is incomplete without application, but that aspiration and application are generated and maintained separately.

7. These three 'bases' (*brten*) or 'supports' (*gzhi*) are set out in the opening section of Asaṅga's *Bodhisattvabhūmi*. See *The Bodhisattva Path to Unsurpassed Enlightenment: A Complete Translation of the Bodhisattvabhūmi*, pp. 3-5.

8. The version of these lines in the Kangyur more clearly distinguishes the generation of bodhicitta from the training in accord with the *Bodhisattvabhūmi*:

'Son of noble family, it is very rare for a sentient being to generate the unsurpassable, completely perfect bodhicitta. For those who have generated the unsurpassable, completely perfect bodhicitta, it is even rarer for them to undertake the bodhisattva conduct.' (H94, 94b-95a.2)

'To undertake the conduct' (*spyod pa yongs su tshol ba*) is, in Sonam Tsemo's version of this quotation, *spyod pa don du gnyer*, and in Lhopa Rinchen Pal (p. 51) *spyod pa chas pa*.

9. *Lhan cig skyes pa'i lha*
10. H129, p. 182b.4-182b.5
11. H72, 352b.4
12. H131, 331b.6-7

2. Confession of Faults

1. This suggests the existence of a commentary by Ratnākaraśānti (c. 1000 CE) at the time of Sonam Tsemo, though no such text is known. It may be one of the anonymous Indian commentaries on the *Bodhicaryāvatāra* (see Brunnhölzl, 2004, p. 831). If someone were to make a careful comparison the relevant passages in these texts (indicated here and at chapter 5, note 14), the author of one them might be discovered to be Ratnākaraśānti.

2. Causal refuge (*rgyu'i skyabs 'gro*), taking refuge in the Three Jewels as objects who provide protection, is juxtaposed with resultant refuge (*'bras bu'i skyabs 'gro*), indicated below as taking refuge in buddhahood as the state to be attained.

3. These two lists are found together in Asaṅga's *Yogācārabhūmi-viniścayasaṃgraha*,

styled as the 'perfected practice of refuge' (*yang dag pa'i bsgrubs*) and 'perfecting practice' (*yang dag par bsgrubs*), respectively. See W1PD95844, p. 465. The former list is also found in the *Abhidharmasamuccaya*. See *Abhidharmasamuccaya: The Compendium of the Higher Teaching*, trans. Walpola Rahula and Sara Boin-Webb, p. 46.
4. *Dge bsnyen*, i.e. lay holder of the prātimokṣa vows.
5. H368, 183b.2-3
6. The pervasion here is the universally quantified conditional, 'Whatever passes away will never be seen again.' See appendix for details of logical subject, pervasion, etc., in the context of logic.
7. *Mahāyānasūtrālaṃkāra*, ch.10 v.8. See *Ornament of the Great Vehicle Sutras: Maitreya's Mahāyānasūtrālaṃkāra with Commentaries by Khenpo Shenga and Ju Mipham*, p.189.
8. Sapan, *sdom gsum rab byed*, chapter 1, verse 204-5: 'Therefore, the sutras and śāstras explain evil deeds with two classifications: inherent misdeeds and attendant misdeeds. Inherent misdeeds are misdeeds for all beings, while attendant misdeeds are subsequent downfalls attendant to [vows].' See Sapan, *A Clear Differentiation of the Three Codes*, trans. Rhoton, 2002, p.67.

3. Fully Holding Bodhicitta

1. I have corrected an apparent textual corruption here, where two similar references to the root text have been elided— '*bdag la zhes pa dang*' should be repeated to indicate both 3.15c and 3.16a.
2. See commentary and notes to v1.16. Though Sonam Tsemo references Jetāri here, there remains a slight difference in their understanding of application bodhicitta. Jetāri and Sonam Tsemo agree however that the two parts of v3.23-24 are: (1) generating both aspects of bodhicitta together—aspiration and application, and (2) undertaking the training, which is distinct from generating (application) bodhicitta.

   Lhopa Rinchen Pal (p. 78) and other commentators have noted that taking the vows of aspiration and application together in this way is characteristic of the Mañjuśrī-Nāgārjuna lineage of the vow, while taking them separately is characteristic of the Maitreya-Asaṅga lineage. Thus if the second part of the vow comprised application bodhicitta, then Jetāri's system, which separates it, would violate the Mañjuśrī-Nāgārjuna (Madhyamaka) tradition of the vow.
3. These causes of losing the prātimokṣa vows are listed by Vasubandhu in the *Abhidharmakośa*. See Sapan, *A Clear Differentiation of the Three Codes*, trans. Rhoton, p.41 and p.74, n.2.
4. While a defeat (*phas pham pa*, Skt. pārājika) warrants expulsion from the monastic saṅgha, a resembling downfall has only the appearance of a violation of the vow. Resembling downfalls are presented in detail below, at the beginning of chapter four.
5. The prātimokṣa, bodhisattva and vidyādhara vows. See Sapan, *A Clear Differentiation of the Three Codes*, trans. Rhoton.
6. H232, p. 21b.4-21b.5
7. *Spang ba'i sems pa*. Though some editions of the text have this as *sems dpa'* (and the term is even repeated), the edition with *sems pa* is evidently correct as can be seen from its close resemblance to Gampopa's discussion of this topic in the *Ornament of Precious Liberation*, which uses the term '*sems pa*'. That resemblance also suggests a common Kadampa origin for these points.
8. According to the vinaya, following the ceremony of full ordination (*bsnyen rdzogs pa*, Skt. upasampadā), the monk preserves the over two hundred rules of monastic observance. After ten years, he may become an 'elder monk' (*gnas pa brten pa*, Skt.

sthavira) who gains certain distinct obligations as well as being relieved of certain others.
9. *Bodhicaryāvatāra*, v5.102
10. *Sdom pa sna 'ga' spyod pa tsam*
11. The five exemptions (*nges pa lnga*), are restrictions upon or exceptions to the maintenance of the vow for specific individuals, acts, places, times or circumstances. See Vasubandhu's *Abhidharmakosabhasyam*, trans. Leo M. Pruden (English), vol. 2, p. 609-610:
    'He who undertakes [any of the five exemptions] does not acquire the discipline [i.e. vow]; rather, he does a good action similar to the acquisition of the discipline.'
    The suggestion is that since the training is intermittent (c.f. *Bodhicaryāvatāra* v1.18-19) the exemption of time is present. Lhopa Rinchen Pal (p. 79), who repeats much of this section on 'method', adds a reference to Asaṅga's *Yogācārabhūmiviniścayasaṃgraha* in which vows of abandonment are distinguished as lesser, middling, greater and perfected according to the limits of their duration, scope, etc. and says that here one should train in applying antidotes in a similar way. See also Sapan's comments on the bodhisattva prātimokṣa:
    'Train in abstaining from the ten nonvirtuous deeds by gradually accustoming yourself to longer and longer periods of practice...' (*Clarifying the Sage's Intent*, trans. David Jackson, p. 432)
12. In the *Śikṣā-samuccaya*, Śāntideva relates this as follows:
    'On this topic, one should not be afraid to take a vow that lasts for all time due to concern about downfalls that may occur in another life, for, in the *Aspiration Prayer of Akṣobhya*, it says:
    "When the Tathāgata Akṣobhya was still a bodhisattva, he said this:
    'If in all my future births I am not ordained, I will have lied to the Blessed Ones, the Buddhas.
    Intelligent ones may purify
    One life through effort,
    But they will purify the rest of their lives
    Through understanding.'" ' (*The Training Anthology of Śāntideva: A Translation of the Śikṣā-samuccaya*, pp. 15-16)
13. Deceiving the lama or those worthy of offerings, causing someone to regret something which should not be regretted, disparaging a bodhisattva who is generating bodhicitta, conducting oneself with pretense and deceit. See Sapan, *Clarifying the Sage's Intent*, trans. David Jackson (2015), pp. 412-413.
14. *'gro ba gzhan gyi rnam rten dge slong gi 'du shes med pa*. Karma Thinley Rinpoche confirmed that this refers to cases such as gods, eunuchs, etc. to whom celibacy does not apply.
15. In certain extreme circumstances, misdeeds such as killing may be committed by bodhisattvas who have a perfectly pure intention. See the section on 'Inherent misdeeds in the moral conduct of the vow' at the beginning of chapter four.
16. While the text here adds *de 'dus ma byas pa yin pa'i phyir* ('because of its being non-composite'), this appears to be a corruption, when compared to Lhopa Rinchen Pal who has *de'ang byas yod yin pas so*, 'because that very function exists' (p. 84).
17. *Shes pa rang bzhin du ma gnas*: the general condition which includes 'beings who are unable to hold a monastic position' (see chapter 3, note 14).
18. Several examples are given in the vinaya texts of Upananda misrepresenting the scriptures in order to trick others, typically old monks (*rgan zhugs*, Skt. mahallaka), into violating the monastic rules for his personal gain.
19. Lhopa Rinchen Pal, p. 85.
20. *Mos pa spyod pa ba*, i.e. the second of the five paths of the Mahāyāna. See e.g. Sapan, *Clarifying the Sage's Intent*, chapter 11.

4. Concern

1. These are given in the *Ākāśagarbha Sutra* and quoted in full by Śāntideva in the *Śikṣā-samuccaya*. See *The Training Anthology of Śāntideva: A Translation of the Śikṣā-samuccaya*, pp. 63-68.
2. *Bzlog pa*, c.f. *cho ga 'jam pos bzlogs* in Lhopa Rinchen Pal (p. 102).
3. *Nyes pa sbom po*, i.e. not a downfall but nevertheless an extremely negative action.
4. *Cho ga btsan po yod kyang sbyor ba las bag yangs su byas*, i.e. a dispensation on the prohibition of killing etc. can apply but only under very special circumstances such as in this example. This type of fault has a homonymic parallel in the vinaya, mentioned in e.g. Dharmamitra's commentary on the *Vinayasūtra*:
   'A formal rule [*cho ga btsan po*] is a strict observance [*bkas bcad dam po*] specified by the Bhagavān, such as bathing in the two-weeks of the full moon which, if not confessed, is a root downfall. There are certain circumstances when this observance is dispensed: during the rainy season, during an illness, when working, when going on a journey, during heavy wind or rain. One may dispense with it at that time.' (D4120, p, 368b-369a).
   In the Mahāyāna, practising the dispensation when it does not apply is a 'heavy fault' of the bodhisattva vow, whereas in the vinaya it is a downfall of the monastic vows.
5. A resembling downfall is an act or omission which seems to be a downfall but is not actually one. A resembling non-downfall is an act or omission which seems to be permissible but is in fact a downfall.
6. The implied attendant misdeed here is destroying plants, one of the monastic rules that can be repaired by confession.
7. Lhopa Rinchen Pal, p. 103:
   'If it was possible to benefit them in some other way but one gave up samādhi, it is practising a dispensation even though a formal rule is available. If in order to accomplish their vast benefit, one abandons yoga, it is resembling downfall. If one remains in yoga having abandoned their benefit, it is a resembling non-downfall.'
8. Lhopa Rinchen Pal, p. 103:
   'If one is accomplishing the benefit of some beings and one sees there would be a cessation of accomplishing qualities and hearing, etc. of a vast country and that country would be harmed for a long time, one can either accomplish all their benefits, or accomplish the benefit of the many beings by another means, or avert the harm for both of them. If it was possible to do so, yet one abandons a benefit, it is the former fault. If there is no other means, without forgetting the benefit, one should continue to benefit of the vast country. That would be a resembling downfall. Otherwise, it is a resembling non-downfall.'
9. In other commentaries, line 4.3d is explained as unhesitatingly practising the bodhisattva conduct, e.g. Prajñākaramati (W21708, p. 79): 'What doubts could remain? Therefore, it is logical to exert oneself fully in such a promise.'
   C.f. Lhopa Rinchen Pal (p. 88): 'Although one may have promised to do something which one has not examined, one should examine it, i.e. analyse whether or not it is beneficial.'
10. Lhopa Rinchen Pal (p. 89) has 'Bhimasena'.
11. Lhopa Rinchen Pal (p.89-90) identifies the *Great Commentary* ('*grel chen las*) as the source of this opinion. Prajñākaramati's *Great Commentary* relates that Ārya Śāriputra abandoned perfect enlightenment but, attaining the 'enlightenment of the śrāvakas', worked for many aeons to benefit sentient beings who were the objects of his former vow to liberate them from saṃsāric suffering (W21708, pp. 81-82). Sapan notes that the śrāvakas had a tradition of 'generating bodhicitta' (*sems bskyed*) where

they resolved to attain the results of arhat, pratyekabuddha or Buddha but this tradition had declined (see Sapan, *A Clear Differentiation of the Three Codes*, trans. Rhoton, p.81). For comments on whether *'grel chen* is indeed W21708, see chapter 6, note 14.

12. Lhopa Rinchen Pal (pp. 89-90) adds,
'My own lama [Sapan] said that since such cases are inconceivable, one should never abandon bodhicitta… In the *White Lotus of Holy Dharma Sutra* (H116, p.52-53) Śāriputra's final enlightenment as the completely perfect Buddha Padmaguru [c.f. 'Padmaprabha (*padma'i 'od*)' in H116] is predicted. Since it is impossible for a Buddha not to previously generate bodhicitta, it seems Śāriputra only appeared to abandon [bodhicitta].'

13. From the *Eight Thousand Verse Perfection of Wisdom Sutra* (H12, 278b). That version has 'morality' (*tshul khrims*) in place of 'the development of bodhicitta' in the third line.

14. I.e. the 'four similar defeats' (*pham pa'i gnas lta bu bzhi*): According to the tradition (see e.g. Sakya Pandita, *Clarifying the Sage's Intent*, trans. David Jackson, p. 412-413), there are four specific acts which violate the bodhisattva vow. They are 'similar' to the four defeats of the śrāvakas in that they constitute breakages of a vow, but they differ in that the bodhisattva vow, unlike the Hīnayāna vows, can be retaken and restored. Thus, abandoning the vow simpliciter is more serious than breaking the vow by these four means.

15. H332, p. 392b

5. Clear Comprehension

1. H232, p. 129b
2. The 'women' here are explained by other commentators including Prajñākaramati (W21708, p. 104) and Thokme Zangpo (W1KG1795, p. 64) to be denizens of the Śālmari (or Śālmali) hell, who entice one into tortures, manifesting as the result of sexual misconduct. Lhopa Rinchen Pal (p. 95) glosses the point as 'one's own nonvirtues are the appearances of mind' and gives a quote from the same sutra:
'One's mind is an enemy, a great enemy. There is no enemy other than the mind. Just like a stick on fire will burn itself, one's own mind is burned by mind itself.'
See also Śāntideva's reference to this in *The Training Anthology of Śāntideva: A Translation of the Śikṣā-samuccaya*, pp. 240-241.
3. This section heading was previously given as 'The reason (*'thad pa*) for guarding the mind'.
4. *Tshangs skud*, known as yajnopavita.
5. *Skyes po bslu ba'i sgyu sum cu so gnyis*—Lhopa Rinchen Pal (p. 97) uses a similar expression, *skyes po bslu ba'i sgyu thabs sum bcu rtsa gnyis dang ldan pa*.
6. Restrictions on monastic eating times are dispensed with in certain cases of sickness and famine. The downfall is afterwards, when the sickness or famine is removed and the monk neglects to apply the restriction again.
7. Sonam Tsemo has *rjes su bsten pa* ('serve') here, while the root text is normally *rjes su brtan pa* ('instruct'), i.e. receive teachings.
8. *Rang bzhin*, i.e. body or mind. Some editions of the Tibetan text erroneously have *rang bzhin med*. Lhopa Rinchen Pal (p. 98) has *rang bzhin*.
9. H176, 209b
10. The text has giving (*sbyin pa*) here, but presumably the intent is to match v5.42d. Lhopa Rinchen Pal, on this same point, has moral conduct (p. 99).
11. There is a minor textual corruption here, with three headings indicated but only

two given. I have replaced the missing second heading based on Lhopa Rinchen Pal (p. 99) who, in the other headings, has followed Sonam Tsemo.
12. Here I have followed Lhopa Rinchen Pal (p. 101) for whom *lus kyi spyod pa* (bodily conduct) becomes *las kyi spyod pa* (conduct of action) and by whom the titles of sections two and three are reversed. Since this seems to fit the content here better than having section two entitled 'bodily conduct', I have assumed a typographical error in the Tibetan version of Sonam Tsemo's text.
13. I.e. six antidotes correlating to the six perfections.
14. See chapter 2, note 1. Lhopa Rinchen Pal (p. 104) also gives this quote.
15. *Ma dad pa'i gnas mang ba*: The translation of this expression is informed by Lhopa Rinchen Pal's comment (p.105), '*gzhan ma dad pa dang nyes spyod gyi rgyur 'gyur bas skyes pa med par zhes so*': '"Unaccompanied" becomes a cause of lacking faith and negative conduct in others.'
16. In Prajñākaramati (W21708, p. 137): '*dpung pa gnyi ga mnyam pa ste dus gcig tu mi mnye ba'o*', i.e. shoulders or upper arms.
17. The text here mentions only confession and dedication, but since Lhopa Rinchen Pal (p. 106) and other commentators have confession, rejoicing and dedication, I have assumed a typographical error.
18. H67, p. 175
19. Lhopa Rinchen Pal (p. 106):
'Therefore, because one should subdue [*tshar gcad*] and protect others and be knowledgeable oneself, one should endeavour in this.'
20. Sadaprarudita's extraordinary devotion and dedication to receiving the Prajñāpāramitā teachings from the bodhisattva Dharmodgata are related in, e.g. Patrul Rinpoche, *Words of My Perfect Teacher*, pp. 153-157.
21. The passage on Śrīsambhava in the *Avataṃsaka Sūtra* (H94, p. 227b) contains the detailed instructions given by the boy and girl bodhisattvas Śrīsambhava and Śrīmati to Sudhana, including the famous instruction:
'Noble son, you should look upon yourself as sick, the spiritual friend as the doctor, the teaching as medicine and practice as the cure.' (*The Flower Ornament Scripture: A Translation of the Avatamsaka Sutra*, pp. 1444-1452)
22. As noted above, these are also quoted in full by Śāntideva in chapter four of the *Śikṣā-samuccaya*. See *The Training Anthology of Śāntideva: A Translation of the Śikṣā-samuccaya*, pp. 63-68.
23. This refers to the *Śikṣā-samuccaya* and the *Sūtra-samuccaya* of Śāntideva and two works of the same titles by Nāgārjuna, of which only Śāntideva's *Śikṣā-samuccaya* (D3940) and Nāgārjuna's *Sūtra-samucaya* (D3934) are extant.

6. Patience

1. See commentary to verse 6.11
2. Primal substance is *gtso bo* (Skt. prakṛti). Individual consciousness is *skye bu* (Skt. puruṣa).
3. Universal flow is *'gro ba* or *'gro ba thams cad* (Skt. jagat). Manifestations are *gsal ba* or *rnam 'gyur* (Skt. vikāra).
4. Outer objects and inner experiences exist like reflections within the two sides of a double-sided mirror, which is itself a material evolution of the primal substance. According to Mipham (*The Wisdom Chapter: Jamgon Mipham's Commentary on the Ninth Chapter of The Way of the Bodhisattva*, p. 133), the 'Great One' itself is the mirror of mind.
5. The Great One (*chen po* or *blo*, Skt. mahat or buddhi) is the first evolution of the disequilibrium of the primal matter. Pride, *nga rgyal*, means misidentifying the

manifestations as self. The five bare elements, *de tsam*, are sounds, smells, tastes, touchables and colours. The five elements, *'byung ba*, are the gross elements of fire, water, earth, air and space. The eleven organs, *dbang po*, are the five senses, five action organs and the mind (*yid*). These twenty-three manifestations, in addition to the primal substance and the individual consciousness, comprise the twenty-five ontological enumerations of this school. See commentary to v9.127 for a more detailed description of this system.

6. The example of the self autonomously creating harm relates to the chapter topic, i.e. patience, and section topic, i.e. 'Stopping impatience with the establishment of suffering for oneself' etc.
7. *Blo sngon du btang*, cognates *blo sngon du gtong ba'i sems pa*, *bsam blo sngon nas gtong ba*, *blo sngon du btang ba*, Skt: buddhī-purvaka, 'preceded by design, intentional' or 'preceded by intelligence' (Monier-Williams). This term is used in Sonam Tsemo's discussion of the Naiyāyikas.
8. Though the text here has 'not matter' (*bems po yang ma yin*), the negation must be a typographical error, for it would not accord with the Naiyāyika doctrine (e.g. Prajñākaramati: '*sems pa med pa yang sems med pa'i rang bzhin te bem po zhe bya ba'o*', W21708, p. 163) or indeed Sonam Tsemo's own subsequent remarks (see commentary to v9.68).
9. The pervader is 'gradual and instantaneous function'. It not supported by the sempiternal self.
10. Qualification: 'The sempiternal self has no gradual or instantaneous function.'
11. Pervasion: 'Whatever has no (gradual or instantaneous) function is not an agent (producing an effect).'
12. The ability to change is not supported by the sempiternal self.
13. Qualification: 'The sempiternal self is unchanging.'
14. In support of this point, Sonam Tsemo quotes the root text at v6.27b here as '*bdag ces rtag pa*', i.e. 'sempiternal self', rather than the more usual '*bdag ces brtags pa*', i.e. 'designated self', found in the extant Tibetan editions of the root text. Lhopa Rinchen Pal, (p. 116) reiterates Sonam Tsemo's point here and attributes it to the author of the *Great Commentary* ('*grel chen mkhan po*). However, he corrects v6.27b to 'designated self'. In the extant Tibetan translation of Prajñākaramati's *Great Commentary*, v6.27b is quoted as '*brtags pa*' (W21708, p. 162) but the treatment of this line seems to be associated with the Sāṃkhyas and not the Naiyāyikas. However, this is the only notable point of difference among several points of direct correspondence between the 'author of the *Great Commentary*' and the extant Tibetan edition of the *Great Commentary* (see chapter 9, note 27). Within the present section, the three topics identified by Sonam Tsemo—refuting the primal substance, manifestations and individual consciousnesses—correspond with Prajñākaramati's commentary. Here they are represented with formal logic, which is absent from Prajñākaramati, but this is a difference of style rather than substance. The Tibetan colophon to the *Great Commentary* (W21708, p. 534) notes that chapters 1, 2, 7, 8 and 9 were translated by the Indian pandita Sumatikirti and the Tibetan translator Darma-drak (dar ma grags), while the remaining chapters, including the present one, were translated by one Lodro Zangdragpa (blo gros bzang grags pa). It is possible a version of chapter six of the *Great Commentary* other than the extant Lodro Zangdragpa translation was available to Sonam Tsemo.
15. The primal substance supports the 'contrary' property of being material, i.e. contrary to intentionality.
16. The individual consciousness does not support the property of being a creator.
17. The creator of experience is temporary.
18. The text here indicates six but gives only five headings. I have treated the title of the

fifth section as the missing one and replaced it. Lhopa Rinchen Pal (p. 119) uses a different schema here, so his text cannot be consulted.
19. Previously this heading was '...the production of negative actions towards my side'.
20. The text here has '*gzhan la mi 'dod pa*', but it is evidently correct in Lhopa Rinchen Pal (p. 122) as '*gzhan la mi gnod pa*'.
21. Pervasion: 'Whatever is a cause of virtue is not an obstruction to merit.'
22. H239, 97b.7

7. Effort

1. H232, p.33a. Sonam Tsemo adds 'and so forth' here, i.e. the passage continues, as quoted in the *Śikṣā-samuccaya*:
  'They did not attain enlightenment while already being tathāgatas. In the same way, I shall strive and in the same way I shall practise diligently. With effort shared with all sentient beings, with effort that takes all sentient beings as its object, I will completely awaken to unsurpassable complete enlightenment.' (*The Training Anthology of Śāntideva: A Translation of the Śikṣā-samuccaya*, p. 58)
2. Reverse pervasion: 'Where there is no virtue, the cause (i.e. motivation) was absent.' Forward pervasion: 'Where there is motivation, the result will be present.'
3. H94, 174a. That version is slightly more descriptive and hence longer than the one quoted here. This sutra passage is also quoted in the *Śikṣā-samuccaya* (D3940, 153a, under v24 of the root verses) in the longer form, though with yet another translation. All the Tibetan editions of Sonam Tsemo's commentary here erroneously have *ri mo mnyams* for *ri mi mnyams* ('the rugged mountains').
4. Lhopa Rinchen Pal (p. 135):
  'Weakening other actions means ceasing conduct, i.e. action diminishing the unattained. Weakening results means not attaining the results themselves, i.e. action diminishing the attained.'
  C.f. Sthiramati's *Mahāyānasūtrālaṃkāraṭīkā* (D4034, 85a.2-3):
  'If a shameless person commits actions such as killing, although he may have virtuous dharmas in the past such as faith and moral conduct, they will be lost. This is called action damaging attained virtuous dharmas (*thob pa las nyams*). Though in future lives one would have attained virtuous dharmas such as faith and moral conduct, they will not be attained. This is called action damaging unattained virtuous dharmas (*ma thob pa las nyams*).'
5. The Tibetan text text here has '*thad* (logic, reason) for the second heading (the first being *bsten par rigs pa*) but later has *thabs* (means), which is confirmed by Lhopa Rinchen Pal (p. 136).
6. Just as the defilement of anger can be productively turned against the defilements (v4.29, 4.43 and 6.46), so pride can be productively used against them. The English word 'pride' is particularly suitable here in having proper (productive, virtuous) and improper (nonvirtuous, defiled) applications. As Thomas Reid expressed it in his *Essays on the Active Powers of Man* (1788):
  'When it is grounded upon a vain conceit of inward worth that we do not possess, it is arrogance and deceit. But when a man, without thinking of himself more highly than he ought to think, is conscious of that integrity of heart, and uprightness of conduct, which he most highly esteems in others, and values himself upon this account; this perhaps may be called pride of virtue, but it is not a vicious pride. It is a noble and magnanimous disposition, without which there can be no steady virtue.' (Quoted in P.M.S. Hacker, *The Passions: A Study of Human Nature*, p. 139. See also pp. 140-151)

7. I have altered the text's apparently erroneous *rkyen nyin* to *rkyen nyen* in accord with Lhopa Rinchen Pal's (p. 137) *nyon mongs nyen gnyen po stobs bskyed*.

8. Meditation

1. Though this section is not listed here, a section of this name is found later covering verses 85-88. Lhopa Rinchen Pal's (p. 145) equivalent section in this list is entitled 'The qualities of solitude', confirming that it belongs here and that its loss in Sonam Tsemo's text is a typographical error.
2. Non-distraction (*mi g.yeng ba*) earlier; here, solitude (*dben pa*).
3. The time taken on the Mahāyāna path to attain buddhahood.
4. Pervasion: 'Whatever is suffering should be abandoned.'
5. Pervasion: 'Whatever is happiness should be established'
6. H129, 200b-222b.
7. *Dpa' bas sbyin*. Lhopa Rinchen Pal (p. 149) has *dpa' sbyin*. H129 has *dpa' bas byin*.
8. The text indicates four sections but only names three; here I have assumed the second one is missing and offered its title.
9. This list is slightly corrupted in the Tibetan text and has been corrected here by reference to Lhopa Rinchen Pal (p. 155). The first heading was missing and the fifth appeared as two separate sections.
10. Lhopa Rinchen Pal (p.156) attributes this interpretation to Puṇyaśrīmitra.

9. Wisdom

1. Sonam Tsemo actually mentions two subsections here—abandoning objections from the relative perspective and from the ultimate perspective. However, he explains later that this distinction, from Ngok Lotsawa, is not correct and adopts the schema presented here.
2. This passage is based on an earlier presentation of the same four prasaṅgas by Chapa Chokyi Sengge, formalizing a passage in the third chapter of the *Saṃdhinirmocana Sutra*. See Tauscher 2003, pp. 213-218. See also Sapan, *Clarifying the Sage's Intent*, trans. David Jackson, pp. 518-519, who gives a brief presentation of the same points.
3. Though I use the generally accepted term 'relative' to translate the Tibetan '*kun rdzob*' (Skt. saṁvṛti), it does not convey the sense of concealment and deception in the original Sanskrit and Tibetan terms. A possible translation of *kun rdzob dben pa* (Skt. saṁvṛti-satya) here could be 'deluded truth'; though this term at first glance may seem paradoxical, it captures the sense of delusion *mistaken for* truth. Distinctions can be made within this kind of 'truth': Candrakīrti, for example, distinguishes between clear and defective perceptual faculties (see Lama Jampa Thaye, *Rain of Clarity*, p. 66-67) and elsewhere consensus is invoked as a differentiator. In the present text, a distinction between the 'yogin's relative' and 'ordinary (person's) relative' is invoked, this being the most soteriologically relevant differentiator. The subtle question of whether the relative truth, especially the relative truth of emptiness, is always a *mere* delusion or whether it can be true in some degree or some sense, is a recurrent concern in the present chapter (see, e.g. v7-8, v106-107, v138-140).
4. Though the qualified comprehension of the ultimate by inferential reasoning is a motif of Svātantrika Madhyamaka, Sonam Tsemo does not use the usual Svātantrika term for this—'approximate ultimate'—but rather distinguishes it from direct perception of the ultimate by calling it an 'ascertainment' or 'making certain'

(*nges pa*), rather than a 'cognition' (*shes pa*). In a slightly later Sakya account of the two truths according to Svātantrika Madhyamaka, Sapan says in *Clarifying the Sage's Intent*:

'The Svātantrika Mādhyamikas say that each of the two truths are approximate and non-approximate, i.e. four in total: Appearances from the perspective of a non-analytical ordinary person are the non-approximate relative. Truth from the perspective of analysis is the approximate ultimate. Non-conceptual wisdom [*mi rtog pa'i ye shes*] of the three kinds of āryas is the non-approximate ultimate [See notes to v9.15 in the present text for more on this point]. Pure worldly wisdom [*dag pa 'jig rten pa'i ye shes*] is the approximate relative.

'This is the position that Buddhas possess wisdom, which is certainly not incorrect [*skyon med*] but the Buddhas' wisdom is beyond existence and nonexistence. Also, the distinction between non-conceptual and pure worldly wisdom is made from the perspective of how we see it, whereas on the level of a Buddha, they are non-dual.' (W4CZ2193, p. 338)

See also Sapan's definition of the two truths in the same text:

'Therefore, in our tradition, the relative is what is established from the perspective of non-analytical conceptual thought [*ma dpyad pa'i blo*], the ultimate is what is not established from the perspective of analytical conceptual thought, and truth [i.e. relative truth and ultimate truth as opposed to merely relative and ultimate] is what is not opposed [*gnod pa med*] from one's own perspective.' (ibid. p. 337. See also the translation of these two passages by David Jackson, 2015, pp. 515-517)

5. The account that follows is presented provisionally. Subsequently, Sonam Tsemo criticizes certain aspects of it, then gives a revised account. The revision concerns whether the differences between higher yogins and those of lower understanding are direct perceptions (first exegesis) or conceptual/inferential (second exegesis). The first exegesis, which treats them as direct perceptions (or non-conceptual realizations), corresponds with that of Prajñākaramati but is probably intended to also include other Indian and Tibetan exegeses. See chapter 9, note 14.

6. *Ser skya* (c.f. *ser skya gzegs zan* in Lhopa Rinchen Pal, p. 174), the founder of the sāṃkhya school.

7. *Snang med pa'i shes rab*. Wisdom not having appearances is juxtaposed with conceptual thought (*blo*) which perceives dualistic appearances (*snang med/snang bcas*). This distinction relates directly to a fundamental issue in Mahāyāna philosophy addressed in this chapter—how Buddhas and bodhisattvas can act for the benefit of beings in saṃsāra without themselves becoming subject to saṃsāric defilements. 'Appearance' in this sense has the essential connotations of delusion, duality and non-analysis, while 'without appearance' means non-duality and wisdom. Thus, non-appearance is not to be understood as mere non-perception or an inert blankness of mind incompatible with the active enlightenment of Mahāyāna.

8. Pervasion: 'Whatever is free from singularity and multiplicity has no essence.'

9. Qualification: 'Appearances are free from singularity and multiplicity.'

10. *Gcig dang du ma dang bral ba'i phyir ro / rang bzhin med de gzugs brnyan bzhin*. This syllogism and its formulation closely resemble the first stanza of Śāntarakṣita's *Madhyamakālaṃkārakārikā* (D3884, p. 53a).

11. While the example is mentioned in the root verse, Tibetan logic seems to have loosened this requirement, i.e. syllogisms can be established without one and indeed this is the norm for subsequent syllogistic applications in the present text. See Tillemans, 1999, p. 15.

12. See chapter 9, note 5.

13. See Sonam Tsemo's section headed 'Distinguishing the types of mind', above.

14. Lhopa Rinchen Pal rehearses the two perspectives but does not specify a preference. The first side, attributed to Prajñākaramati's *Great Commentary*, holds that yogins are āryas and ordinary ones are ordinary people and that the objections (or differences) are direct perceptions, with examples used for abandoning those objections. The second side, unattributed though clearly corresponding to Sonam Tsemo's position, claims, 'Yogins are those who accept the Four Seals as the mark of the Buddha's words and take refuge in the Three Jewels and ordinary ones are those who reject this.' In expressing this latter position, Lhopa Rinchen Pal gives a similar objection to the one set out here:

    'Āryas and ordinary people are not appropriate as opponent and objector. If truth distinguishes those on the path of seeing, how are śrāvakas distinct from Cittamātrins and Mādhyamikas? Moreover, how can one object before or after to the ārya wisdom? It is a contradiction to say someone with wisdom which sees the ultimate is [at first] the objected to and [later] the objector.' (ibid. pp. 173-174)

    Later commentators on the *Bodhicaryāvatāra* seem to have overwhelmingly followed Prajñākaramati's explanation without responding to the objection raised here.
15. *Lhan cig dmigs pa'i nges gnod.* Jamgon Ju Mipham (2005, p. 237) mentions this argument, though from the perspective of the Cittamātra school. Here, the objection to the Vaibhāṣikas is that a blue object and the cognition of it are simultaneous, so the object cannot be a cause of the cognition, for cause and effect must be ordered in time. The Sautrāntika conclusion is that representations must exist as intermediaries between objects and cognitions.
16. *Skyes la 'dra ba la sogs pa'i yul gyi mtshan nyid bkag pa.* Jamgon Ju Mipham (ibid. p. 236) mentions this argument as refuting imperceptible outer objects as the cause of representations of those objects, such as in the example of pressing the eye and seeing two moons but there only being one moon.
17. *Rnam pa bden pa*, often translated as 'True Aspectarians'.
18. Sonam Tsemo explains at the start of the third major section of this chapter, which includes a section structured according to the 'Four Foundations of Mindfulness', that it can be regarded as a teaching on refuting the non-self of the individual. The fourth major section also contains objections to the non-Buddhist doctrines.
19. Nāgārjuna, *Madhyamakālaṃkārakārikā*, v29-30, D3884, 8a6-7.
20. Śāntarakṣita, *Madhyamakālaṃkārakārikā*, v68, D3884, 55b.
21. Kamalaśīla, *Bhavanakrama*, D3916, p. 54a2.
22. The intention is the motive for teaching the indirect meaning. The intentional basis is the teaching device used. The valid cognition refuting the literal interpretation is self-explanatory. See Mathes, 2008, p.13-14.
23. Nāgārjuna, D4158, p. 109b.
24. Pervasion: 'Whatever is illusion-like cannot persist across rebirths.'
25. Pervasion: 'Whatever exists for a long time is real.'
26. Pervasion: 'Whatever is not distinct from saṃsāra in the pure nature is not distinct from saṃsāra.'
27. This is Prajñākaramati's *Great Commentary*. Vose (2009b, p. 304) translates *'grel chen mdzad pa* here as 'Great Commentator' and suggests this is Chapa Chokyi Sengge. I believe this can be ruled out. 'Great Commentator' would surely be *'grel pa chen po*, while *'grel chen* means *Great Commentary*. For further evidence that Prajñākaramati is the *'grel chen mdzad pa*, see notes 14, 57, 90 and 131 to chapter 9. In Sonam Tsemo's commentary, the *'grel chen* is represented as the source of the present objection that Buddhas would be subject to delusion, whereas Prajñākaramati in fact expresses the objection in terms of Buddhas having suffering. This is, however, a distinction that makes no difference, for delusion and suffering are internally related. For an

observation on one notable difference between the *'grel chen mdzad pa* and Prajñākaramati, see chapter 6, note 14.
28. C.f. Sakya Pandita, *Clarifying the Sage's Intent*, trans. David Jackson, p. 573-574.
29. Though not an antecedent text, a related criticism of the Prāsangika position is made by Sapan concerning the Buddha's knowledge of relative truth:

'That [Prāsangika] position would be acceptable if the Buddha remained in nirvāṇa and did not have wisdom [of the relative] but, since we do not accept that the Buddha is only in nirvāṇa, it is not logical to say he does not have wisdom [of the relative]. Because of this, [the Prāsangika position] is slightly illogical [*cung zad mi 'thad do*].' (*Clarifying the Sage's Intent*, W4CZ2193, p. 338, my translation.)

Sapan, as mentioned above, also slightly faults the Svātantrika position for reifying the wisdom of the relative. His preferred position is that 'the appearance aspect is relative, the emptiness aspect is ultimate and the indistinguishable [*dbyer mi phyed*] aspect is their unification regardless of the individual [i.e. regardless of whether it is sentient beings, āryas or Buddhas]'. (ibid.)
30. In using the term 'we' (*kho bo cag*) here, Sonam Tsemo might be thought to be including himself among the Svātantrikas. I do not think such a conclusion is warranted, for this passage begins with an obvious textual corruption (*rnam bdzun pa'i gnod pa spangs pa dang*, a line belonging to the next page and erroneously copied here) and ends with a quotation or attribution indicator (*zhes bya ba*). Though Sonam Tsemo clearly prefers the Svātantrika position to the Prāsangika one on this point, elsewhere he impartially presents both the Svātantrika and Prāsangika perspectives and represents some of Śāntideva's arguments as prasangas despite extant Svātantrika exegeses (see his commentary on v9.17 and preceding v9.116). See also the (second) exegesis of v9.4c in which he responds to an objection that any argument or refutation is conceptual and therefore a delusion, an objection which pertains directly to the use of svātantras to prove emptiness. Given his general impartiality in presenting both Svātantrika and Prāsangika perspectives, Sonam Tsemo probably did not strictly consider himself either a Svātantrika or a Prāsangika, a position in accord with that of Sapan in *Clarifying the Sage's Intent*. Even if Sonam Tsemo were to be counted as a Svātantrika, this should not be understood merely as a preference for svātantras over prasangas, but should be viewed in the broader context of a doctrinal position on how Buddhas, āryas and ordinary beings each perceive relative and ultimate truth (see note 31 below).
31. Lhopa Rinchen Pal also describes both the Prāsangika and Svātantrika Madhyamaka perspectives here but without mentioning the objection to the Prāsangika position, reflecting his teacher Sakya Pandita's impartial stance towards Svātantrika and Prāsangika (see above):

'There are two responses to the objection. According to the Svātantrikas, just as when the causes and conditions of an illusion are not reversed, so it is not reversed, when the causes, etc. of saṃsāra are not reversed, it is not reversed. When the continuity of that which is to be abandoned is reversed, though merely relative, conceptual thought of deluded saṃsāra does not arise, i.e. one abandons its causes. Therefore, since there is no conceptual wisdom [*rtog bcas kyi ye shes med*], there is no remaining in saṃsāra and since non-conceptual wisdom is mastered, there is no remaining in nirvāṇa.

'According to the Prāsangikas, while on the temporary path one has not exhausted karma etc.—the causes of conceptual thought, the various transmigrations are not stopped. When the temporary resultant unawareness, etc. is interrupted, the Buddha does not master a wisdom with appearances as the merely relative—the first two lines. That he has knowledge of what appears is the illusion-like relative and his knowledge of what is is unelaborated like space. By abandoning the causes of delusion, there is fundamentally nothing to master—the second two lines.' (ibid. p. 183)

Earlier, he describes the different opinions of Asaṅga, Bhāvaviveka and Candrakīrti on the relative and ultimate truth and their relation to Buddhas, āryas and ordinary beings, noting the three natures of Asaṅga's works and the two ultimates of Bhāvaviveka. Of Candrakīrti, he says,

'Ācārya Candrakīrti says the Buddha and nirvāṇa are only ultimate, the meditative absorptions of the three āryas are ultimate, but their post-meditation is relative and ordinary people are solely ['ba' zhig] relative. In the commentary [dgongs 'grel, though this quote is also v6.30 of the Mādhyamakāvatāra root text, reiterated in the auto-commentary, W1KG3407, p. 180] it says, "Thus, if the worldly had valid cognition, since they would see reality [de nyid mthong], they would already be āryas, so what would be the point of the ārya path? It is a contradiction to say the ignorant have valid cognition." He says the conceptual thought which cognizes emptiness, etc. is the yogin's relative... My own lama [Sapan] did not think there was a difference between the intentions [dgongs] of the earlier and later ācāryas.' (ibid. p. 172)

Thus, according to Lhopa Rinchen Pal, Candrakīrti and Mādhyamikas generally allow that the three āryas perceive the ultimate, though only while in meditation and not in post-meditation. Hence, Lhopa Rinchen Pal does not accept the criticism made by Sonam Tsemo that Prāsaṅgikas deny that the three kinds of āryas perceive the ultimate. This corresponds with the view of the Sakya hierarch Jetsun Drakpa Gyaltsen (1147-1216) that Svātantrika and Prāsaṅgika agree that the cognitions of the three ārya are all ultimate when in meditation and relative when in post-meditation (see Tauscher, 2003, p. 210).

The idea that āryas perceive the ultimate in meditation and relative in post-meditation is also found in certain commentators of Candrakīrti, including the ninth Karmapa, Wangchuk Dorje (2008, p. 213) and Jamgon Ju Mipham (2002, p. 199). Strictly speaking, Candrakīrti's auto-commentary does not mention the meditation/post-meditation (mnyam gzhag/rjes thob) distinction in relation to the cognitions of āryas. Rather, in commenting on v6.28, Candrakīrti says in the Madhyamakāvatāra-bhasya,

'Śrāvakas, pratyekabuddhas and bodhisattvas have abandoned defiled vision. Visible objects for them are karmic formations—like reflections, etc., their nature fabricated and untrue because truth is not something pretended. The childish are deluded but, for these others, it is the mere relative, arising through dependent origination, like an illusion. Yet, because of mere unawareness, they still have the essential characteristic of the obscurations of cognizables. These āryas remain within the domain of dualistic appearances. They are not the ones who have mastered the domain without dualistic appearances. Those are the Buddhas, who have achieved complete, perfect enlightenment in all dharmas in all their aspects. Mind and mental events are always in error. Therefore, the Bhagavān taught both relative truth [kun rdzob kyi bden pa] and the mere relative [kun rdzob tsam]. What is the ultimate of ordinary people [so so'i skye bo rnams kyi don dam pa]? It is this mere relative of āryas whose domain is dualistic appearances. What is the emptiness of the intrinsic nature of that? It is their [the āryas'] ultimate. The ultimate of Buddhas is the natural state itself [rang bzhin nyid] and the ultimate truth of those who have no delusion. Each of these should be known separately. Relative truth, because it is a delusion, is not ultimate truth. Therefore, having presented relative truth, ultimate truth is presented. But, because it is inexpressible, is a cognition and is not an object, it is not possible to show it directly but, because it is possible to experience it in one's own mind by hearing about it and its nature being clarified, the examples are taught.' (W1KG3407, p. 173-5)

Here, Candrakīrti in one sense allows that āryas experience the ultimate by saying the 'mere relative' of āryas is ultimate, i.e. 'the ultimate of ordinary people'. This position evolved, perhaps in response to the kind of objection raised here by Sonam Tsemo, into a broad consensus among Candrakīrti's commentators that āryas experience the ultimate whilst in meditation and the relative in post-meditation.

In any case, what is certain is that for the early Sakya Mādhyamikas, a central issue in the Svātantrika-Prāsaṅgika distinction is how relative and ultimate are related to Buddhas, āryas and ordinary beings, respectively. For Buddhas, the controversial or difficult point is their cognition of the relative without being subject to delusion; for ordinary beings, it is their cognition of the ultimate while being subject to delusion and, for āryas, it is both. That the Svātantrika-Prāsaṅgika distinction subsequently, from the fourteenth century onwards, became more focussed on the question of whether the Svātantrikas conceptualize emptiness and reify relative truth through their use of logic and negation was, therefore, a centering of the issue solely around its conceptual characteristics—i.e. how the two truths relate to ordinary beings—and away from the questions which encompass the minds and activities of Buddhas and āryas.

32. Sonam Tsemo uses the term 'Yogācārins' (*rnal 'byor spyod pa*) here as synonymous with the term Vijñaptimātrins (*rnam par rig par smra ba*), used earlier.
33. Pervasion: 'Whatever is non-dual is not aware of itself.'
34. *Bya byed/bya ba*. This not the juxtaposition of *gzung bya/'dzin pa*, i.e. beheld/beholder, sometimes translated as object/subject, which relates to primarily to perception. Rather, this juxtaposition relates to acting and being acted upon, so agent/patient is a more accurate dichotomy than subject/object. It should be understood that agency here is not meant in a moral or intentional sense but merely in the sense of active and passive participants.
35. H91, 375b.3
36. H91, 375b.6
37. These are two of the three kinds of reason, i.e. reasoning from a causal property and from an inherent property. See appendix.
38. Forward pervasion from effect to cause: 'Whatever has memory has self-awareness.' Reverse pervasion: 'Whatever does not have self-awareness cannot have memory.'
39. I.e. the reverse pervasion above.
40. Reason: '[Because of] being nonexistent.'
41. Pervasion: 'Whatever is nonexistent has no nature (and hence no function).'
42. Pervasion: 'Whoever is free from duality is a Buddha.'
43. *Don spyi*, which technically can refer to the pramāṇa notion of a universal or abstract object. Less formally, it means any general concept or predicate.
44. Lhopa Rinchen Pal is very brief on these lines: 'Negation depends on a negandum. By its absence, dependent origination.' (p.192)
45. Lhopa Rinchen Pal comments here on the Svātantrika and Prāsaṅgika perspectives on whether Buddhas have primordial wisdom. He comments that the opinion of his own lama (Sapan) is that the two systems have the same intent and there is no real contradiction. Conceptual thought overcomes conceptual thought like an illusory king defeating another illusory king (*Mahāyānasūtrālaṃkāra* XII.29). Buddha's wisdom, like conceptual thought, is non-arising and presented from the perspective of convention (*Madhyamakāvatāra*, XII.4). He concludes:

'Therefore, objections such as that delusion is not abandoned [by Buddhas] are rejected, as well as the other claims that wisdom is solely equipoise, or an alternation [between equipoise and conceptualization], or that the post-meditation stage is conceptualization, or that kāya and wisdom are distinct. This presents briefly the discrimination of what is reasonable and unreasonable in the nature of omniscience of the three times, etc. Although ultimately all dharmas are without intrinsic nature, relative appearances are unceasing, their nature free from all extremes, the great self. Such is the opinion of my lama.' (ibid., p.193-195)

It is evident here, as above, that the Svātantrika-Prāsangika distinction for early Sakyapas essentially concerns the question of the Buddhas' cognition and not merely that of sentient beings.

46. *Sam gu*. In other early Tibetan commentaries, including that of Lhopa Rinchen Pal (p. 197) and Buston Rinchen Drup (p. 420), this is 'Brahmin Shanku' (*bram ze shang ku*) and later commentators have followed them, thereby identifying the protagonist of this story with the author of a short tantric work on Garuḍa in the Tengyur, *Siddhagaruḍaśāstra*, D3703. According to Pawo Tsuglag Trengwa, 'Brahmin Shangku' was the name given in notes (*zin 'bris*) written by Atīśa Dīpaṃkara Śrījñāna (see Brunnholzl, 2004, p. 661, and Pawo Tsuglag Trengwa, W7500, spelt '*bram ze sha ngku*').

47. Lhopa Rinchen Pal (p. 197-198) comments again (see chapter 9, note 31) here on distinction between Prāsangika and Svātantrika doctrines. For the former, the appearances of the Buddha kāyas and wisdoms appear to trainees from the practice of previous bodhisattva conduct and they remain in the vajra-like samādhi without any mental events. Svātantrikas say they exhaust conceptual discrimination (*rnam par rtog pa zad*), but the Buddha kāyas and wisdoms accomplish the benefit of others by manifesting spontaneous and uninterrupted activities—a position with clear affinity to the *Uttaratantraśāstra*.

48. *Seng ge rnam par rtse ba'i mdo*—this is not to be taken as the *Ārya-maitreya-mahāsiṃhanāda Sutra*, where the quote is not to be found, but is the *Ārya-bodhisattva-pitaka Sutra* (H56), p. 379a. Some commentaries correctly give the *Puṣpakūṭadhāraṇī Sutra* (H605, 467b) as an alternative source for this point.

49. Pervasion: 'Offering to the Buddha generates merit.'

50. Though these six sections are listed here, in the subsequent elaboration, section 2 is elided with section 1 and subsequent sections are numbered as 2 to 5.

51. H9, p. 352b and p. 460a, as well as many other similar instances.

52. We find these criteria for the Buddha's teaching in, e.g. *Mahāyānasūtrālaṃkāra*, v2.5 (D4020, p. 2b). Other commentaries say this is the Buddha's own definition (*sangs ryas gyi bka'*).

53. '*dod chags dang bral ba*, Skt. kamavitaraga, i.e. those who are temporarily reborn outside of the desire realm, in the form or formless realms, which is attainable by non-Buddhist paths.

54. This Dānaśrī is probably to be identified with one Dānaśīla who co-translated the first Tibetan edition of Śāntideva's *Śikṣā-samuccaya* during the 8th-9th century and who was invited to Tibet around that time (see *The Sakya School of Tibetan Buddhism: A History*, p. 42, and *The Blue Annals*, p. 229). This is not to be confused with the Dānaśrī who accompanied Śākyaśrībhadra to Tibet in the early 13th century.

Dānaśīla is possibly the author of one of the anonymous Indian commentaries on the *Bodhicaryāvatāra* (see Brunnhölzl, 2004, p. 831). If someone were to make a careful comparison with the relevant passages in these texts (indicated here and at chapter 9, note 72), the author of one them might be discovered to be Dānaśīla.

55. Vibhudatta (*sgur chung*) was an arhat who was unable to take alms due to his negative karma and subsequently died of hunger.

56. *Tshogs drug*, the six kinds of cognition comprising five sense consciousnesses and mental cognition.

57. Prajñākaramati, W21708, p. 397

58. The D3940 edition of the text has:

'This completes the explanation of the foundations of mindfulness. Having prepared the mind in that way, one should then engage in emptiness. Concerning the emptiness of the individual, it is thoroughly established in that way. Because of that, by cutting the root, all the defilements will not arise.' (D3940, p. 133a, my translation. See also *The Training Anthology of Śāntideva: A Translation of the Śikṣā-samuccaya*, p. 233)

This is the edition co-translated by Ngok Loden Sherab (1059-1109), revising the earlier 9th century version of Yeshe De et. al. Sonam Tsemo presumably had access to the Ngok translation, indicating Sonam Tsemo's reference is a paraphrase. The D3940 version of Ngok's translation also elides the extant Sanskrit edition, most notably where 'engage in emptiness' originally reads 'engage in the emptiness of all', i.e. of the individual and of dharmas (see *The Training Anthology of Śāntideva: A Translation of the Śikṣā-samuccaya*, p. 403, n. 1). Lhopa Rinchen Pal (p. 161), whose quotation of the *Śikṣā-samuccaya* is almost identical to that of Sonam Tsemo, makes the same point. Indeed, the point is later repeated with the comment, 'Others have it explained it in the same way and it is also the opinion of my own lama [Sapan].' (p. 211).

59. The sixth chapter of the *Mādhyamakāvatāra* comprises these two sections, i.e. non-self of dharmas and the individual, in that order. See e.g. *Introduction to the Middle Way: Candrakīrti's Mādhyamakāvatāra with Commentary by Jamgon Mipham*, p. ix-x.
60. Though Lhopa Rinchen Pal (p. 162) also attributes this quotation to the Vasubandhu's *Abhidharmakośa*, it is found in Asaṅga's *Yogācārabhūmi-bhūmivastu* (W1PD95844, p. 206b). Other authors identify its source as a 'scriptural fragment' (*lung sil bu*) or 'sutra fragment' (*mdo sil bu*), e.g. Gampopa, *Ornament of Precious Liberation*, pp. 313-314.
61. See chapter 6, note 4.
62. The Sāṃkhyas assert five 'bare elements' (*de tsam lnga*), which correspond to the five senses.
63. Reason: '[Because] it is sempiternal.'
64. Pervasion: 'Whatever is an immutable cognition of sound experiences an immutable, single sound.'
65. *Khyad par du byas*, i.e. the type of sound determines the type of sound cognition.
66. See chapter 6, note 4.
67. *Sems pa gzhan rjes su 'brel ba*, i.e. subsequently 'joined' or 'connected to' a mind.
68. Pervasion: 'Whatever is insentient matter is not an agent.'
69. *Sems can gzhan dang ldan*, i.e. 'have', 'possess', or 'own' a mind. C.f. note 67. Both ways of presenting mind's relation to matter are clearly problematic.
70. See chapter 6, note 7.
71. There are different kinds of ripening karma; the result of maturation refers specifically to the kind of rebirth one takes. Other kinds of ripening karma include the result similar to the action and general results.
72. See chapter 9, note 54.
73. The opposites of the four foundations: the purity of the body, happiness of sensations, permanence of mind and self of dharmas.
74. Lhopa Rinchen Pal:
  'In teaching in detail the meditation of non-self from the perspective of the four foundations, i.e. of the body, sensations, mind and dharmas, each of the four foundations applies to the body, etc. of both self and others... Previously, they were an antidote to decline in conduct under the power of the defilements. Subsequently, they are an antidote to self-grasping under the power of wrong views.' (ibid. p. 211)

  He quotes Maitreya's *Madhyāntavibhāga* v4.1 in support of this perspective on the four foundations of mindfulness (D4021, p.43a).
75. Pervasion: 'Where suffering exists, there cannot be joy.'
76. See chapter 9, note 62.
77. Pervasion: 'Whatever is not experienced is not a sensation.'

Notes | 517

78. Sonam Tsemo paraphrases the root verse here with the term *gzhan 'ga'*, 'some other', while some editions of the text have *gzhan dga'*, 'another joy'.
79. Pervasion: 'If separated, they do not make contact' and 'If unified, they do not make contact.'
80. There is a textual corruption here in the Tibetan text, with four sections numbered but only three named. Based on Lhopa Rinchen Pal's similar four section headings (p. 214) and the content of this passage, it is apparent that Sonam Tsemo's third section heading has been lost.
81. Pervasion: '(x)(y) (~x penetrates y → ~x makes contact with y).'
82. Pervasion: 'Whatever is multiple is not truly existent.'
83. Pervasion: '(x)(y) (x is simultaneous with y → ~x experiences y).'
84. It is a matter of valid cognition and logic that cause and effect are so ordered in time.
85. Pervasion: '(x) (x's nature has ended → ~x is experienced).'
86. Proposition: 'Consciousness exists before its cognizable.' Reason: '[Because] it has no preceding cause.'
87. Pervasion: 'Whatever has no preceding cause has no producer.'
88. *Bskyed bya*, as in cause and effect as produced and producer (*bskyed bya skyed byed kyi rgyu 'bras*).
89. Lhopa Rinchen Pal:
    'Objection: "If there is no arising, relative truth is not established, since of the two truths, the arising of existent objects is relative. Therefore, the assertion that there are two truths is not logical. If [objects arise] through someone else's designation, they would be obscured by their obscurations, so how could there be nirvāṇa?"
    'Response: They may be obscured in their own stream of being but that is the deluded designation of others, not our Madhyamaka mere relative, since the cause of delusion in one's own stream of being is abandoned. If the causes and conditions of delusion such as unawareness are complete, appearances are harmful. Otherwise, they are not.' (ibid. p. 216)
    This explanation treats the 'after' in the root text (i.e. v107c, 'If it [a relative truth] is ascertained as arising after, it exists') as referring to 'after' the causes of delusion have been abandoned. This interpretation is in accord with most of the Indian and Tibetan commentaries, but here draws with subtlety upon Candrakīrti's distinction of the 'mere relative' from 'relative truth' to overcome the objection. According to Sonam Tsemo, 107cd is a response to a further objection (i.e. 'that relative depends upon conceptual thought, which is not logical, for it is negated from the perspective of one who perceives its reality'). This explanation treats 'after' as referring to the effect 'after' the cause, recalling the analysis of verses 9.104-105b. In doing so Sonam Tsemo is consistent with the (anonymously authored) *Small Commentary on the Knowledge Chapter Only* (P5278, see the excerpt from this text in *The Center of the Sunlit Sky*, pp. 740-741). The idea is of an internal relation between relative truth and the analytical understanding of emptiness (achieved through the analysis of cause and effect) as distinct from relative truth as mere delusion. This distinction is acceptable from the Svātantrika perspective but not the Prāsaṅgika, which treats all analysis as delusion (see v138-140). The argument simplified runs as follows:
    Objection: The relative is nonexistent, so there is only ultimate truth.
    Response: It exists as a delusion.
    Objection: Then it does not exist for one who sees reality, so it is nonexistent. If it existed for the Buddha, he would be deluded, so how could there be any nirvāṇa?
    Response: It exists only for the deluded person, not for the Buddha. It exists if the effect arises after cause (as a composite taken as a singular).
90. The explanation which is 'not thorough' probably derives from Ngok Lotsawa, for

the same expression (*ha cang ma yin*) is made in reference to him earlier, in the commentary to v9.15. The 'ṭīkā', a term normally referring to an extensive commentary, is probably that of Prajñākaramati, where the exegesis of this verse broadly corresponds with the one given here (see W21708, pp. 470-471).

91. Lhopa Rinchen Pal distinguishes the Svātantrika and Prāsaṅgika perspectives here:
'According to the Svātantrikas, this means that since there is no basis of conceptual discrimination in appearances, it is not saṃsāric. As Ācārya Dignāga says, "Since you [Mañjuśrī] are free from discrimination of reality, you are indeed in nirvāṇa [D2712, p. 79b]." The Prāsaṅgikas do not speak of Buddhas having wisdom but claim that the analyst's understanding that the analysandum has no intrinsic nature is itself not established.

'Objection: "If this understanding requires another valid cognition that it also has no intrinsic nature, there is an infinite regress. If it does not require that, the agent and patient [analyst and analysandum] would be one."

'This is just a designation. What need is there for another analyst? If the object is not established, the subject is not established. Just as when firewood is exhausted, there is no need for more firewood, so when the object of abandonment is cut off, there is no need for a further antidote.' (ibid., p. 217)

This passage is also notable for associating Dignāga with the Svātantrikas.

92. *Gzhung yi ge'i don du 'di nyid zhugs so*. Lhopa Rinchen Pal (p. 162) reiterates the structure attributed here to Vairocanarakṣita and quotes one '*ga po zhabs*' as saying, 'These are the *only* explanations I accept ['*di kho na gzhung la zhugs*]', surely referring to Sonam Tsemo. Lhopa Rinchen Pal adds that the 'Lord of Dharma himself [Sapan] also corroborates this.'

93. *Deng* in the Tibetan editions has been corrected to *dpe*, i.e. an example.

94. *Rtsa ba'i gtan tshigs*—the syllogism which proves that all dharmas are not established, i.e. the vajra slivers.

95. Pervasion: 'Whatever does not arise from self, other, both, without cause has no intrinsic nature.' Qualification: 'Appearances do not arise from self, other, both, without cause.'

96. The pervader is the composite predicate: '(*x*) arises from self, other, both, or without cause.' The pervader is not true of *x*, the logical subject ('mere appearances').

97. Establishing the reverse pervasion (contrapositive) establishes the forward pervasion *a priori* (see appendix). Reverse pervasion: 'Whatever has an intrinsic nature arises from self, other, both, without cause.'

98. The text deals with arising from self, other and without cause separately in the following sections.

99. Lhopa Rinchen Pal (p. 218-219) restates most of the points here from the identification of the three root syllogisms (as explained 'by the commentators', '*chad pa po dag gis*) to the criticism that they are not compatible with Śāntideva's intent. He remarks in addition that svātantras are incompatible with several of Śāntideva's verses, such as the ultimate not being an object of conceptual thought, as well as verse 34c. He also adds that v118 is 'clearly a proof by prasaṅga rather than establishing a svātantra (*zhes thal 'gyur du gsal gyi rang rgyud bsgrubs pa'i ngag ma gsungs so*)'. The point by both Sonam Tsemo and Lhopa Rinchen Pal that this section is a negative refutation of tīrthika doctrines rather than a positive proof of emptiness is a move away from Svātantrika interpretation towards the Prāsaṅgika, the intention being to accurately represent Śāntideva's text rather than express any general preference on the part of the commentators.

100. Proposition: 'The effect exists without its cause.' Reason: '[Because] the cause does not exist.'

101. Pervasion: 'Every effect has a cause.'

102. See chapter 6, note 7.

103. Reason: '[Because] creator and creation are sempiternal.'
104. Proposition: 'Īśvara's creations can be created/are creatable.' Reason: '[Because] they are sempiternal.'
105. Pervasion: 'Whatever is created by a sempiternal self is contemporaneous with it.' Pervasion: 'Whatever is sempiternal cannot be created/is not creatable.'
106. Pervasion: 'The creations of a sempiternal creator have no beginning/are sempiternal/are contemporaneous with their creator.'
107. Reason: '[Because] it arises from a sempiternal causal power.'
108. Qualification: 'The effects (e.g. happiness and suffering) arise from a sempiternal causal power.'
109. For notes on terminology and Sāṃkhya ontology, see chapter 6, notes 2-5.
110. Pervasion: 'Whatever has three qualities is not singular.'
111. Prajñākaramati (W21708, p. 496):
    'Such things as cloths have no essence of composition [*yan lag can*], have no nature of atoms and have no self of the threefold qualities. In this way, when substances are analyzed and examined, the wise see that although substances appear, they are like illusions.'
112. The three primordial qualities of purity, activity and darkness correspond to the experience by individual consciousnesses of dullness, pleasure and pain respectively. Henceforth in this section 'pleasure' refers to the Sāṃkhya idea that unmanifest pleasure pre-exists in the primal substance as a cause of manifest pleasure, thus allowing them to claim pleasure is self-arising, i.e. both cause and effect.
113. Lhopa Rinchen Pal (p. 226):
    'That the five bare elements create [pleasure, etc.] is contradictory to claiming the primal substance, which has the intrinsic nature of pleasure and so forth, is their cause, for then the five bare elements would be their cause, while pleasure and so forth would be the effect.'
114. Lhopa Rinchen Pal (p. 226):
    'Objection: "The proposition is not that sound and so forth are the cause [of pleasure, etc.] but that they are transformations of the primal substance, which is their intrinsic nature." Then sound and so forth would not be the causes of pleasure and so forth, which violates your own premise.'
    The objections here centre on the Sāṃkhya *satkāryavāda* theory that effects pre-exist within their causes, i.e. if all existence is merely modifications within an existing material reality, which is the ultimate cause of everything, nothing new ever comes into being. Although the Sāṃkhya is a dualist school, their beliefs about the evolution of the material basis into higher order perceptible phenomena is a commitment held in common with all materialist philosophies, including contemporary mainstream philosophical materialism.
115. The heading here is enumerated as *gnyis pa* (2), but it corresponds to the title of section 4 previously given.
116. According to Vose (2009a, p. 57) these two objections (prasaṅgas) are Prāsaṅgika objections to the Svātantrika claim that Madhyamaka analysis is a worldly valid cognition. However, it is clear from the expressions 'You Mādhyamikas say…' (*khyod dbu ma pas blo ni kun rdzob yin par 'dod ces*) and 'If a primal substance were not real…' (*gtso bo la sogs pa mi bden pa na*) that these are substantialist or realist objections made from outside both the Svātantrika and Prāsaṅgika perspectives. Lhopa Rinchen Pal (p. 228) attributes the objections to 'all substantialists' (*dngos po smra ba thams cad*).
117. *Bye brag med pa spyir bkag pa*—c.f. the commentary to 9.33: 'Since one would be negating something without any qualities, the negation is indeterminate, for the object to be negated must be identified.'

118. Pervasion: 'For any x, if x is false, then cultivation of x is meaningless.'
119. C.f. 'The valid cognitions which ascertain those characteristics' near the beginning of the chapter which states that the 'elimination of objects to be negated with inferential reasoning cutting off elaborations' is a valid cognition, i.e. the 'merely analytical aspect'. Here it is said, in accord with the Prāsaṅgika view, that a proof of emptiness is *not* a valid cognition and is, as Śāntideva incontrovertibly says, 'false'. But, according to the Svātantrika view, in just this one respect it is 'not a delusion' (*'khrul pa med pa'i cha yod*), i.e. it is not incompatible (*mi 'gal*) with *analytical* valid cognition.
120. The Tibetan text here has *lus pa*, a misprint for *'dus pa*, as it is in the root text.
121. This section is not found in Lhopa Rinchen Pal (see p. 229).
122. Reverse pervasion (contrapositive): 'Whatever has an intrinsic nature is not dependent (or fabricated).'
123. Transforming (alteration, change) is not supported by a nonexistent object.
124. A nonexistent object does not support cessation or impermanence. A nonexistent object cannot cease.
125. Qualification: 'The nonexistent object cannot abandon its nonexistence.'
126. A nonexistent object does not support duality (of existence and nonexistence).
127. An alternative structure, differing only slightly to this one, is given at the end of this section.
128. Possibly a reference to the story in the Purāṇas where Kāmadeva (*dga' rab dbang phyug*) fired a flower arrow at Maheśvara to cause him to desire Uma, though the correspondence is not exact.
129. Prajñākaramati, W21708, p. 528

10. Dedication

1. *Yu'u thang du* here is in various versions of the root text *u bu'i thad du, 'u bu'i thad du* or *yi bu'i thad du*. Lhopa Rinchen Pal (p. 234) divides this section into finding hope (*dbugs dbyungs pa*) and finding refuge (*skyabs rnyed*), corresponding to the first three lines and remainder, respectively.
2. A bodhisattva whose generosity is unconditional, like space. See *The Training Anthology of Śāntideva: A Translation of the Śikṣā-samuccaya*, p. 257-258.

Colophon

1. Sonam Tsemo's remark here seems to be a reference to the brevity of Chapa's text, the extant W1PD89051 version in the *bka' gdams gsung 'bum* being just fourteen pages.

Translator's Afterword: Logic

1. See Lama Jampa Thaye, *Rain of Clarity*, p. 71.
2. See chapter 9, note 30 on classifying Sonam Tsemo as a Svātantrika. On one occasion (see commentary to v9.148) he presents a syllogism in both logical forms, where the transformation is apparently merely grammatical.
3. The English phrase 'the reason is a property (or quality) of the subject' has been used in this context in certain English translations (e.g. Tillemans 1999, p. 39, Tauscher 2003, p. 234 and passim), to define qualification. This phrase is

ungrammatical in that it treats a singular nominal term ('the reason') as an adjective ('is a property'). It would be more grammatical, not to say correct, to define qualification as obtaining when the reason's *predicate* is a property of the subject.
4. There is a difference in the positions of Svātantrikas and Prāsaṅgikas here, in which the former maintain that pervasion can be known by valid cognition, while the latter assert that only āryas and not ordinary beings can have such knowledge. See Tauscher 2003, p. 225-230. Sonam Tsemo is apparently on the Svātantrika side here (e.g. 'It is untenable for the pervasion not to be established, for it would contradict valid cognition', see commentary to v9.88, and elsewhere). This matter invokes ancient philosophical questions on what makes universally quantified statements true and how they can be known to be true, questions common to the Western and Buddhist philosophical traditions. It is beyond the scope of this essay to touch on this vexed metaphysical topic.
5. Matilal, 1998, pp. 14-18. Tillemans (1988, p. 163) has noted that, since first order predicate logic has quantifiers which 'taken normally (as in an elementary logic textbook)' range over existent objects, it does not meet the requirements of Tibetan logic, which refers to nonexistent objects, like a 'sky-flower' or the 'horns of a rabbit', or space, or as in existence-negating (or emptiness proving) syllogisms, the *sine qua non* of Svātantrika Madhyamaka. Thus, a variant logic in which quantifiers are ontologically neutral and existence is permitted as a predicate (as proposed by e.g. Richard Routley) is required for the formalization of such pervasion statements. Tillemans also proposes that to interpret quantifiers as ranging over a domain composed of mental proxies for existent and nonexistent particulars would be consistent with Dignāga's epistemology. See also Mipham, 2005, p. 155-6, for some comments from the tradition on the relation of 'nonexistence' to lack of intrinsic nature in the context of logic.
6. 'The pervader is not supported' is treated as the third of three kinds of pervasion and hence akin to the relations of the first two kinds, e.g. like the general relation between fire and smoke, or between conceptual imputation and nonexistence. However, 'the pervader is not supported' is the non-satisfaction of the antecedent predicate by the logical subject (i.e. the negation of qualification), not a relation between two predicates. That is to say, 'the pervader is not supported' is not a universally quantified conditional but a singularly quantified negation on x. But then x is often not a singular term but a general kind or mass term and hence in such cases 'the pervader is not supported' is not singularly quantified after all.

Printed in Great Britain
by Amazon